The Iron Age
in Lowland Britain

The Iron Age
in Lowland Britain

D. W. Harding

Department of Archaeology, University of Durham

Routledge & Kegan Paul

London and Boston

First published in 1974
by Routledge & Kegan Paul Ltd
Broadway House, 68–74 Carter Lane
London EC4V 5EL and
9 Park Street
Boston, Mass. 02108, U.S.A.
Printed in Great Britain by
Butler & Tanner Ltd, Frome and London
© D. W. Harding 1974

ISBN 0 7100 7677 0
Library of Congress Catalog Card No. 73–86575

To Eric Birley

Contents

Plates

Figures

Preface

THIS VOLUME was originally conceived in the summer of 1966, shortly before the writer took up his present post in the University of Durham, at a time when he was completing a programme of full-time research at the Oxford Institute of Archaeology. In attempting to compile an undergraduate reading-list to cover the later prehistoric archaeology of Britain, the lack of any adequate general survey of the Iron Age had become acutely apparent, a deficiency which this and other recent books can only at best begin to fill. In tackling this work, it seemed necessary to include a good deal of basic material, including drawings of well-known site assemblages, simply because, as a teacher in a provincial university, the writer has become aware of the difficulties of obtaining specialist or local periodicals, and reports long since out of print, from most libraries outside Oxford, Cambridge and London. At the same time a good deal has been included which reflects purely personal views, and the results of the writer's research into the southern British Iron Age and its relationship with contemporary Continental cultures. It is hoped that this inclusion of personal interpretations will, nonetheless, not invalidate the book's primary purpose as a student textbook.

The early and middle 1960s marked a significant point in the progress of British Iron Age studies. Although the 'invasion controversy' itself now has the smack of a period piece, it nonetheless challenged prehistorians who had come to accept older conventional models either to reject them outright or to justify rigorously their hypotheses to others who were weaned on more recent conventions. The outcome has been, at any rate, that we have all become more circumspect in our use of those terms which imply cultural change in some aspect, and for the most part simplistic invasions are now decidedly démodé. For Britain, however, geographically peripheral to the cultural mainstream of central and western Europe in later prehistoric times, the question how such change was generated remains fundamental to our interpretation of the period. Should we regard novel types as the result of *imposition* by colonists from mainland Europe, as the product of commercial *diffusion*, or as evidence for a process of spontaneous insular *innovation*? Throughout the debate, it seemed a pity to the present writer that the criteria for invasion which were being demanded of the so-called Marnian invasion were not being applied with equal rigour to the Belgic invasions of La Tène 3 in southern England: hence the structure of the present volume, the first half being a survey of settlement patterns and structural types, the second a chronological survey, in which an implied comparison between these two important phases of the British Iron Age may perhaps lead us to the resolution of some of the attendant problems of both.

The author wishes to record his gratitude to the following individuals and institutions for their kind assistance in the preparation of this volume: Mr K. Annable and the staff of

Devizes Museum; the Department of Antiquities, Ashmolean Museum, Oxford; Mr D. M. E. Avery; Mr D. Bonney and the Royal Commission on Historical Monuments (England); Mr J. Brailsford and the staff of the Department of Prehistoric and Romano-British Antiquities, British Museum; Mr J. Allan Cash; Dr J. Close-Brooks and the National Museum of Antiquities of Scotland; Mr P. W. Dixon; Professor S. S. Frere; Miss E. B. Green and the staff of Norwich Museum; Mr J. Hampden of the National Monuments Record; Professor Christopher Hawkes; Professor E. M. Jope; The Ministry of Defence (Air); Dr J. K. St Joseph; Miss D. M. Slow and the City of Liverpool Museums; Mr W. N. Terry, Northampton Museum; Mr F. H. Thompson and the Society of Antiquaries of London; Mr R. Wilkins; Sir Mortimer Wheeler; and finally to my friend and colleague, Mr David Ridgway, who kindly undertook the laborious task of reading the text in draft.

I BACKGROUND TO THE STUDY

I

Culture, chronology, classification

MOST STUDENTS of archaeology will be familiar with Wheeler's famous dictum that archaeology is about not things, but people (1954a, 13). Few serious prehistorians would dispute such an ideal, though its attainment for periods of remote antiquity may seem little more than a pipe-dream. Lacking for the most part the supplementary benefits of literary or epigraphic sources, the prehistorian is especially dependent upon accurate excavation as a primary source of information, and upon the accumulated evidence of excavation for reconstructing distribution patterns of structural and material remains as the foundation for historical interpretation. In processing the evidence thus retrieved, quantitative methods are increasingly being adopted by prehistorians as a means of reducing to some semblance of order a mass of material which otherwise could only be evaluated on a highly subjective basis. That archaeology should progressively transform itself from a pioneer study with a background in the humanities, to a more rigorous, professional discipline, exploring and exploiting the principles and techniques of the natural and social sciences, is as inevitable as it is desirable. More conventional practitioners, however, regret that the coy handmaid of history should flirt, not only with the natural sciences, but with the barely respectable social sciences as well (J. Hawkes, 1968). The outcome of such a union will doubtless include a good deal of turgid publication and computerised data of dubious value, but at the same time it will provide opportunities for greater precision both in field techniques and in subsequent stages of research. Accuracy of observation and recording are an essential pre-requisite to a true evaluation of evidence in human terms, and unless the prehistorian observes the highest standards available at the time, availing himself equally of whatever applied techniques may usefully be adopted from other disciplines, no amount of humanity, no spurious felicity of written style, will raise his work above the level of informed fiction. 'The scope and penetration of our perception of extinct human orders', Isaac aptly observed, 'is directly proportional to the extent and acuity of our primary observation of objects' (1971, 123). However we strive to view our material as the surviving vestiges of a complex human society, the fact remains that we are dealing with a largely artefact-orientated discipline, in which applied techniques and quantitative methods are a necessary part of our equipment.

Conscious of the deficiencies inherent in his data, the prehistorian has hitherto resorted to the concept of *culture* in an attempt to infuse some sense of a living society into the historical anonymity of the assemblages he is studying. Yet often enough even these have been labelled according to their principal diagnostic artefacts, or perhaps from a type-site which fortuitously happened to be the first at which such an assemblage was recognised – the Beaker culture, the Windmill Hill culture, the absurdly disparate Rinyo-Clacton culture and more recently the coinage, worthy of vaudeville, of the Round-based-bowl-culture

(J. G. D. Clark, 1966, 177). According to Childe's oft-quoted definition, an archaeological culture could be recognised by a series of structural and material types which were regularly found in association (1956, 16, 28). But so few are the occasions where a culture is represented on any given site, or even group of sites, by the full range of these types – houses, burials, pottery, metalwork and so forth – that in practice prehistorians, even those who pay lip-service to Childe, are obliged to handle assemblages with just a few, perhaps unrepresentative, structural or material types. The problem then arises that scholars will place a different emphasis upon the significance of individual types, and will discount any historical interpretation which is based upon those which they regard as secondary in importance. For our period – the Iron Age – the evidence for a Marnian invasion, for the Arras culture of eastern Britain, and even for the Aylesford-Swarling (Belgic) culture, can in each case be shown to be defective in terms of Childe's limited definition. Yet this definition itself could take no account of language and oral literature, music and dance, religious, funerary or marriage ceremonials, or structures of kinship and lineage for non-literate prehistoric societies. That such aspects of culture nonetheless must have obtained in prehistory is surely sufficient justification for continued enquiry. But the subordination of accuracy in observation and record, too often noted in even post-war excavation reports, to a grandly subjective vision of history might cause the most conventional research student to abandon the proper study of mankind and resort to the computer.

In an attempt to synthesise the social and ideological systems of prehistoric communities from archaeological evidence, we are more fortunate in Iron Age studies than in remoter periods of antiquity, since by the second half of the first millennium B.C. Britain was on the threshold of history. The impersonal cultures of protohistoric times therefore emerge as historical entities, known to the classical world by their tribal names. For all their limitations, the records of contemporary Greek and Roman writers, or the observations of geographers and historians which have been transmitted through the writings of later classical authors, provide us with an insight into the way of life of the protohistoric Celts which dirt archaeology alone at the present time could not hope to supply. Though we might anticipate a good deal of distortion in these reports, some of the central points in the descriptions of Celtic society, especially in Gaul, are borne out by similar accounts in Irish epic literature (Tierney, 1960; Ross, 1967, 1970). Dating in their earliest extant form probably no earlier than the eighth century A.D., these texts evidently embody traditions of a way of life much older, which have survived unsuppressed by four centuries of Roman occupation to provide us with another window, albeit of frosted glass, upon the Iron Age (K. H. Jackson, 1964). In studying the Iron Age, therefore, we have a further means of approach, that of inferring backwards in time from the better documented state of Britain on the eve of the Roman conquest into the preceding centuries, when the tribal framework of Celtic Britain was in process of formation. With the accumulation of distribution maps of settlement and material remains, therefore, we should anticipate an increasing correlation between the anonymous evidence of prehistoric archaeology and the patterns of settlement which have emerged by the end of the first millennium.

4

Whatever reservations we may have concerning the standards of excavation and scientific accuracy of the earlier years of this century, it is as well to remember that many of the classic type-sites which remain the foundation of contemporary interpretation were pioneer projects of the pre-First World War era. However *avant garde* our systems of classification, it is hard to eliminate all reference to the Aylesford cemetery, published by A. J. (Sir Arthur) Evans in 1890, to the Glastonbury lake-village, published in two volumes by Bulleid and Gray in 1911 and 1915, to Bushe-Fox's pre-war excavations at Hengistbury Head, or the Cunningtons' at All Cannings Cross. Though we tend to treat these reports, probably rightly, today, as no more than outstanding assemblages of reference material, they do represent the first attempts to integrate our insular Iron Age within the wider framework of Continental Europe. In due course, the terms *Hallstatt* and *La Tène* were adopted in the terminology of the British Iron Age, after the famous cemetery and salt-working settlement in the Salzkammergut of Upper Austria (Kromer, 1959), and the rich deposit of metalwork recovered from the shores of Lake Neuchâtel in Switzerland (Vouga, 1923; de Navarro, 1972) respectively. These two type-sites have subsequently formed the basis for the classification of the two principal phases of the European Iron Age, the former in the French system being divided into Hallstatt 1 and 2 (Hallstatt C and D in Germany, where A and B are used to describe the material remains of the Older and Younger Urnfield cultures of the late Bronze Age), the latter into La Tène 1, 2 and 3 (in Germany A–D).

Evidently, in each major geographical region Hallstatt and La Tène culture will not appear with an identical aspect, and, especially in peripheral zones like the British Isles, subdivisions may become blurred and some phases may be absent altogether. In consequence, by 1930, the need was recognised for an independent system of classification of the British Iron Age, which, though acknowledging Continental affinities where they were apparent, would be designed to fit primarily our insular evidence. Hence the coinage by C. F. C. Hawkes of the ABC division (1931), which was meant to correspond broadly with the three principal waves of immigration from the Continent then generally recognised by prehistorians, A Hallstatt, B La Tène and C Belgic (La Tène 3). With the intensification of regional archaeology in Britain in the 1930s and 1940s, local subdivisions of this simplistic system were coined by various scholars, largely on the basis of regional ceramic variations. Such a proliferation of modifications – A_1, A_2 to indicate sub-groups, an AB and even an ABC to convey amalgam cultures, together with their regional prefixes – called for some rationalisation, which was provided by Hawkes in his developed scheme, published in 1959. In this, he divided Britain into six major provinces and, within these, thirty lesser regions, according to physiographical boundaries which he believed could be expected to contain recognisable archaeological entities. The broad ABC categories were then broken down into cultural subdivisions: First A and Second A; First, Second and Third B; and likewise First, Second and Third C, each attested by some modification or innovation in structural or material types. These cultural subdivisions were not to be tied rigidly to an absolute time-scale, since regional conservatism might be expected to induce an irregular process of change. Such a comprehensive scheme for southern Britain would evidently require an

5

intensive programme of regional research in order to sustain or refute it in detail. In the event, the very basis of the ABC system was challenged, principally by Hodson (1960, 1962, 1963, 1964a, 1964b), on the grounds that the Hawkes scheme depended upon a particular historical assumption, namely, that the British Iron Age was the product of successive waves of invasion from abroad. Indeed, it is not hard to recognise the loop-holes of the ABC classification. First, we need not suppose that the provincial and regional boundaries would have remained static throughout the Iron Age; in the post-Caesar period, for instance, Catuvellaunian expansion evidently intruded upon several adjacent regions. Second, the culture changes are frequently denoted by very limited modifications in artefact types, whose significance is not easy to assess in historical terms. At the same time, we might add that the overall chronology of the Iron Age will doubtless also be subject to revision, but the flexibility of the scheme should be sufficient to admit such fluctuations in fashionable interpretation.

The alternative scheme offered by Hodson placed much greater emphasis upon insular continuity from the indigenous Bronze Age into the ensuing era. With the exception of two outstanding assemblages, the so-called Arras culture, centred upon eastern Yorkshire, and the La Tène 3 Aylesford-Swarling culture of south-eastern England, which he was prepared to see as the product of invasion from the Continent, Hodson grouped the whole of the southern British Iron Age under the general heading of a Woodbury culture, named after the type-site excavated by Bersu in Wiltshire. As representative of the Woodbury culture, Hodson recognised three principal 'type-fossils', the permanent large round-house, the ring-headed pin and the bone weaving-comb. To these he added the notable absence of a regular burial type, which he believed was tantamount to a negative type-fossil when compared to those burial forms current in the Iron Age on the Continent. At the same time, Hodson rightly urged the compilation of more detailed distribution maps, and the need for more closely associated groups, a deficiency which has long been recognised by those who have struggled with the frustration of poorly stratified sites in Britain. One of the principal flaws of Hodson's scheme is the bold assumption that the Arras and Aylesford-Swarling groups can be accepted as intrusive, and the failure to insist that these invasions measure up to the same rigorous cultural criteria as he demanded for the Marnian incursion. During the course of this study, we shall have occasion to question the validity of this assumption, which passed unchallenged during the period when the ABC scheme was under critical review. As for the Woodbury culture, it is true that Hodson's type-fossils are in some measure typical of the British Iron Age, but the weakness of these criteria for a workable classification of the insular Iron Age lies not so much in what they include as in what is omitted. A scheme which excludes major field monuments such as hillforts, which takes virtually no account of pottery, and which can only represent the vast body of metal types, including weapons, domestic utensils and ornaments, by the ring-headed pin alone is of little practical value to the majority of fieldworkers in the subject.

More significant than any particular scheme of classification has been the reaction against the traditional view that British prehistoric cultures were the outcome of successive waves

6

Little Woodbury, Wiltshire: air-photograph of settlement enclosure

Thornley, Co. Durham: air-photograph of settlement enclosure

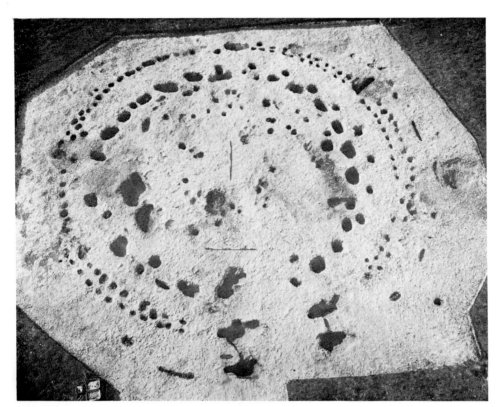

III *Pimperne, Dorset: concentric post-circles o[f] round-house from twent[y] metres*

IV *Uffington, Berkshire: air-photograph of hillfort on White Horse Hill*

of immigration from Continental Europe, and in particular it has become fashionable in recent years to deprecate the notion of an early La Tène invasion from the Marne, which was central to Hawkes's scheme. Clark was even moved to speak of an 'invasion neurosis', under the influence of which British prehistorians felt obliged to ascribe any archaeological innovation to foreign influence rather than an indigenous process of change (J. G. D. Clark, 1966; for a reply see C. F. C. Hawkes, 1966, 1972). More pertinently, Adams has related what he prefers to call the 'theory of successive populations' to the wider context of theories of historical causality which also embraces the evolutionist and diffusionist views of history (1968). The real importance of Adam's contribution is that for the first time attention was focused upon the relative value of different kinds of evidence available to the archaeologist as an index of invasion, and though concerned principally with Nubia this study is of the utmost relevance to British prehistory.

The first step is to consider what we mean by the term 'invasion'. C. F. C. Hawkes once spoke of 'bands of Celtic warriors . . . over large parts of the south country' (1940c, 333); Clark is now doubtful of 'more than local intrusions'. But how many small groups of migrants infiltrating along the coast are required to make up an invasion? Apart from Wheeler's Iron Age beach-head at Lulworth, with its echoes of Anzio and the Second Front, no-one seriously envisages a highly organised sea-borne invasion bringing task-forces into Britain along a wide Channel coastline. The invasion controversy is therefore one of degree, in which each side has been keen to demonstrate the extremity of the other's position. In effect, to explain all innovation in the Iron Age as the result of commercial contacts rather than of any movement of people would be to succumb to the same social-environmental factors to which Clark attributed the invasion obsession of the 1930s, except that today the neurosis has been induced by a preoccupation with trade delegations and the current emphasis upon European economic unity. Study of historical periods indicates amply that invasions need not involve so very many people, and need not greatly or permanently affect the lives or culture of the majority of the population. The immediate effect may in fact be a change in the ruling house or class; the long-term effects will be much more difficult to measure archaeologically. Conversely, if the movement is less organised politically – supposing for instance a refugee migration is involved – then larger numbers of immigrants may have a disproportionately slight impact upon the indigenous culture, which may absorb it with very little trace in terms of material remains. To what extent is an invasion from abroad likely to reflect itself in the material culture of the native population, or of the amalgam population which possibly results from immigrant movements? Should we expect a radical change in objects of a non-political significance such as domestic pottery? Need there be a change in burial rites, or might the invaders concede to the native custom out of political expediency, or in deference to their native wives? Need we expect a change in settlement pattern or house-types, if the indigenous forms had evolved as a natural consequence of that particular environment? With regard to martial invasions, there is the primary consideration of whether or not any particular incursion is successful. If it is only a partial success militarily, the native elements in material culture may well emerge as the dominant ones within a relatively short space of time. Alternatively, if the invaders, though superior in arms, have a lower standard of material culture – in terms of pottery manufacture or domestic architecture, for instance – they may well adopt the higher standards of the people they have suppressed. This, indeed, may be the motivation behind such a military invasion.

Defective though the case for Iron Age invasions may be, it is sobering to reflect upon the number of invasions or substantial military raids which would pass unremarked if we were solely dependent upon the record of the soil. Without the testimony of the *Chronicle*, how many archaeologists would remotely entertain the Viking penetration of 893–5 into the Marches and the Wirral? Within our own period, could we even sustain Caesar's invasions of 55 and 54 B.C. without the written record of the event? It may be argued that Caesar's expeditions were not followed by systematic conquest, and therefore rank as raids rather than invasions. But how much greater were the organisational efficiency and capacity for colonisation of the Roman army than those of any previous invading band which may be conceived in the Iron Age!

From all this we might be justified in concluding that there is so little chance that the archaeological record will reflect historical actuality that even to attempt a reconstruction of events from excavated material in the absence of literary or epigraphic evidence becomes a meaningless exercise. We may sympathise with the predicament of the prehistorian, but Adams's retort is here pertinent: 'It may be that historical interpretation in archaeology will never amount to more than "making the best of a bad job". But are we really making the best of it?' (1968). Certainly it is incumbent upon the advocate of invasions to demonstrate his case; but in Iron Age archaeology it is easier to destroy than to create, and we may perhaps be justified in regarding Hawkes's ABC scheme as the 'best of a bad job' as a working hypothesis in preference to the limbo of Hodson's Woodbury culture. Of course we must begin with the evidence and proceed to its interpretation, rather than approach our material, vice-versa, with a preconceived view of its historical significance: no serious scholar would assume otherwise. But a refusal to venture a tentative historical interpretation once the evidence has been examined is the mark of an unimaginative and impoverished discipline. The real danger is that what one scholar advances as a tentative suggestion is eagerly seized upon by others who suppress its qualifications and peddle it as proven fact.

In an attempt to evaluate the evidence for archaeological invasions, we might consider a number of categories which may be relevant to European prehistory. Seven are here proposed, of which some would clearly be of greater significance as an index of invasion than others:

(1) new physical type
(2) new language
(3) written record of the event
(4) new burial types
(5) new settlement types
(6) new artefact types
(7) continuity or otherwise in site-location and distributions

Probably the most direct evidence which may be adduced for the arrival of new people in substantial numbers would be the widespread appearance in graves of a new phylogeneric type. In the later prehistoric period in Britain, the only instance of such a change is the arrival towards the beginning of the second millennium B.C. of Beaker-using metallurgists, whose brachycephalic skulls distinguish them from the shorter, long-headed people who inhabited the British Isles in the Neolithic phase of prehistory. Though changes in 'racial' characteristics may remain a substantial basis for an invasion hypothesis, we may take Adams's warning that any well-established theory of such change may still require radical revision. By and large, the genetic characteristics of skeletal material are unlikely to afford much help to the student of restricted periods and geographical regions such as the Iron Age in Britain.

Language may here be treated equally briefly. As an indicator of new people, the appearance of a new language may be fairly decisive. But the historical incidence of Norman French or ecclesiastical Latin should be sufficient to warn us against assuming that any given text or inscription reflects the language of the majority of the population. Indeed, the probability is that the very converse is true, and that such inscriptions or fragmentary texts as are available to the archaeologist represent either an official language, or what Parkes has called in another context 'pragmatic literacy' (1973), rather than vernacular usage. The value of apparent linguistic change in assessing population movements on a large scale must, therefore, be qualified. Once again evidence for the prehistoric period is defective. In fact, *direct* evidence is totally lacking in Britain, and the only linguistic information available is that of Celtic proper-names, including place-names, which have been preserved in Latin, and occasionally in Greek, texts.

The written record of an invasion I have deliberately relegated to third consideration, lest it should be assumed to be the most reliable witness to a historical fact. Such records may well be distorted, perhaps as a result of inaccurate information or biased sources; or facts may have been deliberately perverted in the interests of self-justification or propaganda. Even if the motivation is honest enough, we may doubt whether any general's war memoirs, for instance, can be relied upon for their objectivity. For our period, the most important reference is Caesar's statement that the maritime tribes of Britain had crossed from 'Belgium' into Britain in search of plunder by invasion (*de bello Gallico*, 5, 12). The date conventionally assigned to this event was c. 75 B.C., leaving a respectable twenty years for the inter-tribal warfare which the Belgae had been waging up to the time of Caesar's first raid in 55 B.C. Few archaeologists would doubt that there was indeed a Belgic invasion, though Dr Birchall has demonstrated that the *archaeological* evidence for invasion before Caesar is sparse in the extreme; sparser, we might add, than the evidence for Marnian invaders! The dating of the earliest Belgic incursion has been subject to considerable debate, following Mr D. Allen's analysis of the sequence of Gallo-Belgic A–E coinage and British derivatives (1958, 1962). If Allen's dating of Gallo-Belgic A and B coins before 100 B.C. is to be accepted as evidence for intruders at that date, then so far the numismatic evidence has been unsupported by any structural or material remains which might conclusively be assigned to Belgic invaders of this period. It seems probable that Caesar was fundamentally correct in asserting the Continental origins of the tribes of south-eastern Britain. But the identification of which tribes were the intruders, and of when they came, remains a matter for some discussion. On balance we may now regard the idea of a single historical invasion as erroneous; a succession of migrations – corresponding perhaps to the successive waves of coinage – may seem more plausible, and would certainly account for the political unrest among the tribes of south-eastern Britain of which Caesar had heard rumours. It seems unlikely in this instance that Caesar would have fabricated his account for purposes of propaganda or self-justification, as has been suggested in other contexts, though the reliability of his sources in matters relating to Britain should perhaps be questioned. For the present, however, the early migrations of Belgae into Britain are not adequately attested in terms of Childe's definition of an archaeological culture, to which we are all supposed to pay lip-service.

The remaining four categories introduce evidence which more directly is the province of the archaeologist, though its interpretation might be regarded as equally the business of an anthropologist or sociologist. Particularly is this so with regard to burial customs. It would not seem unreasonable to assume that prehistoric communities were fairly conservative in their burial customs, and that in consequence they would adhere to traditional rites in spite of superficial political upheavals. On this basis, the absence of burials of Continental type in southern England in the Iron Age might well be taken to argue against any invasions in this period; and conversely, the Yorkshire cart-burials and cremation cemeteries of the Aylesford-Swarling group stand out as clear indications of intrusive populations. Yet in earlier periods we find quite radical changes, to account for which no-one demands an invasion, such as the introduction of cremation in collared urns in the later Wessex culture, superseding the practice of inhumation. And if burial customs are to be regarded as a reliable index of a cultural or tribal group, how are we to account for the widespread distribution of megalithic tombs in cultural and historical terms? Burial practices clearly are not confined within tribal or cultural boundaries, nor are changes dictated solely by practical or functional considerations. A grave of Continental type may well be that of an invader or his sons; but a change in burial type need not mean different people. The problem of the early Iron Age, with its notable absence of burials (Hodson's 'negative type-fossil') remains, of course, a very special case; but it must be said that this apparent absence of a distinctive grave-type is as much out of keeping with the insular Bronze Age tradition as it is with Continental practice in the Iron Age, and for this reason does not seem to the present writer to be conclusive either way in the invasion controversy.

The pre-occupation with grave-archaeology has in part contributed to the problem of identifying cultural groups, since it has often been to the detriment of settlement excavation. This is especially true of those regions of France and the Low Countries from which any invasion might be expected to have originated. Comparison between domestic pottery of the British Iron Age and grave ceramics from Continental sites is bound to reflect the apparent poverty and insularity of British wares, simply because we are comparing the broken relics of kitchen pans with often complete vessels which were perhaps the best, or even specially designed, for funerary purposes. In fact, the paucity of settlements excavated adequately north-west of the Rhine is bound to create an artificial contrast with the British Iron Age. The apparent distinction between the round-houses of the British Iron Age and the tradition of rectangularity on the Continent has been invoked as evidence of the insularity of the British Iron Age, uninterrupted by incursions from without. But in fact, house-plans of any shape or design are a positive luxury in France, and we may be permitted a wry smile when Hodson declares that 'it is not likely now that this fairly distinct continental pattern will be seriously changed by future discoveries' (1964b, 103). Even within the last five years the pattern in France has been significantly modified by the discovery of several settlements which included circular as well as rectangular buildings. In Britain meanwhile, rectangular buildings, if not yet conforming to a recurrent domestic type, have at least been recognised on several sites in the south and west. Can we be so sure, therefore, that the absence of rectangular houses in greater numbers in Britain betokens no invaders? If so, how can we continue to regard the Arras culture of eastern Yorkshire as the product of an intrusive movement? Or does a cart-burial compensate for a house-plan in the invasion points-tally? The problem is not confined to the Iron Age. Why are there no Neolithic long-houses in Britain comparable to the distinctive Continental types? Why, indeed, have we failed to identify more than a handful of houses for the entire Neolithic and early Bronze Age in southern Britain? When we can answer these questions, the way may be open to a reappraisal of the evidence for the Iron Age.

Apart from house-types, settlement remains are more likely to have been determined by particular regional circumstances and environment than by a predetermined pattern characteristic of any given population group. One major class of monument which cannot here be omitted is the hillfort, particularly since the apparent wave of hillfort construction in southern England in the Iron Age was a principal factor in C. F. C. Hawkes's original exposition of the Marnian invasion thesis. With the extended chronology for the Iron Age now current, it is evident that the building of hillforts was spread over a much longer period of time than seemed possible formerly: the impact politically of their appearance has consequently been diminished, and with it the credibility of Hawkes's argument. It is questionable, in any case, whether hillforts need imply a military threat from abroad. Might they not equally suggest inter-tribal warfare, of the kind which Caesar records?

But if the mere presence of hillforts is insufficient to substantiate an invasion from abroad, the techniques of construction incorporated in their defences may provide a stronger basis for postulating Continental influence. The technique of reinforcing hillfort ramparts internally with a timber framework, for instance, practised already in Central Europe in the late Bronze Age (e.g. at the Wittnauer Horn in Switzerland (Bersu, 1945b), and elsewhere. See below, pp. 54 ff) was apparently adopted in the early Iron Age more extensively throughout southern Britain than has hitherto been suspected. Such a technical innovation need not be explained solely as the product of invasion from abroad, of course, though an invasion, or its potential imminence, may well have provoked a period of activity in hillfort construction and renovation. Unlike potters or metalsmiths, however, a team of itinerant military architects seems less plausible in the context of the British Iron Age. (An instructive example of such innovation is afforded by the use of mud-brick defences at the Heuneberg on the upper Danube (Dehn, 1953). Yet even here the essential conservatism of prehistoric chieftains in such matters is demonstrated by the retention of traditional building techniques for the most vulnerable face of the hillfort.) And though we may be able to define certain regional groupings in hillfort design and distribution, it is seldom possible to equate such distributions with particular tribal or cultural entities. Across the Channel, Hawkes was able to show a correspondence between the distribution of earthworks of Fécamp type and the territorial limits of Belgic Gaul on the eve of the Gallic wars (1968, Fig. 2b). But in Britain even this equation is less apparent. Fortifications here, which have been modified according to the Fécamp model, are relatively few in number, and are located, not in the territory north of the Thames which is conventionally regarded as the Belgic heartland, but in Sussex and Kent, the regions of Caesar's 'maritime' tribes. Upon reflection, perhaps, we may believe that this limited distribution has greater significance as an index of Belgic invasion than we have hitherto imagined.

The introduction of new artefactual types is perhaps the category whose interpretation is most subject to debate. In general, prehistorians are happier with metalwork than with pottery, simply because objects of bronze and iron are more amenable to typological analysis and classification than is pottery, which, in the British Iron Age in particular, is subject to the vagaries of local domestic and non-commercial production. In consequence, pottery is deliberately excluded by Hodson from his series of type-fossils for the British Iron Age. 'Fine-pottery styles', he maintains, 'are so numerous in Britain and western Europe during the Iron Age that any cultural division based primarily upon these would immediately provide too much fragmentation, too many cultures. Coarse pottery, on the other hand, is so unspecialised and difficult to treat as types that a classification based on this would be far too generalised and subjective.' He therefore recommends that in formulating a first general classification for the Iron Age, we should 'avoid pottery as far as possible . . . or if pottery is used, (to) select really distinct pottery types' (1962, 154). With this rejection of pottery the present writer is in profound disagreement. The hazards facing a treatment of Iron Age pottery are admitted: but its unavoidable merits are its quantity, and the fact that it is frequently the only class of material remains represented, whereby the chronology and cultural affinities of a site may be assessed. And as an aid to the construction of regional chronologies, we may anticipate that ultimately, with the improvement of laboratory dating-techniques, the very diversity of pottery will prove its strength by facilitating a greater degree of precision in local classification.

By contrast, the very fact that bronze and iron working are professional industries may prove their fundamental weakness as an index of population groupings or movements. The distribution of a particular brooch- or weapon-type, which displays Continental features, may reflect nothing more than the activity of a single bronzesmith or armourer whose arrival had set a new trend in the craft. And in metalworking in particular there is always the danger that new ideas may be deliberately borrowed or sought from abroad for commercial reasons, such as the desire and need to keep up to date in a competitive market. On the other hand, from the consumer's viewpoint, the restricted availability of metal goods may well result in their being hoarded or handed down as heirlooms over several generations from the time of their original production. The re-use or repair of metal artefacts may further result in a composite piece which combines stylistically the typical elements of several periods or regions. Such complications can hardly apply to pottery, which is worthless once broken, and is unlikely therefore to have had a very long period of use. Furthermore, as the product of domestic or local craftsmen, it is much more likely to reflect the cultural traits of a given region than is a more widely-based commercial industry. Pottery, therefore, cannot be ignored or relegated to a minor role in classification. It is the bread-and-butter of Iron Age archaeology, and forms the closest contact we have with the domestic culture of actual population groups.

With the introduction into Britain in the Belgic period of wheel-thrown pottery, and with it, evidently, a more highly organised commercial pottery industry, classification and typology become a simpler process. The significance of this development in cultural or historical terms is not so obvious as it may seem, however, and is subject to the same qualifications as apply to the bronze- and iron-working industries. The comparatively late introduction of the wheel has been taken as a further demonstration of the insularity of the pre-Belgic Iron Age cultures in Britain, since wheel-thrown pottery was current in certain parts of the Continent from a much earlier date (Dehn, 1963). But would an invasion from the Continent automatically result in the introduction of the potter's wheel? Are we to assume that British potters before the Belgic period were ignorant of this device? Or could it be that the market for commercially produced pottery in Britain was just insufficient to sustain the capital costs involved in setting up a professional pottery industry? It is clear that the bulk of Iron Age coarse-wares were manufactured domestically, either by the women of the household, or possibly by a local craftsman, the equivalent to the village blacksmith. But some Iron Age fine-wares do have a wider distribution, and though still hand-made, imply techniques beyond those of the locally produced wares. An example of the latter is the fine-ware angular pottery from Long Wittenham, Berks, which stands out from the coarse native pottery made in imitation of it and found on the same site. In such circumstances, several possible interpretations present themselves. We may claim that these finer vessels were the work of invaders, producing in Britain pottery which approximated to that to which they were accustomed in their Continental homeland. Alternatively, it may be argued that this was the work of a group of skilled potters – the embryo of a professional industry – who had contacts with the Continent, whence they borrowed new ceramic fashions. Our ultimate preference in each instance will in part depend upon the nature of the British distribution, and its relationship to Continental antecedents. But if such innovations in pottery and even metal types are to be explained as the result of trade or other commercial contacts with the Continent, it is surprising that so few actual imports have been recognised in Britain. In general, both pottery and metal types in Britain show obvious similarities to Continental assemblages, but nonetheless display individual characteristics which mark them out as British products: this view has been taken of the early La Tène daggers from the Thames for instance (Jope, 1961). It could be argued that such circumstances are more likely to indicate the influx of a limited number of people, who were responsible for the new idea, but who thereafter broke off further contact with their homeland to develop their crafts along individual and insular lines, than commercial connections which would almost certainly have resulted in the appearance of more obviously exotic articles of Continental manufacture. Such objects have been recorded in Britain, of course, but their uncertain provenances have led them to be generally dismissed as modern imports or collectors' pieces.

Finally, we should consider site continuity. If British Iron Age cultures were indeed as J. G. D. Clark claimed 'rooted in a Bronze Age past', we might well expect to find some element of physical continuity in the situation of settlements. The fact is that the remarkable paucity of authenticated late Bronze Age settlements – with the exception of a small group in the south-east of England – has made continuity much more difficult to demonstrate. With the removal of the Deverel-Rimbury culture, formerly regarded as representative of the late Bronze Age in southern England, back into the later middle Bronze Age, following M. A. Smith's reappraisal of its metal associations (1959, and see below, p. 129), we have been left with an embarrassing hiatus which has proved difficult to fill. It is, of course, conceivable that permanent settlement was less common in the late Bronze Age than in the ensuing Iron Age, perhaps for economic or even social reasons. But if this was so, we must ask what precipitated the change? Certainly the sheer numbers of known Iron Age sites in contrast to the late Bronze Age argue a much increased population, either as a result of a more sedentary society, or swelled by an influx of immigrants from the Continent.

The updating of the Deverel-Rimbury culture has in turn had its repercussions upon the chronology of the Iron Age itself. In an attempt to bridge the gap between the decline of the Deverel-Rimbury phase in the centuries following 1000, and the inception of the Iron Age in Britain, prehistorians have been inclined to extend the time-scale of the Iron Age, so that an initial date in the seventh century B.C. would no longer be regarded as excessively *avant garde*. Clearly we must ensure that our insular sequence is consistent with the Continental chronology from which it is derived, but hitherto there has been a tendency to exaggerate the effects of time-lag between the appearance of new ideas on the Continent and their introduction this side of the Channel. The progressive extension of Iron Age chronology has had the effect of diminishing the apparent impact of innovations, which may no longer be attributed to single historical events but to a protracted series of intrusions from abroad or even simply a cumulative process of change. Examples of this have already been noted in the Belgic invasions of the La Tène 3 phase, and the Marnian contacts of La Tène 1. But the expanded time-scale has further implications. It is becoming increasingly apparent that settlements which were assigned by their excavators to a single phase of occupation may in fact have been abandoned and re-occupied in several distinct structural periods, which, without the advantages of deep stratification, will not be distinguished by clearly defined stratigraphic horizons. Random cases could be cited at All Cannings Cross in Wiltshire (Cunnington, 1923), at Mount Farm, Dorchester, Oxon (Myres, 1937), and at Hawk's Hill, Fetcham, Surrey (Hastings, 1965), where the ceramic evidence of haematite-coated or finger-tip ornamented pottery on the one hand, and globular bowls and jars, or even so-called saucepan pottery of Iron B on the other, argues convincingly for two distinct periods of occupation, rather than continuous settlement over a span of several hundred years.

With hillforts, our task is potentially simpler, since here we may anticipate a stratigraphic sequence corresponding to the principal structural phases of the site in rampart sections. Unfortunately, hillfort engineers seldom scattered their broken artefacts in the earthworks under construction so liberally as the archaeologist might hope, with the result that we can rarely recover as abundant a pottery sequence as we would wish. And throughout it must be remembered that pottery from such a sequence of levels can only be used as a *terminus post quem* for the layers in which it was found, and may well include sherds scraped up from the ground where the rampart material was quarried. A reliable assessment of actual date – at best a subjective process by this means – will therefore depend upon the recovery of pottery or associated metalwork in sufficient quantities for the odd rubbish survivals of earlier periods to stand out as intrusive. Where circumstances and resources permit, of course, samples from key levels within such a *relative* site-sequence may be subjected to laboratory dating techniques such as radio-carbon analysis, in an effort to tie the sequence to what are euphemistically called *absolute* dates. (For a recent summary of progress, see Allibone et al., 1970.) In practice, however, the standard deviation quoted for radio-carbon determinations is generally too great to allow the measure of precision required within the half millennium of comparatively recent prehistory with which we are concerned, though in highland Britain, where pottery evidence for the majority of sites is virtually non-existent, the technique has been applied with greater success (MacKie, 1969).

Apart from hillforts, the opportunities in Britain for the construction of vertical sequences of stratified and associated material are limited, since the majority of settlements are located on exposed downland sites where there has been little soil accumulation since Iron Age times. Indeed, where a settlement has been intensively ploughed, there may be no un-disturbed layers at all between ploughsoil and the natural subsoil or bedrock in which the structural features are exposed. Where a settlement has been occupied, continuously or intermittently, over a long period of time, the superimposing of structures of one phase upon another may afford the opportunity of distinguishing an earlier from a later occupa-tion, as in the case of the houses at Longbridge Deverill Cow Down in Wiltshire. Likewise, with intensive occupation of a site, there may have been a physical shift in the location of the domestic nucleus which could facilitate the construction of a sequence. In general, however, the principles of horizontal stratigraphy, which have been applied so successfully to Continental cemeteries, for instance (Close-Brooks, 1965; Hodson, 1968), are not so easily adapted to Iron Age settlements in Britain where the range and volume of material remains is so much more restricted.

It is this lack of a wide range of dateable artefacts that causes us to rely so heavily upon pottery classification as a means of assessing the date of Iron Age occupation sites in Britain. The hazards of pottery classification may be illustrated by the erroneous chronology which has in the past resulted from the assumption that pottery profiles must 'develop' or 'degenerate' in an entirely regular fashion. I have attempted to show elsewhere (1972, 73 ff, 86 ff) the fallacy of this approach in the supposed progression from jars with angular shoulders to slack- or round-shouldered jars, which long formed the basis for assigning pottery of the early Iron Age in the Upper Thames valley into an earliest or A_1 phase and a subsequent A_2 phase. If indeed there was a professional pottery industry in the pre-Belgic period, the distinction may arise simply from the efforts of a local domestic potter attempting to imitate the superior efforts of a skilled craftsman. Certain traditions, or ceramic conventions, may be reflected in the work of a number of individual potters, but it is unlikely that there would have been any conscious attempt to produce a jar of 'Type X' or a bowl of 'Type Y'. Occasionally a pottery vessel may have been made in imitation of, or as a cheaper substitute for, a metal prototype, though hitherto this aspect of pottery manufacture has been much over-emphasised, with little serious effort to identify specific metal originals for the alleged pottery derivatives. The term 'type' is therefore avoided here in discussing pottery; where vessels with similar characteristics can be distinguished, the terms 'group' or 'class' are considered adequate.

In spite of the abuse of pottery classification, it nonetheless seems perfectly legitimate to the present writer to group together artefacts which upon inspection have a number of salient characteristics in common, and to make observations on the group as a whole. Typology in this aspect is purely a matter of observation and identification, and is an essential preliminary to the preparation of distributions. Such a process must take account of as many aspects of pottery as possible, not only the pot form, but also its fabric, surface treatment and decoration, if a valid basis for comparison is to be established. In the following classification, therefore, an attempt will be made to bring together certain outstanding groups of Iron Age pottery, having regard for their circumstances of manufacture in so far as it is possible to assess them, but not to erect these into formal numbered types.

The second stage in the classification of Iron Age pottery is to relate the groups so identified to their appropriate chronological or historical framework. This may be achieved in three ways – by constructing a relative sequence from stratified deposits; by means of associated artefacts whose dating is already established; by the use of close parallels from contexts where dating evidence is available. The desirability of stratified deposits and archaeological associations has long been recognised, though the lack of such contexts in Britain affords little prospect of rapid progress by this means. We may be obliged, therefore, to resort to 'Continental parallels' as an aid to chronology, since the Continental framework is in general more reliably established by Mediterranean imports than our insular chronology (Dehn and Frey, 1962; Rowlett, 1969). That this procedure has been deprecated by innuendo by the opponents of the invasion hypothesis in no way reduces the validity of observing Continental affinities for certain principal pottery groups, and thereby inferring a date for the appearance of that group in Britain. Such a process of objective comparison need in no way prejudice the question of relationship between the insular and Continental assemblages. This treatment of pottery necessarily entails a considerable element of hypothesis, and will produce at best a notional framework which is unlikely to satisfy the purist. But the gradual accumulation of evidence in this manner, sustained by the evidence of metalwork and dateable associations where possible, should eventually result in a system which, though notional in detail, is substantially sound in outline. And in an imperfect discipline such as archaeology, little progress will be made unless we are prepared, with Adams, to 'make the best of a bad job'.

II SETTLEMENT AND SOCIETY

2
Enclosure types and structural patterns

IN BRITAIN in the early Iron Age, civil settlements fall into a variety of categories. Though not defensive in the strictest sense, the majority are defined by some kind of perimeter works, either stockade or boundary ditch. The area which these settlements enclose may vary from less than half an acre to ten acres and more, and though the smallest invariably contain only a single house, it does not follow that the larger enclosures are villages with multiple buildings. Though we may group these sites according to their extent, or the nature and scale of their boundary works, there is no guarantee that such a typological classification will bear any relation to chronological development. The fact that, in a number of cases, stockaded camps appear to have preceded hillforts on the same site, for instance, affords no grounds for assuming that palisaded enclosures generally will have antedated ditched settlements, or that the latter in turn will have led to the construction of hillforts. Each could have been adopted at any phase in the Iron Age in response to local circumstances and requirements. Not all Iron Age settlements seem to have been so rigidly defined by palisades or ditches. Hence the term 'open settlement' has been adopted by prehistorians for a number of Iron Age sites, including some of the more outstanding like All Cannings Cross, in Wiltshire (Cunnington, 1923). Whether such sites were really unenclosed, or whether the absence of boundary ditches or gullies which retained a stockade is merely to be attributed to our failure to excavate on a sufficiently extensive scale to locate them, remains questionable. Even where extensive stripping, in advance of commercial development, for example, has revealed the lack of an immediate enclosure, we cannot be sure that individual farms and hamlets were not part of a larger system of enclosure embracing several such units. There is always a danger in assuming, in any case, that enclosure ditches necessarily mark the outer limits of a settlement: conceivably such a boundary could delimit only the nucleus of occupation.

Ever since the publication in 1940 of Bersu's excavations, it has been customary to cite Little Woodbury as typical of Iron Age settlement in southern Britain: indeed it was singled out by Hodson to stand as the type site for his native Iron Age 'Woodbury culture' (1964b). This slavish reiteration of the typicality of Little Woodbury has obscured the fact that it is typical only of a limited region of southern Britain, the chalk downs of Wessex, and may indeed be typical only of a particular kind of economic and social structure. Misapprehensions about the Woodbury settlement have stemmed from the failure, too often, to recognise, first, that the excavated enclosure is part only of a larger complex (Fig. 1), and second, that this more extensive settlement was evidently subject to structural modifications over successive phases of occupation. The major part of Bersu's excavation was concentrated upon stripping an area across the interior of the smaller of the two principal enclosures, that of Little Woodbury. The complex and cumulative nature of the occupation is immediately apparent from the mass of overlapping and intersecting features revealed by this area-excavation (Bersu, 1940, Pl. I), and though Bersu recognised that a prolonged occupation was represented, he made no serious attempt to subdivide the structures into successive building periods. Enclosing the houses, pits, granaries and working hollows was a perimeter ditch, some 3–4 metres in width and around 2 metres in depth. Such an earthwork can scarcely be regarded as defensive in the same sense as a hillfort rampart and ditch provided a military defence; at best it would function, with the bank on its inner lip, as a protective boundary against intruders or wild animals at night. Just within the line of this ditch, at the

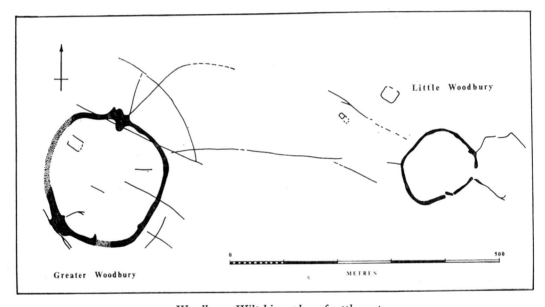

Little Woodbury

Greater Woodbury

0   500

METRES

1. *Woodbury, Wiltshire: plan of settlements*

east end of the excavated area, was a length of palisade trench, through which a small gateway gave access to the interior. Though the main ditch also terminates in close proximity to this gate, it seems improbable that they formed part of the same phase of construction, as Bersu himself acknowledged. The stockaded camp, he concluded, was earlier and had itself been preceded by a yet earlier palisaded feature which the stockade trench intersected. On the western side of the site, neither palisade was located; their continuation at this point was presumably either diverted outside the subsequent ditch, or had followed directly the course taken by their successor. In each phase, the area enclosed probably remained much the same, in the order of $3\frac{1}{2}$ acres. One distinctive feature of the Little Woodbury enclosure – probably to be associated with the ditched phase – is the system of 'antennae' ditches which lead outwards from its east entrance (Pl. I). Comparable ditches may be cited elsewhere in Wessex (Bowen and Fowler, 1966, Fig. 1), where, as at Little Woodbury, their function was most probably to funnel animals from the surrounding pasture into the enclosure.

Leading away from the Little Woodbury enclosure is a further length of ditch, which extends westwards towards the larger ditched enclosure which O.G.S. Crawford originally named Woodbury, but which we might for convenience call Greater Woodbury to distinguish it from its smaller neighbour. Relatively little is known of this second site, since Bersu's resources were largely concentrated for practical reasons within the one area. A single cutting, excavated by C. W. Phillips, across the ditch of Greater Woodbury, however, revealed that the defences of this enclosure had attained significantly larger proportions, the ditch itself being 7 metres in breadth and nearly 4 metres deep. A pronounced 'bleaching' effect on the air-photographs of the site, immediately inside this ditch, doubtless corresponds to the position of the former bank, now completely levelled. Without further excavation it is impossible to tell whether this more substantial earthwork, which enclosed an area of some 10 acres, was once again only the last in a series of structural phases. But typologically, it would be possible to envisage a progression from stockaded camp to one protected by a small bank and ditch, followed, with a shift in physical location, by what amounts to a small univallate hillfort.

Other features, however, are revealed by the air-photographs of the Woodbury settlement and may well belong to one or other of its phases of occupation. To the north-west of Little Woodbury are two sub-rectangular enclosures, separated from each other by a linear ditched feature. The larger of the two is barely 25–30 metres in length and breadth, but has a clear entrance on its north-east side; the other is too faint to plot with any accuracy. A similar enclosure, however, may be traced just inside the north-western corner of Greater Woodbury, apparently of comparable proportions. The function of these enclosures cannot be firmly established, of course, without excavation. But their similarity in plan to the small sub-rectangular enclosures of the Lower Windrush and Lower Evenlode settlements in Oxfordshire suggests that they may have contained a single house, and need not perhaps have been simply animal pens (D. W. Harding, 1972, Pls 27, 28). Other lengths of ditch may be traced from the air-photographs, some intersecting the major enclosure-ditch of Greater Woodbury, and therefore reinforcing the notion that this was a later addition to the structural complex. What chronological span is represented by these various features is impossible to tell, particularly in view of the inadequacies of the pottery evidence from Little Woodbury, but it is conceivable that the two principal ditched enclosures at Woodbury overlay the fainter remnants of earlier, even late Bronze Age, occupation.

The importance of viewing the Woodbury settlements as a whole, and not Little Woodbury as an entity, is reinforced by a comparison with the early Iron Age settlement at Pimperne Down, Dorset (D. W. Harding and Blake, 1963). Here, the basic layout also included two enclosures, one very much larger than the other, with the two effectively linked by a shallow linear ditch (Fig. 2 A, B). At Pimperne, however, it is the larger enclosure, of which the perimeter bank survived in one sector, which has been the subject of excavation. Here, the ditch was of similar proportions to that at Little Woodbury, averaging 2 metres in depth,

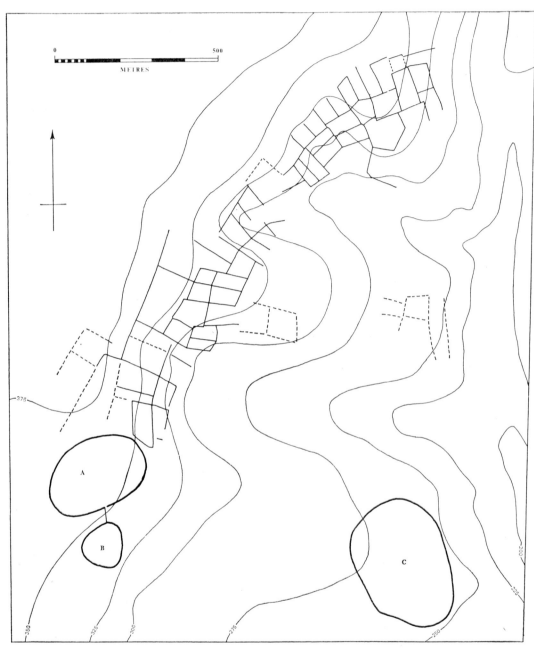

2. *Pimperne Down, Dorset: plan of settlement. Enclosure A excavated 1960–3, with limited trial cuttings in Enclosure B*

though the area it enclosed, over 11 acres, was considerably greater. Access to the settlement was provided by three entrances, two of which have been excavated on the east and south-east sides of the camp, while a third to the north has been identified from air-photography and geophysical surveys. Extending into the interior from the causeway of the eastern entrance was a passage-way, flanked on either side by a line of timber posts, several of which had been renewed in a subsequent building phase. Fragments of human skull had been placed in the packing of these postholes, apparently as deliberate foundation offerings. The ditches of the eastern entrance had likewise been subject to structural modification; north of the causeway, the last 30 feet of ditch had been backfilled, and covered with a capping of heavy flints. Beneath this stony cairn had been placed a human femur and half a human skull, split vertically, and lacking the lower jaw. There can be little doubt that these deposits of fragmentary human remains were part of a deliberate ritual, and they stand in sharp contrast to another form of burial which distinguished the south-eastern entrance at Pimperne. Here the timber gateway itself was of much simpler design, though the arrangement of ditches was complicated by the shallow antenna ditch which led south-eastwards to the secondary enclosure. The intersection of this antenna ditch had rendered redundant the butt-end of the primary enclosure ditch, in the filling of which were found the semi-articulated remains of ox and horse skeletons, buried with two small chalk lamps. This burial had itself been partly mutilated by the recutting of the antenna ditch in a later phase of occupation. It would be tempting to regard these deposits as reflecting the principal functions of the two entrances, the one being for normal human traffic in and out of the camp, the other more specifically for transferring animals from the primary to the secondary enclosure. The shallow antenna ditch which linked the two would certainly have been sufficient to serve as a cattle-grid to prevent a herd from wandering, while they were being driven by a single herdsman, or perhaps by a child, from one to the other. The eastern or northern entrances, on the other hand, provided ready access to the arable fields, most probably situated to the north of the main enclosure, where the remains of a Celtic field-system are still extant. The evidence argues convincingly that the entire settlement was planned with the careful and systematic division of the surrounding land into arable and pasture in mind. Studied as a whole, settlements like Pimperne and Little Woodbury would, therefore, reveal a great deal more about the social and economic aspects of Iron Age communities in Wessex than the excavation of internal structures alone can do, and we can only regret that the resources available to British archaeology have as yet permitted only very partial excavation of these two key sites.

From more recent air surveys, other settlements have been discovered in the near vicinity of Pimperne which appear to repeat this enclosure pattern. The accumulation of such sites would seem to imply a recurrent form of Iron Age settlement on the chalk downs of Wessex, based upon single-family units engaged in a mixed cereal and pastoral economy. Though it has been argued that such sites were the seats of local tribal dignitaries (G. R. J. Jones, 1961; Alcock, 1962, 52–3), there seems no real evidence to show that their owners were more than independent, and perhaps at times prosperous, farmers and ranchers.

Whether this kind of homestead represents new settlers from abroad at the outset of the Iron Age, or whether it embodies elements which are already indigenous in the late Bronze Age, is questionable. But it is certainly by no means a typical form of farming settlement through southern Britain.

A contrast with Wessex is provided by the Iron Age settlements of the Upper Thames basin. Intense commercial activity, directed principally at the exploitation, over a number of years, of the gravel terraces on the northern bank of the river above Oxford, has exposed an area of fairly dense Iron Age occupation, particularly concentrating in the Lower Evenlode and Lower Windrush districts. These sites are normally described as 'open settlements'. Though apparently random lengths of gully, or even small ditched features, are recurrent, none before the Belgic period incorporates a continuous enclosure ditch which might be compared with either of the principal Woodbury enclosures, or that at Pimperne. At the same time, the individual sites display a number of features in common, sufficiently so to suggest that they should be treated, not in isolation, but as multiple entities of settlement.

The best illustration of this pattern is the Lower Windrush multiple settlement, which clusters around Stanton Harcourt in Oxfordshire (Fig. 3). Each of the component sites, extending southwards from Beard Mill across the former aerodrome towards Linch Hill corner, includes at least one small, sub-rectangular or sub-square ditched enclosure, measuring sometimes no more than 30 metres across, and seldom more than 60 metres in breadth internally, generally with a single entrance across its ditch on one side. The function of these enclosures is not certain in every instance, though the Beard Mill example did contain centrally within its area a small circular hut (Williams, 1951, Fig. 4). In the circumstances of excavation, it is quite possible that traces of other such buildings have been obliterated by the mechanical stripping of topsoil prior to quarrying, and we might therefore be justified in inferring that other such enclosures had originally contained dwellings. The ditch, with its bank, was evidently not defensive in a military sense, since the enclosure is so small that a handful of raiders could surround it and raze any buildings to the ground without ever needing to breach the slight earthworks. On the other hand, it would provide a certain measure of protection against the odd intruder, or perhaps a deterrent to beasts which might otherwise prey upon domestic livestock.

The second principal element in the layout of the Upper Thames settlements is the linear gully or palisade trench, which evidently retained fencing whereby the land adjacent to the house-enclosures was divided into individual fields or separate holdings. Since their foundations required no great depth, these gullies are frequently extremely intermittent. At Beard Mill, however, again the best preserved unit in the series, lengths of fencing join at right angles, and furthermore, at one point, appear to flank an approach road to the nucleus of the settlement. Elsewhere, in the absence of gullies, linear spreads of pits achieve a similar effect of land-division, perhaps because they were formerly aligned along a field-boundary which has not survived in the ground. Finally, of course, these pit-clusters themselves are a structural common denominator of all the component settlements of the group, though not one of any special significance in terms of settlement pattern, except in so far as they reflect land-divisions, as on the aerodrome site and perhaps even at Linch Hill (South). The linear spread of settlement from Beard Mill to Linch Hill may well have been planned so that the house-enclosures and farm buildings themselves served as a barrier between arable land, towards the modern village of Stanton Harcourt, and pasture where

3. *Lower Windrush multiple settlement, Oxfordshire*

the cattle could graze along the flood plain of the river Windrush to the west. It is, at any rate, difficult to imagine that sites within such close proximity of each other, which have most of their basic structural features in common, and which appear from pottery evidence to have been broadly contemporary, should have been anything other than coherent settlement units. In such a structure, the question of security would not be dealt with by building earthworks or stockades around each individual farm. By its very location at the confluence of the Windrush and the Thames, it would require little more than a barrier of

27

stakes or thorn-bushes across the principal access-routes from the north-east to protect the settlements from intruders. Quite clearly this would provide no protection against armed invaders; but neither would the Little Woodbury or Pimperne enclosures, when the scale of anticipated assault demanded the construction of a hillfort. We have become so accustomed to ditched enclosures as an element of the prehistoric landscape that we may underestimate the extent to which a thick, thorn hedge could provide an adequate substitute, with very much less labour. Even 'open settlements', therefore, may have been much less vulnerable than that name implies.

Elsewhere I have attempted to show (1972, 11 ff) that there is a division in the Upper Thames between this kind of settlement north of the Thames and west of the Cherwell, and the enclosed settlements which characterise the district around Dorchester-on-Thames, where new cultural influences from the south-east were more readily absorbed or imposed. Here 'open settlements' may have existed, but if so, they were soon superseded by ditched enclosures, which might assume defensive proportions, as at Allen's Pit, Dorchester (Bradford, 1942a), or might be on a lesser scale, as, perhaps, at Radley (Leeds, 1931a) or Mount Farm, Dorchester (Myres, 1937). In view of this contrast, it would be tempting to regard the settlements of the Lower Windrush and Lower Evenlode districts as reflecting, in something of a cultural backwater, an older, insular, Bronze Age tradition. Certainly this is the district of the Upper Thames basin which, both ceramically and structurally, shows itself throughout the Iron Age to have been most conservative.

It is, in fact, precisely the small sub-square ditched enclosures which form the principal component of the Oxfordshire multiple settlements which characterised the later Bronze Age settlements of north Wiltshire (C. M. Piggott, 1942). In particular, the enclosures at Preshute Down and Ogbourne Maizey, together with the sites at South Lodge and Boscombe Down, with which they were compared, show a remarkable affinity in shape and size to the Stanton Harcourt examples. So far, of course, none of the Wiltshire enclosures has been shown to contain a dwelling, and the conventional interpretation has been that they were cattle kraals. Whatever their immediate function, their layout and relationship to adjacent lynchets seems to reinforce the notion that the Upper Thames multiple settlements were based upon an indigenous Bronze Age pattern of settlement. The widespread occurrence of such an enclosure type in Wessex in later Bronze Age contexts may cause us to speculate further concerning the Bronze Age antecedents of Woodbury itself, since it is this selfsame form of sub-square ditched feature which we noted earlier on the air-photographs of that settlement, as a possible forerunner of the main Iron Age enclosures.

An even more outstanding example of this loosely-knit pattern of settlement may be illustrated (Fig. 4) at Plumpton Plain in Sussex (Hollyman and Curwen, 1935). Because the sites on Plumpton Plain are distinguished superficially from the gravel-terrace settlements of the Upper Thames by the fact that their structural features survive as extant earthworks, the same relationship between the house-enclosures and surrounding fields may be seen with greater clarity. Site A included four quadrilateral banked enclosures, the smallest measuring some 20 metres square, the largest no more than 33 by 42 metres. Three of these enclosures were partially excavated in their interiors, to reveal the postholes of small, circular huts of rather irregular plan: their function as domestic occupation sites is therefore, in this instance, beyond doubt. These hut-enclosures were linked by a system of trackways, which presumably not only provided access for human traffic, but also enabled

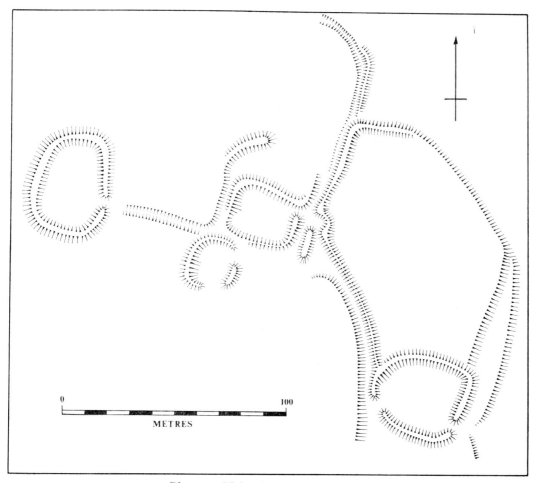

4. *Plumpton Plain, Sussex: plan of settlement*

cattle to be moved from the enclosures to pasture without their wandering into arable land. Similar enclosures have also been traced at two points further to the west of Plumpton Plain, where less of the surrounding earthworks has survived. From the proximity of extensive field-systems, however, it is clear that each of these concentrations of farming units must have had its cultivated fields and pasture in the near vicinity. Not all these individual units need have been in simultaneous occupation, however; indeed, a comparison of the pottery from Sites A and B indicates a prolonged period of settlement, probably from the later middle Bronze Age well into the first millennium B.C. Nonetheless, we would surely be justified in regarding the Plumpton Plain settlement, like its Iron Age counterparts in Oxfordshire, as a continuing and perhaps expanding entity.

A similar pattern of settlement can be cited in the late Bronze Age on Itford Hill, Sussex (Burstow and Holleyman, 1957, Pl. XVI and Fig. 2), though here the individual house-enclosures are clustered together in a more cellular manner. That this form of settlement continued into the Iron Age, however, is best exemplified in Wessex by the site on Figheldean Down, Wiltshire, which was studied in some detail by Applebaum (1954). Working from the evidence of air-photographs only, he subdivided the several groupings of field-enclosures at Figheldean Down, and devised a sequence for the development of the cultivated areas. The settlement sites, however, which must have been associated with these fields and paddocks, he was unable to trace. But in the light of accumulating evidence from other regions, we must surely now suspect that the two small sub-square enclosures, captioned A and B by Applebaum, were two hut- or house-enclosures of the kind which have been enumerated above. It would be unreasonable to suppose that the occupation areas would be far removed from the arable land and pasture which this farming community worked, and the small enclosures at Figheldean are certainly reminiscent of the quadrilateral hut-enclosures from Plumpton Plain or Stanton Harcourt.

The distribution of small house-enclosures of this type is by no means restricted to Wessex and the Upper Thames region. One of the most exceptional illustrations of the small ditched enclosure, serving as a compound for a single house, has been excavated at Vinces Farm, Ardleigh in Essex (Erith and Holbert, 1970), a site which has become better known on account of the middle Bronze Age urnfield nearby. It was first located from the air, when the perimeter ditch of the enclosure and the shallow ditch which marked the position of the circular house within showed clearly as a crop-mark in a field of oats. The layout of the structures is unique (Fig. 5). The ditch of the outer sub-rectangular enclosure, which varied in depth from about a metre to nearly 2 metres, was interrupted on its south-east side by a narrow causeway which served as the entrance into the compound, the terminals of the ditch itself turning to project outwards at this point. The shallowest section of the ditch was its long side, directly opposite this entrance, where the alignment had been deliberately curved outwards to provide an apsidal recess into which fitted the back of the ditch surrounding the house itself. Unlike the ring-groove houses of the north of England, however, this penannular ditch apparently did not retain the outer wall of the building as such, being in any case rather wider and deeper than is usual for such foundation-slots. Evidence for the house was provided by a series of postholes, within the area defined by the penannular ditch, which, together with a curving post-slot, formed an incomplete and rather irregular circular outline. The intervening space between the house and its enclosing ditch was around 2 metres, sufficient to permit the earth quarried from the latter to be heaped upon its inner lip to form a low bank. The advantage of such a construction is not entirely clear. If the house itself was to be divided by an earthen bank from its surrounding ditch, the latter can scarcely have served as a means of draining water from the eaves.

30

v *St Catharine's Hill, Winchester, Hampshire*

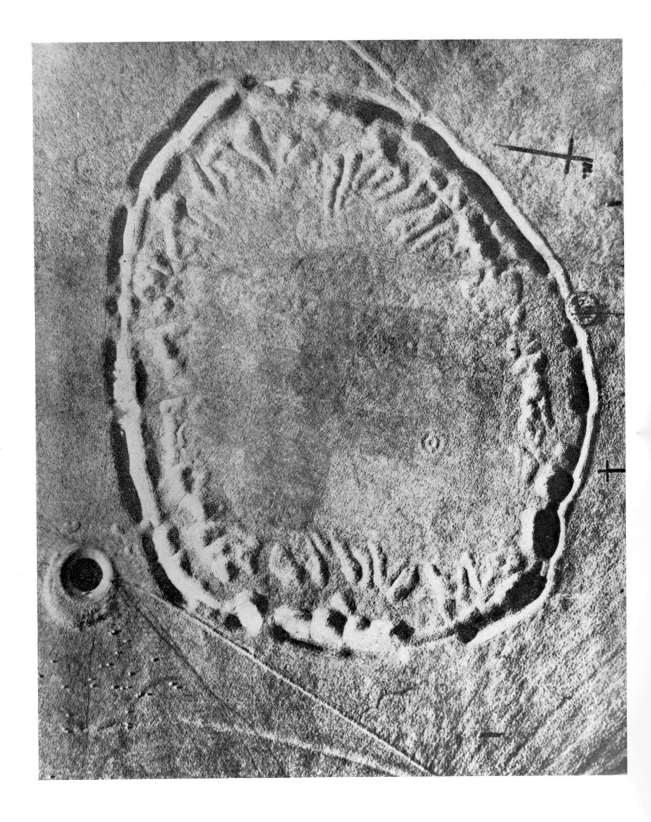

The excavators were doubtless right, therefore, in assuming that this bank was an integral part of the house, serving to retain the main rafters of the roof, in a manner which has been suggested under similar circumstances for the building at West Harling in Norfolk (R. R. Clarke, 1960, 94 and Fig. 25). Further internal support for the roof may have been provided by a tower of uprights, based upon six postholes arranged centrally within the building. The porch of the house was clearly marked on one side by a length of gully, which

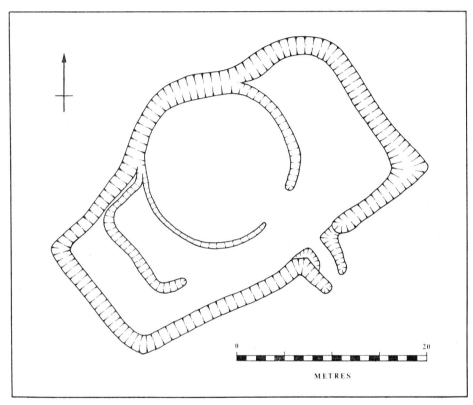

5. *Vinces Farm, Ardleigh, Essex: plan of house enclosure*

projected outwards towards a corresponding gap in the circular ditch. Both entrances faced south-eastward, towards the gateway to the outer enclosure. The entire layout, in its final form, therefore, comprised a timber round-house within a penannular ditched enclosure, measuring 15 metres in diameter, which was itself contained within the outer, sub-rectangular enclosure, some 33 metres in length and approximately 18 metres in breadth. Some structural alterations may have taken place during the occupation of the site. To the south-west of the house-circle, a further length of ditch may have been part of an earlier outer enclosure; but if so, it evidently was still contemporary with the occupation of the circle, around which it bent quite deliberately, like its successor.

The site once again is clearly not designed as a defensive work; the proximity of the house to the perimeter ditch precludes any practical function as a protection against martial assault. In fact, the plan gives an impression of contrived architectural grandeur. Certain details it shares in common with other Iron Age settlements in southern Britain; but its arrangement with a house, surrounded by a penannular ditch recessed in this fashion into the main enclosure, is without parallel at the present time.

Recent work in the Nene valley in Northamptonshire has shown that the sub-rectangular enclosure is likewise a feature of Iron Age settlement in the south-east Midlands. At Twywell (D. A. Jackson, 1970, 43–4), for instance, such an enclosure was accompanied by three small circular houses, whose foundations were revealed by their ring-groove construction. The ring-groove technique, however, is more frequently associated with Iron Age houses in the north of England and Scotland, where it is the dominant method of construction. Though the settlements of northern Britain are not strictly within the scope of the present study, one particular regional group in the north-east of England should be included here, since it displays a significant variation upon the quadrilateral-enclosure theme which has been the subject of this section. The excavated homestead at West Brandon, in County Durham (Jobey, 1962), will serve as a type-site for the group. Its sub-rectangular ditch, which averaged 4 feet in depth, enclosed an area three-quarters of an acre only in extent (Fig. 6). The earthworks were interrupted on the east side by a single entrance, on the inside of which four postholes flanked a passage-way 10 feet in width. The position of the gate itself was marked by a well-cut trench, between 20 and 30 inches deep, which extended across the causeway between the inner terminals of the ditch. Centrally within this compound were located the footings of a large circular timber house, whose overall diameter of 58 feet exceeded those of even the Wessex round-houses. Ancillary structures within the compound included pairs of postholes, possibly for drying-racks, and two rock-cut bowl furnaces for iron smelting. The West Brandon type of enclosure, therefore, represents typologically a combination of the small sub-rectangular house-enclosures of the indigenous Bronze Age tradition and the large circular house, with its symmetrical groundplan (or a compromise between them), which is more characteristic of the larger settlements of Wessex like Pimperne or Little Woodbury. In fact, this type of small *Einzelhof* settlement would seem to be especially characteristic of the Tyne-Tees region. Almost identical settlements have been located from the air at Whickham, near Gateshead and more recently at Thornley (Pl. II), and at Broomside, near Durham City, and at Brawn's Den, Brandon, a few hundred yards only from the settlement excavated by Jobey.

Though we have selected it as the type-site for this region, West Brandon in its original form was not a ditched, but a stockaded, enclosure. Immediately within the line of the ditch were the parallel palisade trenches of this earlier camp. With the parallel of Hayhope Knowe, Roxburghshire (C. M. Piggott, 1949), in mind, Jobey was inclined to regard these palisades, not as successive stockade-enclosures, but as part of a contemporary unit, which deliberately incorporated the closely-spaced double palisade as a protection against wild animals. The entrance to this earlier camp was, like its successor, on the east side of the enclosure, though offset slightly from the alignment of the causeway through the subsequent ditch. Presumably contemporary with this earlier enclosure was the occupation of House A, likewise somewhat offset from the position of the later house, but otherwise of similar proportions. The superstructure of this building was supported entirely by uprights bedded in postholes, without the aid of a ring-groove, arranged in four concentric settings.

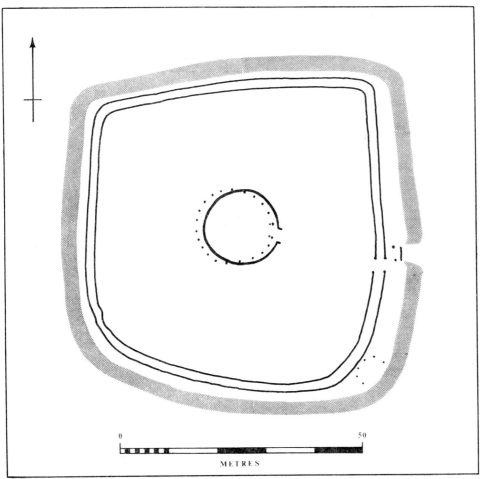

6. *West Brandon, Co. Durham: plan of settlement*

So far, those instances which we have examined of palisaded settlements, at Little Woodbury and West Brandon, have in each case preceded a subsequent ditched phase of construction. An example which never developed beyond a stockaded camp is the classic settlement at Staple Howe on the northern fringe of the Yorkshire Wolds (Brewster, 1963). Here, in spite of the impression which the palisade trench gives of being double around most of the camp's perimeter, like West Brandon and its Scottish counterparts, the inter-

33

section of the trenches on the south side of the site, adjacent to the entrance, clearly indicates that more than one phase of building is involved (Fig. 7). Within the enclosure three huts were excavated, of which one apparently incorporated a low outer wall of stone derived from the levelling of its foundations into the sloping bedrock. Rather less regular in plan than is usual for Iron Age houses in southern Britain, the Staple Howe huts are comparable with middle and late Bronze Age buildings at Shearplace Hill in Dorset (Rahtz and ApSimon 1962, Fig. 5; Avery and Close-Brooks, 1969, Fig. 1) or at Itford Hill in Sussex (Burstow and Holleyman, 1957, Pl. XVI). The pottery from Staple Howe likewise is suggestive of Bronze Age antecedents, including fragments with slack profile and applied cabled

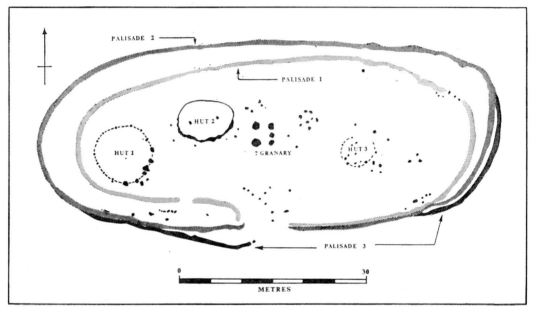

7. Staple Howe, Yorkshire: plan of settlement

cordons which are more than usually reminiscent of bucket-urn forms. These factors, together with the structural complexities of the palisaded enclosure, argue a prolonged occupation of the site; the sixth century Hallstatt C bronzes, and the radio-carbon determination of 450 b.c. ± 150, derived from a sample of carbonised grain, need not, therefore, be representative of the earliest occupation on the site.

In the south of England, palisaded enclosures of this kind are frequently found on sites which subsequently developed into proper hillforts with rampart and ditch. An example of such a sequence is provided by Blewburton Hill, Berks (A. E. P. Collins, 1947, 1952, 1959, D. W. Harding, 1967, 1972, 46), where the stockaded phase occupied only about one half of the 10 acres subsequently embraced by the univallate hillfort itself. These stockaded camps, which apparently preceded a number of the Hampshire and Sussex hillforts, evidently derived from a later Bronze Age tradition of palisaded hill-top settlements, which may be compared to the *Hohensiedlungen* of central Europe. In considering the possible Bronze Age origins of the Iron Age hillforts, in due course, therefore, we should take into account the possibility that such sites represent only the final outcome of a longer sequence of occupation, in which the hill-top position had served as a focal point for tribal activities.

Finally, we should not overlook a more specific type of settlement, which in southern Britain has been conventionally illustrated by the so-called lake-villages of the Somerset levels (*Glastonbury* I–II; *Meare* I–III). According to Bulleid and Gray, the twin settlements at Glastonbury and Meare had comprised numerous circular dwellings, erected on mounds of clay upon a base of timber and brushwood, whose foundations were thus raised to form an artificial island in the surrounding marshes. Recent research, however, including the re-excavation of limited areas of the East village at Meare, has led to a radical re-interpretation of these 'lake-villages'. First, Godwin and others have shown that the Meare settlement was not built in a lake at all, but on a raised bog which was already dry and dessicated by the beginning of the Iron Age (1941; Dewar and Godwin, 1963). The nearest water would have been the Meare Pool, a few hundred yards from the village itself, which Avery has therefore suggested (1968) should be termed a 'Lakeside Village' rather than 'Lake Village' as hitherto. Second, the excavations of 1966 and 1968 have necessitated a revision of the structural interpretation proposed by Bulleid and Gray. Evidently much of the timber, which they had believed formed the substructure of the village below a layer of cut and artificially-laid blocks of peat, was in fact buried by a natural growth of peat, and any phase of occupation which it represents should be assigned to a much earlier date than the Iron Age settlement. It has also now become apparent that the number of huts which made up the Meare East village was considerably smaller than the previous excavators had supposed. Their identification of huts had rested not solely upon the recognition of post-circles, but also upon the presence of the clay mounds (which they believed formed the foundations of individual dwellings) and superimposed layers of clay within these occupation areas, which they interpreted as domestic hearths. In fact, the supposed hearths show no evidence of ever having been subjected to heat, the reddening noted by Bulleid and Gray being due to oxidisation of iron compounds in the clay. In several instances, these clay deposits were stratified beneath the larger clay mounds, and therefore cannot have been contemporary with houses built upon them. Many of the mounds themselves are not associated with postholes or upright timbers, and hence cannot be shown to have served as house foundations. As a result of this re-examination, less than a dozen huts can at present be postulated for the Meare lakeside village, where previously over forty had been presumed. Most of these belonged to the earliest Iron Age occupation of the site, probably in the third century B.C. When the settlement was abandoned, perhaps in favour of an alternative site on higher ground two or three hundred metres to the south, it seems only to have been used as a dump for domestic and industrial refuse, until it was re-used in the first century B.C. for the construction of the clay mounds. No houses can yet be firmly assigned to this period, and indeed the function of the clay mounds remains unsolved. At the beginning of the first century A.D. the site became waterlogged, and was abandoned altogether. A layer of mussel-shells, some of which were unopened bi-valves, clearly indicates that the levels were at this stage under water. But this event is established by the stratigraphy at Meare as a late development there, and we can no longer sustain the view that the Iron Age village was composed of artificial crannogs raised up above the surrounding waters. The conclusions which apply to Meare, of course, may not be equally valid for Glastonbury, where peat sections have shown a wetter base than that of the Meare village. But in the light of these developments, we would be well advised to keep an open mind on the subject of 'lake-villages' in the Somerset levels.

With notable exceptions such as these, then, the Iron Age settlements of southern Britain conform very largely to one or other of the principal classes outlined above. The examples which we have examined in Wessex, the south-east, and the south Midlands are sufficient to show that the loosely-knit arrangement of small house-enclosures, associated with arable fields and pasture, and sometimes linked by a network of trackways which divided the two, was a pattern widely represented throughout the country in the first millennium B.C. It is difficult to resist the conclusion that it is these settlements, and the palisaded enclosures, which demonstrate continuity from the insular Bronze Age into the Iron Age, by comparison with which the more positively defined protected settlements of the Woodbury or Pimperne class would appear to represent a novel departure. The latter still need not be seen as the product of invaders, however, so much as innovation brought about by changing social and economic circumstances. By the first century B.C., further change is imminent. With the abandonment of fortified hill-top positions in favour of lower-lying defensive earthworks, comes a parallel development in the structure and orientation of domestic settlements. Relatively few early Iron Age settlements show direct continuity into the Belgic period, and those which do, like Langford Down near Lechlade (A. Williams, 1946), or the site at Linch Hill, Stanton Harcourt, Oxon (Grimes, 1943), may well have been occupied by basically non-Belgic communities who had only adapted superficially to the Belgic way of life by adopting certain of their material innovations. The major La Tène 3 settlements of the south-east, by contrast, show a significant move towards communal settlements on a larger scale, which eventually assume the aspects of urbanisation. In describing the native settlement of Kent, Caesar declares that the buildings were situated in close proximity to each other, and very similar to the settlements of the Gauls (*de bello Gallico* 5, 12). But precisely what he intended to convey by the term *aedificia* remains in doubt, since the isolated farm-settlements of the Belgic invaders of the south-east have yet to be adequately recorded by excavation. The structural innovations of the Belgic period are better demonstrated by defensive earthworks and large *oppida*, which will be the subject of another chapter.

3
House types:
round and rectangular

BY CONTRAST with the apparent paucity of house-sites of the Neolithic and Bronze Ages in Britain, Iron Age houses are relatively common, either in settlement-enclosures of the various kinds discussed in the previous chapter, or sometimes clustering within the precincts of hillforts, as in Wales and Northumberland. The number of such sites which have been excavated or located from the air in recent years tends to obscure the fact that, only forty

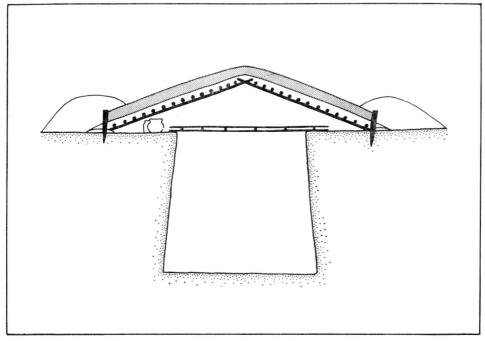

8. Reconstruction of 'pit-dwelling', Fifield Bavant Down, Wiltshire

years ago, prehistorians regarded the subterranean pits which are littered across Iron Age settlements in southern England as a regular form of living-quarters of Iron Age men. The 'pit-dwelling' theory is well illustrated by Clay's reconstruction (1924), complete with roof and access-ladder, of such primitive habitations on Fifield Bavant Down, Wiltshire (Fig. 8), and as late as 1940 it was still possible for Wheeler to interpret some, at least, of the rock-cut pits at Maiden Castle, Dorset, as dwellings, on the evidence of a continuous ring of mutton bones around the walls of one such pit, 'showing how the eaters had squatted in the centre round the fire and had thrown the gnawn bones over their shoulders' (1943, 52). In fact, the notion of a semi-subterranean house is not in itself an entirely fanciful one. In Central Europe, from the early Bronze Age to the La Tène period, sub-rectangular buildings are known which are partially built into the ground in order to provide greater headroom under the eaves, and much the same idea persists in the *Grubenhaüser* of the Anglo-Saxon period. But the much more confined space – the greater depth-to-width ratio – of Iron Age pits in southern Britain unquestionably argues another function.

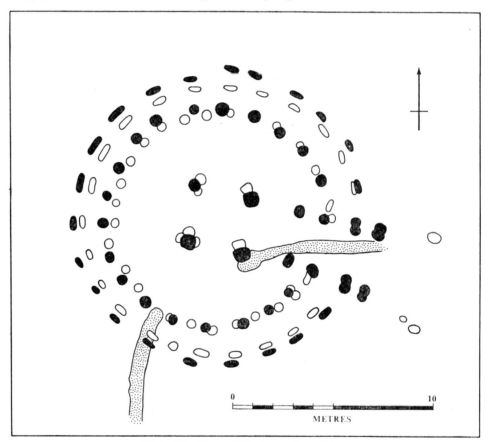

9. *Little Woodbury, Wiltshire: plan of house I*

The death-knell of the pit-dwelling era had, in fact, already been sounded by the time Bersu published the report of his excavations at Little Woodbury in Wiltshire, where large-scale stripping of the interior of a ditched enclosure had revealed a circular timber house, with an overall diameter of nearly 15 metres (Fig. 9). In essence the Little Woodbury house comprised two concentric circles of postholes, an outer wall and an inner weight-bearing circle of roof-supports, supplemented by a central arrangement of four posts in a square. Access to the interior was afforded by a wide tunnel-like porch, flanked on either side by four substantial posts. The entire structure had been renewed in a second phase, the post-settings being placed so close to their original positions that we may imagine that the occupation of the building was in fact continuous. A few yards from the principal house was a second circular hut, of smaller overall dimensions and simpler in design. Though the excavator viewed this structure as an incomplete attempt at a round-house of comparable proportions, it is quite possible that its Iron Age occupants never intended that it should be more than an ancillary building. While its true function is unlikely ever to be resolved, it is significant that comparable houses of reduced dimensions have been recorded in proximity to large round-houses at West Harling, Norfolk (Clark and Fell, 1953, Fig. 7), and Longbridge Deverill, Wiltshire (Notes in Frere, 1958, 18–20; *PPS*, 27, 1961, 346–7).

Subsequent excavations, principally at Pimperne, Dorset, and at Longbridge Deverill, have revealed circular houses very similar to the principal house at Little Woodbury. A feature which the houses on each of those sites display in common is the elaborate porched entrance, the object of which was surely more than mere architectural ostentation. One of the major hazards of living in a timber and thatched building of the Pimperne type must surely have been fire. Provided the hearth was shielded, and the timbers allowed to smoulder slowly, there would be little risk of conflagration, and the gradual accumulation of soot on the ceiling of the building would provide some additional insulation. But a sudden draught and a shower of sparks flying into the roof could spell disaster within seconds, as Hansen's experiments in Denmark have demonstrated. The purpose of the tunnelled entrance, therefore, was surely to support double doors, the outer of which could be closed before the inner one was opened. Such a device is by no means inconsistent with the standard of design and construction which the round-houses display.

The layout of the Pimperne post-circles (Pl. III) certainly reflects the meticulous attention to symmetry and detail which the builders of Iron Age houses expended upon their engineering and carpentry. In so far as it was possible to establish the position of the post itself within its hole, the upright roof-supports appear to have been spaced at regular intervals around the circle, presumably laid out accurately from a central peg. The significant factor in their erection is that the posthole-depths below bedrock vary progressively to compensate for a marginal slope in the ground, amounting to no more than 6 inches over 50 feet. Such attention to the depth of the hole was evidently to ensure that the lintels, which were presumably to bond the uprights together into a rigid framework, were horizontal, but from this evidence we can make the important inference that all the uprights had been previously cut to the same length. Carbonised remains from the postholes showed that the principal uprights were of oak. Elsewhere on the site, pine was found in Iron Age levels, suggesting that the builders were able to select their timber to suit the purpose in hand. It is evident that the large round-houses of Wessex were indeed much more sophisticated structures than the exponents of the pit-dwelling theory would have conceived possible.

In one respect the Little Woodbury house remains unique: in its use of a central arrangement of four posts in a square. In all his hypothetical reconstructions of the Little Woodbury house, Bersu made use of this central feature as the principal means of supporting the roof. Quite evidently, such a system has merits over a single central posthole, since it solves the problem of making rigid the roof-rafters as they converge upon the central point at the apex. Ironically, however, none of the large round-houses excavated since Little Woodbury has been found to contain this central square of postholes, nor a single central post, and for this reason some prehistorians have doubted whether such round-houses were totally roofed. An alternative interpretation was put forward by R. R. Clarke for the West Harling house, in which the central area was seen as an open courtyard in which animals could be coralled, or basic farm activities could be conducted (Clarke, 1960, Fig. 25. For an interesting modification of this reconstruction, see Hamilton, 1968, Fig. 30b). If Little Woodbury appears in retrospect to have been atypical, however, it may not have been so in practice. Since the principal forces exerted upon the central tower of uprights would have been evenly distributed downwards by virtue of the conical roof, the timber framework may well have been a free-standing structure, which, in the early stages of construction, could have served as a portable scaffold, and which would finally be built in to the centre of the round-house as a support for the roof. The area of large flints which were spread across the centre of the Pimperne house might well have supported such a free-standing timber tower. An additional merit of this system is that, when replacements became necessary, these could be installed without riddling the centre of the floor with postholes as at Little Woodbury. On the perimeter of the building, by contrast, it might be necessary to dig the upright posts into the ground in order to counteract outward thrust of the roof, but here it is a relatively simple task to replace rotting timbers, without distorting the symmetry of the circle, by moving to one side on the same diameter.

Though Bersu's attempts at reconstructing the superstructure of the Little Woodbury house may seem to be a trifle implausible, he evidently appreciated the relative sophistication of Iron Age architecture and engineering, and in this respect his somewhat eccentric efforts are infinitely preferable to the rustic conception produced at the Pinewood Studios in 1944 for the film *Beginning of History* (J. Hawkes, 1946), which regrettably has been reproduced in nearly every standard introduction to prehistory since. Rising like an ant-hill from the middle of the compound, the studio reconstruction displays little finished carpentry and belies any architectural skill on the part of its builders. Is it likely that a people whose metalwork, for instance, displays a high degree of technical proficiency and artistic sense would be satisfied with such squalid buildings, when the attention to symmetry and detail witnessed by the ground-plans of the Wessex round-houses argues the very reverse? Is it not more probable that the thatch-makers and carpenters would have exercised the same craftsmanship in their own field as the metalworkers did in theirs? Where evidence for woodworking and allied crafts survives – in the Somerset 'lake-villages' for instance – there is every reason to suppose a high degree of skill. The Wessex round-houses may well have been impressive landmarks in their heyday – perhaps with their roofs thatched ornamentally in zig-zag patterns, and with their upright timbers or porch-posts carved in a totem-like fashion. The external walls of wattle and daub would likewise present a surface for garish ornament, perhaps comparable to the mosaics of gaudy colours which Tacitus alleges the Germans smeared over their houses (*Germania*, 16). Such a vision must of course remain speculative, but surely it is one which is more consistent with the admittedly meagre evidence that survives, than is the humble and rustic view which prehistorians have hitherto favoured for the British Iron Age?

Large timber houses of the Pimperne type are not confined in their geographical distribution to Wessex. Further north, at West Brandon in County Durham (Jobey, 1962), and at West Plean, in Stirlingshire (Steer, 1955) are examples of similar proportions, which

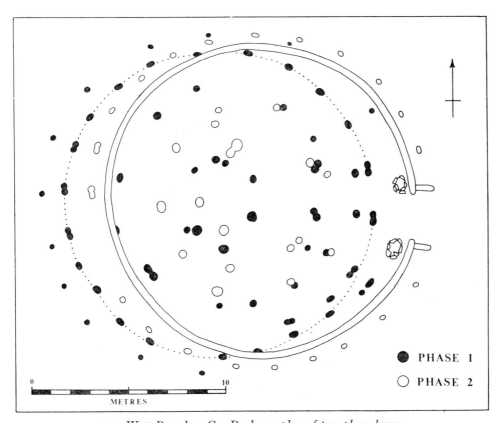

10. *West Brandon, Co. Durham: plan of two-phase house*

likewise have undergone a period of reconstruction on the same site. The particular characteristic of these northern round-houses is the combination of post-circles with the 'ring-groove' technique whereby the upright timbers are placed in a continuous bedding trench, which was presumably easier to construct in bedrock than were individual postholes (Fig. 10). This method further facilitated a tighter fitting of the post into the ground in the radial direction, even if tangentially there was greater room for movement. The space between the uprights would then be packed tightly with stones, as at West Brandon, where broken quernstones were used for this purpose. The use of the 'ring-groove' is not exclusively northern; examples have been excavated in Northamptonshire at Draughton

(Note in Frere, 1958, 21–3, and Fig. 5), and more recently in the Nene valley at Twywell, and I have suggested elsewhere that round-houses built in this fashion may be deduced from fragmentary evidence in the Upper Thames valley (1972, 26 ff). But more commonly in the Highland zone the principal building material is stone, sometimes combined with timber, as at Trevelgue Head, in north Cornwall. This latter example is of particular interest, since its use of alternate orthostat and horizontal drystone walling in the perimeter wall of the house might be seen as the counterpart in stone of a series of upright timbers interlaced with wattling.

Though the very apparent similarities in ground-plan between the round-houses of the Highland and Lowland zones of Britain attest their common cultural tradition, they may have differed in one significant aspect, namely, in the manner of their roofing. Bersu argued ingeniously (1945a) that the Manx round-houses were roofed with turf, an interpretation which has been adopted for other sites in northern Britain. Though turf may have been readily available to the round-house builders, its principal disadvantage is one of weight, a factor which is reflected in the multiple circles of upright posts required in the Ballacagen house to support its roof. References to cattle straying upon the roof of houses in old Irish literary sources become credible in terms of such a broad, low round-house roofed with turf. Furthermore, the reduced importance of the porched entrance at West Brandon and West Plean, by contrast with the Wessex examples, would be consistent with the use of a less inflammable roofing material, if the double-door theory advanced above is accepted.

By contrast, it is generally assumed that the southern British round-houses would have been thatched. The steeper pitch required to render a thatched roof effectively weatherproof necessarily entails a much higher apex, which, in the case of Little Woodbury and Pimperne, would have stood up to 25 feet above the ground. In consequence, it is unlikely that the Iron Age builders of the Wessex round-houses would have attempted to span the distance from apex to eaves with single continuous rafters. More probably the roof would have been erected in two stages, the completed first stage, once braced and rigid, forming the basis for the construction of the upper canopy of the roof. It seems unlikely, anyway, that the occupants would have wasted the considerable space afforded by such a steep-roofed building, when the addition of a catwalk or hay-loft would provide valuable extra room for storage. Perhaps this too was the reason for the exceptional width of the entrance passages at Little Woodbury, Pimperne and Longbridge Deverill – surely much wider than normal domestic use required – which enabled a hay-wain to be driven into the house itself at harvest time for unloading directly into the loft. The provision of fodder and bedding for beasts must surely have been no less important to the community than the provision of such necessities for the human population.

Any attempt to infer the superstructure of Iron Age houses from their ground-plans is bound to be speculative, but in some measure the exercise is necessary for an understanding of how such buildings could have been utilised in daily life. Comparison between the timber houses of Wessex and the stone-built wheelhouses of northern Britain (Fig. 11) would suggest a communal living-area in the centre of the building, surrounded by a series of separate rooms or cubicles for use as sleeping quarters. Such a layout internally would not be inconsistent with the indirect evidence of Irish sources (see Ross, 1970, 89–91), though there is very little archaeological evidence to determine whether access to such cubicles was from the central hall directly, or by an external entrance, or conceivably via the porch.

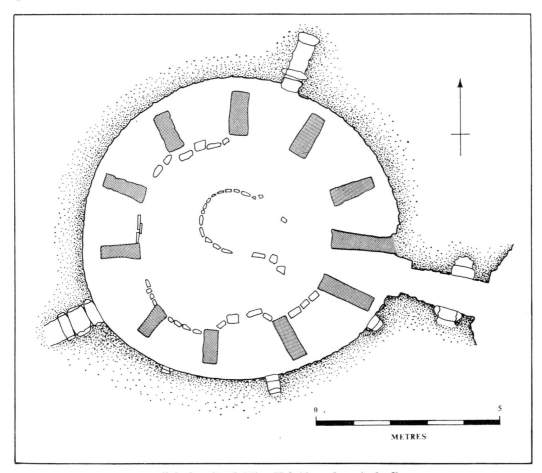

11. *Kilpheder, South Uist, Hebrides: plan of wheelhouse*

The attention which naturally focuses upon these outstanding homestead sites should not be allowed to obscure the existence of many settlements where the characteristic form of building is a smaller circular hut, with a diameter ranging from 15–25 feet commonly. Such huts may be found in isolation within a small ditched enclosure, as at Beard Mill, Stanton Harcourt, Oxfordshire (Williams, 1951, Fig. 4), or in groups of two or three, as at Standlake (Riley, 1946, Fig. 9), a mile or so to the west. Structurally, they are less complex than their larger counterparts, displaying generally a single circle of postholes, which could have supported a conical or bee-hive-shaped roof in a single unit. Though such huts are found in 'open settlements', their most significant occurrence is within hillforts, as in the hillforts of Northumberland or the Welsh Marches. Within one hillfort in Caernarvonshire alone, at Garn Boduan, traces have been planned of 164 stone-built circular huts which may be assigned with reasonable confidence to the Iron Age occupation (Hogg, 1960). In southern England, where huts would have been built of timber, occupation within hillforts is less easily demonstrated, but notable examples may be cited at Chalbury (Whitley, 1943, Fig. 2), and at Hod Hill in Dorset (Richmond, 1968, Figs 2, 3), where the outline of hut-circles could still be identified in some numbers as depressions in modern ground-level. Within the same category may be treated those small circular huts from Glastonbury and Meare whose authenticity has not been eroded by recent reappraisal of the lakeside village settlements (see above p. 35).

Whatever local or regional variations in settlement patterns there may have been, a broad distinction emerges between the nature and context of large round-houses of the Pimperne type, and the smaller round huts like those from Hod Hill or Meare. The division should not be overemphasised, but the relative infrequency of circular buildings of inter-mediate dimensions is certainly quite striking. What, then, is the basis which underlies this distinction? First, we should consider the question of chronology. Round-houses of the large variety are evidently a feature of Iron Age settlements in Wessex at least from around 600 B.C. when the settlement at Longbridge Deverill was established. By the fifth and fourth centuries respectively, the homesteads at Pimperne and Little Woodbury were probably flourishing, continuing in use for perhaps a century or more. For the later Iron Age, well-attested examples are comparatively rare in southern England, though the circular structure on Langford Down, near Lechlade, Glos (Williams, 1946, Fig. 5), might be tentatively identified as an example for the para-Belgic period. North of the Roman frontier, on the other hand, stone-built variants of the round-house type continued in use for several centuries, developing independently architectural complexities of their own. The chrono-logical range spanned by the smaller class of round huts is equally broad, though it perhaps stems from an older indigenous tradition. The large Wessex round-houses might be seen as the culmination of a long-established insular tradition of circularity in domestic architecture, but there is no evidence that this grander type of building universally superseded the smaller variant of round hut.

If the distinction between round-house and hut is not chronological, therefore, could it relate to the social and economic circumstances of their occupation? Was size an indicator of social status? The view that protected settlements like Little Woodbury were the *llys* of a chieftain or seat of a local tribal dignitary has been challenged by Alcock (1962) on grounds of the poverty of finds at Little Woodbury by comparison with certain 'open settlements' such as All Cannings Cross. But the wealth or status of the occupants of Little Woodbury or Pimperne may have been measured in terms of land-holding and stock, rather than pottery and metalwork; and, in any event, the nature and quantity of material finds re-covered from a site may depend very much upon the extent of excavation, and particular site conditions. That size of building and social status are not necessarily synonymous is suggested by the disposition of huts at Hod Hill, where the hut claimed by Richmond as that of the tribal chieftain was in itself no more distinguished architecturally than those which surrounded it. (Richmond, 1968, 23 and Fig. 14. The identification was based partly on the location of the hut, within a large private compound, and with direct access to the Steepleton gateway of the camp, and partly on the discovery within it of iron spearheads rather than simply slingstones.) But if a hillfort was occupied, as we may reasonably suppose, in time of unrest and political instability, it is unlikely that the greater effort of constructing a large round-house would be undertaken at the risk of having it razed to the ground, when a smaller hut, which could be rebuilt more readily, would suffice for temporary residence. What does seem to be implied, therefore, by the existence of large round-houses, is a degree of political and economic stability, since the greater structural problems involved would only be worth undertaking if permanence appeared assured for their occupation. That this was so is indicated by the succession of houses at Longbridge Deverill, and the fact that the houses at Little Woodbury, Pimperne, West Brandon and West Plean all lasted through at least two building phases on the selfsame plot of ground.

If progress is to be made in this field, it is evident that more extensive excavation of Iron Age settlements is required, devoted not merely to the recovery of more house-plans, but to an informed assessment of the relationship between settlements and their spatial environment – how much land was controlled or farmed from one centre, how many people each settlement supported, and whether differences in settlement-type reflect a divergent economic or social structure. At Little Woodbury only about one third of the total area enclosed has been excavated; at Pimperne the proportion must be infinitely smaller, and we must certainly concede the possibility of further houses existing within the 11-acre primary enclosure. Even where more than one large round-house has been found, however, as at Longbridge Deverill, it need not follow that any two were contemporary. Before we relegate the *Einzelhof* theory to the category of Iron Age mythology, as Alcock has urged (1965, 192), we should remember that in northern England and Scotland at any rate, where nearly total excavation of settlement-enclosures is practical on account of their reduced area, West Brandon and West Plean have certainly been shown to be essentially single homesteads. In lowland Britain, on the other hand, large round-houses of the Little Woodbury type have yet to be located in a village settlement of the Itford Hill or Plumpton Plain kind (see above pp. 28–30). Distributionally, single homesteads and nucleated villages need not have been mutually exclusive. Though perhaps derived from differing social, economic or cultural traditions, they may well have co-existed at any given point in time in the Iron Age. Until such questions can be clarified by much more intensive field research, we should perhaps desist from treating Little Woodbury as if it were typical of the British Iron Age as a whole, rather than of just one aspect of settlement in a region which happens to have received a disproportionate attention from field archaeologists.

The use of a circular ground-plan for domestic buildings in the British Iron Age, in contrast to the regular occurrence of rectangular houses in Urnfield, Hallstatt and La Tène culture contexts on the Continent, evidently derives from a long-established insular practice. In adopting the round-house as one of the principal 'type-fossils' of his Woodbury culture, Dr Hodson was led to remark that the contrasting distribution of circular houses in Britain and rectangular houses on the Continental mainland was one which was so firmly established that it was unlikely to be seriously challenged by future discoveries (1964b, 99–100). Outside the British Isles, circular houses occurred regularly in one extremely peripheral region only, in the *castros* of north-western Iberia, whence the British examples could scarcely be derived, since the stone-built houses of the peninsular forts were thought all to have been of late Iron Age date. For those who rejected the conventional view that insular Iron Age cultures were the product of immigration from the Continent, here was a further demonstration that Britain in the Iron Age stood in splendid isolation from the rest of Europe.

If Continental parallels for the round-houses of the British Iron Age were lacking, insular antecedents were not hard to find. With circular buildings at the late Bronze Age settlements on Itford Hill (Burstow and Holleyman, 1957) and New Barn Down in Sussex (Curwen, 1934), and at Shearplace Hill, Dorset (Rahtz and ApSimon, 1962), in a later middle Bronze Age Deverel-Rimbury culture context, it was evident that there had been in Britain a long-established practice of building circular dwellings, which could be traced well back into the Bronze Age, if not as far as the Neolithic period. But by comparison with the small and irregular ground-plans of Bronze Age huts, the enlarged and symmetrical layout of circular houses like those at Little Woodbury and Pimperne still appeared to represent a considerable innovation of the Iron Age. Not only were the proportions of the latter much greater, and the arrangement of their concentric circles of postholes much more regular, but also they incorporated structural elements not present in their Bronze Age predecessors. The elaborate porched entrance, possibly sustaining a double set of doors, was not a feature of earlier huts, and the absence of a single central post in the larger Iron Age round-houses, or the absence of any visible central support in the case of the Pimperne house among others, argued a degree of constructional and engineering skill which was not displayed by any of the similar Bronze Age plans.

A timely boost to the case for continuity was then provided by Avery's and Close-Brooks's re-interpretation (1969) of the structures excavated at Shearplace Hill. Their revised – and surely true – sequence for that site (Fig. 12) has not only shown that the use of a double ring of upright roof-supports, hitherto recognised only in Iron Age houses, was a practice already current in the later middle Bronze Age, but has also evidently opened the way to a similar review of circular buildings at Itford Hill, New Barn Down and Plumpton Plain among others. Evidently, we can no longer regard the exceptional size of the Iron Age round-houses of Wessex as an entirely novel departure, if houses approaching 12 metres in diameter, and incorporating a porch which might be seen as the prototype of the elaborate Iron Age examples, were already being built in the middle Bronze Age. But at the same time, the symmetry and regularity of layout of Iron Age round-houses, which, at Pimperne in particular, indicate an extremely sophisticated level of engineering, greatly exceed those

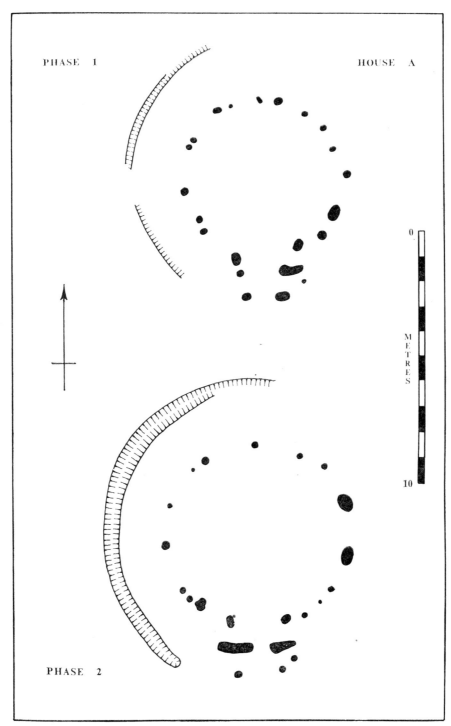

PHASE 1   HOUSE   A

PHASE 2

METRES

0

10

12. *Shearplace Hill, Sydling St Nicholas, Dorset: House A*

of the still very irregular Shearplace Hill buildings. No more so than we should expect, however, for the insular tradition of circular buildings in Britain is scarcely in doubt. The question remains whether this tradition was in such total isolation from the Continental mainstream as we have always supposed. And it is one which can be asked from both viewpoints: whether there are not on the Continent circular houses, other than the peninsular group, which have hitherto escaped our attention, and, conversely, whether there were not in Britain some rectangular dwellings which have been overlooked in our pre-occupation with houses of the Little Woodbury class. To point the way towards a resolution, we must return to the Continental evidence.

First, it must be emphasised that statements concerning the 'Continental' tradition of rectangular building really refer to the Central European convention, rather than one which has been adequately demonstrated in those areas which border upon the Atlantic or the Channel. Until a great deal more fieldwork, involving extensive stripping of Iron Age settlements, is undertaken, particularly in France, it is by no means an assured conclusion that domestic houses in this region will conform exclusively to the rectangular pattern which has been demonstrated further inland at Mont Beuvray, in the Côte d'Or (plan reproduced in Piggott, 1965, Fig. 124), where already the distinctive long rectangular house, which characterises the classic Central European sites, such as the *oppidum* at Manching (Krämer and Schubert, 1970; Krämer, 1960, 1961, 1962), has given way to smaller and rather less regular ground-plans. In the background of the archaeological debate we have the literary record of Strabo, who states quite unequivocally of the Gauls: 'Their houses are large and circular, built of planks and wickerwork, the roof being a dome of heavy thatch' (*Geography* 4, IV, 3), a description which, even to the use of planks as well as wattling, might equally have been written of southern British buildings like that at Pimperne. Without placing undue emphasis upon a single literary reference, the literary record has so far been at variance with the archaeological evidence.

One further source of information – and one which has been long available to, though insufficiently made use of by, prehistorians – should perhaps be introduced in this point, the sculptured reliefs on the column of Marcus Aurelius (Caprino, 1955; Bellorius, 1704). The frequency with which circular huts, as opposed to the rarer rectangular buildings, are shown on the column being fired by Roman soldiers argues convincingly that in the Upper Danube this form of building in the mid-second century was not only present but common. Our problem is to reconcile the evidence of excavation with that of literary sources and sculpture and at the same time to bring the apparently peripheral distributions of circular houses, insular and peninsular, into a more coherent archaeological framework for western Europe.

From older Continental excavations, in fact, it has been evident that rectangularity in house-plan was never there an invariable pattern, though the relatively few circular examples have since been overlooked in our pre-occupation with the more common rectangular buildings of Central Europe (Fig. 13 A, B). More than fifty years ago, Bersu and Goessler had excavated an oval hut at Lochenstein bei Balingen in Baden-Württemburg (1922, 73–103 and Taf. IV), while a more symmetrical plan from a Gallo-Roman context at

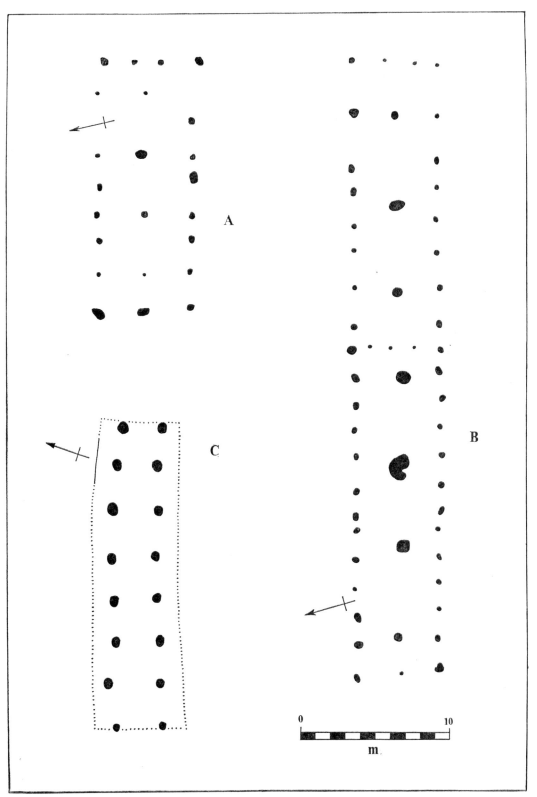

13. *Rectangular houses. A and B, Manching, Bavaria. C, Crickley Hill, Gloucestershire*

Achenheim (Hatt and Heintz, 1951) argued an alternative tradition of circular building. More recent excavations, however, especially in France and Belgium, indicate that these houses need no longer be regarded in isolation or dismissed as freaks. Among the more numerous rectangular or quadrilateral buildings from Dampierre-sur-le-Doubs (Pétrequin, Urlacher and Vuaillat, 1969, Figs 22, 25), south-east of Dijon, was a circular hut, nearly 5 metres in diameter, and clearly defined by a ring of fifteen postholes. It belonged to the earlier occupation, beginning around 1000 B.C., of a two-period settlement of the late Bronze Age, and evidently had been superseded on that site as an architectural type by the final phase of occupation. A significant element of the Dampierre roundhouse, in comparison with British examples, is its incorporation of a porched entrance, projecting outwards from the circle of postholes which formed its perimeter wall.

Among the earliest Continental round huts are those from middle Bronze Age Hilversum culture contexts in the Netherlands. Excavation of a settlement site at Nijnsel (Beex and Hulst, 1968) revealed not only rectangular buildings, but also a circular hut whose function was evidently domestic. Measuring approximately 8·50 metres in diameter, it is once again distinguished by a porched entrance which projects outwards from the main circle of postholes. Internal support for the roof was provided by a number of other posts, arranged rather irregularly in a ring. North of Nijnsel, comparable huts of circular or sub-circular plan have been discovered in recent years at Zijderveld (Hulst, 1965) and Dodewaard (Hulst, 1966), which, in spite of their irregular disposition of postholes, nonetheless retain the outward projecting porch as a prominent feature. In view of the recognised cultural links between Britain and the Netherlands in the middle Bronze Age (I. F. Smith, 1961), it could be argued that the notion of circular building was implanted there as a result of emigration from Britain. At the same time, it does not seem altogether convincing to derive a much wider distribution of Continental round huts from such localised origins in the Netherlands. Oval buildings of the late Bronze Age from the Aude in southern France, at Baous-de-la-Salle (Lauriol, 1958) and the 'Boussecos' settlement (Lauriol, 1963), recovered from motorway construction near Bize, are clearly indicative of another distinctive regional group within a broader tradition in north-western Europe. The oval ground-plan likewise reappears in a late Bronze Age context at Sérézin-du-Rhône in dépt Isère (Combier, 1961). That the circular model had not by the Iron Age been ousted universally in France, however, is demonstrated by a hut of slightly irregular circular plan from Berry-au-Bac, dépt Aisne (Chevallier and Ertlé, 1965), where fragments of *vases carénés* indicated a dating broadly contemporary with the rectangular structure excavated further north in the Aisne at Chassemy (Rowlett and Boureux, 1969), and regarded generally as much more characteristic of the Marnian culture. The origins and development of this tradition of circular or sub-circular building will evidently require further research on the Continent, but we can no longer doubt that such a tradition was much more widespread in France and the Netherlands than British prehistorians have hitherto been prepared to admit. In consequence, the contrast in building practice between Britain and north-western Europe has been more apparent than real, and its importance in the invasion controversy has been much exaggerated.

What really distinguishes the British Iron Age round-houses from the Continental examples which we have cited here is still their greater size, which not only involves a greater structural symmetry and superior engineering skills, but also may well reflect certain social differences – a contrast to a community which occupied a series of smaller, but individual, dwellings. On the Continent, only one site which included sub-circular houses of dimensions comparable to the large British round-houses has so far come to the present writer's notice, that at Lommel, Hoever Heide (de Laet, 1961). Both buildings lack the symmetry of layout of the Wessex round-houses, and both lack the regular settings of post-holes which in the British examples provide the principal roof-support. But whatever their structural differences, the size of the Lommel houses affords the only corroborative evidence yet available for Strabo's claim, itself quite possibly based upon an observation by Posidonius, that the Gauls occupied *large* circular houses. What recent excavation has demonstrated beyond doubt is that circular building was not the exclusive prerogative of the British Iron Age. Contrary to Dr Hodson's belief, we may be confident that increasing attention to the problems of settlement archaeology on the Continent, and in France in particular, will reveal an increasing number of circular houses and huts in later Bronze Age and Iron Age contexts, just as in Britain Bersu's excavation at Little Woodbury sounded the final death-knell of the pit-dwelling, and opened a new phase in the study of the settlement archaeology of the British Iron Age. Whether Strabo will be fully vindicated by the findings of field archaeology, or whether it will transpire that the large and symmetrical round-house really was an innovation, in isolation, of the British Iron Age, remains to be seen. But it is now evident that the view of total contrast between the circular British tradition and the rectangular Continental building fashion is an erroneous simplification. Rather we should see the emphasis upon rectangularity as an aspect of Central European settlement, in contrast to an Atlantic preference for circular building. The issue being no longer one of black or white, we may reasonably anticipate a penumbra across France and the Low Countries, in which elements of both traditions meet. And indeed, from the dating of the examples so far discovered, we might infer that there was in these regions, as in Britain – and perhaps in the Hispanic peninsula as well – a long-established tradition of circular domestic construction, extending back into the Bronze Age, from which in Britain to the north-west and in the Peninsula to the south-west the round-house subsequently developed its special characteristics in the Iron Age, insulated to a degree from the rectangular architectural fashion which dominated central Europe.

If we are to exhort our Continental colleagues to new endeavours in the field of settlement archaeology, we should at the same time question how total was that isolation in Britain from the Central European tradition, and to what extent the absence of rectangular buildings of the British Iron Age is to be attributed to our failure to anticipate their presence. Rectangular houses had been claimed by both Smith at Park Brow (Wolseley, Smith and Hawley, 1927) and Wheeler at Maiden Castle (1943, 124 and Fig. 22), on the basis of groups of paired postholes, of which neither structure seems particularly convincing by comparison with classic Central European long-houses. In fact, both these posthole groupings would currently be explained as settings for timber granaries, corn-drying racks, or perhaps even domestic shrines. Elsewhere, similar attempts have been made to explain somewhat irregular groups of postholes as rectangular buildings, at Ivinghoe Beacon, in Buckinghamshire (Cotton and Frere, 1968, Fig. 8), at West Plean, Stirlingshire (Steer, 1955), or in Wiltshire at Budbury (Wainwright, 1970). A problematical contender is the group of rectangular structures excavated by Stanford in the hillforts of Herefordshire (1970), though even here proper appraisal of their function must await fuller publication. Undoubtedly the most convincing examples, however, have come from the interior settlement of the hillfort at Crickley Hill, Gloucestershire, where the proportions of the buildings compare favourably with those of Central European sites (Fig. 13 C and Pl. XI).

A major factor in our failure to locate rectangular houses of the Iron Age in Britain has been the tacit assumption that a house cannot exist without postholes. In consequence any structure whose foundations did not penetrate into bedrock is unlikely to be recognised in the majority of contemporary excavations. One of the principal merits, however, of a rectangular plan as opposed to a circular one is that it is possible to construct the entire building free-standing, by using an arrangement of sleeper-beams jointed into a solid framework, thereby obviating the need for posts sunk into the ground, and consequently reducing the probability of timbers rotting so soon. The likelihood of recovering evidence of such a building is slight: the best we might hope for would be the faint traces of the sill-beams themselves, where these had been recessed into the ground, or buried under an accumulation of wind-blown sand or vegetable debris. The incomplete outline of a rectangular structure at West Harling (Clark and Fell, 1953, Fig. 9) might be the only surviving evidence for such a building. An alternative but related method of building is the log-cabin technique, which requires only a minimum of vertical timbers – a substantial rectangular house measuring 30 feet in length by 15 feet in breadth might be supported by only six uprights at the four corners and the middle of the two long walls. With its postholes so widely spaced, the plan of such a building could easily be obscured on most Iron Age settlement sites by other intrusions, such as working hollows or pits belonging to another phase of occupation, even if the area opened in the first place was large enough to detect its presence.

Whilst our preoccupation with circular houses, built on a foundation of postholes, may have obscured the potential existence of alternative forms of construction, it is hard to imagine that we have overlooked large long-houses of the classic Central European type. It has been the purpose of this discussion, however, to suggest that, even on the Continent, there is a good deal of variation in house construction, and that we should not expect, further west, buildings as substantial and clearly outlined as those at Manching. Examples cited above (p. 50) from the Aude, and from Sérézin-du-Rhône, were defined, not by settings of postholes, but by oval hollows into which their foundations were recessed. A sub-rectangular pit at Long Wittenham, Berks (Savory, 1937), dated by a series of distinctive angular bowls and jars to the early La Tène period, could well have been a structure of this kind. Elsewhere, floor levels may furnish the only surviving evidence for small rectangular houses. Less than a mile from Long Wittenham, below the Sinodun hills, excavation in 1947 uncovered the corner of what was surely a rectangular house-floor (Rhodes, 1948), the sides of which were traced within the area opened for nearly 3 metres in one direction and just under 2 metres in the other. The eaves of this building were presumably supported on a low wall of chalk blocks, the rubble footings of which were traced along the perimeter of the floor. Examples could doubtless be multiplied by a study of older excavation reports, and what more appropriate starting-point than the classic site at All Cannings Cross, where a series of oblong floors, interpreted by the Cunningtons (1923) as forecourts of houses which had not survived, themselves closely resemble in dimensions and design the rectangular buildings at Mont Beuvray?

We have already seen that the apparent contrast in house-types, between the circular tradition in Britain and the predominance of rectangular plans in Central Europe, has been taken by some prehistorians as a measure of the insularity of the British Iron Age, devoid of intrusive elements from abroad. This contrasting pattern now being qualified, on the one hand by the discovery of circular buildings on the Continent and on the other by a reappraisal of the evidence for rectangular houses in Britain, we must now also question the inference that Iron Age settlements in Britain stemmed from solely insular origins. That the tradition of circular building was already well-established in Britain at the outset of the Iron Age is not in doubt. But we can no longer argue conversely against the invasion hypothesis on the grounds that immigrants would necessarily have brought with them their characteristic rectangular buildings, since they could well have come from parts of the Continent where both circular and rectangular houses were in use. Throughout this discussion, we have been concerned with houses of the pre-Belgic period in Britain. When we encounter a phase of prehistory in which few prehistorians would doubt that there were substantial waves of invaders into south-eastern Britain, the marked absence of an innovating house-type is instructive. Indeed, from examples excavated at the *oppidum* of Camulodunum (C. F. C. Hawkes and Hull, 1947, 46 ff), and beneath the early Roman villa at Lockleys, Welwyn (Ward-Perkins, 1938b, Pl. LXX), 'Belgic' structures would appear to have been even less sophisticated than their native predecessors. Much the same could be said of the Arras culture of eastern Yorkshire, the Continental origins of which are hardly in dispute, but which has so far yielded only minimal evidence of settlement-remains. Why are we lacking here rectangular buildings of a distinctive Continental type, if this is to be regarded as the invariable mark of an intrusive population? Were the invaders content to defer to native practice in domestic building, or were they already using a similar form of house in their homeland? Or should we attribute the lack of rectangular houses in greater numbers in Britain solely to a deficiency in field techniques? Whichever solution we opt for, it must be equally applicable to other periods and regions where no innovating house-type has survived to bear witness to newcomers. And though we may still cherish the roundhouse as a type-fossil of the British Iron Age, it would be unwise in the light of recent excavations on the Continent to regard the circular-building tradition in Britain any longer as an exclusive index of insularity.

4
Fortifications
and warfare

FOR CENTURIES before the advent of scientific archaeology, prehistoric earthworks had attracted the attention and speculation of antiquaries and travellers. To those for whom these fortifications were not the work of giants or of the devil himself, it seemed logical to attribute them to the Roman legions or Viking raiders. Such spurious attributions are reflected in a variety of place-names: Devil's Dyke, Caesar's Camp, Danes Camp and so forth. The sheer size of these monuments made them less vulnerable to the depredations of enthusiastic clergy and country squires, for whom barrows offered more prospect of reward with less expenditure of effort. It was not until the second half of the nineteenth century that serious fieldwork was undertaken to establish the historical context of hillforts, with Martyn-Atkins's excavations at Uffington Castle around 1850 (Pl. IV), and more especially Pitt-Rivers's investigations of Sussex earthworks in the 1860s and 70s. An attempt to classify earthworks in both typological and chronological terms was made in 1908, with the publication of Hadrian Allcroft's *Earthwork of England*, a major landmark in the development of hillfort studies. The basis for modern research, however, remains C. F. C. Hawkes's paper of 1931, which not only considered variations in rampart and entrance construction, but also for the first time produced distributions of hillforts which could be attributed to specific phases of the Iron Age.

In retrospect, as we might expect, Hawkes's views require some modification in the light of further excavation and revisions in Iron Age chronology. Though the structural sequences worked out for Quarley Hill (1940a), Bury Hill (1940c) and St Catharine's Hill (Pl. V) (Hawkes, Myres and Stevens, 1930) remain essentially valid, many archaeologists would now question whether the apparent proliferation of hillforts of the Iron B phase can be so confidently assigned to Celtic immigrants from the Continent. In 1940, Hawkes had argued that the Hampshire hillforts, including the unfinished earthwork at Ladle Hill (Pl. VI), together with the forts which Curwen and Wilson had excavated in Sussex (Curwen, 1927, 1929, 1930, 1931a, 1931b, 1932; Wilson, 1938), were erected by the native population of southern England as a result of a war-scare in the third century B.C. 'That invasion', he wrote, 'must have let loose bands of Celtic warriors from across the Channel over large parts of the south country, and against them the A₂ inhabitants had to undertake the great work of building these hillforts and settlement defences' (1940c, 333). With the extended chronology for the Iron Age now current, and a consequential extension of the date-range assigned to specific hillforts, the activity represented by their construction now seems rather less intensive, though the infiltration of immigrants in early La Tène times may nonetheless have provoked the re-occupation of existing forts, or even the construction of new defensive works in certain instances. But Dr Grace Simpson's reiteration of the view that the hillforts

54

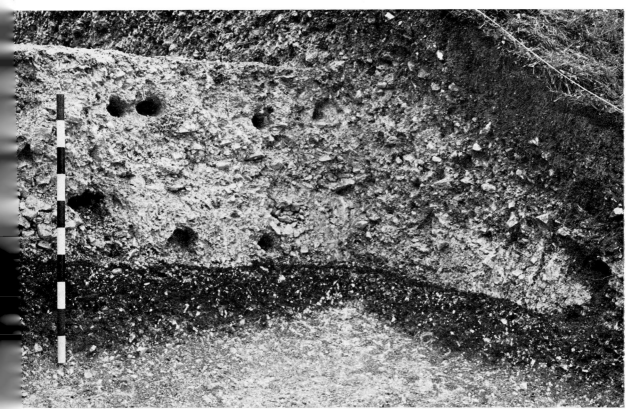

I (a) and (b) Blewburton Hill, Berkshire: cavities of timber-lacing in face of primary rampart

of southern England were designed to repel an invasion of Continental settlers in the third century (1964, 209) would carry little conviction among most prehistorians today. Recent research, on the other hand, has gone a long way toward reinforcing the links between British hillforts and their Continental counterparts. It is now evident that techniques such as timber-lacing of ramparts, a recurrent feature of Continental fortifications, were adopted more extensively in Britain than was hitherto supposed. Furthermore, it is now apparent that the construction of hillforts was not an exclusive innovation of the Iron Age in Britain, but that, as on the Continent, such earthworks may already have existed in the late Bronze Age. Before we can assess the significance of hillfort distributions in terms of historical movements of people, we shall need to consider what other evidence may exist to suggest that they were built to combat a martial invasion from abroad rather than inter-tribal raids in Britain.

As a result of the researches of the Committee on Ancient Earthworks and Fortified Enclosures at the beginning of this century, three classes of camp were distinguished, according to their topographical location – promontory forts, contour forts and plateau forts. At a time when relatively little excavation had been conducted on these sites, it is understandable that classification should be based upon superficial observation. Such a classification, however, provides no sound basis for supposing that the builders of a certain kind of earthwork were related culturally or politically, or even that forts of any particular group were occupied contemporaneously. The location of a defensive earthwork will have been very largely dependent upon factors of local topography, and need not therefore be especially significant in cultural or chronological terms. A natural promontory, either coastal or inland, clearly presents opportunities for fortification without the massive labour required by an enclosed hillfort; examples of widely disparate date and cultural affinities may be cited at Hengistbury Head, Hants (Bushe-Fox, 1915), Leckhampton near Cheltenham (Burrow et al., 1925; Champion, 1974), and on the north Cornish coast at Trevelgue Head (Note in *PPS*, 5, 1939, 254, and information by courtesy of Mr C. K. Croft Andrew). If promontory forts are readily identified by their situation, the distinction between contour forts and plateau forts is by no means so clearly defined.

In view of these difficulties, in the preparation of the Ordnance Survey Map of Southern Britain in the Iron Age, Rivet adopted an alternative means of classification, based upon size and rampart construction. This system, too, evidently had its limitations, since both criteria will again have been determined in some measure by local conditions. He demonstrates, for instance, that the simplest means of constructing a univallate plateau fort is by throwing the material excavated from the ditch inwards to form the bank. If the fortification is being constructed around the contour of a steep-sided hill, on the other hand, the effort of throwing the upcast on to the inner lip of the ditch is much greater, and for this reason the inner rampart is often built of material from a smaller quarry ditch inside the perimeter of the camp, as in the final phase of Scratchbury, Wilts. The bulk of rubble excavated from the main ditch may then be thrown down the slope to form a counterscarp. This technique, Rivet argues, produces a result not far removed from the defences of a multivallate hillfort, and affords a very plausible sequence to account for the introduction of multivallation in Britain (1958, 31–2). In certain instances, however, rampart construction may have a cultural or at least regional significance; this is most apparent in the case of hillforts with widely spaced ramparts and allied groups in the south-west of England which have been recognised by Lady Fox (1958). A detailed consideration of south-western types, and their relationships with fortified sites in Brittany, however, is beyond the scope of the present study. We must now turn our attention to the hillforts of southern and south-eastern England which are our primary concern.

Largely for economic reasons, hillfort excavators in Britain have generally concentrated their efforts upon the ramparts and entrances, and neglected the extensive stripping of the area enclosed by the earthworks. The merits of excavating a cutting through the defences of a hillfort as a preliminary to work elsewhere are obvious, for only by this means can the archaeologist unfold the structural history of the site. This procedure has the additional advantage that it can be repeated if the complexities of the structural sequence are not fully understood from the first section, whereas an area excavation of the entrance, for instance, allows no such room for error. Armed with information gained from rampart cuttings, the excavator is then in a position to tackle the entrance with a greater probability of correlating the structural sequence revealed there with the overall history of the forti-fications. This standard practice, however, results in only a partial knowledge of the nature and occupation of hillforts, neglecting both the occupation within the defences and the areas outside the hillfort, where settlements dependent upon it for their security may nonetheless have existed. The allocation of adequate resources to tackle these problems is one of the principal responsibilities of archaeological research in the future.

Excavations of hillfort defences have at least provided us with a good deal of information regarding the construction of Iron Age fortifications. Ramparts were built by one of two principal methods: either as a simple 'dump' bank of rubble, or by retaining the material quarried from the ditch within a front-and-rear revetment to form a 'box'-rampart (Fig. 14). On *a priori* grounds, we might be tempted to regard the former as the earlier type, which was subsequently developed into the structurally more elaborate box-type, but excavation has shown that such a typological sequence would be erroneous. Indeed, the stratigraphy of rampart-cuttings has frequently demonstrated that the sequence was the other way round, as at Blewburton Hill, Berks, for instance (Collins, 1947, 1952, 1959; D. W. Harding, 1967). For the present, therefore, we shall consider each type separately, without prejudice to the question of chronology.

In essence, the box-rampart is designed to achieve a greater height-to-width ratio, which will give the defender on the parapet a tactical advantage over his enemy, and to present the assailant with a vertical face which must be scaled once he has successfully bridged the ditch. Postholes or gullies which would have retained upright timbers have been found in alignment along the front and rear of the ramparts of a number of hillforts in southern England, including Hollingbury (Curwen, 1932) and Cissbury in Sussex (Curwen, 1931b, 22 and Pl. IV), Bindon Hill (Wheeler, 1953) and Maiden Castle in Dorset (Wheeler, 1943), and Blewburton Hill, Berkshire. In other instances, comparable features almost certainly existed, but have perhaps been missed by excavators whose rampart cuttings were narrower than the interval between the uprights, so that the failure to locate such postholes by excavation does not necessarily prove their absence. Only by extensive stripping of the bank can

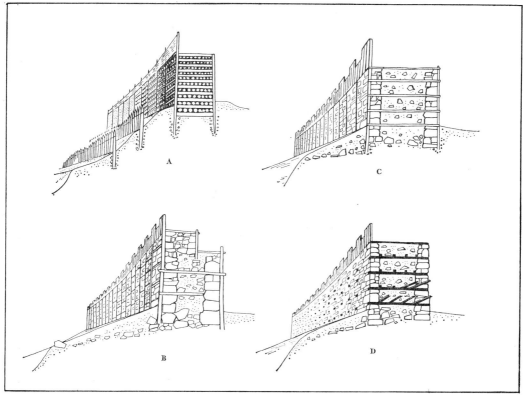

14. *Reconstruction of box-ramparts in Britain and Europe. A, timber wall of log construction, with rows of stakes as* chevaux de frise, *Lausitz culture, e.g. Niederneundorf, Middle Germany. B, timber-laced rampart with timber-framed stone facing, Lausitz culture, e.g. Schafberg at Löbau, Middle Germany; La Tène culture?, Hunsbury, Northamptonshire. C, timber-laced rampart with timber-framed stone facing, La Tène culture, e.g. Preist, near Bitburg, Rhineland. D, timber-laced rampart with longitudinal and lateral framework, with stone facing, La Tène culture, e.g. Le Camp d'Artus, Huelgoat, Finistère, cf. Caesar's description of the* murus Gallicus *at Avaricum*

the issue be clinched, as was demonstrated so effectively by C. F. C. Hawkes at Buckland Rings, Hants (1937), and more recently by Stead at Grimthorpe (1968), in the East Riding of Yorkshire. The principal disadvantage of a box-rampart constructed in this manner must have been that the weight of the rubble core would cause the uprights both front and rear to bulge outward, unless they themselves were reinforced or braced in some way. The most effective means of strengthening the structure is by the use of horizontal cross-ties, binding the front and rear revetments into a single framework. This technique of timber-lacing is extensively employed in Continental hillforts, but until recent years had been recognised on remarkably few sites in southern England. It is scarcely conceivable that box-ramparts with timber-lacing would be built without this additional reinforcement, since otherwise their effective life would surely have been reduced to a matter of months if not weeks. The paucity of known examples in southern England must therefore be attributed to our failure hitherto to detect the faint residual traces of horizontal timbers, the survival rate of which is no greater than that of the actual timbers which we know must have existed within the vertical postholes of the front and rear revetments. Whereas the position of a vertical timber can be readily traced from the point at which it penetrates the old ground surface or natural bedrock, once a horizontal beam in the body of a rampart has decayed, the core material will in most instances compress to eliminate all trace of the former cross-ties. The only exception to this process will be where the core, as for instance in chalk, sometimes has already compressed itself like a plaster mould around the timber framework, so that

15. Blewburton Hill, Berkshire: section through northern defences

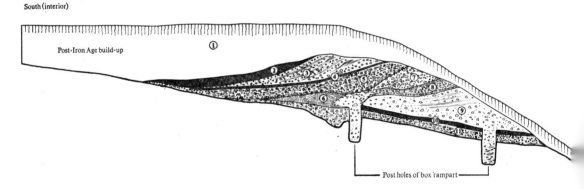

South (interior)

Post-Iron Age build-up

Post holes of box rampart

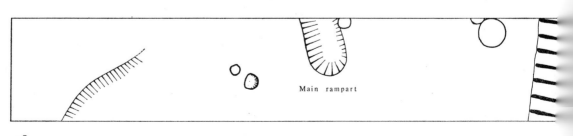

Main rampart

the horizontal cavities remain after the timber has decayed. Such appears to have been the case at the Caburn, where, in 1937, Wilson (1938, 174) found cavities in the chalk rampart, hollow for lengths of up to 4 feet, containing a few grains of dark powder which was all that remained of the horizontal timbers themselves. Similar traces of a timber-laced framework were located on a more extensive scale at Blewburton Hill, Berkshire in 1967 (D. W. Harding, 1967; 1972, 47 ff). Along the front and rear of the primary rampart was a series of postholes, spaced at intervals of approximately 4 metres, which would have supported the upright revetment of the bank (Fig. 15). When the front face of the rampart was cut back to expose a vertical section behind the timber revetment, a number of

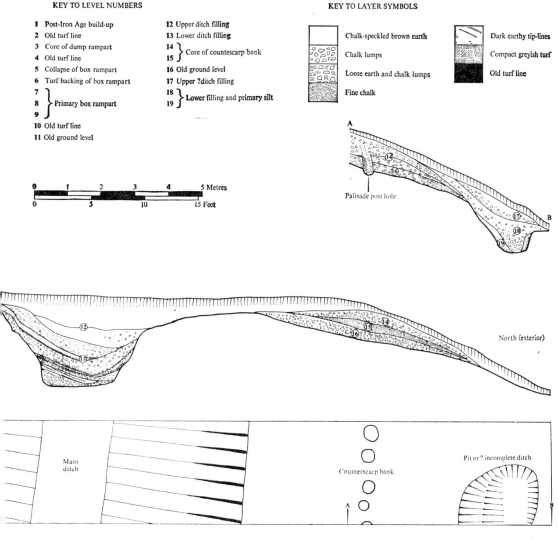

KEY TO LEVEL NUMBERS

1 Post-Iron Age build-up
2 Old turf line
3 Core of dump rampart
4 Old turf line
5 Collapse of box rampart
6 Turf backing of box rampart
7
8 } Primary box rampart
9
10 Old turf line
11 Old ground level

12 Upper ditch filling
13 Lower ditch filling
14
15 } Core of countescarp bank
16 Old ground level
17 Upper ?ditch filling
18
19 } Lower filling and primary silt

KEY TO LAYER SYMBOLS

Chalk-speckled brown earth
Chalk lumps
Loose earth and chalk lumps
Fine chalk

Dark earthy tip-lines
Compact greyish turf
Old turf line

Palisade post hole

North (exterior)

Main ditch

Counterscarp bank

Pit or ? incomplete ditch

cavities appeared, extending horizontally into the core of the bank, in some of which traces of charcoal clearly indicated that they had contained timber cross-braces (Pl. VII). By carefully exposing the rampart from above, it was then possible to reveal the timber-lacing in plan. The horizontal cross-members had apparently been introduced in several levels, though the weight of the rampart had subsequently distorted the symmetry of the structure. The dating evidence of this rampart at Blewburton is not conclusive in itself, but it certainly succeeded the earlier palisaded camp on the site, which on pottery evidence should belong to the sixth century or thereabouts, and possibly with no great lapse of time between the two phases of occupation. It also remains to be seen whether this method of construction was used extensively around the defences – whether it was missed by accident in other cuttings, or whether it really was restricted to the rampart which flanked the entrance on the western side of the fort.

In the light of experience at Blewburton Hill, it is a reasonable inference that many, if not most, of the hillforts on the chalk downs of Wessex and the south-east which display upright timber revetments at the front and back of the rampart would originally have had horizontal members as well. In some instances, however, the front revetment posts are not matched by a parallel line at the back of the bank, as in the case of the inner rampart at Wandlebury (Hartley, 1956), though this does not necessarily preclude the possibility that horizontal or sloping ties were incorporated within the bank behind the timber facing as a variant of the normal timber-laced design. The discovery of charred timbers behind the front stone-facing of the Leckhampton rampart (Champion, 1974), where there is no corresponding wall at the rear, reinforces this possibility. Even given internal bracing, the danger of the vertical timber revetments bulging under the weight of the core must have been considerable. It is conceivable that turves may have been stacked in front of the timber facing, to reduce the risk of collapse. Without greatly reducing the effective angle of the obstructing earthworks, such a measure would have the additional merit of eliminating the foothold which the *berm*, separating the front row of timbers from the ditch, might otherwise have afforded to an assailant.

Most impressive of the British box-ramparts are those in which the front- and rear-facing walls are constructed of stone. The distribution of such camps evidently reflects in some measure the local availability of building materials, with the majority of examples off the chalks – Leckhampton, Glos, Maiden Castle, Bickerton and Eddisbury in Cheshire (Varley, 1948, 60; 1964, 95–7), and Dinorben in Denbighshire. One of the finest illustrations of this technique excavated in recent years is at Rainsborough Camp, Northants (Avery *et al.*, 1967). Here the rampart of the earliest hillfort was reinforced along its inner edge by three tiers of stone walling rising to a height of over 2 metres above ground level within (Pl. VIII). The outer edge of the rampart was apparently reinforced in the same manner, with the topmost tier supporting a timber parapet which towered some 7 metres above the bottom of the ditch. The principal sections in which this remarkable construction was exposed were immediately adjacent to the entrance to the camp, and it is possible that the tiered effect on the inner edge of the rampart was here exaggerated, as it curved inwards to join up with the framework which embraced the guard-rooms in the entrance (Fig. 16). Nonetheless, the introduction of a stepped revetment along the outer face of the bank is provocative, since we might imagine that this would surely have impaired the effectiveness of the defences. In order to explain this phenomenon, we must either accept Avery's contention that turves were stacked in front of the walls to produce a steep sloping rampart, or conclude that military efficiency in the construction of the Rainsborough hillfort played a secondary role to architectural ostentation! And if this seems a flippant motive to attribute to early Iron Age hillfort-builders, we may recall that the Celtic chieftain who ordered the construction of the Heuneberg on the Upper Danube was apparently prepared to adopt from the eastern Mediterranean architectural fashions which in a Central European hillfort may be regarded as more ostentatious than practical (Dehn, 1953).

One of the most massively defended, and, in its hey-day, visually spectacular hillforts in southern Britain was the univallate camp which occupied a spur on the western scarp of the Cotswolds overlooking the Severn valley at Crickley Hill in Gloucestershire (Dixon, 1972; 1974). Here the original rampart (the excavator's Period 2) was reinforced front and back by walls of limestone slabs, which still survived at one point to a height of 1·8 metres, revealing in the face three tiers of sockets for horizontal timber braces. The walls had evidently been built in sections, indicated by the differing thickness of limestone slabs which had been derived from different depths within the quarry ditch. Furthermore, two building breaks were visible in the front wall, behind which low foundation walls extended from front to back, creating a box effect in the body of the rampart. The horizontal cross-ties were further supported by an internal arrangement of timber uprights, based upon a double row of post-holes which were traced along the alignment of the bank. This defensive system was apparently destroyed by fire, which reduced the rubble core to quicklime, subsequently slaked by water action to form the hard white concretion which faced its excavators. North of the entrance, at any rate, it appeared that the conflagration had been generated from the interior of the camp, probably in a deliberate slighting of the defences after the capture or abandonment of the camp.

In due course the front wall of the rampart was rebuilt on the collapsed footings which survived demolition (Period 3A). At its rear, however, it is not entirely clear whether the revetment wall was refurbished at this stage, or whether it simply sloped down into the interior of the camp. The principal development of Period 3B was the massive refortification of the entrance. First, semi-circular bastions were constructed on either side of the entrance passage, replacing on its southern flank the end of the Period 3A rampart, and enclosing the end of the Period 2 wall to the north. The northern bastion was founded on a stone raft filling the earlier ditch end, and abutted directly upon an inner hornwork which led to the outer gateway. The whole defensive system was completed by a vast outer hornwork which closed off direct access to the inner gates, and which was built, like the earlier ramparts, with construction breaks and incorporating timber-lacing. Material for this extension was derived from an outer ditch embracing the outer hornwork. At the same time, the main ditch to the south of the entrance was widened and its inner edge was reinforced

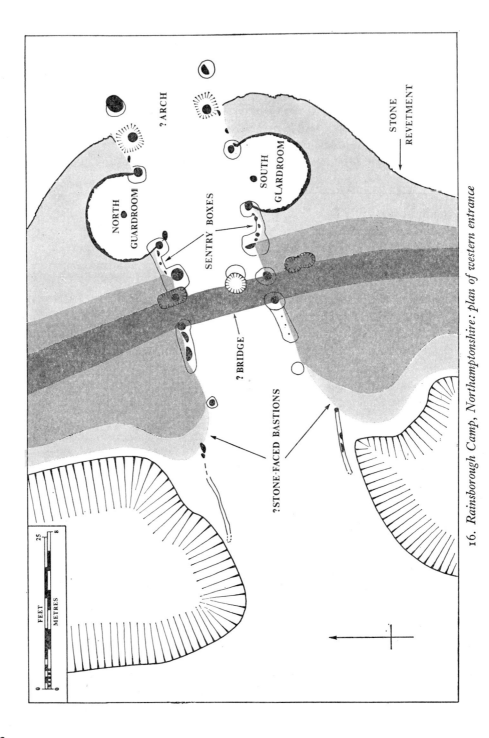

16. *Rainsborough Camp, Northamptonshire: plan of western entrance*

STONE REVETMENT

?ARCH

NORTH GUARDROOM

SOUTH GUARDROOM

SENTRY BOXES

?BRIDGE

?STONE-FACED BASTIONS

FEET
METRES

by a wall which, on excavation, still rose 3·3 metres from the foot of the ditch. Such defences would be exceptionally impressive for any Iron Age hillfort; more so at Crickley, however, since the entire occupation appears to have come to an end by the fifth century B.C. or thereabouts. All credit is due to the excavators for their skill in recovering the intricate details of the construction technique of this complex fortification which, for both its structural grandeur and its remarkable series of rectangular houses, must rank as one of the most important hillfort excavations conducted since the war.

With fully timber-laced ramparts being recognised more extensively in southern England the distribution of hillforts with timber-laced defences in Britain begins to conform more meaningfully to an overall European picture. Hitherto the Scottish examples appeared sufficiently out on a limb to warrant Childe's interpretation of the Abernethy culture as the product of a sea-borne invasion from the Continental mainland (1935, 195 and 236–7; 1946, 129–30). An alternative interpretation, proposed by Hawkes and Piggott (1948, 47), derived the Scottish timber-laced and vitrified forts from southern Britain by an overland route through Cheshire and the Welsh borders, and thence by sea into south-western Scotland. But even so, the paucity of truly timber-laced ramparts in the south of England seemed scarcely sufficient to sustain such a view. It is becoming increasingly evident that timber-lacing is not restricted to a few sites in southern England, with outliers in Cheshire and the Welsh marches. In particular, unpublished excavations at Hunsbury, Northants and Alton, Staffordshire, provide crucial evidence for an intensification of the Midland distribution. Ultimately it may be possible to relate the Scottish timber-laced forts to a cultural continuum in north-western Europe, without invoking a sea-borne invasion to explain their presence in Scotland, virtually detached from their Continental origins.

In her classic study of British camps with timber-laced ramparts, Mrs Cotton (1954; 1957) distinguished two principal Continental prototypes, which she named after the La Tène 2 hillfort at Preist, near Bitburg in the Rhineland, and the alternative form of timber construction, described by Caesar, at Avaricum. The Preist rampart (e.g. Fig. 14, C) was retained by a timber revetment along its front and rear faces, reinforced between the vertical timbers by dry-stone walling. The verticals themselves were braced by horizontal cross-ties extending from front to back, to form a solid framework which held the core of the rampart. At the same time, the front vertical timbers may have been sufficiently substantial to support a breastwork along the crest of the fortification. At Avaricum, by contrast, the body of the rampart contained a framework of transverse and longitudinal timbers arranged alternately in layers (e.g. Fig. 14, D). Furthermore, vertical timbers form no part of the front and rear revetment; these are composed entirely of stone, through which the lateral timbers project, to leave upon decay a series of cavities resembling putlock holes in a medieval fortification. This latter form of construction Mrs Cotton attributed to the period of the Gallic campaign, noting that the distribution in France corresponded broadly to the territory occupied by Caesar during the period 58–51 B.C. Its development out of earlier Hallstatt and La Tène forms of box-rampart could be attributed, on the basis of Caesar's comments, to the need for an effective counter to assault by fire and the battering-ram: 'The masonry protects it from fire, the timber from destruction by battering-ram, which can neither pierce nor knock to pieces a structure braced internally by beams running generally to a length of forty feet in one piece' (*de bello Gallico*, 7, 23). This description of the classic *murus gallicus*, which evidently was sufficiently effective to attract Caesar's professional and detailed attention, is a clear tribute to the engineering skill of the Gauls; indeed the ability to manipulate and utilise timbers up to forty feet in continuous length might well be remembered in any discussion of Iron Age domestic carpentry and architecture.

We should not, however, make the mistake of regarding these two 'classic' types as rigorously dictating the rampart construction adopted by hillfort engineers on the Continent throughout the Iron Age. Even Caesar admitted some variation within his definition of the *murus gallicus*: '*muri autem omnes Gallici hac* fere *forma sunt*', and indeed Dehn has pointed out that vertical timbers, a characteristic of the Preist type of defensive wall, are incorporated in the entrances of the Gallic wall forts at Otzenhausen, Le Petit Celland and Le Camp d'Artus (1960, 50–1). At the same time, the use of nails to bind together the transverse and horizontal timbers of the Avaricum type of rampart, well illustrated by Wheeler's excavations at Le Camp d'Artus, Huelgoat and Le Petit Celland (Wheeler and Richardson, 1957, Pls III, XVII), is by no means a *sine qua non* of the *murus gallicus*. Neither of the terms used by Caesar (*revinciuntur* and *coagmentatis*) specifically imply a metal binding or nail, so that the use of nails alone should not be regarded as sufficient to justify the identification of a Gallic wall-fort. A salutary warning in this respect is afforded by the example of Burghead in Morayshire, where nails were claimed to have been found at one point in the construction of the timber-laced rampart. Formerly regarded as the only true example of an Avaricum-type fort in Britain, Burghead has more recently been assigned to the Pictish period on the basis of radio-carbon dates (Small, 1969). The dating of other earthworks of 'devolved Avaricum'-type recognised by Mrs Cotton, including Corley Camp, Warwickshire and Almondbury III, remains very much a matter for debate. In Britain, at any rate, it seems fair to conclude that availability of materials as well as local circumstances and traditions will equally have governed the particular technique adopted in the construction of timber-laced ramparts, and that typology should not, therefore, be invoked too rigidly as an indicator of chronology.

What we can say regarding the chronological relationship of timber-laced ramparts and the simpler *glacis* construction is that in certain instances, notably at Rainsborough Camp and Blewburton Hill (Fig. 15), excavation has clearly demonstrated that an earlier box-rampart was reconstructed in a subsequent phase as a dump-rampart. It is difficult however, to conceive of any other method whereby a box-rampart, which has been allowed to fall into a state of dilapidation, could be reconstituted, other than simply by clearing the collapsed debris and silt from the ditch and throwing it over the broken-down rampart to form a dump. For this reason, site sequences such as those from Blewburton and Rainsborough need not prejudice the earlier dating of dump-ramparts elsewhere. Once again, the confident identification of early dump-ramparts is hampered by the inadequacies of older excavations, whose narrow cuttings might easily have been sited between the postholes of a timber framework; but Bury Hill (Phase 1), Quarley Hill and St Catharine's Hill in Hampshire are possible examples where the dump-technique was employed in an early phase of the Iron Age. The construction of box-ramparts in the later Iron Age in southern and south-eastern Britain is less easy to substantiate, though in Cornwall the case of Castle Dore (Radford, 1951) and the Rumps (Brooks, 1964) argues for continued use into the second and first centuries B.C. The most likely instance at present is the Caburn, where Wilson assigned the outer timber-laced rampart to the first century B.C., on the basis of pottery in the old turf line which sealed the ditch of the previous phase (1938, 188–9). Our conclusions, therefore, concerning the relationship of the two techniques must remain fluid: typology alone provides no sound basis for suggesting the chronological priority of either one over the other. The *glacis* technique may well have commended itself for simplicity and speed of construction in times of unexpected unrest, when the imminence of attack did not permit the more elaborate preparations required for a box-rampart to be built. This consideration alone may account for the reconstitution in dump-technique of the ramparts at Blewburton and Rainsborough and elsewhere on the fringes of the Belgic south-east, in the later second or first centuries B.C. To explain these refortifications, Avery has argued convincingly that they were designed, not to repel actual Belgic invaders, but to afford some measure of protection against marauding bands, dispossessed of their own lands by the Belgae, who were moving west in search of plunder and new dominions (Avery *et al.*, 1967, 292). In this instance, then, the *glacis* technique might have been adopted purely out of expediency, without regard for the finer points of military tactics. By contrast, the use of dump-ramparts in association with a broad, shallow ditch, on the lines of the Fécamp earthworks, certainly was tactical, and will be dealt with in greater detail in due course.

While recognising the obvious merit of a box-rampart – that it presented a vertical face to the assailant, and at the same time enabled the builders to achieve greater height without increasing the width of the base of the rampart – we should not minimise the effectiveness of the *glacis*-type earthwork. Less pretentious in design, it nonetheless presented a formidable obstacle to assault, and nowhere more formidable than the Iron B refortification of Maiden Castle, Dorset (Pls XII, XIII), where, burdened with its weapons and shields, a hostile force had to scale a slope which rose 80 feet from the bottom of the ditch at an angle of nearly 40 degrees, without foothold or shelter from the hail of fire launched by the defenders on the summit. It was these same Iron B occupants of Maiden Castle who there introduced the concept of multivallation, a technique which, though known elsewhere, is especially characteristic of the later Iron Age hillforts of Wessex and the south-west. Wheeler claimed that the refortification of Maiden Castle was designed to afford protection in depth against the use of the sling, and that this tactical innovation, together with evidence for new ceramic forms, indicated that Iron B culture was introduced into Dorset from Brittany (1943). The stimulus for this immigration from across the Channel was seen as the defeat of the Veneti by Caesar in 56 B.C. For Maiden Castle, therefore, and by implication for Wessex as a whole, multivallation was apparently to be regarded as a first-century innovation. The subsequent publication by Wheeler and Richardson of their researches in northern

France was already sufficient to cast doubt upon the ceramic affinities of Wessex and Brittany, though it served to reinforce the validity of a link between the multivallate cliff-castles of the Breton coast and the cliff-castles of Cornwall. More significant, however, was the discovery in 1957 of the coin-hoard at Le Catillon in Jersey, itself dated to the period of the Gallic campaign, the implications of which for the Maiden Castle chronology have been summarised by Frere (1958, 84–92). At Maiden Castle, coins only appear in Wheeler's Iron C phase, which he had dated to A.D. 25; their absence from any B context can scarcely be coincidental, since no less than fifteen coins were found stratified in Iron C levels. The appearance of Durotrigan coins, comparable to those from Maiden Castle, in the Le Catillon hoard, therefore, has crucial implications for the Maiden Castle chronology, and consequently for the question of multivallation. Evidently, the coin-using Iron C culture of Dorset must be dated at least to the mid-first century B.C., and, consequently, the Iron B phase might well be pushed back into the second century. Multivallation could still be derived ultimately from Brittany via the south-west, since a Venetic link with Cornwall could still be maintained. But there is no longer any requirement to invoke an invasion into Wessex to account for its appearance there. It is not proposed here to elaborate upon the south-western regional variants of multivallate fortifications, which have been dealt with in detail by Lady Fox (1958), nor upon their various Continental affinities. The fundamental difference, however, between the wide-spaced ramparts of south-western earthworks, and the close-set pattern of the multivallate Wessex forts, is sufficient to indicate that any relationship between the two was indirect at best, and we may prefer alternatively to regard multivallation simply as a natural and logical stage in the development of more complex fortifications and modes of warfare.

Once again, the excavation of Rainsborough Camp has proved instrumental in our reassessment of the phenomenon of multivallation. On the basis of comparison between the stratigraphy of the outer and inner banks, Avery (Avery et al., 1967) concluded that the Rainsborough hillfort had been bivallate from the end of the fifth century B.C. There is no reason to suppose that all or even the majority of hillforts with bivallate defences would have been built so early, and in particular, the Rainsborough evidence need not prejudice the chronology of multivallate earthworks in Dorset or the south-west of England. But Avery is surely right to insist that we should now abandon the equation of box-ramparts with univallation and dump-ramparts with multivallation, and allow a greater flexibility in the dating of each of these defensive techniques. The origins of multivallation remain obscure. Though the concentration of multivallate earthworks in the south-west has led us to look in that direction for their origins, it would perhaps be more accurate to regard multivallate defences as a characteristic of hillforts in the highland zone generally, not excluding those of north Wales, Northumberland and lowland Scotland. Since the evidence – in the form of visible hut-circles – for habitation within these camps is rather more intense than for the hillforts of midland and south-eastern England, it could be that more regular, though not necessarily permanent, occupation of the hillforts of the highland zone resulted in the elaboration of their defences to a degree which was never considered worthwhile for the majority of sites elsewhere. Such a proposition need not be influenced by vulnerability to invasion from abroad so much as by local factors, such as the degree of political stability within a given region. What is abundantly evident is that problems of this kind cannot be effectively resolved until a good deal more excavation has been directed towards the interiors of hillforts and the settlements in their immediate environs.

From this brief survey, it will be apparent that a good deal of information regarding rampart construction has been derived from hillfort excavation since C. F. C. Hawkes's study of 1931. Equally, attention which has been devoted to hillfort entrances has shown that Iron Age engineers, conscious of the vulnerability of the gateway to direct assault unimpeded by an intervening ditch, devised elaborate structures to prevent a breach of the defences. From a superficial survey of extant earthworks, we may see a number of examples where the ends of the rampart adjacent to the entrance have been turned inwards to form an elongated passage, which would have enabled the defenders to repel an attack upon the gates from behind the cover of the flanking banks. In his report on excavations at St Catharine's Hill, Winchester, Hawkes (Hawkes, Myres and Stevens, 1930, 81–2) recognised that this form of entrance was not an innovation of La Tène 3, though structures of this period tended to be elaborated to a degree which was not common previously. Excavation has demonstrated that the banks on either side of the entrance passage-way were generally reinforced by a timber or stone revetment, which enabled the builders to maintain the height of the rampart without risking its collapse upon the main thoroughfare into the camp. At the same time, the timber revetment may well have supported a foot-bridge across the entrance, so that sentries could patrol the entire perimeter of the defences without descending at the gateway. The introduction of a timber passage is an early development in the Iron Age, and one which is not solely dependent upon the military nature of the site. At Pimperne, in Dorset, for instance – where the enclosure bank and ditch can only have served a protective rather than a fully defensive function – the east entrance is flanked by a double row of postholes which evidently retained the inturned banks.

Among early hillforts with timber passages, Rainsborough presents a particularly fine example. In Phase 2A, the passage extended for nearly 60 feet inwards from the entrance causeway, and was flanked for most of its length by postholes supporting a timber revetment (Fig. 15). Two pairs of more substantial posts, sited centrally between the topmost tiers of the rampart, probably sustained a catwalk, 5 feet wide across the passage, directly in front of the main gate itself. Behind the gate, two semicircular guard-rooms (Pl. IX) of dry-stone construction, were set into the internal framework of the rampart; their roofs were apparently of wood, and ladders doubtless provided access for the sentries from the chambers to the parapet above. Finally, the inner limits of the entrance were demarcated by two pairs of massive post-pits, of which the largest was 4 feet in diameter and nearly 5 feet in depth below bedrock. Such huge sockets must have retained either a second, inner gate, as a last line of defence once the outer gates had been stormed and taken, or conceivably a great triumphal arch in timber to impress newcomers on their arrival with the architectural grandeur of the fort.

Unique in the Midlands, the Rainsborough guard-rooms may be adequately paralleled by the sub-rectangular guard chambers at Dinorben, in Denbighshire (Gardner and Savory, 1964, Fig. 5), and comparable sites in north Wales and the northern Marches. When Gardner first uncovered the entrance at Dinorben, he not unreasonably – at that time – assumed a measure of influence from Roman military architecture. As a result of subsequent research, however, Savory recognised that guard-rooms of this type were a recurrent feature of hillforts in the territory of the Cornovii and Deceangli, and in the publication of Gardner's excavations, he was inclined to attribute them to an advanced phase of Western B culture. The existence of such structures at Rainsborough by the end of the fifth century may now cause us to consider an earlier currency for the type elsewhere, and with the additional example of Leckhampton, Gloucestershire, which had formerly appeared to be peripheral to the main distribution, we may question whether the use of guard-chambers was an exclusively Cornovian practice. It is scarcely credible that such a substantial structural element in the layout of hillfort entrances could have been overlooked by excavators elsewhere in southern and midland England, but with the example of Eddisbury (Varley, 1950, 29 ff, Fig. II) in mind, where the first-phase guard-rooms were constructed solely of timber, it is conceivable that timber-framed chambers existed elsewhere, which have been obscured by the collapsed debris of the flanking ramparts.

The purpose of guard-chambers deserves comment. Their location, invariably recessed into the internal framework of the ramparts, affords no obvious advantage in repelling an assault upon the entrance. On the other hand, flanking the roadway just inside the main gates, they could usefully serve as guard-posts for sentries whose business it was to check traffic passing in and out of the fort. Such an interpretation has the obvious implication of permanent occupation of the camp, in which such inspections were part of the regular routine of the resident garrison. This view is further supported by the fact that a good deal of effort had evidently been expended, both at Rainsborough and at Blewburton Hill, to maintain a metalled surface through the entrance, a labour which would scarcely seem worthwhile if only periodic or intermittent occupation were anticipated. The fact remains, of course, that there is relatively little evidence in the form of structural remains for such occupation within these camps. At Blewburton, however, the quantity of domestic pottery recovered from the interior suggests that extensive stripping might well reveal house-foundations which have so far eluded the excavators.

Though Blewburton did not, apparently, boast guard-rooms, its entrance nonetheless displays considerable originality in design (Fig. 17). A few yards inside the entrance, and at right angles to it, a steep-sided ditch was excavated, six feet in depth, which would have effectively impeded a direct assault upon the interior through the entrance passage. Once the main gates had been forced, those who were not impelled by the force of their own charge headlong into the cross-ditch would have been obliged to turn to one side, thereby exposing their flank to a hail of missiles from the defenders, lined up behind the bank beyond. Simple in design, this device is without close parallel to date in Iron Age Britain. At both St Catharine's Hill (Hawkes, Myres and Stevens, 1930, Fig. 5) and St Mawgan-in-

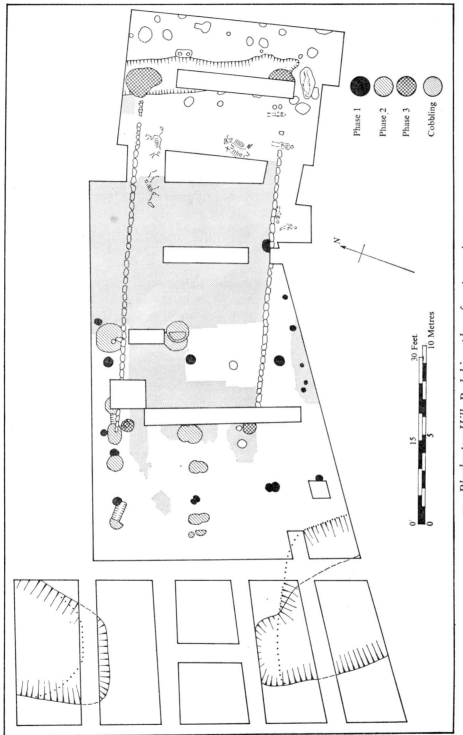

Phase 1
Phase 2
Phase 3
Cobbling

N

30 Feet
10 Metres

15
5

0
0

17. *Blewburton Hill, Berkshire: plan of western entrance*

69

Pyder, Cornwall (Murray-Thriepland, 1956, plan facing p. 52), gullies were found, extending across the width of the entrance, but neither reaches defensive proportions. It must be remarked, however, that the cross-ditch at Blewburton is situated 90 feet inside the entrance causeway, and it is doubtful therefore whether a small scale area excavation of a hillfort entrance would extend sufficiently far into the interior to locate comparable features. With the limited resources available for excavation, it is nonetheless possible that geophysical methods could be usefully employed to determine whether this technique was adopted elsewhere in Iron Age fortifications.

In the final phase of occupation at Blewburton, dating probably from the end of the second century B.C., the earlier timber structures were replaced by a long passage with flanking dry-stone walls to retain the ramparts. A number of comparable examples could be cited from southern Britain, including Bredon Hill, Worcestershire (Hencken, 1938), Cherbury Camp, Berks (Bradford, 1940), and Phase 4 of the east entrance at Maiden Castle (Wheeler, 1943, 46, Fig. 9). The type is evidently analogous to those excavated by Wheeler in northern France, and to the Continental *Zangentore* (Dehn, 1961), though any cultural affinity between the latter and insular examples has yet to be demonstrated. Though the twin passages at Maiden Castle employ a similar stone construction, the elaborate external framework with which they are associated is apparently a corollary of the development of multivallation.

In view of the effort and ingenuity which was evidently lavished upon Iron Age hillforts, we might imagine that this was a time of repeated incursions from abroad, or of widespread civil discord within Britain. The fact remains, however, that there are relatively few hillforts which betray clear signs of violence, whether in the form of ruined fortifications or burials of battle casualties. For Rainsborough the evidence is unequivocal. The gateway was destroyed by a fire, the intensity of which reddened the stonework, and burnt red and purple the soil in several postholes below bedrock level, and the stone revetment-wall along the front of the rampart was tumbled into the ditch. No accidental calamity could have embraced the defences so thoroughly, and the fact that the camp was abandoned for two centuries after its destruction bears silent witness to the totality of its political and military eclipse. Few other hillforts showed comparable traces of violent sack, apart from those like Maiden Castle itself, where the final assault came at the time of the Conquest, and which, therefore, can scarcely be viewed as representative of inter-tribal Celtic warfare. Indeed, Alcock has rightly emphasised that our knowledge of Celtic warfare, as derived from literary records, very largely relates to engagements with the Roman army, or to Roman attacks upon Iron Age strongholds: very little information survives regarding the assault and capture of hillforts by Celtic forces. In view of this, he points tentatively to a Homeric model, imagining 'the defences thronging with non-combatants – the young and old and those of inferior social status, women and slaves – while the warrior classes, chiefs and freemen, challenged and fought in chariots and on foot on lower ground' (1965, 185). In the event of defeat, the hillfort might fall as a prize to the victors, and 'we might expect a massacre of non-combatants like that uncovered at the War Ditches, Cherry Hinton

(Cambs)'. Such an interpretation could well be applied to the evidence from Maiden Castle itself, where a third of the skeletons uncovered in the war cemetery (Pl. XIV) outside the east gates was of women, and the remainder included both young and very old. Though the graves included offerings of food and drink, none contained the weapons of the dead to indicate warrior status. We may speculate, therefore, whether the massacre of the non-combatants at Maiden Castle was not more savage and ruthless because the Celtic troops had acquitted themselves to good effect in defeat elsewhere.

Literary accounts of Celtic methods of warfare place great emphasis upon the convention of single combat between champions. Diodorus Siculus, quoting Posidonius, outlines the procedure (5, 29):

> When the armies are drawn up in battle-array they are wont to advance before the battle-line and to challenge the bravest of their opponents to single combat, at the same time brandishing before them their arms so as to terrify their foe. And when someone accepts this challenge to battle, they loudly recite the deeds of valour of their ancestors and proclaim their own valorous quality, at the same time deriding and making little of their opponent and generally attempting to rob him beforehand of his fighting spirit.

We should exercise caution, however, before assuming that such accounts accurately reflect the normal battle routine of the Celts. Doubtless the prestige of a tribal leader would be greatly enhanced among his own troops if he could demonstrate his fighting prowess publicly by overcoming an opposing champion, but it seems doubtful whether individual combat would decide the outcome of the conflict, except insofar as the morale of the defeated champion's forces would be reduced before the main engagement. Had the issue of a challenge to single combat been a regular formula, we might have expected to find more instances where the Celts challenged the Roman army in this fashion. Such a performance might well be fitting for epic poetry, and may indeed have happened in reality when a chieftain judged he could boost his reputation accordingly, but we should no more believe that this constituted an invariable practice among the Celts than we should accept the speeches put into the mouths of Boudicca or Byrhtnoð as bearing upon historical actuality.

The use of chariots, on the other hand, is well authenticated in the archaeological record. Diodorus' account of chariot warfare among the Gauls (5, 29), based upon Posidonius, and reflecting a practice which had been abandoned on the Continent by the first century B.C., bears a striking similarity to Caesar's description of a chariot charge in Britain in 55 B.C. (de bello Gallico, 4, 33). The chariot, as Powell rightly observed (1958, 104; for further references, see Harbison, 1971), was not essentially a machine of war, but a vehicle to convey the warrior speedily to the front and away again, should circumstances necessitate a hasty withdrawal. Hence the charioteers had the mobility of cavalry and the stability of infantry ('ita mobilitatem equitum, stabilitatem peditum in proeliis praestant'). Significantly, Caesar adds that their skill was such that they could control their teams in full gallop down the steepest of slopes, and manœuvre them abruptly for action ('in declivi ac praecipiti loco incitatos equos sustinere'), suggesting that hillforts could have served as strongholds from which a mobile force could issue swiftly to join battle with an approaching enemy on lower ground. Other than by this means, the hillfort could in no effective sense control the territory surrounding it, and without the aid of long-range artillery, could not command a strategic position such as a pass or river-crossing, as Hod Hill and Hambledon Hill in Dorset were surely intended to do.

In this respect, therefore, an Iron Age hillfort bears little affinity to hill-top strongholds of subsequent periods, such as Corfe Castle, Dorset or Monte Cassino. In Iron Age Britain, an enemy force could simply ignore a hilltop in which the local tribesmen had barricaded themselves, and continue to plunder and pillage at will. The defenders, on the other hand, were hardly likely to be content to remain behind the safety of their ramparts while their villages were razed and their crops destroyed, and hence would be obliged to mount a counter-attack in which the topographical location and elaborate defences of their hillfort would afford them no advantage. We can only conclude, therefore, that the camp itself served simply as a military base, and as a refuge for old men, women and children, whose task was to gather as much as possible of their possessions and livestock within the safety of the walls until the outcome of the conflict was decided. Should the defending force be overwhelmed, then the victors might well mount an assault upon the camp itself, garrisoned only by old men and womenfolk, supplemented perhaps by those who had fled in defeat to the temporary shelter of its defences.

Under such circumstances, an assault upon the stronghold itself was probably not a prolonged engagement. It is unlikely that the attacking force would have the resources necessary to mount a siege, and the location of hillforts alone, often without an immediate supply of water, is sufficient to suggest that their occupants did not anticipate indefinite incarceration within their walls. Nor is there any evidence to indicate the introduction of siege-engines, against which the narrow-ditched hillforts with box-ramparts would have been especially vulnerable. The speed with which the Suessones, in spite of their initial success in repelling the Roman attack, capitulated at the sight of siege-works at Noviodunum seems to corroborate Caesar's statement that the Gauls were unfamiliar with such devices (*de bello Gallico*, 2, 12). To what extent an Iron Age army was capable of co-ordinating attacks upon several different points around the perimeter of a hillfort, in order to effect the initial breach of the defences, is open to speculation. Offensive tactics against early Iron Age hillforts in Britain might very well have been similar to those employed by the Belgae against the *oppidum* of the Remi at Bibrax. In one of the few instances on record of an inter-tribal engagement, Caesar explains the method of attack adopted by the Belgae and other tribes in Gaul: 'A host of men is set all round the ramparts, and when a hail of stones from all sides upon the wall has begun, and the wall is stripped of defenders, they lock their shields over their heads, move up to the gates, and undercut the wall' (*de bello Gallico*, 2, 6).

That the entrance formed a focal point for assault is clearly demonstrated by the Rainsborough evidence, though the extent of the burning of the gateway is not necessarily a measure of the ferocity of the attack. Once the main gates had been burnt or broken down, a simple expedient for keeping the assailants at bay would be for the defenders to fire the passage, and continue to heap fuel upon the blaze. Whatever tactics were regularly adopted in inter-tribal wars among the Celts, it is evident that they soon realised the ineffectiveness of conventional forms of earthwork against the artillery and apparatus of the Roman army, and in consequence the policy of surrender, and deception in breaking treaty, is a particular reaction to the circumstances of the Gallic campaign.

That the Belgae in Gaul did react to the introduction of siege-engines is demonstrated by the development of the Fécamp type of earthwork, with broad ditch and massive dump-rampart. In proposing this view, Wheeler (Wheeler and Richardson, 1957, 12) recalled Caesar's failure to capture the fortress of Noviodunum, the rallying-point of the Suessones in 57 B.C., in spite of the fact that it was garrisoned by a relatively small force; this setback Caesar attributed to the breadth of the ditch and height of the rampart (*'propter latitudinem fossae murique altitudinem paucis defendentibus expugnare non potuit'*). Reference to Wheeler's sections across the defences of Fécamp and allied earthworks reveals the nature of the obstacle (Fig. 18). First, the ditch is much too broad to be spanned by timbers and hence

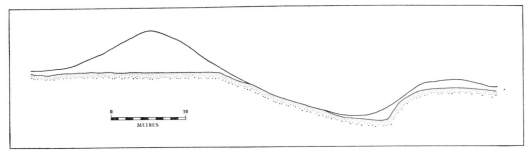

18. *Section through defences, Camp du Canada, Fécamp, Seine Inférieure*

the siege machinery must be man-handled into the ditch before advancing to the walls. Second, the dump-rampart cannot be fired, or even undermined, so easily as a box-rampart, and furthermore, the lack of a vertical face renders the siege-towers virtually ineffective. In his recent study of the Belgae, C. F. C. Hawkes (1968, Fig. 2) has shown the relationship in distribution between forts of Fécamp type and the territorial limits of Belgic Gaul, and the extension of Fécamp-derived earthworks into south-eastern Britain. The best illustration of this technique in Britain, at Oldbury, in Kent, was dated by Ward-Perkins (1944) to the eve of the Roman Conquest, though the idea of a broad ditch with massive dump-rampart may well have been introduced elsewhere earlier in the Belgic period. It is significant, however, that the distribution shows a clear emphasis south of the Thames, in the region occupied by Caesar's 'maritime' tribes, rather than to the north in the Catuvellaunian heartland. The introduction of Fécamp type of earthwork is not the only innovation in fortification in the Belgic period in Britain which is indicative of a change in military tactics: both the situation and layout of defensive sites in several instances reflect a fundamental reappraisal of the problems of fortification, which must now be considered in detail.

I have suggested elsewhere (1972, 54 ff) that many early Iron Age hillforts in southern Britain were not re-occupied in the Belgic period, but that, instead, new camps were established in lower-lying positions like the site at Cassington Mill, in Oxfordshire. In some instances, the loss of a commanding hilltop situation is compensated for by the choice of a natural promontory formed by the course of a river, as in the case of the Dyke Hills camp at Dorchester-on-Thames. The native tribes realised the advantages of incorporating natural features such as streams, woodland and marsh into a defensive network, since this provided opportunity for both ambush and escape in terrain with which the enemy was unfamiliar. These tactics were employed against Caesar in 54 B.C., not without success. Shortly after landing, the Seventh Legion engaged the tribal forces, who, after an initial clash with cavalry and chariots, withdrew into the woods, where they had a stronghold well fortified by nature and by man-made defences ('*locum nacti egregie et natura et opere munitum*') (*de bello Gallico*, 5, 9). Access-routes into the stronghold had been blocked by felling trees, rather than by elaborate formal entrances as in earlier hillforts, and Caesar emphasises that the enemy engaged his troops in small bands, instead of confronting them in a pitched battle. In a subsequent encounter, he reiterates the same point: the enemy never fought in close order, but separated in small parties ('*numquam conferti sed rari magnisque intervallis proeliarentur*') (*de bello Gallico*, 5, 16), with detachments of reinforcements ready to relieve individual groups. The guerilla tactics of the Britons evidently confused the Roman forces and lowered their morale by harassing foraging parties and luring cavalry away from their infantry support by feigned retreat. Finally, Caesar was obliged to launch an assault upon Cassivellaunus' headquarters, north of the Thames in the Catuvellaunian heartland, which he describes in terms comparable to the earlier account of a woodland stronghold: defended by forest and marsh ('*silvis paludibusque munitum*') and incorporating both natural and man-made barriers ('*egregie natura atque opere munitum*'). This, he states, is what the Britons called an *oppidum* ('*oppidum autem Britanni vocant, cum silvas impeditas vallo atque fossa munierunt*') (*de bello Gallico*, 5, 21).

This kind of fortification is developed into more extensive systems of dykes, streams, marsh and forest in the period between Caesar's invasions and the Conquest. It is well illustrated by the complexity of earthworks at Colchester, Cunobelinus' capital of Camulodunum (Hawkes and Hull, 1947, Pl. I). Here three sets of linear ditches, the Gryme's Dyke, the Triple Dyke and the Lexden Dyke, extending from the Roman river to the Colne, form a defensive barrier across the neck of a natural peninsula, encompassed by river and forest. The area enclosed by these defences is over three miles across, and would have required a massive and mobile army to hold it against a co-ordinated attack from several directions. But if the defenders employed the same guerilla tactics which apparently had such a demoralising effect upon Caesar's troops, such a stronghold would present a formidable target to capture and subdue. Further from the area of primary Belgic settlement, similar fortifications were adopted by the tribes living in north Oxfordshire, and by the Dobunni at Bagendon (Clifford, 1961). The north Oxfordshire Grim's Ditch is perhaps the most extensive of these strongholds. Dating to the final decades before the Conquest, its earthworks are of relatively small proportions, though the territory embraced by their inter-mittent sections covers an area of twenty-two square miles. That such a site could not be garrisoned and held in the same way as an early Iron Age hillfort might have been is self-evident; but, with forest or marsh providing additional hazards for the enemy and cover for the defenders, small bands of guerillas could ambush and harass an invading force, inflicting upon it severe losses, before withdrawing whence they came. The fact that the earthworks are discontinuous supports the notion that chariots were used in mounting such swift, mobile attacks upon an enemy's flank or rear. Outside the main dyke at Callow Hill, Model Farm, Ditchley and Blenheim park, excavation has revealed lengths of palisade trench, which probably supported an additional barrier of stakes, designed to impede a chariot or cavalry charge. Though the excavators doubted the antiquity of these features, a perfectly good precedent may be found, on a larger scale, in the stakes, sunk into pits, with which Caesar protected his camp at Alesia from cavalry attack (D. W. Harding, 1972, 57–8; Caesar, *de bello Gallico*, 7, 73). A similar technique was adopted by Cassivellaunus when he attempted to impede Caesar's passage across the Thames by driving stakes into the bed of the river, with their sharpened ends, upon which both horses and men might be impaled, concealed beneath the water (Caesar, *de bello Gallico*, 5, 18).

In sum, the forest fortress, with its hidden troops and unexpected obstructions, probably afforded greater protection than did earlier hillforts, for all their structural elaborations, situated as they frequently were in exposed positions from which there was no escape if the stronghold fell. The greater area enclosed by the north Oxfordshire Grim's Ditch would enable the defenders, like Cassivellaunus, to bring their herds within the fortified zone in time of unrest; indeed the dykes may even have enclosed regular pasture and arable fields, as well as woodland in which pigs could forage freely. Though there is abundant evidence for occupation within these strongholds, specific habitation-sites are difficult to identify on account of the vast area available for settlement. At Camulodunum and Bagendon, how-ever, material remains, including coin evidence, are sufficient to indicate that they were major tribal capitals, whose chieftains exercised considerable political sway over the sur-rounding regions.

To what extent pre-Belgic hillforts served similarly as tribal centres, for purposes other than defence, is not easy to estimate. Attempts to demonstrate the regional pre-eminence of a particular hillfort, on the basis of acreage or complexity of earthworks, over adjacent 'satellite' forts, are fraught with dangers, the most obvious of which is that the sites in question may not have been in contemporaneous occupation. It is clearly foolish to assume that the largest or grandest was necessarily the most important: the extent of the enclosure may be dictated solely by the contours of the hill, or by the purpose which the hillfort was intended to serve in addition to its primary military function. In many cases, the hillfort would evidently have been a prominent local landmark, and therefore the most suitable rendezvous for tribal gatherings, festivities, markets or legal and religious ceremonies.

Finally, there remains the question of chronology. The construction of hillforts in Britain must evidently have spanned a far longer period of time than was formerly imagined, with origins in the later Bronze Age. For Scotland, MacKie (1969) has argued on the basis of radio-carbon determinations that certain hillforts with timber-laced defences, including Finavon in Angus, Dun Lagaidh in Wester Ross and Craigmarloch Wood, Renfrewshire, were derived from Continental Urnfield antecedents, and were already in existence in the eighth or seventh centuries B.C. Likewise in southern Britain, a late Bronze Age occupation has been postulated at Mam Tor, in Derbyshire (Coombs, 1973), at Portfield, Whalley, Lancashire, at Ivinghoe Beacon, Bucks (Cotton and Frere, 1968), and in north Wales at Dinorben in Denbighshire (Savory, 1971). The fact remains, however, that for the most part we are still lacking direct associations to demonstrate that the fortifications themselves were constructed in the late Bronze Age; subsequent research may lead us to the conclusion that the earthworks were generally a later addition to hilltop sites where the late Bronze Age settlement had been undefended on the Central European *Hohensiedlungen* model. While there is no *a priori* reason why hillforts should not have been built in Britain in the late Bronze Age, as on the Continent, we must nonetheless await the accumulation of closely-dated examples before they can be recognised as a widespread phenomenon of the insular late Bronze Age. Whatever the outcome of future research in this respect, it is evident that hillforts should now be viewed as part of a progressive sequence, with a progressively intensifying distribution, for which a single historical explanation no longer appears valid, as it may have done forty years ago.

5
Economy, industry and crafts

FOR A MODEL of the economy of the Iron Age in lowland Britain, archaeologists convention-ally turn to the farmstead at Little Woodbury in Wiltshire. Serving once as the type-site for Hodson's Woodbury Culture, it is pressed into commission again as a model for Piggott's Woodbury Economy (1961). It was Piggott's contention that the Iron Age economy of Britain divided broadly into two zones, that to the south and east of the Jurassic Ridge which he named after the type-site at Little Woodbury, in which a cereal crop element predominated, and that to the north and west of the Jurassic Ridge, typified by the economy at Stanwick, which was apparently based principally upon pastoralism. As a starting-point, therefore, we may take the settlement at Little Woodbury and examine the nature of its agricultural economy, before considering to what extent it can be regarded as typical of lowland Britain as a whole.

One of the principal characteristics of the settlement at Little Woodbury – and one which had attracted attention particularly on the air-photographs of the site (Pl. I) – was its con-centration of pits and working hollows, which Bersu associated with a variety of harvest activities. Without excluding other possible functions, it is clear that pits were used in the Iron Age as underground silos, and indeed in some instances, as at Little Woodbury and at Itford Hill in Sussex (Helbaek, 1957), samples of grain have been recovered from them. In addition, the Little Woodbury enclosure produced quantities of heat-crazed flints ('pot-boilers'), ash, and fragments of clay ovens in excess of what we might expect for normal domestic usage. The agricultural application of such hearths and ovens could have been twofold. The two principal kinds of wheat grown in the Iron Age, emmer and spelt, are, as Helbaek has pointed out (1952, 233), species in which it is difficult to separate the husk from the grain simply by threshing in a natural state of ripeness; parching is therefore essential to crack the spikelets and make them brittle first. Alternatively, it would have been advisable to parch grain which was intended for consumption prior to underground storage in order to allay subsequent germination.

In view of this risk, and the danger of contamination by mould, we might wonder how practical underground storage of grain would have been in a damp British climate. Cer-tainly Tacitus (*Germania*, 16, 4) refers to the practice among the Germans of excavating underground cavities for storing produce, while modern ethnographic parallels in Somali-land, Nigeria and Cyprus were recorded by investigations on behalf of the Colonial Office (Hall, Haswell and Oxley, 1956) during the period 1939–45. The principal necessity for successful underground storage of grain is to maintain the air-tightness of the pit, and thereby to reduce bacterial activity. Under such conditions, the heat generated by bacteria in the pit would eventually be self-destructive, and, provided that the pit was not opened in the interval, grain stored in this fashion could last with only minimum wastage for up to seven years. The sterilising process could apparently be accelerated by firing the pit immediately prior to use, and we may wonder whether, in Britain, this was not essential to the successful storage of grain: charcoal found in pits on a number of sites could have resulted from such a process. The lid of the pit would doubtless have been sealed with layers of clay, straw and dung; internal lining with wickerwork frames, the impressions of which have been traced occasionally in Britain, is a refinement for which there are ethnographic parallels, though the technique is by no means universal. Doubtless such a wickerwork frame or container would have made subsequent removal of the grain a simpler operation. The essence of underground storage was to maintain the seal until the entire content of the pits was required: where partial emptying has been employed, the loss-rate through mould and mildew is very much higher.

In consequence, an alternative means of storage would have been required for everyday domestic supplies of corn. This need could have been met by the construction of upstanding timber granaries of the kind which Bersu suggested for Little Woodbury, and which has been recognised at Staple Howe and elsewhere in Britain and on the Continent (Brewster, 1963, Fig. 28; Joffroy, 1960, Pl. 7). Current opinion, however, has favoured the interpretation of these four-poster structures as small domestic shrines (Piggott, 1968, 61), and it may be that grain for day-to-day requirements was simply stored in large pottery jars, with wooden or flat stone lids to conserve the contents from vermin. In fact, Bersu believed that it was the grain for consumption which was stored in pits, while his raised granaries would have contained seed-corn for the following spring. This view was based upon the quantities of burnt debris found in and around the pits, which he reasonably inferred indicated that grain had been roasted in the near vicinity prior to storage. Such grain would naturally be for consumption, not for seed. But the debris of the roasting-hearths would scarcely be scattered into pits which had just been prepared to receive the grain itself; only after they had been emptied and abandoned would pits have been used as rubbish tips in this way. Hence we can infer no special relationship between the pits and grain which had been roasted, rather than seed-grain. Furthermore, seed-grain contained within pits could remain untouched until sowing time, whereas domestic supplies would need to be transferred *en bloc* to storage jars, perhaps stacked in the timber granaries, as soon as the seal of the underground silo was broken.

It is evident that grain-storage was not the sole function which these subterranean cellars could have performed. Other produce could equally have been stored in semi-airtight conditions, while, even without a permanent seal, such cool cellars could well have provided a temporary store for salted meat. The articulated portion of an animal carcass from a pit at City Farm, Hanborough, Oxon (Case, 1964, 48), might perhaps be the remnants of a side of meat which went rotten in storage, and was buried as it stood to prevent further contamination. Some pits – as at Little Woodbury and Maiden Castle (Wheeler, 1943, 54, 91) – could have contained water-tubs. Others could even have been cess-pits. Some were certainly used as rubbish-dumps for domestic refuse, as quantities of animal-

...ckley Hill, Gloucestershire:
...n entrance (a) main rampart
...uth entrance bastion (c) north
...ce bastion (d) outer hornwork
...ter gateway

...ickley Hill, Gloucestershire:
...otograph of interior of camp,
...g circular and rectangular
...gs partially excavated

XII *Maiden Castle, Dorset: air-photograph of hillfort from the east*

XIII *Maiden Castle, Dorset: air-photograph of western defences*

bones together with fragments of pottery found in them indicate. But this was probably only a secondary function, when the pit was no longer considered serviceable for storage, and had to be filled in anyway. As a primary function, pits for the disposal of rubbish would have been a hygienic luxury, particularly since domestic garbage, which did not include tin cans or bottles, would have decomposed fairly rapidly if thrown into a compost heap, to be spread subsequently over the fields for manure. When we consider the potential danger of a group of open pits, both to the community and to its livestock, it is scarcely surprising that we find many pits with clean filling that were apparently refilled before waiting for quantities of household rubbish to accumulate.

In view of the many imponderables which surround the nature and use of storage pits, there seems little point in attempting elaborate calculations of population, or even acreage of land tilled, from an estimate of the volume of grain stored on any given Iron Age settlement. With regard to Little Woodbury itself, Bowen and others have demonstrated (1967; 1969, 12) that Bersu's calculations were based upon an incorrect conversion from cubic metres to bushels, resulting in a radical under-estimation of the true capacity of the pits. But any estimate of the number of pits in use in any single year must depend upon how many were cleaned down and re-used, as they quite well could have been, simply by scraping back a few inches of the pit walls until a clean face was exposed. This process in itself would result in the enlarging of a pit from its original size, which is therefore more difficult to calculate. The length of time that the pits remained sealed, and differences in the annual yield, introduce further variables, while the possibility of winter- as well as spring-sown crops could radically affect any calculation. Finally, the average consumption of grain per head of population depends so much upon a knowledge of the diet of an Iron Age community, whose basic starch requirements were not met by potatoes, that it seems a remote chance that a realistic conclusion could be reached by calculation on this basis.

The importance of cereal crops to the Iron Age population of southern Britain, of course, does not depend solely on evidence for the storage of grain. 'Working hollows', shallow scoops cut into the chalk at Little Woodbury, Pimperne and elsewhere, are conventionally regarded as sites for a variety of post-harvest activities such as threshing and winnowing. Paired postholes, again represented at Little Woodbury, but also quite clearly at Standlake, in the Upper Thames (D. W. Harding, 1972, Fig. 2; Riley, 1946, Fig. 9), were regarded by Bersu as the foundations of timber racks, over which the harvested corn could be draped for drying. At Stanton Harcourt (D. W. Harding, 1972, Fig. 7; Williams, 1944, Fig. 6. See also Hamlin, 1966, Figs 1 and 2) in Oxfordshire the proximity of hearths to such clusters of paired postholes certainly lends weight to this view of their function, though whether it was corn rather than hay which was being dried on the racks is open to question. The crop was apparently harvested with short-bladed sickles, and was most probably cut high below the ear. If so, the racks were more probably for drying hay or straw.

Apart from the short-bladed sickles, mounted in their wooden, bone or antler handles, few material artefacts relating directly to agricultural activities could be expected from Iron Age settlements. The most durable are fragments of quernstone for grinding corn, and occasionally iron shares from a light form of plough. Ploughs themselves were of a 'beam' **or** 'bow' ard type, without coulters (Fig. 19), and most probably drawn by two oxen (Payne, 1947, 1957; Aberg, 1957). The introduction of the heavy plough has conventionally, but on rather slender evidence, been attributed to the Belgae, partly on the grounds that Belgic settlement seemed to show a shift towards lower-lying situations on heavier soils from the ownland locations favoured by their predecessors. This view, however, has been challenged

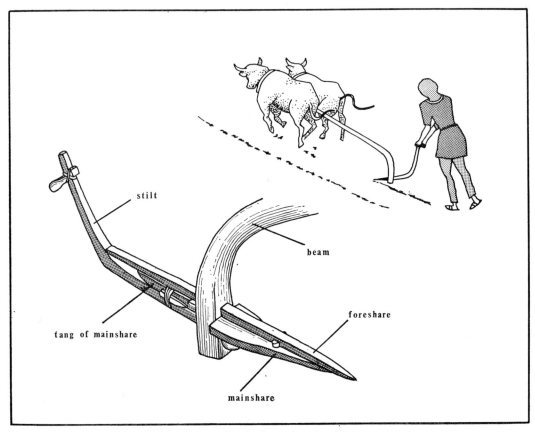

stilt

beam

foreshare

tang of mainshare

mainshare

19. Early Iron Age plough

by Bowen (1969, 18) and Manning (1964, 62–3), who have underlined the inadequacy of the material evidence, which still includes no iron coulters from convincing pre-Roman contexts.

The land which was cultivated by means of these ox-teams was evidently in close proximity to the settlements themselves, and in a number of cases, such as Pimperne in Dorset, the outline of field systems, which must surely be regarded as contemporary with the occupation of the early Iron Age camp, still survives as extant earthworks immediately adjacent to it. Such so-called 'Celtic' fields (Bowen, 1961) (Pls XV, XVI) – normally square or sub-square in shape and ranging in size individually from $\frac{1}{3}$ to $1\frac{1}{2}$ acres – are particularly common on the chalk downs of Wessex where modern agriculture has not obliterated them. Where a direct relationship with a settlement cannot be demonstrated, their dating can only be established less certainly from broken and abraded sherds of pottery scattered across them as a result of manuring from domestic compost heaps. Nonetheless, there can be little doubt that field-systems of this kind can be traced at least as early as the Middle Bronze Age, when the 'Celtic' affiliations implied by their name could scarcely be sustained. Where earthworks of this kind have survived in the vicinity of Iron Age settlements it may be possible to supplement the very tentative speculations concerning the capacity of grain storage-pits with an estimation of the acreage under regular cultivation. A site not unlike Little Woodbury on Farley Mount, Winchester (A. C. Thomas, 1966, Pl. VI), for instance, had a minimum of 60 acres of 'Celtic' fields within its immediate environs.

Information concerning the cultivation of cereal crops can be derived from one further principal source – the grain itself. In the immediately post-war years, Helbaek (1952; Jessen and Helbaek, 1944) devoted a good deal of research to the essentially very simple method of examining carbonised grain samples and the impressions of grain left embedded in the fired clay of prehistoric pottery. With the development of more sophisticated laboratory techniques for dating and analysis of other materials, the study of cereals has attracted less attention in recent years, though Helbaek's basic conclusions are fundamental to our interpretation of Iron Age economy in Britain. At the outset of the Neolithic, to judge by the impressions from Windmill Hill, the vast majority of cereals grown were of the two categories of wheat, emmer and eincorn, the former being dominant. Less than 10 per cent of the samples identified were of barley, and those mainly of naked barley. With the Beaker invasions of Britain, the pattern is sharply reversed, and throughout the Bronze Age barley remained in the ascendancy, with the increasing dominance of the hulled variety. Examination of carbonised grain from late Bronze Age and Iron Age contexts revealed at this period yet another significant innovation, the introduction of spelt, a particularly hardy variety of wheat which could be winter-sown, and therefore afforded the opportunity of an early as well as a later harvest. Hence, of the large deposit of grain from Fifield Bavant Down in Wiltshire (Clay, 1924), two-thirds of that examined was barley, almost all of which was of the hulled variety, while the remaining third was spelt. Emmer, the staple form of wheat in Britain up to this time, was totally absent. Elsewhere, spelt certainly did not oust emmer to the same degree. Indeed, on the Fifield Bavant evidence, Helbaek was inclined to see there 'the agricultural habits of immigrants recently arrived from the Continent', perhaps from the spelt-growing region of the middle Rhineland (Helbaek, 1952, 210). The presence of rye, though represented by just a single grain which could be certainly identified, tended to confirm this point of origin for the Fifield Bavant settlers. Some regional variation might well be expected in the relative percentages of cereals. In the settlements of the Somerset levels at Glastonbury and Meare the principal cereal was apparently barley, exclusively of the hulled variety, though both emmer and spelt were present in significant proportions. Particular emphasis was placed by Helbaek upon the appearance for the first time at Meare,

Glastonbury and Worlebury of the Celtic bean which, outside these examples, is not generally known in Britain until the Roman period. Uncultivated weeds are found among a number of samples, and in several instances wild oats and chess occurred among deposits of spelt. Further research would doubtless result in modifications to the conclusions of Helbaek's pioneer study, but is unlikely to diminish the significance of the introduction of spelt at the outset of the Iron Age, and the agricultural advance which it reflects. Whether or not we would be justified in attributing such an economic shift to new settlers from the Continent, or, further, in attempting to pin-point their homeland in Central Europe, may be debatable.

The conclusions reached by Helbaek on the basis of cereal research gain some support from literary sources. Hecataeus, writing in the sixth century B.C., for instance, was aware of the practice in Britain of reaping two harvests in one year (Diodorus Siculus, 2, 47). But such a fundamental change in the agricultural pattern of prehistoric Britain has further implications. It is normally assumed that limitations of winter fodder would have obliged Iron Age communities to utilise the stubble of arable fields for grazing livestock. Hence, the cultivation of a winter-sown crop was taken by Applebaum to 'imply that there was sufficient winter pasture elsewhere, or more probably that part of the arable was fallowed on a two- or three-course system and grazed in winter' (1954, 105). This new cropping system, in which the winter-crop enclosure was distinguished from the summer fields, he believed could be traced in the earthworks of Figheldean Down, in Wiltshire. During the summer cattle and sheep would have grazed the open downland, where they were prevented from encroaching upon arable land by a system of dyked droveways; in winter the livestock would be moved to the stubble of the summer fields, while an enclosed winter field was under cultivation (1966). Such a system could be equally applicable to certain parts of the Upper Thames basin, where lengths of fencing, apparently forming sizeable enclosures immediately adjacent to Iron Age settlements, may perhaps have defined similar infields for winter-sown cereal crops (D. W. Harding, 1972, 18).

Following Bersu, prehistorians hitherto have regarded the cultivation of cereal crops as the dominant element of the 'Woodbury economy', and in our preoccupation with storage pits and estimates of the annual yield, it is easy to overlook the equally important part which was undoubtedly played in the mixed-farming economy of lowland Britain by stock-raising. In listing the principal exports of Britain, Strabo included cattle and skins as well as corn, minerals, slaves and hunting-dogs (Geography, 4, v, 2). The importance of meat to the Celts is further emphasised by Athenaeus' remarks, quoting Posidonius: 'Their food consists of a small number of loaves of bread – (one is reminded of the carbonised buns from Glastonbury) – together with a large amount of meat, either boiled or roasted on charcoal or on spits' (4, 36). There is absolutely no reason to suppose that such comments applied exclusively to areas like the highland zone of Britain, where pastoralism was especially important. Indeed, at Little Woodbury itself, the so-called 'antennae ditches' which converge upon the entrance to the settlement must surely have been for funnelling stock into the camp from open pasture or grazing lands. If cattle or sheep were kept in sufficient numbers to merit the construction of such ditches, we may well reconsider the function of Bersu's racks, serving to dry hay for fodder rather than ears of corn. Little Woodbury, of course, was not unique in its antennae ditches; similar devices for guiding stock into the enclosure may be seen at Gussage All Saints (Bowen, 1969, Fig. 1, 1), and less conspicuously at Farley Mount, near Winchester. The arrangement of primary and secondary enclosures at Pimperne, outlined earlier, and in particular the use there of a separate entrance with antenna ditch apparently designed for the use of stock, show a degree of deliberate planning in the layout of the settlement which is not consistent with a view which relegates the pastoral element to a minor or subsidiary role in the mixed economy of that farming community.

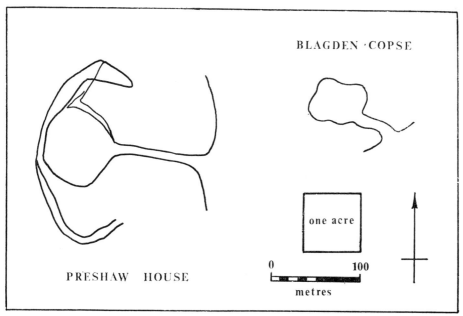

20. *Stock enclosures of 'banjo' type*

Recent fieldwork in various regions of southern England has tended to confirm the importance of cattle-breeding or sheep-rearing in lowland Britain. In Hampshire, a distinct class of earthwork has been identified whose function was quite clearly pastoral. These so-called 'banjo' enclosures (Fig. 20) are seldom larger in area than an acre or an acre and a half, and therefore are much smaller than the settlement sites of the Little Woodbury or Pimperne type. They are characterised by a long funnel-like track leading from the entrance, flanked by twin ditches which may flare outwards at their terminals in the shape of a flask or glass beaker. Well-defined examples have been recognised at Preshaw House, Exton (Perry, 1966), at Blagden Copse, Hurstbourne Tarrant and at Bramdean (Bowen, 1969, 23), of which the last two have been assigned by excavation to an occupation in the middle or later Iron Age. A feature of several sites within this group is their univallate construction

83

with *internal* ditch, a factor which precludes a defensive function in the military sense, and suggests that the enclosure was designed to retain rather than to exclude. In the light of this, the view that these enclosures served as cattle corrals seems unexceptionable.

Elsewhere in Wessex, long linear earthworks or 'ranch boundaries', sometimes enclosing areas of 50 acres or more, argue a similar emphasis upon stock-breeding. Not necessarily forming an enclosure in themselves, their primary purpose may have been to divide arable fields from pasture or grazing land. Other forms of linear earthworks may have fulfilled a similar function, whether they were designed initially as ranch boundaries or not. The territorial divisions of the eastern Chilterns, skilfully reconstructed by Dyer (1961), though certainly supported by earthworks of defensive proportions at Dray's Ditches, Bedfordshire, could nonetheless have greatly facilitated the division of land for agricultural usage as well. Comparable to the Mile Ditches, with their arrangement of triple ditches and quadruple banks, which form the eastern limit of Dyer's Region 5 in his Chiltern series, is the system of multiple banks on Thickthorn Down, Dorset (D. W. Harding, 1959). Technically, the latter should not be termed 'cross-dykes', and topographically their situation is undistinguished. At their north-east end, the Thickthorn banks continue for a short distance parallel to the southern butt-end of the Dorset *cursus*, perhaps incorporating the Neolithic earthwork as part of the later dyke system. To the south-west, the dykes of Launceston Down could have been conceived as part of the same network of ranch boundaries. One aspect of the Thickthorn banks, however, is instructive. The section excavated across bank IV revealed very clearly a v-shaped wedge of humus which extended along its crest, perhaps the result of constructing the earthwork by throwing up rubble from both adjacent quarry ditches to form a pair of 'twin banks' and leaving the humus to accumulate subsequently between them (Pl. XVII). Alternatively, such stratification could be regarded as the product of a thorn hedge, laid along the summit of the bank as an obvious reinforcement of the earthwork. As such, it affords some evidence for a practice which must surely have been quite common in the Iron Age, for both defensive and non-defensive earthworks.

Linear earthworks or ranch boundaries, like small pastoral enclosures, are not a feature exclusive to the Iron Age in southern Britain. Indeed, some years ago C. M. Piggott recognised a group of small ditched enclosures of the middle and late Bronze Age in Wessex (1942), which have been generally regarded as stock-corrals, and more recently Bradley has shown that in Sussex rectilinear enclosures of this kind are associated with linear boundary ditches (1971a). Furthermore, Bradley has argued that certain classes of Iron Age hillforts may be derived directly from such stock-enclosures, while others were apparently developed from arable farms of the Little Woodbury or Pimperne kind. The former, arising from stock-compounds or tracts of enclosed pasture, he regards as earlier in date than the latter, and he accounts for this pattern in lowland Britain 'against a background of social change and arable intensification, both brought about by population increase and an attendant shortage of land' (1971b, 71). In effect, with a growth in population at the beginning of the Iron Age, accelerated by the arrival of bands of settlers from the Continent, there was an urgent need to utilise land to its maximum capacity for the production of food. To speak of a Bronze

Age economy which was essentially pastoral, in contrast to an Iron Age agricultural system based principally upon arable farming may perhaps be an over-simplification, but it is evident that there was at least an intensification of cereal cultivation, as Bradley has argued, and indeed such a process may well have been stimulated by the arrival of spelt-growing settlers from abroad, introducing into Britain the practice of winter and spring sowing. Such a process of arable intensification, with perhaps a consequent element of social change, would scarcely have been achieved in all regions equally or without resistance and upheavals. The various boundary ditches discussed above, therefore, may well have served a dual function, not simply as a practical means of defining areas of pasture from arable land, but providing also a measure of protection in the event of unrest between farmer and rancher. As a corollary to Bradley's thesis of arable intensification, the contrast between the Woodbury economy of the lowland zone and the Stanwick economy of highland Britain surely needs qualification to take account of the progressive effect of agricultural change upon regions further north. And although the concept of a retarded Bronze Age culture lingering on, little changed, in the north until the Roman period has been largely discredited by fieldwork and research in recent years, it is conceivable that agricultural practice, determined as much by environmental factors as by technological innovation, may have retained there a bias towards pastoralism longer than elsewhere.

The principal stock bred in Iron Age Britain comprised cattle and sheep. The cattle were of the small 'Celtic shorthorn' variety (*bos longifrons*), apparently introduced into Britain in the later Bronze Age, and doubtless kept to supply milk as well as meat to supplement the cereal and vegetable diet. Sheep were of a small type, comparable to those which today are bred in semi-wild conditions in the Orkneys, Shetlands, Hebrides and in particular on the island of Soay. The female of this breed is characterised by its goat-like horns, which has led in the past to confusion between the excavated remains of sheep and those of domestic goats. Apart from providing a further supply of meat, sheep were evidently bred for their fleeces, while the ewes may well have been milked as well as cows and goats. In the absence of evidence for shearing in the Iron Age, we must assume that the wool was plucked, for there is ample evidence of its subsequent processing. Spindle-whorls of chalk, baked clay or even Kimmeridge shale, for spinning the wool into a yarn, are common on Wessex settlements, some of which, like Longbridge Deverill and Little Woodbury, have also produced post-settings which were most probably the foundations for wooden looms. Triangular loomweights of stone or baked clay were used to keep taut the vertical warp threads in the loom, while the horizontal strands were beaten down into a tight weave by using bone weaving-combs of the kind which Hodson has taken as one of his type-fossils for the British Iron Age (Fig. 21, E, F).

One of the principal difficulties in prehistoric times of maintaining herds and flocks must have been the supply of winter fodder. Clark has quoted medieval and early modern instances of this same problem in Denmark and the Western Isles of Scotland, where only a bare minimum of animals, required for breeding the following year, could be kept over the winter, and where even these survived into the spring in a weak and emaciated condition.

85

The solution which prehistorians have conventionally inferred has been that cattle and sheep were rounded up at autumn, and, with the exception of those animals selected as breeding stock, were slaughtered. The meat would then have been salted for preservation, or perhaps smoked by hanging the carcasses over a domestic hearth. Support for this

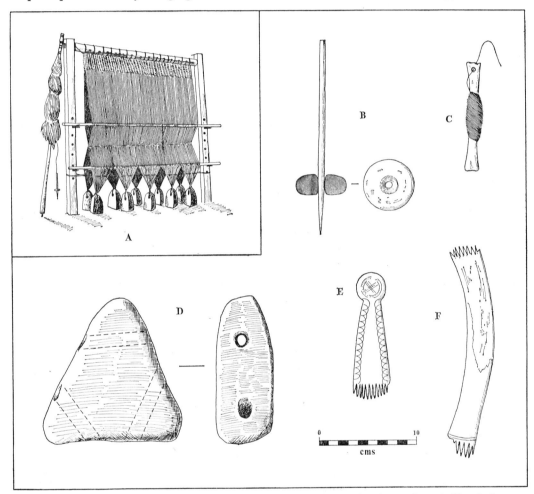

21. *Weaving and spinning utensils. A, reconstruction of primitive loom. B, spindle. C, bone bobbin. D, baked clay loomweights. E and F, ? weaving-combs*

theory, archaeologically, was derived from evidence of the bones of young animals – too often recorded only in very vague terms – found by excavation, and in particular Watson's analysis of the animal bones from the Neolithic settlement at Skara Brae in the Orkneys, published by Childe in 1931. In citing this report, Clark claimed that, of the cattle bred at Skara Brae 'nearly three-fifths were slaughtered at less than six months, and (that) less than a fifth reached maturity' (1952, 125). Since the total number of specimens was only seventeen, it is evident that no firm conclusions could effectively be drawn from such a statistic; and as two of these were animals that died at birth, and hence scarcely merit inclusion in the number deliberately killed, the proportion of cattle slaughtered under six months falls to approximately half. In fact, a re-examination by Higgs and White (1963) of the entire question of autumn slaughter has cast doubt not only upon the necessity for such a practice in prehistoric times, but also upon the method used to determine the seasonal rate of killing stock. The ageing of animals is largely based upon dentition, the period of eruption of the molars and pre-molars, itself calculated by reference to present-day cattle. A further complication is introduced by the intervening periods between these eruption points, which can only be calculated by assessing the degree of wear on the teeth which are present. Allowing, furthermore, a range from the beginning of February to the end of March for the lambing season, or perhaps March and April for the birth of cattle, it is virtually impossible to assert that any reduction of livestock was achieved systematically in an autumn round-up, rather than as need demanded throughout the winter.

In the absence of total analysis of animal bones in quantity from more excavated settlements, it is difficult to be sure to what extent the samples retained really represent the true proportions of stock maintained by Iron Age communities in lowland Britain. For the most part, cattle seem to have been most numerous, though an extreme contrast at Glastonbury would suggest there a local emphasis upon sheep-rearing. At Blewburton Hill (Collins, 1947; 1952; 1959; Harding, 1967), on the northern edge of the Berkshire Downs, a series of deliberate burials of horses – of a kind resembling an Exmore pony in size – perhaps suggests that horse-breeding was of particular importance in that region. Horse-coping on a large scale must have been a significant activity in lowland Britain in the later Iron Age, at any rate, if Caesar's estimate of the numerical strength of Cassivellaunus' chariot force is even remotely credible (*de bello Gallico*, 5, 19); though it has been suggested that such teams would have been traded from ranches in the north of England (Piggott, 1961, 15–16), it is hard to imagine that a tribal war-lord would rely upon external sources for stock, other than perhaps stallions for stud. Finally, of the principal domestic breeds, pigs are found on Iron Age settlements in small but not insignificant numbers, particularly in regions of deciduous forest where they could forage freely for beech-nuts and acorns.

Apart from the meat or milk for which cattle were reared, their hides would have been utilised for leather goods, and the bones provided a workable material for small domestic artefacts like weaving-combs, needles, awls, and toggles, and perhaps even for ornaments or gaming-counters. The basic diet of meat, cereals and vegetables – probably peas, beans and lentils – could doubtless have been supplemented by hunting and fishing, though the bones of wild animals are comparatively rare on settlement sites. The hunting of hare, fowl and geese for sport is recorded by Caesar (*de bello Gallico*, 5, 12), while Britain is reputed to have been famous for its hunting dogs (Strabo, 4, v, 2). Wicker traps or nets could doubtless have been employed in the pursuit of game, and perhaps also weapons which entangle, like the bolas. Evidence for throwing spears and slings is more common than evidence for archery, though two small iron arrowheads from Pimperne indicate the use of the bow there. The gathering of wild honey was apparently practised from earliest prehistoric times (Clark, 1952, Fig. 12), and by the end of the Bronze Age bees had probably been domesticated, not only for honey, but also for the wax which was used in the *cire perdue* method of bronze casting. Equally, a variety of berries and wild fruit could have been gathered, though there is no evidence for the cultivation of fruit trees. Flax, however, was certainly grown in Britain by Iron Age times, both for textile fibres and for its oil-bearing seeds. In spite of Strabo's assertions to the contrary (4, v, 2), it is hard to imagine that Iron Age farmers did not produce cheese, and pottery vessels from many sites in lowland Britain which have holes pierced in their bases could well have been designed to strain off whey. The making of fermented drink is certainly well documented in literary sources (for a list of references, see Piggott, 1965, 266, note 82). Strabo refers to the production of drink from honey and grain, and, in addition to mead and beer, by the end of the Iron Age wine was being imported into south-eastern Britain at any rate. Not only is this trade attested by the frequency of *amphorae* from burial sites, but also we have the evidence of the coinage of the Belgic king Verica, which incorporated the vine-leaf as an emblem in contrast to the native ear of barley.

A variety of other local crafts can be inferred indirectly either from literary sources, or from our knowledge of developing techniques in central and western Europe that are not well attested archaeologically in Britain. Ship- and boat-building, for instance, was evidently a highly developed craft, judging from Caesar's comments concerning the robust but shallow-draughted vessels of the Veneti, well adapted to the stormy conditions of the Atlantic (*de bello Gallico*, 3, 13). Their prows were high and stoutly built to meet the force of the waves, the cross-members were constructed of oak beams nailed together, their anchors were secured by iron chains rather than cables, and their sails were of leather rather than canvas for added strength against the Atlantic gales. Whether ocean-going vessels in Britain were so sturdily built we cannot be certain, though the remains of two vessels which were apparently used as ferries across the Humber estuary in the eighth century B.C. were evidently the work of a team of highly skilled local shipwrights (Wright 1947). A recent radio-carbon determination for the Ferriby boats of 750+150 (Barker and Mackey, 1960) places them considerably earlier than the excavators had supposed (Wright and Churchill, 1965). The more complete of the two boats from North Ferriby was probably some 15 metres in length originally, and was constructed of adzed planks, sewn together with yew withes around a central framework of three stout oak timbers. Both were shallow-draught vessels but, unlike the Venetic warships encountered by Caesar, we have no clue to their superstructure or rigging. Dug-out canoes continued in use, and, especially on inland waterways, skin-covered curraghs or coracles would doubtless have been common.

Among the rural settlements of lowland Britain, thatching, hurdling, netting and basketry were undoubtedly commonplace local crafts, though archaeology will seldom afford direct evidence for any of these skills. Under exceptional conditions, like those of the late Bronze Age site at Minnis Bay, Birchington, Kent (Worsfold, 1943, Pls IX and X), or in the Somerset levels at Glastonbury and Meare (Meare II, e.g. Pl. XXX), sections of hurdling have been preserved (Pl. XVIII). Indeed, it is from Glastonbury and Meare that we have the best-preserved evidence for carpentry in the British Iron Age, not only in the form of iron tools – saws and chisels for instance (Fig. 22) – but also in the shape of the products themselves. A finely turned wooden tub, decorated with curvilinear ornament of the later La Tène style, and carefully designed axle-boxes (Fig. 22, A), indicate furthermore the

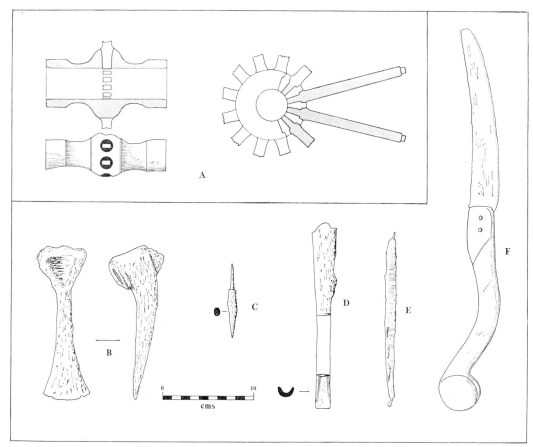

22. *Wooden axle-box and carpenter's tools, Glastonbury, Somerset. A, reconstruction of axle-box. B, adze. C, awl. D, chisel. E, file. F, saw*

use of a lathe, which is otherwise witnessed by the presence of lathe-turned bracelets of shale. But if the industries and crafts of Iron Age Britain have achieved a high level of technical attainment, at the same time older skills like flint-working no doubt persisted in many quarters. The use of a flint boring-implement at Pimperne, probably for piercing leather, reflects the continuance of well-tried and serviceable methods which the newer technology of iron had not superseded.

If crafts such as weaving, basketry and hurdling were skills normally practised in every household, more specialised trades like metalworking (Tylecote, 1962; Coghlan, 1956; Cleere, 1972), were evidently in the hands of professionals, who not only had access to the mineral ores necessary for their industry but who also controlled the marketing of their products. At what level in Iron Age society such skilled craftsmen operated we can only speculate. Doubtless local agricultural communities would have required the services of a blacksmith for their basic tools and equipment, and would have acquired their relatively few luxury goods – small personal bronzes and so forth – from pedlars distributing them from a professional centre. But it seems doubtful whether the master craftsmen who produced lavish parade-armour like the Witham and Battersea shields or exotic ornaments like the Snettisham and Ipswich torcs could have sustained production except under the patronage of a wealthy tribal aristocracy. Of the production centres of ironwork – still less of silver or gold – we know comparatively little in pre-Roman Britain.

Sources of iron ore in Britain, including outcrops which would have been readily exploited by open-cast mining, are plentiful. The iron deposits of the Weald are specifically mentioned by Caesar as one of the industrial regions of Iron Age Britain (*de bello Gallico*, 5, 12); the quantities of ironwork at the Hunsbury hillfort (Fell, 1936) doubtless reflect the use of local resources from Northamptonshire extending north-eastwards into Lincolnshire; and by the Roman period at any rate, iron was being extracted from the ores of the Forest of Dean. If there were indeed centres of iron production, however, these have yet to be located. The only evidence available to us at present for the extraction of iron from its ores comprises a handful of sites scattered throughout Britain at which small bowl-furnaces, operated by a simple bellows system, have been recognised. The example from Kestor, in Devon (Fox, 1954), is fairly representative. Not much over a foot in diameter and about 9 inches deep, the furnace contained some quantities of iron slag and charcoal. At Chelm's Combe, Cheddar (Penniman *et al.*, 1958), a comparable bowl-hearth was equipped with a *tuyère* in one side for the insertion of the bellows. Excavation at Purberry Shot, Ewell, Surrey (Lowther, 1946) also produced slag which had accumulated in the bottom of furnaces where no means had been provided for tapping it off. This was apparently normal practice in Iron Age smelting-hearths; only at All Cannings Cross have fragments of tap slag been found. Elsewhere, remains of iron smelting have been found at Rowberrow Cavern in Somerset (Taylor, 1922), at Catcote, Co. Durham (information by courtesy of Mr C. D. Long. Final report forthcoming), and in several instances there are traces of pre-Roman smelting activity in the Weald. In the Upper Thames region, two sites have produced evidence for iron-working, though not for smelting as such. At City Farm, Long Hanborough, two pits were recorded by Case (1964, 42–4, 94–5), both of which were lined with rammed, stony loam, and both of which contained quantities of iron slag. The slag itself did not appear to have been heated in the range necessary for tapping 'molten' from the furnace (1000°–1200°) and this factor, together with the difficulties of achieving, with a primitive bellows, smelting conditions in pits of such a size suggested that the City Farm pits had been for ore-roasting rather than smelting. The object of this exercise would be to reduce carbonate ore – in this instance probably derived from the north Oxfordshire ironstone region – into the more easily reducible oxide. A further pit, containing ash, stones and iron slag, from the nearby settlement at Cassington (note in *Oxoniensia*, 2, 1937, 201) may have served a similar function, though in this case the presence of extraneous animal bones perhaps suggests that the pit itself was merely a receptacle for rubbish from an adjacent working-area where there had been a roasting-pit or smelting-bowl.

Of the various metal industries known to have been active in prehistoric times, only iron-working could have been supported on any scale by the natural resources of lowland Britain in the Iron Age. But in spite of this innovation, the demand for bronze, particularly for ornamental and non-utilitarian goods, undoubtedly persisted. The natural resources of copper in Wales, Scotland and Ireland were apparently supplemented by Cornish tin, the mining of which was remarked by Diodorus Siculus (5, 2), probably drawing upon the observations of the fourth century Greek explorer, Pytheas. Small crucibles which show traces of bronze smelting have been found at both Glastonbury and Meare, and elsewhere in northern and western Britain principally. Of the precious metals, gold likewise was the product of western and northern Britain. Relatively few precious ornaments of the early Iron Age have been shown to be of unalloyed native gold; many, like the torcs from Snettisham, include alloys of silver or copper. Native silver is seldom found in prehistoric contexts, since it occurs in deep seams which would have been practically inaccessible; as in the Roman period, therefore, silver would probably have been derived from lead, from deposits like those of the Mendips. Silver and gold, at any rate, are included by Strabo, together with iron, skins, slaves and hunting-dogs, among the exports which were traded from Britain in exchange for exotic ornamental goods from the Continent.

By contrast with metalworking, the manufacture of pottery has conventionally been regarded as a domestic industry for the most part in the Iron Age, the traditional function of women, as it still is among some primitive communities today. Even so, recent research has made necessary a reappraisal of this view, as evidence is accumulated for the activities in certain areas of professional potters, whose wares can be distinguished by analysis of the grit inclusions which were added by the maker to temper the clay. In particular, Peacock (1970) has attempted to show that the later Iron Age pottery of south-western Britain can be attributed to specific centres of manufacture, whence it was distributed commercially, sometimes over quite wide marketing areas. The pottery of his Group 1, for instance, including vessels with curvilinear ornament, internally grooved rims, and stamped 'duck' impressions, he traces to the gabbro outcrops of the Lizard in Cornwall. Other groups contain inclusions which could be derived from geological sources closer to the ceramic-distribution zones: Group 2 from the red sandstone of the Mendips; the calcite-gritted pottery of Group 3 from the Mendip limestones; the shell-gritted wares of Group 4 from the Jurassic outcrops of Somerset and Dorset. For Groups 5 and 6 (sanidine and volcanic grains) a source near the permian of the Exeter district has been suggested. Peacock's research and conclusions evidently have implications of the utmost importance, not only for our view of Iron Age pottery manufacture as a professional industry, but also relating to our interpretation of ceramic evidence in cultural and historical terms. But before we leap to the conclusion that all Iron Age pottery was the product of such professional centres, it is as well to remember that the pottery with which Peacock has been concerned has been largely fine-wares of a late and particularly distinctive kind. Similar groups might well be located by further research in central southern and south-eastern England: the stylistic uniformity and limited distribution of the cordoned haematite bowls of Wessex, for instance, suggests perhaps a school of semi-professional potters in operation already by the fifth or fourth centuries B.C. But for the vast majority of coarse-wares of the early Iron Age, there can be little doubt about their domestic and localised manufacture.

In the Belgic period the proportion of commercially manufactured pottery is far higher. Now for the first time the concept of pottery typology becomes relevant, with the production of vessels of standardised shape – pedestal urns, cups or *tazze*, platters, imported butt- or girth-beakers, and so forth. Though there is still a recognisable sub-stratum of coarser, domestically made pottery, the greater degree of uniformity in commercially produced ceramics greatly facilitates the business of classification. Whether cause or effect, this intensification of the professional element in pottery manufacture may be related to the adoption in south-eastern Britain of the technique of throwing pottery on a fast wheel. Previously, all pottery of the British Iron Age had been hand-made, with the sole aid of the turn-table or *tournette* (Childe, 1954, 196–7), a device for rotating the vessel in order that the potter might have before him the face at which he wished to work. The turn-table, however, did not permit the construction of a pot by means of the centrifugal force exerted by rotation; this could only be achieved with the introduction of the wheel proper, either a simple wheel or a footwheel. The former comprises a disc of wood or stone, pivoted on a vertical spindle, which rotates in its socket like a spinning top. It may be started by a simple device such as pulling sharply a strap wound around the spindle, and thereafter relying upon the weight of the wheel itself to maintain momentum. Using a footwheel, the potter can control the speed of rotation by use of his feet, whilst leaving his hands entirely free to build the pot (Jope, 1956, 288 and Fig. 271). The notion that the turntable represents an intermediate stage towards the introduction of the fast wheel is an over-simplification. There is no real evidence that the footwheel developed from the turntable, or that its introduction in the Iron Age universally displaced the latter. Indeed, it is most likely that a piece of capital equipment like the kick-wheel remained an expensive asset in which only professional potters could afford to invest.

An equally important distinction between pottery manufacture of the early and later Iron Age concerns the process of firing. Evidence for kilns in the pre-Belgic phase is virtually non-existent, unless we imagine that ovens like those from All Cannings Cross (Cunnington, 1923, Pl. 3, and 2) were multi-purpose affairs that served for baking pottery as well as bread, or drying corn. Even 'Belgic' kilns are comparatively rare, and those that have been excavated and recorded are late within the period. Two examples salvaged from a quarry at Long Hanborough, Oxfordshire, are typical of their general layout and construction (D. W. Harding, 1972, Fig. 9, from salvage excavation conducted by D. Sturdy. See note in *Oxoniensia*, 25, 1960, 133). The first was little more than an elongated pit in which the stoke-hole was scarcely separated from the main oven-pit, but comprised an extension of one end of it. Around its perimeter the baking-chamber was lined with clay, and in its centre was a raised platform of clay, the edges of which were reinforced by large stones. A number of fragmentary kiln-bars were found in the pit, suggesting that they had spanned the gap between its sides and the central platform, to form a floor-level upon which the sun-dried pots could stand, and beneath which the heat from the furnace could circulate. The main chamber of the kiln was presumably roofed over, with a central vent in the dome to facilitate an updraught. The furnace chamber, on the other hand, was probably open, to enable the potter to feed the fuel into the kiln. Kiln 2 was apparently of a modified, and slightly more efficient design. It had a proper flue leading from the stoke-hole into the baking-chamber, in which the kiln bars, found radially around the pit, were supported in the centre not upon a platform of clay, but upon three mushroom-shaped pillars of baked clay, around which the heat could circulate much more freely. A series of late Belgic or early Roman kilns from Hardingstone, Northants (Woods, 1969, Figs 5–7), displays a similar design, with the stoke-hole removed only by a short flue channel from the firing chamber. An even more striking similarity in plan may be seen, however, between the Hanborough kilns and the Anglo-Saxon examples from Purwell Farm, Cassington, Oxon (Arthur and Jope 1962, Figs 2 and 3), both of which were little more than elongated pits.

In the absence of convincing kiln-plans for the pre-Belgic period, we can only assume that the majority of domestic pottery was clamp fired – that is, it was fired at ground level by piling the fuel over the green-hard clay vessel. This method can be perfectly adequate – indeed it is still used to good effect today by certain Arab potters in North Africa – though there is a danger that the pot will be damaged by a jet of flame, or by the fuel collapsing as it burns. The principal disadvantage, however, of clamp firing is that the temperature cannot be controlled so effectively as in a kiln. Heat is therefore generated very rapidly as the wind causes the fuel to blaze up, to the possible detriment of the vessel being baked. Steam may be trapped in the clay, causing the pot to warp or crack. There would clearly be some advantage in removing the fire from the direct blast of the wind by sinking it into a pit; indeed the earliest kiln-pits may have been little more than a means of sheltering the firing-area from excessive or irregular draught. Thereafter, the next stage of development, the removal of the pots from the fire itself into a separate firing chamber, requires no major technological innovation.

The lack of an efficient kiln-firing process in the earlier Iron Age does, however, account for the regular use of temper in the manufacture of pottery. It is a common misapprehension that temper serves to bind the clay, whereas any non-plastic material like flint, quartz, calcite or shell-grit is bound to reduce the plasticity of the clay rather than the reverse. Its principal function in prehistoric pottery was to facilitate the process of dehydration by opening the texture of the clay and permitting more even evaporation throughout (Shepard, 1961). Otherwise the evaporation of water on the surface of the pot will proceed more rapidly than it can be replaced by capillary action from the interior, resulting in uneven shrinkage of the pot wall which will then lead to warping and cracking. In much coarse pottery of the earliest Iron Age, the grits which are introduced for this purpose amount to sizeable inclusions: some of the calcite and shell grits in the Upper Thames region, for instance, are over 10 mm in width, occasionally reaching 15 mm. Grits of this size could have the reverse effect of producing a flaw in the surface of the pot which would be exposed by firing. In view of this, the contrast between such coarse pottery and the fine haematite-coated wares of the early Iron Age, for instance, might well reflect differences in the quality of materials and equipment available to the domestic potter on the one hand and the professional on the other.

Finally, we should consider the actual methods of manufacture available to pre-wheel potters of the early Iron Age. First, the simplest method of construction, by hand-modelling, may occasionally be illustrated by small pots which are little more than lumps of clay into which the potter has pressed his thumbs to fashion a crude and asymmetrical vessel. Second, there is the 'classic' method of pot construction of coil building, either by placing individual rings of clay upon each other, or by building up the walls in a continuous spiral. Under normal conditions it is extremely difficult to detect coil building simply from an examination of pottery sherds (Hodges, 1962, 60), though occasionally the hand-modelled base of a jar will have broken away from the body of the vessel in such a way as to leave an impression on the base of the initial coil. Sharply angular profiles like the carinated bowls from Long Wittenham must have been more difficult to achieve. Here the lowest section may have been modelled first up to the carination, and then allowed to dry until sufficiently rigid to sustain the neck. When this had likewise dried adequately, the flaring rim could then be added. Though it is generally held to be impractical to construct a pot in independent sections thus, the method is operated successfully by North African Bedouin, provided that the actual joint between the successive stages is kept moist by leaving a damp cloth over the vessel while the walls are allowed to dry. The technique of slab-building, we might, on the basis of ethnographic parallels, have expected to feature more frequently in prehistoric European contexts than it actually does. Two unpublished examples only are known to the present writer from the British Iron Age, from neighbouring sites at Minnis Bay, Birchington, Kent (unpublished material in the Powell-Cotton museum at Birchington), and at Margate a few miles to the east. Both are rectangular vessels with the corners rounded by smoothing the junction of the slabs, and both are of a fabric and finish which is generally associated with medium-fine burnished wares of Iron B. In view of their coastal contexts, these vessels could be interpreted as salt-evaporating pans; but whatever their purpose, their rectangular shape and method of construction are quite alien to the mainstream of British Iron Age pottery.

Once the vessel was complete, it would be left to dry in the sun until it was green-hard, a process which may have taken several days, until its walls would nearly ring if tapped with the knuckles. At this stage the surface of the pot could be burnished with a smooth stone to a high lustre, and any decoration which was required would be added by incising, or excising, the clay. Slips, too, could be added, in the form of a coloured clay wash to the outer surfaces of the vessel, or, in the case of haematite-coated wares, applied probably as a powder and then burnished into a deep metallic sheen. Only the finer pottery would have received such attention; perhaps these too, were skills restricted to the professional craftsmen and seldom available to the domestic potter. Stylistic characteristics of fine-pottery may, therefore, suggest the existence of local schools of skilled craftsmen; only laboratory analysis an ultimately demonstrate whether such groups of professional potters were a significant phenomenon in pre-Belgic Iron Age society.

6
Celtic religion and ceremonial monuments

EVIDENCE FOR religious practices in Iron Age Britain derives from two principal sources: literary records and a handful of archaeological monuments. Both must be treated with caution, providing at best a fragmentary impression of the role of religion in Iron Age society. The literary sources themselves divide into two major groups. In the first instance, there is a considerable body of information in early Irish writings relating to the activities of the priesthood, the names of Celtic deities, and the principal religious festivals of the Celtic year. Though none of these records in their extant form can be dated earlier than the seventh or eighth centuries A.D., in the absence of Roman colonisation of Ireland it is conceivable that they embody beliefs and practices which have a much older ancestry in the pre-Roman Iron Age. We may be encouraged in this inference by numerous analogies which may be drawn between the Irish records and the second major group of literary records relevant to this study, namely the writings of Greek and Roman geographers and historians, whose observations were based upon the religious traditions of Celtic tribes in Gaul at the time of the Roman occupation. This latter source is further supplemented, both on the Continent and in Britain, by epigraphic evidence, principally monumental inscriptions incorporating the names of both Celtic and Roman deities set up under Roman rule. How far information derived from these sources accurately reflects the state of affairs in Britain or on the Continent in the later Iron Age is questionable. In considering the recorded role and activities of the druids, for instance, we must surely take account of inaccuracies which might arise out of the writer's ignorance of foreign and strange customs, or even deliberate embellishment motivated by propaganda purposes or political expediency. The Romans would not have been unique in invoking the argument that they brought civilisation to replace savagery as a justification of colonialism. In view of such qualifications, it is unfortunate that the archaeological evidence for religious monuments in Iron Age Britain is itself so defective. Sites have certainly been found for which a religious purpose seems probable, most notably the timber temple excavated some years ago by Grimes at Heathrow airport (Fig. 23) (1948, esp. Figs 3 and 4; 1958, 25 and Fig. 7), and the dual shrines at Frilford in Berkshire (Fig. 24) (Bradford and Goodchild, 1939; D. W. Harding, 1972, 61 ff, Fig. 8 and Plates 33, 34). Others may exist for which a similar interpretation might be valid. But in the absence of prolific cult-finds or dedicatory deposits, it would be a bold archaeologist indeed who would invoke such an interpretation at the risk of being accused of abandoning scientific objectivity and permitting nineteenth-century romanticism to cloud his judgment! The fact remains, however, that in Iron Age contexts it is hard to imagine what kind of evidence we should expect to demonstrate a ritual function, and several cases where such an interpretation may seem justified depend less upon any intrinsic evidence in the character of the structures, than upon their relationship to Romano-British religious buildings which were subsequently constructed on the same site (Lewis, 1966). So far it has proved impossible to correlate fully the evidence of excavated sites with our knowledge of Celtic religion derived from literature. For the present, therefore, we can only examine the available information from both independently, in the hope that future research may yet provide some basis for drawing the two together into a coherent picture of Iron Age religion.

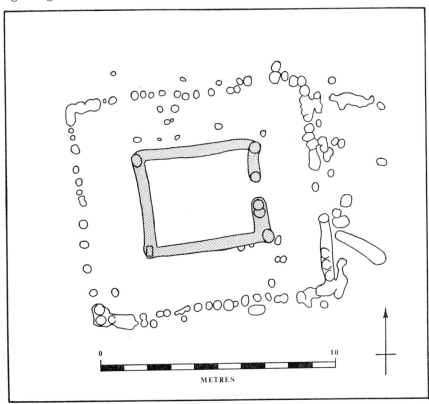

23. *Heathrow, Middlesex: plan of early Iron Age temple*

From the Irish records it is evident that Celtic religious festivals were closely related to the changing seasons and principal events of the agricultural year. The most important of the four festivals was *Samain*, celebrated at the beginning of November, when flocks and herds would have been rounded up from their summer pasture, and perhaps reduced to the bare breeding-stock for the winter months ahead. Second in importance to *Samain* was the festival of *Beltine* on 1 May, when the animals that had survived the winter were driven out to open range. From the emphasis upon these festivals, rather than those which might be associated with the agrarian cycle, it is evident that the economy of Celtic Ireland was based upon pastoralism primarily. Though we might infer similar seasonal practices in the rest

97

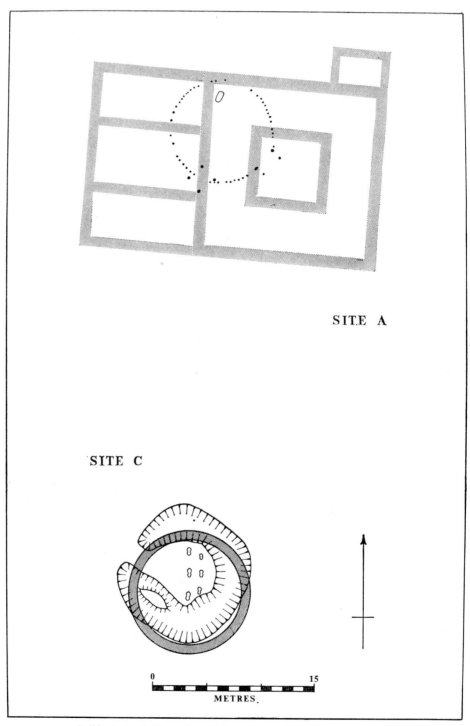

SITE A

SITE C

0   15

METRES.

24. *Frilford, Berkshire: plan of Iron Age and Romano-British temples*

of Britain, therefore, we should not assume that these particular festivals were accorded equal emphasis in lowland England, for instance, where the cultivation of cereal crops undoubtedly played as great a role in the agricultural economy as pastoralism in Ireland.

The remaining two festivals known from Irish records were *Imbolc* at the beginning of February, and *Lugnasad* on 1 August. The latter, presumably associated with the worship of the god Lug, – whose name was incorporated in the place-name Lugudunum, Lyons – could well have been connected with the agrarian cycle, marking the beginning of the season of harvest. Though this sequence of events may seem odd to a society for whom the harvest festival is principally one of thanksgiving for the successful gathering of crops and produce, we should remember that religious ceremonies and dedications among the Celts were mainly designed to guarantee the efficacy of either soil or beasts in advance of the event. It is perhaps significant that the principal non-pastoralist festival of the Irish calendar should be related to a god whose origins were foreign to Ireland; indeed, Powell has put forward the suggestion that Lug may have been introduced to Ireland by Gaulish immigrants in the first century B.C. (1958, 120).

Such festivals and magical rituals were presumably initiated and conducted by the druids, who feature prominently in both Irish and classical literary sources (Kendrick, 1927; Piggott, 1968). In fact, the Irish texts mention several related groups in addition to the druids. Of these the *fáthi* (singular: *fáith*) is the cognate of the *vates* or prophets of Strabo (Jackson, 1964, 24 ff). Finally, in the early Christian period another category of trained poets achieved predominance, the *filid* (singular: *fili*), a term which etymologically implies the ability of these prophets or seers to predict the future. Accounts of the lengthy and rigorous training of the *filid* in early Irish sources are reminiscent of Caesar's account of the instruction of potential druids in first-century Gaul, which, he reports, could take up to twenty years, involving the learning by heart of a great number of verses. In describing the principal classes of Gallic society, Caesar distinguished two groups, among which the druids were accorded equal status and dignity with the knights or *equites*. The common people, as in early Irish literature, were considered to be of no account, and utterly subservient to the nobility. The function of the druids, on the other hand, evidently extended beyond purely religious ritual to include jurisdiction in civil and criminal matters:

[The druids] are concerned with divine worship, the due performance of sacrifices, public and private, and the interpretation of ritual questions . . . in fact, it is they who decide in almost all disputes, public and private; and if any crime has been committed, or murder done, or if there is any dispute about succession or boundaries, they also decide it, determining rewards and penalties: if any person or people does not abide by their decision, they ban such from sacrifice, which is their heaviest penalty. Those that are so banned are reckoned as impious and criminal (*de bello Gallico*, 6, 13).

Contrary to the Irish evidence, which indicates that druids were entitled to be householders and to bear arms, Caesar emphasises that druids in Gaul were exempt from military service and war taxes; indeed he suggests that many young men voluntarily took up druidic training in order to dodge the draft, or at least to claim the privileges of the priest-hood. The druidic practice of human sacrifice is also recorded by Caesar, though he places a different interpretation upon such practices from that of other Roman writers:

> They believe, in effect, that, unless for a man's life a man's life be paid, the majesty of the immortal gods may not be appeased. . . . They believe that the execution of those who have been caught in the act of theft or robbery is more pleasing to the immortal gods; but when the supply of such fails they resort to the execution even of the innocent (*de bello Gallico*, 6, 16).

The final comment in this passage, added by way of an afterthought, gives the impression of a deliberate piece of propaganda, included to disgust a sophisticated Roman audience. Though much of Caesar's record of druidic practices must have been based on first-hand experience, or upon direct reports during the Gallic campaign, it is possible that he included also traditional elements, particularly when dealing with the more horrifying practices which were attributed to the druids by Posidonius and his successors. His reiteration, for instance, of the Gaulish practice of constructing a great wickerwork colossus, in which sacrificial victims were burnt, is probably not based upon personal experience of such an event, but upon Posidonius' narrative, which was apparently the source of the same story in Strabo (*Geography*, 4, IV, 5).

One of the principal objects of human sacrifice, according to both Strabo and Diodorus Siculus, was evidently not the appeasement of the gods, but the divination of the future. Both repeat Posidonius' account of the sacrifice of human victims, from whose convulsions and death-throes the seers made their predictions (Strabo, *Geography*, 4, IV, 5; Diodorus Siculus, 5, 31). Both sources, however, must be treated with caution, for, as Tierney reminds us, they are themselves capable of confusing what Posidonius reported, even if the latter himself were accurate in the first place. For instance, the ability to reconcile two opposing armies on the verge of combat is attributed by Diodorus to the bards, and by Strabo to the druids. Indeed, it is not easy to distinguish in terms of precise functions and powers between the threefold ranks of druids, bards and seers (*vates*) who are mentioned by Strabo, Diodorus and Ammianus Marcellinus (Ammianus Marcellinus, 15, IX, 8), all depending directly or indirectly upon Posidonius. It is not the purpose of the present study to compare in detail the texts of these various classical writers, a task which has already been undertaken else-where (Tierney, 1960, 223) with great skill and scholarship; it is sufficient for our purposes to conclude that the parallelism between the threefold structure in Celtic Gaul and the Irish triumvirate of *bard*, *fáith* and *druí* argues convincingly that such a division did exist among Celtic peoples in the immediately pre-Roman period.

There can be little doubt that Caesar exaggerated the importance of the druids, to the extent of attributing to them powers and functions that elsewhere were divided between the three classes. His motive in doing so was presumably to demonstrate the politico-religious threat which they represented to Rome, and to justify their suppression. It is difficult to imagine that their ritual was his only reason for wishing to stamp out the druids, and, in spite of his exaggeration for the purposes of propaganda, it is possible that the druids did indeed incite political resistance to Rome. An important element in this situation was the druidic belief in an after-life: 'The cardinal doctrine which they seek to teach is that souls do not die, but after death pass from one to another; and this belief, as the fear of death is thereby cast aside, they hold to be the greatest incentive to valour' (*de bello Gallico*, 6, 14). This statement is dismissed by Tierney, who argues that the 'Pythagorean belief in the immortality of the soul with its peculiar utilitarian motivation of valour in battle may be suspected of being an aetiology superimposed by Posidonius on the one great fact known about the Celts from the time of Aristotle onward, that is, their quite reckless valour in battle' (1960, 223). Contrived the philosophy may have been, but more probably by the druids than by Posidonius; and its effect in fanning resistance to Rome, like the analogous belief in immunity to fire-power of Mau Mau terrorists, could nonetheless have been extremely real. The most surprising factor in Caesar's emphasis of druidic authority in general is that he makes no further reference to their activities throughout the remainder of his *Commentaries*, which might well be regarded as evidence that his account in Book 6 was an exaggerated one.

One further comment made by Caesar has particular relevance to this study, namely, that the origins of druidism were to be traced to Britain, whence all who wished to perfect their knowledge of the cult travelled. Tierney dismisses this as totally improbable, preferring a source for druidism somewhere in the Middle Rhine or Bohemia. Of course, it is conceivable that, having established druidism as a cause for repression, Caesar could derive further justification for extending his campaign into Britain by inventing a spurious connection with the cult; but were we to accept this view, we should have to explain the lack of further reference to the druids, which might have been expected for the sake of political consistency. On the other hand, we may recall that in the *Cattle Raid of Cooley*, Medb encounters a female *fili* or *fáith* who has just returned to Ireland after studying the arts of the *filid* in Britain (Strachan and O'Keefe, 1912), a passage which serves to emphasise the tradition that Britain was the place for post-graduate studies. The only literary reference to druidism specifically in Britain remains Tacitus' description in the *Annals* (14, 30) of the priesthood of Anglesey inciting the native population to resist the forces of Suetonius Paulinus, which they apparently did with a fanatical fervour of a kind familiar to historians of the Sudanese campaigns of more recent times.

No less problematical than the structure of the priesthood is the identification of particular deities. Caesar singles out the worship of a native god in Gaul whom he equates with Mercury, adding the names of Apollo, Mars, Jupiter and Minerva as a subsidiary group (*de bello Gallico*, 6, 17). In this more than in any other field, however, we should question the authenticity of Roman documentation – the emphasis placed by Lucan (*Pharsalia*, 1, 445–6) upon the gods Taranis, Teutatis and Esus, for instance, is totally at variance with the archaeological record afforded by Gallo-Roman inscriptions. The simple equation of a native deity with a Roman god can in itself be confusing, since the attributes of the one may correspond only partially or marginally to that of the other, and the attempt at approximation could therefore lead to an exaggeration of one particular facet of the native deity. In this context, such Celtic names may represent no more than a local manifestation of a wider and as yet undifferentiated divine power, and it may have been the imposition of Roman culture that assisted in the creation of Celtic deities as individual personalities. We should not assume, therefore, that all these individual names can be transposed back into the pre-Roman Iron Age in any meaningful sense.

Though the concept of localised deities focused in some natural context such as a sacred grove, spring, river or mountain would appear to be central to Celtic religion, nonetheless certain elements of Romano-Celtic iconography recur with sufficient frequency over a wider geographical distribution to reinforce the view that such deities are indeed local manifestations of a wider divinity. The widespread cult of a horned god is a good illustration of this. Variously equated with Mars, Mercury and Silvanus, and frequently depicted in the north of England in phallic representations, it can be traced northwards from Yorkshire and eastwards along the line of Hadrian's Wall. Among examples of horned gods in Britain, Dr Anne Ross had drawn attention to a relief from Cirencester, depicting a stag-god in squatting posture, comparable to the Gaulish stag-god, identified as *Cernunnos* (1967, 139, Pl. 43a and Map VIII). From the same site a second representation has been recovered in which the stag-god is portrayed as an antlered head. On the Continent the notion of a stag-god with antler-horns may be traced as early as the Bronze Age in the rock carvings and phallic figures of Denmark. Dr Ross has pointed out, however, that the rock carving at Val Camonica in northern Italy, which she attributes to the mid-fourth century B.C., affords the earliest evidence for a Cernunnos cult in a demonstrably Celtic context (1967, Fig. 90). The figure is depicted in a standing pose, with arms uplifted and bearing at each elbow a pendent ornament which has been identified as a torc. The torc is certainly an important element in the iconography of horned deities, and is well represented on the inscribed Cernunnos relief from Paris and on the famous silver cauldron from Gundestrup in Denmark, where a squatting god with antler-horns holds a torc in his right hand and a symbolic serpent with ram's horns in his left (Klindt-Jensen, 1959; 1961).

An important element in Celtic religious iconography which likewise transcends the local distributions of individual cults is the notion of triplism. In Britain tricephalic sculptures are not so common as in Gaul, though examples have been found in Scotland, Northumberland and Guernsey. Two three-faced sculptures are known from Ireland, one from Woodlands, Co. Donegal, the other better known example from Corleck, Co. Cavan, which Dr Ross has aptly compared stylistically with the tricephalos from Roquepertuse, France. The concept of triplism carries with it no particular implications of a trinitarian theology, but is merely an expression of the omnipotence of the deity portrayed. At the same time the number three evidently had some basic magical quality, which is exemplified by the divine triads of early Irish mythology whose origins most probably are to be traced to the pre-Roman Celtic period.

If much of our knowledge of Celtic religion derives from iconographic or epigraphic evidence, itself dating to the Roman occupation of Britain and Gaul, we might anticipate a

Maiden Castle, Dorset: war-cemetery: (above) general view; (below) skeleton with ballista-arrow in spine

xv *Fifield Down, Wi*
shire: air-photogra
of 'Celtic' fields

xvi *Burderop D*
Wiltshire: air-ph
graph of 'Celtic' f

comparable element of continuity in the location of sacred sites. That there was such physical continuity is suggested very strongly by the number of Romano-Celtic temple sites in lowland Britain where objects of pre-Roman rather than simply Romanised Celtic character have been found, though in most cases it has not yet proved possible to relate such discoveries to Iron Age structures for which a ritual function might reasonably be claimed. The difficulty of demonstrating such a purpose has been mentioned earlier, and the nature of the problem is well illustrated by the excavations at Worth, Kent (Klein, 1928; C. F. C. Hawkes, 1940b). Beneath the *cella* of the Romano-Celtic temple were located postholes and an area of flooring, from which pottery with finger-tip ornament in the Iron A style was recovered, together with other fragments with pedestal bases, which should probably be attributed to a slightly later phase. In addition, the underlying levels of the temple produced a bone weaving-comb and a La Tène 1 brooch, attesting Iron Age occupation at least as early as the fourth century B.C. For the present discussion, however, the most relevant discovery was that of three bronze votive shields – two of them fragmentary – which were identified in the pre-Roman levels beneath the temple site (Fig. 25, C, D). Votive objects such as these probably afford the most convincing evidence which we are ever likely to obtain to demonstrate the sanctity of an Iron Age site. Clearly the environs of the Worth temple would merit further excavation, in an attempt to recover a plan of any pre-Roman structures which may have existed on the site.

Iron Age pits and postholes have more recently been excavated around and beneath the circular Romano-British shrine at Muntham, near Findon, Sussex (Holleyman, 1958), while traces of pre-Roman material have been recorded from Romano-British temple sites at Thistleton (Lewis, 1966, 84; note in *Arch. News Letter*, 7, no. 10, 238), Lancing (Frere, 1940, 160–3 and Fig. 11), Harlow (Lewis, 1966, 49. For references to Belgic coins see *VCH Essex*, III, 1963, 139), Farley (*VCH Surrey*, I, 1902, 248–9) and Sheepen Hill, Colchester. At Gosbecks (Hull 1958, 259, 263–4 and Fig. 13) the Romano-British temple, built or rebuilt in the second century A.D. in stone, was located in the corner of a square area which was itself surrounded by a ditch of pre-Roman date, suggesting that the ditched enclosure or *temenos* sanctuary itself might have been of pre-Roman origin, perhaps enclosing features, such as a sacred grove, which would not leave structural remains, but which could account for the temple's displacement to the corner. Quite probably sacred in pre-Roman times was the site at Woodeaton, Oxfordshire (Goodchild and Kirk, 1954; Kirk, 1949; D. W. Harding, 1972, 64 ff.), where quantities of fine angular pottery, recovered from excavation beneath the Roman levels of the *temenos* enclosure, together with numerous small bronzes of pre-Roman date, including swan's-neck pins and involuted brooches, argue an occupation in the pre-Roman period at more than a domestic level. So far structural evidence in terms of postholes and floor-levels cannot be classified into a coherent ground-plan, but the quantities of material remains certainly suggest intensive Iron Age occupation in the immediate proximity of the subsequent Romano-Celtic temple.

The most convincing evidence for continuity from the Iron Age into the Roman period in the traditional sanctity of a site comes from Frilford in Berkshire, first excavated in

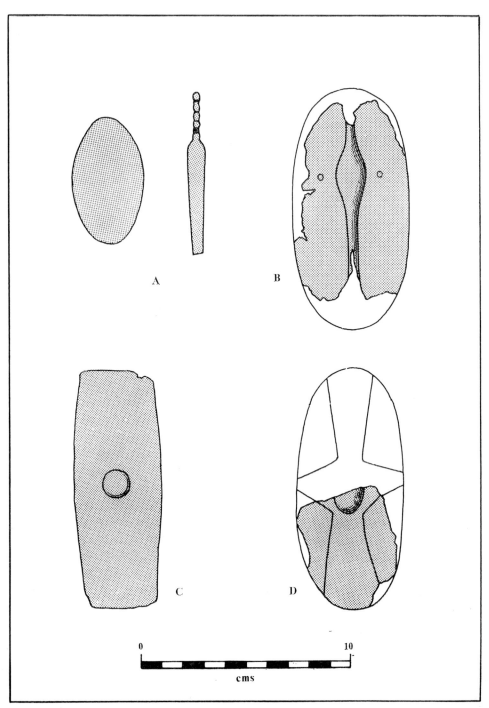

25. *Votive swords and shields. A, Frilford, Berkshire. B, Hod Hill, Dorset. C and D, Worth, Kent*

1937–8, and re-examined in 1964, when further structural features came to light. The structural details of the site have been described elsewhere (D. W. Harding, 1972, 61 ff., Fig. 8 and Pls 33, 34), and it is not proposed therefore to elaborate upon them here. It will be sufficient for our present purpose to note that two Romano-British temples were recorded at Frilford, one a circular stone-built shrine, the other a square temple with portico of the Romano-Celtic variety, both situated within a few yards of each other on the north bank of the river Ock. Beneath the Roman rotunda, the pre-war excavations had confirmed the existence of a penannular ditched shrine, dated by pottery in the primary silt to the early Iron Age, but otherwise resembling a small henge monument of Atkinson's Class I (Atkinson, Piggott and Sandars, 1951). As a result of further examination, it is now apparent that the second Romano-British temple was also constructed on the site of a pre-Roman building, in this case a circular ceremonial enclosure, within which two child-burials were located. Though direct structural continuity could not be demonstrated stratigraphically in this instance, as it could between the penannular ditched enclosure and its Romano-British successor, nonetheless it seems probable that the tradition of the sanctity of the timber circle in the first century B.C. had lingered on until the foundation of the Romano-Celtic temple at the end of the first century or the beginning of the second century A.D. Among the small votive objects found buried within the stone rotunda were a miniature sword and shield (Fig. 25, A), presumably deposited, like the Worth examples, in dedication to a Celtic or Romano-Celtic god of war. Significantly, however, the same shrine contained a small pit, in the bottom of which was buried an iron ploughshare, perhaps a cult-offering of a more pacific, but no less important, nature by the Iron Age inhabitants of the Upper Thames region.

Frilford is of particular importance for a study of Iron Age religious monuments in Britain, since it is the first site to have produced two adjacent, and perhaps complementary, shrines. From the evidence which has already been inferred from literary or iconographic sources concerning Celtic religion, we might anticipate that Iron Age sacred sites would include a multiplicity of shrines with a variety of individual dedications. Frilford affords the most positive archaeological evidence to date that this was so. Equally important is the fact that one of these shrines, unquestionably of Iron Age date, preserves the form of a religious monument which was current and unique in Britain in the late Neolithic period. Clearly, it would be premature on present evidence to claim continuity in religious practice from the Neolithic into the Iron Age, in view of the absence of tangible evidence in the intervening centuries of the Bronze Age. But, recalling Caesar's conviction that Britain was the traditional home of the druidic priesthood, we may speculate whether there was here an environment of religious stability in which cult practices could have survived from remote antiquity into the proto-historic period.

Though the circular plan of both the Iron Age shrines at Frilford is within the insular building tradition of circularity, a Continental parallel for the timber enclosure may be cited at S Margarethen-am-Silberberg in Austria (Pittioni, 1954, Abb. 530), a shrine which is also dated to the first century B.C. The principal difference is that the S Margarethen circle was only 20 feet in diameter, and therefore rather smaller than the Frilford structure, and in consequence was reckoned to have supported a roof, a comparatively rare feature in pre-Roman shrines or temple enclosures. The penannular ditched enclosure at Frilford can likewise be compared in general terms with the very much larger enclosure at the Goloring (Röder, 1948), in the Koberner Wald between Koblenz and Mayen. Here the circular area enclosed by the bank and ditch was 625 feet in diameter and contained a raised dais some 295 feet across, which clearly served as the focus of ritual. As at Frilford, there was no evidence of habitation or burial inside the ditched enclosure, and the only internal structural feature was a substantial posthole at the centre of the dais, which apparently held some sort of totem. It is becoming increasingly evident that postholes, and sometimes ritual pits, are the only recurrent features to be found within Iron Age religious monuments, and from such unsubstantial remains it is difficult to reconstruct the nature of the ceremonial performed within them. The proximity of funerary monuments to the Goloring, however, in the form of two groups of tumuli, dating from Urnfield to Hallstatt times, may indicate that the henge monument itself fulfilled some role in connection with funerary rites.

Comparable to the structural sequence at Frilford from penannular ditch to stone rotunda is the sequence of buildings recorded on Site L at Maiden Castle, Dorset (Wheeler, 1943, Pl. XX). Only 40 feet from the Romano-Celtic temple, Wheeler uncovered a circular stone structure some 23 feet in diameter, constructed somewhat crudely of unmortared limestone blocks. This in turn had been built directly upon the levelled remains of a pre-Roman circular structure, the walls of which were partly of limestone blocks and partly of chalk, but similar in its general form to other circular dwelling-huts excavated elsewhere within the hillfort. Finds apparently indicated that this feature was contemporary with the Iron C or Belgic occupation of the site, and, though there were some coins and pottery of the intervening period, direct structural continuity from pre-Roman hut to late Roman rotunda could not be demonstrated. Though Wheeler regarded this late Roman building as belonging within the same complex as the temple itself and the 'priest's house', he made no claims for its own sanctity. In Lewis's classification (1966, 83), however, the Maiden Castle rotunda is cited as a shrine, and though no particular deity can be assigned to it, the abundance of coins from within its precincts possibly provides some justification for this interpretation. The relationship between it and the Belgic building within the walls of which it is built, and the question of possible continuity in the sanctity of the site, remain a matter for speculation, but the parallel with Frilford is certainly provocative. Indeed, as Wheeler suggested, the siting of late Roman temples within prehistoric earthworks in itself implies a harking back to Celtic cults in the late Roman period, and may well have caused former sacred sites to be deliberately sought out and refurbished.

In the absence of votive deposits, it is possible, of course, that circular shrines of the pre-Roman period have hitherto been confused with dwelling-houses, which they could quite closely resemble. At Winchester (Biddle, 1965, Pl. LXVIII), for instance, a circular building uncovered in 1964 displayed constructional features reminiscent of Iron Age round-houses, including a rectangular setting of four substantial postholes as at Little Woodbury, and a circular gully around the perimeter, as on many Iron Age sites in the north (Fig. 26). Two factors, however, inhibit its interpretation as a round-house. First, the rectangular setting was not central, as might be expected if it were an integral part of a roofed building. Second, the circular gully contained no postholes, nor, within a diameter of 35 feet, were

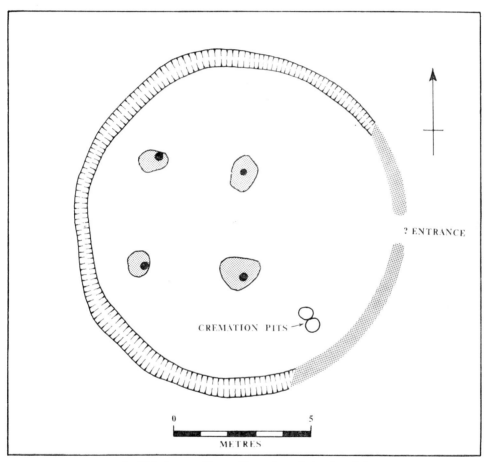

26. *Winchester, Hampshire: plan of circular shrine*

there any traces of further concentric post-circles. Within, and spreading beyond the area of the enclosure, were a number of pits, of which some could well have been contemporary with it, including two that contained human cremations. Other than those which were demonstrably medieval, the pits did not intrude upon the area of the rectangular setting of postholes, but were clustered around the eastern half of the enclosure. The most plausible interpretation of this structure is surely that put forward by the excavator, that it was the site of a shrine. We may then imagine that the sacred area was defined by the circular gully, the rectangular structure within forming the focus of ritual, in front of which pits had been used for dedicatory libations or even sacrificial burials.

The need for further field-work is self-evident, particularly on those Romano-British temple-sites where the occurrence of Iron Age material as surface finds, or in the lowest levels of earlier excavations, is suggestive of continuity from pre-Roman times. But with such qualifications as the present state of knowledge demands, we may provisionally recognise a class of Iron Age shrines, distinguished by their circular ground-plan, for which the Frilford structures will serve as a model. In due course, it may be possible to differentiate between those which are enclosed by a ditch, as on Site C at Frilford, at Winchester and possibly also at Brigstock (Fig. 27), and those which were defined by a circle of timber stakes, as on Site A at Frilford. If the identification of the Belgic circular building at Maiden Castle as a shrine is accepted, a third category with stone foundations might be added. The Winchester example, however, raises a further issue, which must now be considered in detail, namely, the extent to which rectangular buildings were used for Iron Age religious architecture, either independently, or incorporated within a circular enclosure.

Of the rectangular buildings of the British Iron Age for which a religious function has been postulated, the most outstanding is the temple excavated during the war by Grimes on the site of Heathrow Airport. The plan of the Heathrow temple (Fig. 23) displays an obvious structural resemblance to the square Romano-Celtic temple with portico, but translated into timber. Indeed, Powell regarded it as the 'explicit wooden prototype' of the Romano-British form (1958, 146), but, in spite of superficial affinities, any attempt to derive the latter from a pre-Roman type, exemplified at Heathrow, would have to be reconciled with the dating of the early Iron Age pottery found on that site, which places the prototype several centuries before the earliest of its Romano-British successors. Grimes suggested alternatively that the Heathrow plan was a crude copy of a Greek temple (1948), a view which is supported by the very slight elongation of the building into a rectangle rather than a true square. This interpretation is favoured by Lewis, though the unique position of Heathrow in a British prehistoric context remains outstanding, whichever view is accepted.

In fact, the notion of a square plan, as opposed to the more usual emphasis upon circularity in the domestic architecture of the insular Iron Age, is not unknown in religious or allied contexts in Britain. The quarry ditches of the La Tène barrows of Lincolnshire and Yorkshire characteristically form a square or rectangular outline (Stead, 1965), as do their Continental counterparts, some of which also contained internal timber structures (Brisson and Hatt, 1955; Piggott, 1968, Fig. 12). Within the ditched enclosure at Fin d'Écury, Marne (Fig. 28), for instance, were four postholes arranged in a 5-foot square, which presumably supported a structure at which some funerary ritual was performed before the final interment of the dead within the barrow mound. Piggott has compared these structures with similar settings of postholes, from about five to eight feet square, in the Netherlands, which have there been interpreted as Iron Age shrines. Few rectangular barrows in Britain have produced any traces of internal timber structures, though the arrangement of four posts in a simple square has already been noted at Winchester. The same device recurs at

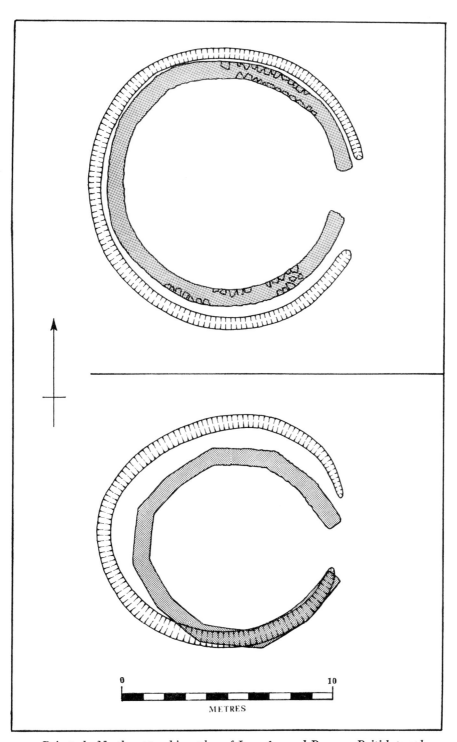

27. Brigstock, Northamptonshire: plan of Iron Age and Romano-British temples

South Cadbury in Somerset (Alcock, 1969, 36 and Fig. 3), where a setting of four (or perhaps six) postholes, forming a rectangle 5 metres by 4 metres, was provisionally identified by the excavator as the site of a shrine. Clearance of a wide area around this structure revealed a series of pits, in which the complete skulls of oxen and horses had been buried, in the manner

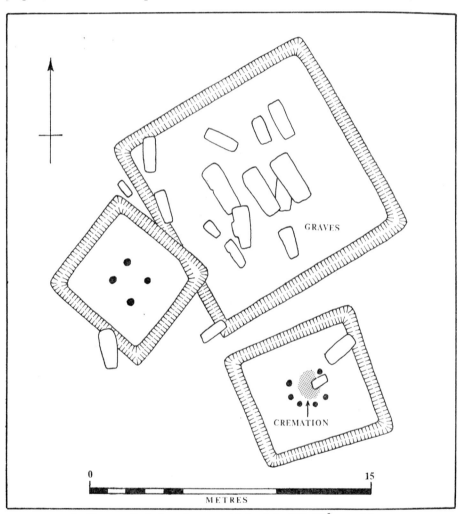

28. *Square-ditched enclosures with burials, Fin d'Écury, Marne*

of deliberate deposits rather than casual household debris. The parallel with the Winchester site is convincing, and raises the question whether other four-poster structures, formerly identified as free-standing granaries, might not equally be regarded as small shrines. Piggott has suggested that the arrangement of four posts containing a hearth, immediately west of the Romano-Celtic temple at Maiden Castle (Wheeler, 1943, Pl. VII) might be a candidate for reinterpretation; we might even add the Staple Howe structure (Brewster, 1963,

47–55 and Plan inside back cover), which would be singularly appropriate as a small domestic shrine in its prominent situation between the two principal houses. Nor should we overlook the fact that there was also such a four-poster structure at Frilford (Fig. 24), which, though not contemporary with the stake circle which intersected it, might nonetheless have been an earlier shrine, contemporary with the earliest occupation of the penannular ditched temple on Site C. As with the circular structures considered above, there is a very real possibility that buildings which served quite different functions shared a common ground-plan, and in certain instances their interpretation as granaries or domestic shrines would be equally apposite. At any rate, we may now propose a second class of Iron Age shrine, smaller than the circular variety considered earlier, and characterised by a square ground-plan. The circular and square types should not, however, be regarded as mutually incompatible: at Frilford they apparently were erected in close proximity to each other, while at Winchester both were incorporated within a single structural unit. Both are found in association with pits containing burials, both human and animal, perhaps suggesting a sacrificial ritual comparable to that attributed by Caesar to the Celtic priesthood.

Those rectangular structures so far cited, for which a ritual function has been proposed, were evidently individual shrines. Rectangular cult enclosures of the kind known on the Continent have not yet been confirmed in Britain. Of the Continental sites, two outstanding examples have been excavated, at Aulnay-aux-Planches in the Marne (Schwarz, 1962, 55; Piggott, 1965, Fig. 132; 1968, 73, Fig. 20) and at Libenice in Czechoslovakia (Rybová and Soudský, 1962). Both were elongated rectangular earthworks, about 300 feet in length, and both were recognised as sacred enclosures on account of human and animal burials, which could well have been sacrificial offerings. At one end of the Libenice enclosure was a series of pits, which may have been dug to receive libations, and several postholes. Besides two of these were the remains of charred posts and a pair of bronze neck-torcs, which perhaps had adorned the gods whose figures were perhaps carved upon the upright timbers. The site at Libenice has been dated to third century B.C., that at Aulnay-aux-Planches belongs more probably to the tenth century, indicating a considerable antiquity for this form of Celtic ceremonial enclosure. Allied to these sites are the so-called *Viereckschanzen* of Central Europe (Schwarz, 1958. For a recent example and bibliography, see Zürn, 1971), known principally from examples in southern Germany. Again, there are no confirmed parallels in Britain, though it is conceivable that some of the rectilinear enclosures listed by Mrs Cotton in Berkshire, of which the excavated site at Robin Hood's Arbour produced Iron B and Belgic pottery, may perhaps have been related to this class of monument (1961). In addition, Piggott has suggested that the three ditched enclosures containing ritual shafts at Fox Furlong, Long Wittenham, Berks (Pl. XIX), should be included, representing a category of Iron Age and Romano-British sacred sites hitherto unrecognised in southern England.

A recurrent element in many of the sites which have been considered here is the use of the ritual pit or shaft. The ritual purpose of the more outstanding Continental examples, such as those from Holzhausen in Bavaria (Schwarz, 1962), has been established from the variety and nature of the deposits found within them, which would scarcely be consistent with a normal well. Some attain a very considerable depth – in excess of 100 feet – and were presumably regarded as a means of making offerings to the gods of the underworld. Others may indeed have been wells, but equally could have been adapted to a secondary ritual purpose. In Britain, shafts of this kind are known at least from the middle Bronze Age, while a series dating to the Belgic Iron Age has been the subject of particular study by Dr Anne Ross (1968).

There remains the question of isolated deposits, particularly of metalwork, which may have been votive offerings. Those hoards which have been found in or beside lakes, for instance, as at Llyn Fawr, Glamorganshire (Crawford and Wheeler, 1921; Fox and Hyde, 1939), Llyn Cerrig Bach in Anglesey (C. Fox, 1946), or on the Continent at the type-site of La Tène itself (Vouga, 1923; de Navarro, 1972), could well have been ritual deposits. Powell has suggested that finds of metalwork, such as the daggers and shields that have been dredged from the Thames, were far too elaborate and valuable to have been lost through carelessness, with no attempt to retrieve them from the river, and that these, too, might be regarded as deliberate offerings to a water deity. I have suggested elsewhere that the same inference could be drawn from the occurrence of groups of weapons from the Upper Thames as well. At any rate, the notion seems consistent with what we have learned concerning Celtic religion in the pre-Roman period.

To draw together all the available information, fragmentary as it is, into a coherent picture of Iron Age cults and religious practices would be a formidable task, and, until the way has been clarified by a good deal more research, we can only select certain salient points which have emerged as fundamental elements in Celtic religion. It can be acknowledged that early Irish literature provides a valuable source of information from which we may reasonably infer something of the structure of pre-Roman religion, the diversity of its deities and its close relation to the seasonal cycle. With the aid of classical literature, the authenticity of which must be weighed critically, depending upon the source of information and the motivation of the writer, a good deal of evidence can be accumulated concerning the priesthood and divine orders, and their function within Celtic society. And finally we can trace the lasting effects of ritual and worship in a number of enclosures and structures which have been identified archaeologically as potential temples, shrines or ceremonial sites, together with inscriptions or dedications set up by native Britons under the influence of the *interpretio Romana*. To those Romano-British sites where an element of continuity from the Iron Age can be anticipated from the presence of finds of pre-Roman date, special attention might be devoted in the future, since it is here that we stand most chance of establishing for earlier structures a religious function, which may elude us, for lack of conclusive finds, elsewhere.

7
Burials and funerary practices

THE APPARENT PAUCITY of burials in the British Iron Age has long been recognised as a facet of insular Celtic culture which distinguishes it from related groups in Continental Europe. With the exception of two outstanding La Tène assemblages, those of the Arras culture of eastern Yorkshire and the Aylesford-Swarling (Belgic) group in the south-east of England, no consistent grave type has yet been recognised which could be claimed as characteristic of the indigenous Iron Age culture of the pre-Belgic phase. Indeed, we have already seen that this lack of burials has been erected by Hodson into a 'negative type-fossil' of his insular Woodbury culture (1964, 105). The implications of this apparent absence of burials in terms of population movements or cultural diffusion have been considered in an earlier section: it is now time to question how total was this lack of graves, and whether it is not so much the absence of burials which has proved the source of confusion as our inability to isolate a distinctive and recurrent type of inhumation or cremation burial.

Though by no means so numerous as the barrow cemeteries of the Bronze Age, Iron Age burials are in fact not so rare as is sometimes supposed, as a cursory check through the gazeteer compiled by the Ordnance Survey (1962, 53–5) will indicate. Unfortunately, many of these burials were recognised as a result of exploration in the nineteenth or early twentieth century, like those listed by C. Fox from East Anglia, and hence records of their contents or structural form are far from reliable. In some instances the graves contained so little in the way of pottery or material artefacts that dating itself is problematical, a factor which may well have prejudiced chances of recognising a larger body of funerary monuments for the British Iron Age. It would be natural to assume, for example, that round barrows which contained no grave-goods were poor relations of their Bronze Age neighbours, rather than that they belonged to a subsequent era when the use of grave-goods was no longer fashionable. Yet such an interpretation might well prove preferable to the view which has been proposed by some prehistorians, that Iron Age communities had such little interest in their dead that they flung out their corpses unceremoniously for the birds and scavengers to pick clean and dismember like any other form of domestic garbage. Certainly isolated skeletons in pits are known from a number of Iron Age settlements in southern Britain, including Fifield Bavant (Clay, 1924, 489–90) and Longbridge Deverill in Wiltshire, Twywell in Northants, and half a dozen different sites in the Upper Thames region (D. W. Harding, 1972, 68). But these can scarcely be regarded as representing the normal manner of disposing of the dead. In fact, the bodies might well have been those of criminals or social outcasts who had been deliberately denied whatever was the customary funeral ceremonial.

By comparison with contemporary Continental assemblages, the British Iron Age may seem provincial and relatively impoverished; and in this respect, burials prove no exception. But we should not be misled by really outstanding tombs like Vix (Joffroy, 1954) and the Hohmichele (Riek and Hundt, 1962), or the early La Tène *Fürstengräber* of the Rhineland (e.g. Reinheim, Keller, 1965), into assuming that all burials of the Continental Iron Age were of comparable grandeur. Whatever the particular structural details of the barrow, however, there was established by late Hallstatt times in Central Europe a tradition of aristocratic burial in which the dead man – or quite frequently woman – is accompanied by a wheeled vehicle or funeral wagon. By the early La Tène period, this custom had been adopted west of the Rhine, in the region of the Aisne and the Marne, whence it was transmitted into north-eastern England in the area of the so-called Arras culture. Prior to these early or middle La Tène incursions, there is no trace in Britain of the wealthy wagon-burials of Hallstatt Europe. Only in one instance has a related grave been tentatively suspected, on a much lesser and poorer scale than its Continental neighbours, at Beaulieu in Hampshire (Piggott, 1953). Here a small and inconspicuous mound, only 15 feet in diameter and standing less than 2 feet at its centre above the old ground level, was assigned an Iron Age date on the strength of a sherd of pottery and a cast bronze ring. The grave had originally rested on the old ground surface, where the remains of timbers were found, including fragments which showed evidence of joinery. Of the inhumed remains themselves no trace survived: that such had been the manner of burial was inferred from the fact that elsewhere in the New Forest, in earlier barrows, inhumations had suffered severely from the acidity of the soil and rarely survived even as a stain in the sand, whereas cremations had proved more durable. The timber-work of the Beaulieu grave was fragmentary in the extreme, and the excavator's argument that this could have been 'a poor relation of the rich Hallstatt cart burials of the Continent' does not account for the absence or total corrosion of the iron wheels which are normal in such burials. Nonetheless, the possibility that this was a modified burial in the Hallstatt tradition cannot be totally discounted.

Any attempt to identify further burials of the Hallstatt period in Britain from existing archaeological records is plagued by the inadequacy of old excavations and the paucity of convincing – or even properly stratified – material. C. Fox was evidently tempted to speculation by the description of a possible Hallstatt brooch said to have come from an inhumation cemetery at Pirton, near Hitchin (1923, 80), in the early nineteenth century. Likewise we might recall that one of the Italic style brooches from the Roman site near Castor, Northants, illustrated by the antiquary E. T. Artis (1828, Pl. XXXI, 8), was apparently unearthed in the course of excavating a tumulus. For another possible example, the barrow at Oliver's Battery, near Winchester, in spite of its subsequent history, could be assigned, on the basis of the pottery found within it, to an early phase of the Iron Age in its original form. (Andrew, 1933. The excavator ruefully records that the barrow had been re-used in the Civil War, and was 'full of the skeletons of human bodies thrown upon the natural surface of the soil in any direction' which 'proved a complete and unwelcome surprise to us'.)

For the remainder of the pre-Belgic period – excluding for the moment the distinctive Arras group of eastern Yorkshire – Iron Age burials are so disparate in character and so thinly, yet widely, distributed, that it would be easy to end up simply with a meaningless catalogue of dubious sites, without any indication of a dominant type or even salient traits in early Iron Age burial customs. To begin with, many early Iron Age burials are under barrow mounds, and the manner of burial includes both inhumation and cremation. Timber structures, comparable to the circular and concentric post-settings frequently found in Bronze Age tumuli have yet to be recognised, though in the case of Peake's exploration of the Woolley Down barrows (Peake and Padel, 1934) they were specifically sought in the initial stages of excavation. At Chronicle Hills, near Whittleford (Fox, 1923, 78; Thomas, 1971, Fig. 25) in Cambridgeshire, however, a similar purpose was doubtless served by the low chalk walls which surrounded the burials in two barrows, defining circles 22 feet in diameter. Within this area in both mounds was a central pit – in one case 5 feet square, in the other 4 – in which the burials had been deposited. Both pits reached a depth of 8 feet, and apparently had contained grave-goods including weapons of iron and bronze which have since corroded and decomposed. Not all burial pits attain the size and depth of those at Chronicle Hills, but the existence of some form of grave-pit is certainly common to a number of barrow burials of Iron Age date. At Woolley Down, only one of the three barrows which may be presumptively assigned to the Iron Age incorporated a central pit, though that contained no evidence of burials. But in this case, even the shape of two of the barrow mounds was unusual, comprising a circular earthwork with central hollow that appeared not simply to be the result of robbing since antiquity. In spite of the poverty of recorded grave-goods, the Woolley Down barrows introduce us to the idea of an Iron Age barrow cemetery, albeit on a fairly limited scale, comparable to those of the preceding Bronze Age.

Between inhumations and cremations under barrows of the pre-Belgic period, there seems to be little chronological significance. Among those which covered cremation burials, however, there was considerable variation in the size of the barrow mound, from the slight earthworks of the King's Weston barrows, near Bristol (Tratman, 1925), to the mound at Warborough Hill, Stiffkey, Norfolk (Clarke and Apling, 1935), which was 50 feet in dia-meter. Cremations under barrows are known elsewhere in East Anglia at Weeting Park, Norfolk (Fox, 1923, 79), and on Thriplow Heath in Cambridgeshire (Fox, 1923, 79–80), where one of a group of three barrows produced Iron Age pottery in association with a primary cremation interment. More recently, cremated remains have been recovered from a low barrow at Handley, Dorset (White, 1970), to which we shall return again in due course.

Not all known burials of Iron Age date are indicated by a surviving barrow mound, of course, and some may never have been so clearly defined. At Park Brow (Wolseley and Smith, 1924), a cremation in a small urn was deposited in an undistinguished grave, which was no more than an irregular excavation in the chalk bedrock. Likewise with inhumations, at Worthy Down, near Winchester (Hooley, 1930, 181–2, Fig. 30; 193–5), a pit-grave was found without trace of any upstanding monument within the environs of an early Iron Age settlement. The grave itself was clearly of deliberate construction, consisting of a narrow trench 1 foot 6 inches wide leading towards a circular pit, a little over 2 feet in diameter in which had been buried a closely contracted skeleton. The purpose of the funnel-like channel which led to the burial chamber is not evident; nor can we be sure that this, together with a second skeleton found within a pit at Worthy Down, was not an unusual burial of the kind which earlier was tentatively linked with criminals, witches or similar social outcasts. Possibly within the same category was the inhumation from Egginton in Bedfordshire (Gurney and Hawkes, 1940). Though it was already partially destroyed by workmen quarrying sand, the excavator of the Egginton grave was able to reconstruct an oblong burial pit, some $5\frac{1}{2}$ feet in length, in which the body had been laid with its legs drawn up into a semi-foetal position. Two small Iron Age pots were recovered from the grave, which date it broadly to the middle or Iron B period.

Until more sites are located, excavated and recorded by modern standards, our knowledge of pre-Belgic burials is likely to remain inconclusive. It is clear, however, that barrow burial continued in some measure, with interment by both inhumation and cremation. At the same time, to account for the greatly increased population in Britain in the Iron Age, some other supplementary form of burial must surely be envisaged, which has hitherto evaded archaeological record. If we imagine that funerary practice required the total release of the spirit from the flesh after death, it is conceivable that the dead were cremated and their remains subsequently scattered without the erection of a permanent monument. Alternatively, bodies may have been exposed – perhaps on platforms mounted upon four-poster foundations of the kind commonly interpreted as granaries. The association of such structures with barrow enclosures on the Continent (Piggott, 1968, 60–1, Figs 11 and 12) might well sustain such an interpretation. At any rate, we need feel no compulsion to seek a simple solution to this complex problem. Throughout this study it has been apparent that the Iron Age was a period of profound social, cultural and economic change, with innovation from the Continent fusing with insular tradition to produce regional patterns which were far from uniform, and in which intrusive or indigenous elements could in turn emerge as dominant. In such circumstances it would not be surprising to find a similar complexity in funerary customs, the political and tribal upheavals of the period resulting in a breakdown of regularised practice, and the adoption of a more transient attitude towards the dead. In such a climate, it is perhaps less surprising that we find so few really wealthy graves, compared to the Continental chieftains' graves of the late Hallstatt or early La Tène periods. Equally, where such do exist, their significance is perhaps enhanced. For this reason it is especially regrettable that the contracted inhumation discovered in 1903 at Newnham Croft in Cambridgeshire (C. Fox, 1923, 81), was not recorded in greater detail. The accompanying grave-goods (Fig. 29) included a jointed bronze armring with ornament based ultimately on the Continental Waldalgesheim style and an elaborate ornamental brooch, the parallels for which, stylistically and technically, are from late La Tène 1 and early La Tène 2 contexts on the Continent, together with a pair of small penannular brooches and an unusual tazza-shaped bronze casting with chains for suspension or attachment, which could have been a harness or vehicle mount of some kind. As with the earlier series of daggers from the Thames, the Newnham Croft metalwork is regarded by Jope as an insular product of a craftsman who was yet in close contact with Continental fashions. If not the grave of an actual invader, therefore, the Newnham Croft burial must surely have been that of a wealthy tribal aristocrat, and furnishes us with some slight evidence of social stratification in early Iron Age burial customs.

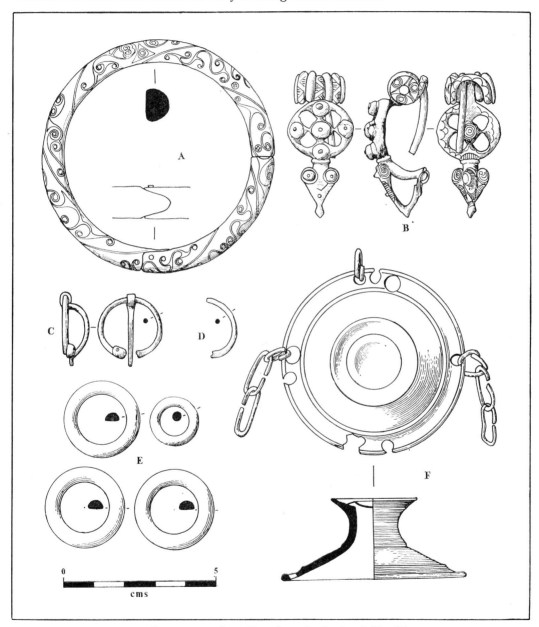

29. *Grave-group from Newnham Croft, Cambridgeshire*

In spite of the presence of more exotic grave-goods at Newnham Croft than is usual in the pre-Belgic Iron Age, there is, as Stead has pointed out, no real justification for classifying the burial as a cart-burial, in the absence of wheels or other substantial fittings. Likewise the grave unearthed in 1812 at Mildenhall, Suffolk (C. Fox, 1923, 81), can scarcely merit its inclusion in the Ordnance Survey's list of chariot-burials, despite its accompanying horse skeletons: the presence of horse-burials at Blewburton Hill, already noted above, is sufficient to indicate the special status of the horse, and need not be directly indicative of a vehicle burial. Though dubious claims have been made elsewhere for the existence of such graves, the main distribution of cart-burials is concentrated in eastern Yorkshire, where they have been the subject of thorough study by Dr Stead (1965). The occurrence of cart-burials however, is not the sole distinguishing feature of the La Tène burials of eastern Yorkshire. Largely as a result of nineteenth-century exploration, a peculiar type of barrow, in which the mound is surrounded by a quarry ditch which is not circular, but square in outline, has come to be regarded as characteristic of this region of eastern England. Both these traits were present at the famous Arras cemetery in the parish of Market Weighton, from which the culture conventionally derives its name. The Arras cemetery, like that at Danes Graves, north of Driffield, probably originally comprised several hundred barrows, some of which were as small as 10 feet in diameter. Of these, only a limited number of graves, presumably those of the tribal aristocracy, contained the remains of wheeled vehicles (Fig. 30). The normal method of burial was inhumation, either crouched or extended, and the grave-goods included a range of personal ornaments such as bracelets, rings, and brooches, which enable the majority of graves to be dated from the La Tène 2 period onwards, from around the third to first centuries B.C. The earliest burial in the Yorkshire series would seem to be one of the five excavated by Canon Greenwell at Cowlam, which included among its grave-goods a fragmentary brooch of La Tène 1a type, a form which was current from around the fifth century B.C. in southern Britain. The implications of this find for an interpretation of early La Tène contacts with Continental Europe will be considered more fully at a later stage (pp. 174–5). For the present it will be sufficient to note that the origin of this particular type of square ditched barrow would appear to have been the Champagne, though for the practice of burying in the grave a wheeled cart in dismantled state Stead has proposed an origin further south and east in Burgundy or even Switzerland.

Not all the barrows of the Yorkshire series are of the square ditched variety: indeed, the recognition of this as a type characteristic of the Arras culture is a relatively recent development. Both square ditched barrows and the more usual circular kind are sometimes represented within the same cemetery, as at Rillington (Pl. XX), though, without excavation, we cannot be certain that they are contemporary in every case. Outside Yorkshire, square ditched barrow enclosures have been recognised by air-photography in Lincolnshire, while allied enclosures surrounding a barrow are known at Leckhampton in Gloucestershire (Burrow et al., 1925, Fig. 5) and at Handley in Dorset. The hub of distribution, however, remains centred upon eastern England, a pattern which is unlikely to be greatly affected by the discovery of occasional outliers elsewhere.

In our pre-occupation with these distinctive types of grave, we should not overlook the existence of an equally outstanding class of burial, well represented in Yorkshire, though few in number – the so-called warrior-burials of the western Wolds (Stead, 1965, 67). In this case the term seems justified, since each of the three principal sites at Grimthorpe,

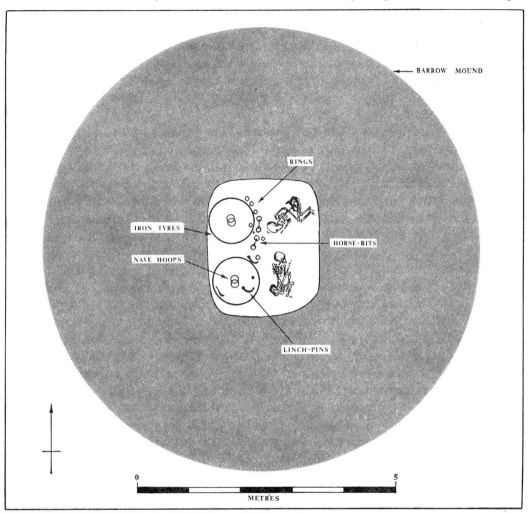

30. *Danes Graves, Yorkshire: plan of burial mound*

Bugthorpe and North Grimston included burials with swords among their grave-goods. The three sites are located along the western edge of the Yorkshire Wolds, and are geographically quite separate from the concentration of cart-burials and square ditched barrows which occupy lower ground between the Wolds and the Hull river. None of these warrior-graves is distinguished by a barrow mound. All were therefore the result of chance finds in the nineteenth or early twentieth century. At Grimthorpe the recovery of four crouched inhumations between 1868 and 1871 was due to the acuity of the local antiquary, J. R. Mortimer; one of them was exceptionally rich in grave-goods, boasting a bronze shield, an iron spearhead, an iron sword and a lavishly ornamented scabbard, as well as a number of bone points apparently used to pin the material of a shroud. Weapons were prominent also among the grave-goods from Bugthorpe (Fig. 61) and North Grimston, the latter including, in addition, a short anthropoid hilted sword of a type which we shall consider in some detail in due course (pp. 183–6). Over in the West Riding, at Clotherholme, another anthropoid sword may conceivably have been from a similar warrior-grave. Outside this Yorkshire group, a comparable burial was discovered in 1944 at Shouldham in Norfolk (Clarke and Hawkes, 1955), where an iron anthropoid sword had been placed across the chest of an extended inhumation.

Equally distinctive are the late La Tène cremation burials of the Aylesford-Swarling culture. This series derives its name from two Kentish cemeteries, published by Evans and Bushe-Fox in 1890 and 1925 respectively. The Aylesford site was first brought to Evans's notice as a result of sand and gravel quarrying, which had exposed a number of exotic pieces of metalwork which had been buried as grave-goods in a circular cremation pit. In fact this was by no means the first discovery to be made on the site; other grave-finds, unearthed over a period of several years, had attracted less attention. In consequence, the impression which we can reconstruct of the Aylesford cemetery is necessarily fragmentary and poorly documented. The method of burial, however, is evident enough. The cremated remains were buried in small roughly cylindrical pits, which Evans believed had been disposed, in one instance at least, in a circular arrangement which he termed 'family circle' (1890, 1 ff. and Fig. 4). Each pit contained grave-goods, generally a group of wheel-thrown pottery vessels including the characteristically La Tène 3 pedestal urn form. Three graves stand apart from the majority, and have been designated X, Y and Z by Dr Birchall in her survey of the Aylesford-Swarling culture (1965, 244–5). These graves are distinguished by the fact that the ashes were contained, not within pottery vessels, but in wooden and metal buckets. In grave X the cremation bucket had been constructed of wooden slats bound with hoops of iron; in grave Y the wood itself had originally been plated with sheet bronze ornamented in repoussé; and, finally, in grave Z the container was a cylindrical wooden tankard with bronze handles. Of these three, grave Y was by far the wealthiest (Pl. XXVI). In addition to its decorated bucket, the grave-goods included a bronze jug or *oenochoe*, a bronze ladle or *patella*, and two bronze brooches of a type paralleled in the north Italian cemetery at Ornavasso (Bianchetti, 1895, Pl. XVII, Figs 6, 9 and 10). These, together with the bronze vessels, which likewise are of types widely distributed in Europe in late La Tène contexts, were evidently imported into Britain, probably within the second half of the first century B.C.

The Swarling cemetery (Bushe-Fox, 1925) was likewise first brought to light as a result of gravel-digging, though in this instance rather better provision was made for its excavation. Nineteen cremation pits were recorded by Bushe-Fox, dividing into an eastern and a western group. Here, his grave 13 was the most impressive for its associated grave-goods.

As well as six pottery vessels, it included fibulae, of imported Ornavasso type as at Aylesford, and the remains of a wooden bucket, comparable to that from Aylesford grave X, in which the ashes were contained.

North of the Thames, no extensive cemetery of the Aylesford or Swarling kind has yet come to light, though such may well have existed formerly at Welwyn Garden City (Stead, 1967), for instance, where modern development and conditions of rescue impeded a full examination of the area around the graves which were salvaged. The graves at Grove Mill, Hitchin (Birchall, 1965, 249–51 and Fig. 14) and those from the 1906 excavations at Welwyn (Smith, 1912) may likewise have been part only of much more extensive cemeteries of flat cremation-burials. Isolated cremations with diagnostic wheel-thrown pottery are widely distributed in Essex, Hertfordshire and Bedfordshire, with outliers in East Anglia and across the Chilterns. Among these, a series of eight graves have been grouped by Dr Stead into his class of 'Welwyn-type burials', which are distinguished by the wealth of their grave-goods, rivalling or even exceeding the grandeur of the rich graves at Aylesford and Swarling. Examples include Welwyn and Hertford Heath in Hertfordshire (Holmes and Frend, 1959), Snailwell in Cambridgeshire (Lethbridge, 1953), Mount Bures in Essex and Stanfordbury in Bedfordshire (Smith, 1912, 8–12). More recently, his own salvage operation at Welwyn Garden City has added another, better documented, burial to the series (Fig. 31). The grave itself comprised a pit, some 10 feet 6 inches in length and 7 feet 3 inches wide, the walls of which sloped slightly inwards towards the floor. The cremated remains were not contained within a vessel, but simply heaped at the northern end of the pit; at the same time there had apparently been some attempt to keep the floor of the grave relatively clean at this point, since the accompanying grave-goods had either been stacked against the wall of the pit to one side, or had been concentrated in the southern half of the grave. The size of the pit itself was more than justified by the goods which it contained. In pottery alone there were three dozen vessels, including five wine *amphorae*. These were supplemented by a bronze dish and strainer, and a wooden vessel of which only the bronze attachments survived. Relaxing with his imported wine, the chieftain whose grave this was evidently enjoyed gambling, for with him had been buried a set of gaming-pieces and also a wooden board with iron binding. Glass beads and bracelets satisfied his love of personal ornaments. Finally, the grave-goods included a silver cup of a handled variety which is found widely distributed throughout the Roman world in the late first century B.C. and the early first century A.D. Though not identical, this vessel is very similar to a pair of imported silver cups which were found in 1906 in one of two cremation 'vaults' at Welwyn (Pl. XXVII), and which are generally dated to the Augustan period. The first grave, like that at Welwyn Garden City, contained *amphorae* as well as a pedestal urn and pottery tazza, together with a handle from a bronze jug, three bronze masks and a bronze bowl. The list of grave-goods is completed by a pair of iron firedogs, whose upper terminals are shaped characteristically into horned animal heads. The second grave – that which contained the silver cups – also produced a pair of firedogs, this time accompanied by a substantial iron frame which was presumably used to suspend vessels or spits over a hearth. Among an assortment of bronze goods were a handled jug and *patella*, comparable to those from Aylesford, and a bronze-handled tankard like that from grave Z at the Kentish cemetery. The remainder of the burials of the Welwyn class have produced similar sets of grave-goods, though not perhaps in such abundance. In spite of the inclusion of a wide range of domestic utensils and tableware, and

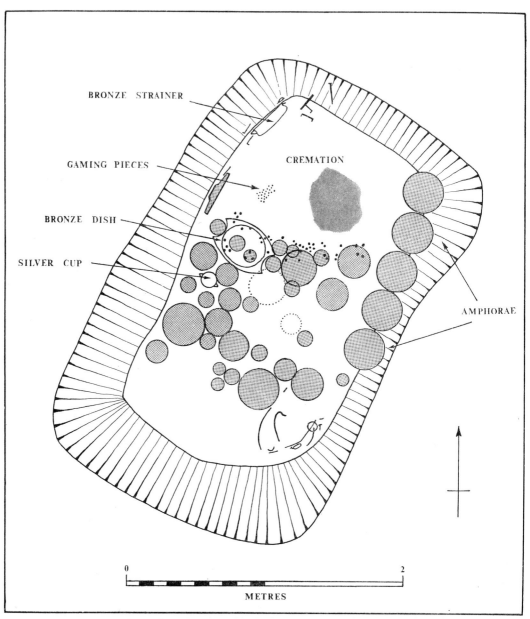

BRONZE STRAINER

GAMING PIECES

BRONZE DISH

SILVER CUP

CREMATION

AMPHORAE

0   2

METRES

31. *Welwyn Garden City, Hertfordshire: plan of La Tène 3 burial*

the clear emphasis upon drink, the lack of any trace of a funeral feast has been remarked by Stead. Hearth furniture in the shape of firedogs is quite commonly represented (Fig. 75); but cauldrons or cooking-pots are absent. And if the Celts' reputation among classical writers for excessive drinking is matched by the rows of wine-*amphorae* in the Welwyn graves, their equally notorious love of fighting is not witnessed archaeologically by weapons in any of the rich graves of the Welwyn series. That these were exceptional – the graves of tribal aristocrats – is further demonstrated by the proximity of other burials at Welwyn Garden City, in which the urn containing the cremated remains was the only item deposited with the dead. The dating of the group is evidently facilitated by the wealth and variety of its grave-goods. Spanning a period of up to a century, Stead has proposed a twofold division. The primary group, represented by the 1906 finds from Welwyn, he assigns to the period from c. 50 B.C. to around 10 B.C.; on the basis of Werner's classification (1954) of such vessels, the principal bronzes found there should fall within that span. The graves of his secondary phase included among their grave-goods imported Gallo-Belgic pottery and Samian ware, and should therefore belong to the period from 10 B.C. (see below, p. 214) until the Conquest. The burials at Welwyn Garden City and Hertford Heath are evidently intermediate in this sequence, since they lack evidence of an early date, but do not yet contain imported Gallo-Belgic wares.

All the Belgic or La Tène 3 burials which we have considered so far have had one element in common. Rich or humble, isolated grave or cemetery, they have all been flat graves, that is, they have not been demarcated by any kind of barrow mound. That the custom of erecting an earthwork over the dead was not totally alien to the tribes of south-eastern Britain, however, is demonstrated on a superlative scale by the Lexden tumulus at Colchester (Laver, 1927), situated within the environs of the *oppidum* of Camulodunum. Among a number of lesser graves, the Lexden tomb stood at the time of excavation 9 feet high, and over 100 feet in diameter. Beneath the mound was a central grave, an oval pit some 30 feet by 18 feet, the floor of which was recessed 7 feet below the former ground surface. Only a very few small fragments of human bone were recovered by Laver's excavation, which was mounted as a salvage operation before the site was destroyed. But the grave-goods were more than sufficient to show that here was the grave of an important tribal chieftain. Ornamental bronzes in abundance reflect the luxury and status of the tomb – a model Cupid, the neck and head of a griffon, a small bronze bull and boar, a 'table' and other furnishings. Further, unlike other La Tène 3 burials, this contained fragments of iron wheel-rims and chain-mail. Of precious metals there were small trefoil silver ornaments, a silver buckle and studs, and fragments of gold tissue. Finally, a silver medallion of Augustus, which must be dated subsequent to 17 B.C., confirms the ceramic evidence of fragmentary butt-beakers and *amphorae* that the grave belonged to the close of the first century B.C. With their proclivity towards historical identifications, prehistorians have sometimes taken the wealth of this grave, and its situation in the later tribal capital of the Catuvellauni, as a clue to the equation of the Lexden tumulus with the tomb of Cunobelinus himself. Attractive though this notion may have been, we must surely now recognise

123

that the Lexden tumulus was erected several decades before the death of Cunobelinus, around A.D. 40, and, if an equation with any historical figure is possible, Peacock's suggestion of Addedomarus of the Trinovantes is the more plausible (Peacock, 1971, 178–9).

Broadly contemporary with the Lexden tumulus is the barrow at Blagdon Copse, Hurstbourne Tarrant (Hawkes and Dunning, 1930, 304–9) in the territory of the Wessex Atrebates. Here a much smaller barrow mound, some 27 feet in diameter, covered a substantial central interment comprising a cremation in a wooden bucket in a manner comparable to those of the Aylesford-Swarling series. The burial itself was surrounded by pottery vessels including pedestal urns, butt-beakers and platters, together with a bronze brooch and bracelet and the remains of a glass vessel. Beyond these regions of primary or secondary Belgic settlement, several outstanding sites of the late La Tène period deserve inclusion here, though records of their circumstances of discovery are very largely defective. Of these, the well-known bucket found in 1807 at Marlborough, Wilts (C. Fox, 1958a, 68; Pls 34–6), most probably contained a cremation burial in the Aylesford fashion (Pl. XXVIII); its size alone, some 52 cm in height and 60 cm in diameter, would suggest a ceremonial rather than a practical function. Like the Marlborough find, Birdlip in Gloucestershire (Smith, 1909; Green, 1949) is better known on account of its ornamental grave-goods (Pl. XXXVII) than for the burials in which they were found. Quarrying in 1879 had uncovered three graves in alignment, each comprising a cist lined and covered with slabs of limestone. The centre burial proved to be a female inhumation, flanked on either side by two inhumation graves of adult males. It was the female burial, however, which contained the lavish grave-goods, as frequently appears to have been the case in Celtic society. Apart from the famous bronze mirror, with its ornamental backing, the grave-goods included two bronze bowls, four bronze rings and a tubular bronze bracelet, together with a necklace of amber, jet and marble beads. A silver brooch, plated with gold, is of a particular distinctive type, known also in Central Europe, in which the bow above the spring is modelled into a grotesque face with eyes and projecting beak. Finally, the grave contained a bronze handle with terminal shaped like the head of a horned animal, whose eyes were sockets originally designed to receive some form of enamel or glass inlay. Mirrors also ranked among the grave-goods from Stamford Hill, Plymouth and Trelan Bahow, St Keverne, Cornwall, where likewise the burials were in stone-lined cists. In Cornwall, the practice of cist-burial can be traced back to a much earlier phase in the Iron Age at Harlyn Bay, where a cemetery of over a hundred graves conformed to this pattern.

Finally there are several war cemeteries, deserving consideration, associated with the sack of hillforts in Wessex and its western margins. Of these, the massacre at Maiden Castle, Dorset, can certainly be attributed to the Roman Second Legion shortly after A.D. 43, while the destruction of Spettisbury, Dorset, Battlesbury, Wilts, Bredon Hill, Worcs, and Sutton Walls, Herefordshire, was quite probably the result of the Roman military advance westwards. At Maiden Castle (Wheeler, 1943) the war cemetery, or that part of it which has been excavated, was located immediately outside the eastern entrance of the hillfort, where the final assault was apparently focused. Here, amid the debris of huts which had been fired in the onslaught, a series of roughly cut graves had been excavated in the chalk, and the bodies of the dead hurriedly inhumed. A number of the skeletons bore marks of severe mutilation from the battle, including one in which an iron arrow-head from a *ballista* was still embedded in the spine (Pl. XIV, b). In spite of the evident signs of tumult, most of the graves were accompanied by pottery vessels, presumably containing drink, and in two cases offerings of joints of meat had been included as well. Several of the dead had been buried wearing ornaments – armrings of iron and shale, and even bronze toerings. Of the thirty-four skeletons in the cemetery, all but one were adults, and ten of these female. Whether these few represent a last token resistance by a handful of natives, or whether the hillfort was the focal point for a more massive show of resistance, only further excavation can reveal. But the apparent savagery of the massacre may perhaps be a measure of the degree of resistance which met the legions as they advanced through Wessex. Spettisbury likewise may well have been one of the twenty *oppida* which Suetonius (*Divus Vespasianus*, 4) records were reduced by Vespasian. Here, in 1857 (Gresham, 1939; Hawkes, 1940d) workmen excavating a cutting for the Central Dorset Railway unearthed a pit, said to have been about 35 feet in length and some 15 feet broad, by the silted-up ditch at the north-eastern extremity of the camp. In it they found nearly a hundred skeletons, haphazardly buried, but nonetheless with a considerable quantity of metal goods, including a sword, currency bars, brooches and a bronze cauldron. Some of the skeletons, as at Maiden Castle, had suffered blows to the skull, and the presence of Roman weapons certainly suggests a comparable engagement. In the remaining instances cited here, the date and agency of the destruction is less easily determined. At Battlesbury (Cunnington, 1924, 373) the cemetery was situated, as at Maiden Castle, just outside the entrance of the hillfort, but here the graves included those of men, women, and children, and, in the absence of conclusive evidence for a Roman assault, they could equally well have been the result of inter-tribal skirmishes which might well have been provoked by those dispossessed of their lands by either Belgic or Roman invaders. At Sutton Walls (Kenyon, 1953), the victims evidently included not only those who had fallen in battle, but also prisoners who had been summarily decapitated, and thrown unceremoniously with the bodies of their fellows into the ditch of their hillfort. Here there had been no attempt at formal burial, and the dead had been stripped of any possessions they may have carried or worn in the final struggle. On evidence which can only be described as equivocal, the excavator nonetheless inferred that the victors of this engagement had been Romans. Such an inference would seem to be valid for Bredon Hill in Worcestershire (Hencken, 1938), where the destruction of the fort was dated by metal finds to the early first century A.D. Once again, no attempt had been made at proper burial of casualties from the battle, and in consequence the bodies of over fifty defenders who had fallen in the assault upon the main inner entrance of the camp had been badly mauled and mutilated by predators in the debris of their tumbled stronghold.

What we can learn of Iron Age burial practices from war cemeteries of the period of the Conquest is, of course, strictly limited. Apart from the Dorset cemeteries, there had been little or no attempt to bury the victims of Roman assault, not even to the extent of protecting the corpses from the ravages of scavenging beasts. Yet at Maiden Castle the aftermath of defeat allowed some attempt at burial. 'From few graves', wrote Wheeler, 'were omitted those tributes of food and drink which were the proper and traditional perquisites of the dead.' That this measure of respect was shown for the dead at Maiden Castle, even in the confusion of military rout, is the more ironic since archaeology affords so little evidence in the earlier Iron Age for any such 'proper and traditional' practices. Here surely is evidence that the apparent lack of regular burial sites in the British Iron Age, outside the Arras and Aylesford groups, is not simply a question of casual disregard for the after-life, but more probably the result of a complex and sophisticated rite which has simply failed to register in the archaeological record.

II *Thickthorn Down, Dorset: section across multiple banks*

III *Glastonbury, Somerset: wicker-work exposed by excavation of lake-side village*

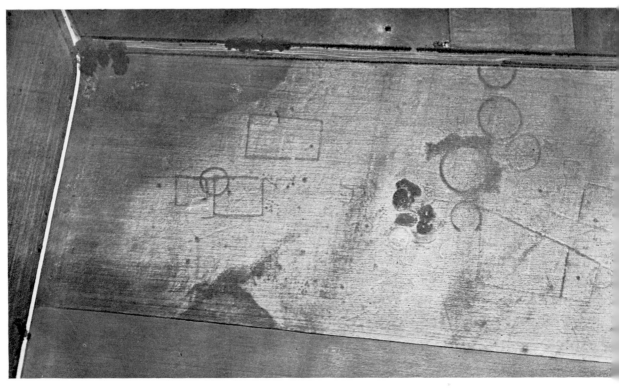

XIX *Fox Furling, Long Wittenham, Berkshire: air-photograph*

XX *Rillington, Yorkshire: air-photograph of La Tène cemetery*

III MATERIAL REMAINS AND CHRONOLOGY

8

The late Bronze Age problem and the transition to the early Iron Age

UNTIL THE later 1950s, insular antecedents of the British Iron Age were conventionally traced in the so-called Deverel-Rimbury culture of southern England, a loosely defined group which derived its name from two characteristic cemeteries in Dorset. Invaders from the Continent of the eighth century B.C., as it was believed, these people supplied a stimulus to insular agriculture by introducing ox-drawn ploughs, regular field-systems and extensive ranches with rectangular kraals for cattle and sheep. Their dwellings were circular, like the huts at New Barn Down in Sussex (Curwen, 1934), and their pottery included coarse-ware urns upon which the poorer fabrics of the early Iron Age might well have ensued. Radical reappraisal of this assessment of the later Bronze Age was initiated by the publication in 1959 of Margaret Smith's study of 'ornament horizon' metalwork in southern and south-western Britain, and its relationship to the Deverel-Rimbury culture. Miss Smith demonstrated that the series of bronzes which constituted her 'ornament horizon', and whose distribution overlapped that of the Deverel-Rimbury finds, with which they were sometimes associated, were most closely paralleled on the Continent by bronzes of Montellius III, or even late II, and should therefore on current chronology be dated to the closing centuries of the second millennium (1959). Furthermore, spectrographic analysis of bronzes, which had already demonstrated a distinct division in the technique of lead-alloying between the middle and late Bronze Age, further indicated that the increased quantities of lead characteristic of the late Bronze Age were only just appearing when the Deverel-Rimbury occupation of sites on Cranborne Chase was coming to an end (M. A. Smith and Blin-Stoyle, 1959). If this updating was to be applied generally to Deverel-Rimbury and allied sites of southern England, formerly regarded as late Bronze Age, the hiatus thereby created would clearly have severe repercussions upon the early Iron Age. Sites like Shearplace Hill, in Dorset (Rahtz and ApSimon, 1962), with its circular houses (Fig. 12), weaving-comb, shallow storage pits and adjacent Celtic fields, which would formerly have been regarded as an immediate fore-runner of the earliest Iron Age settlement pattern in Wessex, must now represent an insular rural tradition already well established in the later middle Bronze Age. Radio-carbon determinations for Shearplace Hill would seem to confirm this conclusion. The loss resulting from the updating of the Deverel-Rimbury culture is represented in two principal areas: first, in the scarcity of settlement-sites for which a late Bronze Age date can still be claimed, and second, in the lack of a substantial body of ceramic evidence for this period which might provide a springboard for a study of early Iron Age pottery.

The apparent paucity of settlement-sites and pottery in the late Bronze Age is curiously at variance with the evidence of metalworking. From the tenth century B.C. in south-eastern England, smiths of the Wilburton school were producing a wide range of bronze-types, including leaf-shaped swords, spearheads and socketed axes, and were exploiting the new technique of alloying their bronzes with lead. These innovations eventually spread further north and west by the eighth century in what Burgess has described as a kind of industrial revolution (1970, 214). Such activity amongst professional craftsmen, stimulated by parallel developments across the Channel, seems scarcely consistent with an apparent stagnation in other aspects of late Bronze Age culture.

The first step in resolving this problem must be to examine those settlements for which a late Bronze Age date could still be argued. With the elimination of sites like the Vinces Farm urnfield at Ardleigh (Longworth, 1960) and the settlement at Mildenhall Fen (Clark, 1936), which can no longer be regarded as any later than middle Bronze Age, we are left with only a limited number of sites whose late Bronze Age occupation is attested either by radio-carbon dating or by the evidence of associated bronzes. At present, radio-carbon dates for this period are relatively few. The cemetery at Bromfield in Shropshire, outside the primary Deverel-Rimbury zone but otherwise evidently in an allied cultural tradition, has produced dates of 762 ± 75 and 850 ± 71, suggesting that in some regions, at any rate, middle Bronze Age modes lingered on well into the first millennium. Following this lead, it may well transpire that other sites in the Deverel-Rimbury tradition might have to be reinstated to a lower terminal dating in due course. In Yorkshire, the timbers used in the construction of the Barmston dwellings in Holderness (Varley, 1968) produced radio-carbon dates, centred upon 1010 b.c. and 950 b.c., for the establishment of the settlement, which may therefore have continued in occupation well into the late Bronze Age. Ironically, the pottery fragment found on the upper surface of the peat deposit on Site B at Barmston, from a variety of furrowed bowl, might otherwise have been taken to indicate an early Iron Age occupation contemporary with the classic Wessex settlements like All Cannings Cross. At Weston Wood, Albury, Surrey (J. M. Harding, 1964), a single date in the sixth century B.C. was obtained for a settlement, the late Bronze Age character of which is attested by a fragment of a bun-shaped copper ingot, comparable to the type found in late Bronze Age founders' hoards. The pottery from Weston Wood may be compared in general terms to material from late Bronze Age sites in the south-east of England. Of these sites, one of the most outstanding is Plumpton Plain B, which yielded a number of distinctive pottery vessels and fragments, together with a fragmentary late Bronze Age winged axe (Hollyman and Curwen, 1935, Fig. 16). For the Plumpton Plain bowls, which are not especially like any of the early Iron Age range of bowls, C. F. C. Hawkes quoted parallel contexts in the Bronze Age IV phase of the Fort Harrouard (1935, 55, and Figs 11, 12), though he insisted at the same time upon their local manufacture. Also in Sussex is the settlement at Itford Hill (Burstow and Holleyman, 1957), where excavation revealed the posthole footings of more than a dozen small, and rather flimsy, circular huts, together with lengths of stockade trenching. Lacking conclusive metal finds, Itford Hill nonetheless produced pottery of a sufficiently crude and indeterminate kind to assign it tentatively to the later Bronze Age.

From other sites where pottery has been found in association with late bronzes, the form of the vessels does not provoke immediate comparison with the Iron Age pottery forms which succeeded them. The sherds from the Heathery Burn Cave, County Durham (C. F. C. Hawkes and M. A. Smith, 1957, Fig. 6; Greenwell, 1894; Britton, 1968; 1971), dated by associated bronzes to the seventh century B.C. or thereabouts, show fewer affinities with early Iron Age pottery from southern Britain than with the so-called 'flat-rimmed' wares of northern England and Scotland. Likewise it is not easy to regard the jar which contained the Isleham hoard as an obvious forerunner of early Iron Age coarse-ware jars; its gently curving body-profile, which becomes slightly concave towards the bottom of the pot-wall, and the short everted rim are broadly paralleled in the late Bronze Age vessel from Run-ar-Justicou, in Brittany (Sandars, 1957, Fig. 82, 3); but the latter lacks handles, whereas the Isleham jar most probably had a single handle mounted between its shoulder and rim, comparable to the example from Écury-le-Repos (Sandars, 1957, Fig. 47, 6). The pot from Worthing (Powell-Cotton and Crawford, 1924, Pl. XXX; Wilson and Burstow, 1948, Pl. III, B5; Musson, 1954, Fig. 9, 510), which, like the Isleham jar, was found actually to contain late bronzes, has a curving body-profile, flat base and short everted rim, but the parallel can only be drawn in the most general terms. These examples, however, actually containing dateable bronzes, provide as reliable an association of pottery with metalwork as we are likely to encounter. At Minnis Bay, Birchington, Kent (Worsfold, 1943), the relationship between the well-known assemblage of bowls and jars and the bronze hoard (Fig. 37) was by no means so conclusive, since it might be claimed to be one of sequence, with the pottery being later than the latest of the scrap bronze pieces that composed the hoard.

A number of other instances are known where late Bronze Age fragments have been found on the same site as, though not in stratigraphic association with, pottery which has otherwise passed as early Iron Age. The assemblages from Castle Hill, Scarborough (Smith, 1927) and from Sheepen Hill, Colchester are cases in point, where the proximity of the pottery to the bronzes is tantalising but inconclusive. We may be more inclined to describe such pottery as late Bronze Age when its form and fabric are not entirely in keeping with what we commonly regard as characteristic of early Iron Age wares, as for instance the jar from Brigg, Lincolnshire (C. F. C. Hawkes, 1946, Fig. 3). But the danger here is that pottery forms, already current in the late Bronze Age, may have been confused hitherto with subsequent Iron Age groups, which may therefore themselves require re-appraisal in the light of the new chronology. Even if the pottery from these sites is not associated directly with the late Bronze Age bronzes, the problem which their proximity of location poses cannot simply be dismissed. Either we must acknowledge them to be contemporary in the broad sense that they were deposited by the same phase of occupation, or we have to conceive two phases of occupation, the one represented by metalwork but no pottery, the second by pottery but no metalwork. When the late bronzes are fragmentary scraps left over from a bronzesmith's hoard, we may be inclined to accept the latter alterna-tive. But in cases such as Sheepen Hill and Scarborough, and possibly even Minnis Bay, the evidence for a late Bronze Age date for both pottery and bronzes is surely more plausible than evidence to the contrary.

Perhaps the clearest illustration of this problem is the hillfort at Ivinghoe Beacon in Buckinghamshire (Cotton and Frere, 1968). Here, in addition to a late Bronze Age winged axe, recorded as having been found on the site some years ago, excavations carried out between 1963–5 produced a number of small and fragmentary bronzes for which a later eighth- or seventh-century dating seems appropriate. In the circumstances it is difficult to dismiss them as survivals, though they could conceivably have been simply the remnants of a late Bronze Age founder's hoard. The alternative would be to grasp the nettle firmly and declare them contemporary with the occupation of the hillfort itself, and with the pottery which that occupation produced. The concept of late Bronze Age hillforts in Britain, in fact, would no longer be regarded as excessively controversial; though formerly they were seen as a phenomenon of the Iron Age exclusively, there is now sufficient evi-dence for hillforts on the Continent extending back into the Urnfield period to render their absence in Britain in the later Bronze Age increasingly implausible. But the question remains at Ivinghoe Beacon, whether we assign the fortifications as such to the earliest phase of occupation, or whether we view these as a subsequent addition to an undefended late Bronze Age hill-settlement of the central European *hohensiedlungen* type. The accumu-lation of radio-carbon dates in due course, however, will doubtless establish the introduction of hillforts as a feature of the later Bronze Age in Britain.

Among unfortified settlements of the late Bronze Age, that at Eldon's Seat, Encombe, Dorset (Cunliffe and Phillipson, 1968), clearly ranks as one of the most likely candidates. A number of pottery vessels from the phase 1 occupation of this site was recognised by the excavators as potential late Bronze Age forms, though their dating of this initial occupation to the seventh and sixth centuries B.C. was perhaps a trifle conservative. The barrel-like jars with slack profile and applied finger-tip bands are evidently derived from later middle Bronze Age antecedents, and the appearance side by side with these of shouldered forms need in no way be tied to the subsequent recrudescence of angular wares in the late Hallstatt or early La Tène phases. Culturally the settlement is evidently late Bronze Age, and there is no reason why it could not have been occupied at virtually any point in the opening centuries of the first millennium B.C.

From those sites which we have considered here as potential late Bronze Age settlements, it is clear that the ceramic evidence is singularly undistinguished. This may well account for our inability to recognise outstanding late Bronze Age forms, though equally it could be argued that we are not simply dealing with funerary wares, and that domestic pottery could have been supplemented by vessels made of perishable materials, such as leather (Ryder, 1966), or even wood. Certainly the Isleham jar, which had already lost its base by the time it was deposited in the ground, had incorporated a wooden disc instead as a base to the pottery vessel. For cooking a stew, of course, wooden or leather containers would hardly be practical. Communal stews were doubtless prepared in a large sheet-bronze cauldron, too valuable and too capacious to be the property of a single household. With the decline of the sheet-bronze industry, these vessels were evidently repaired over and over again to keep them in service. Attempts were even made to produce pottery substitutes, as we shall see in the next chapter. As water-carriers and storage vessels, however, leather bottles and wooden tubs would doubtless have served equally well, with the added advantage of being less brittle than pottery. In some measure, therefore, the relative paucity of domestic pottery, as perhaps in the Iron Age in northern Britain, could be a reflection of a strong pastoral element in late Bronze Age economy. If, alternatively, the lack of distinctive pottery forms is really the result of our failure to recognise them, then it can only be assumed that examples of late Bronze Age pottery have been confused hitherto with subsequent early Iron Age groups – in effect, that a sequence of pottery has been conflated into a single period, a situation which might well arise if one had developed from the other. Throughout the Iron Age, indeed, there is a sub-stratum of coarse pottery which shows very little change in form and fabric from the less distinguished wares at Itford Hill or Ivinghoe Beacon, with which it might easily be confused in the absence of diagnostic forms of fine or decorated pottery. The contrast between this sub-stratum and such distinctive fine-wares not only underlines the basic insular continuity from Bronze Age to Iron Age, but further throws into highlight those intrusive ceramic elements whose appearance in Britain is the result of external stimulus.

9
The primary Iron Age: native, refugee, colonist?

WITH THE relative absence of late Bronze Age settlement-sites in lowland Britain, the equal lack of a consistent form of burial, and the scarcity of diagnostic pottery types, it may be inconsistent with the available evidence to speak in terms of insular continuity into the ensuing Iron Age. But however defective the archaeological record may be at present, there can be little doubt that the British Iron Age from its inception retained a strong native component. Whether we envisage widespread colonisation from the Continent, or merely a sporadic influx of refugees, prospectors and traders, the end result must have been to supplement numerically, to enrich culturally, and technologically to improve rather than to supplant the native population by a totally alien culture from abroad. Patterns of settlement, methods of agriculture and the basis of the economy are unlikely to have been immediately influenced, even by a change in local rulers, and in technological development the arrival of ironsmiths made no great impact upon many of the farming communities of southern Britain. For evidence of incursions from the Continent, therefore, we are very largely dependent upon innovations in pottery styles, supplemented occasionally by metal artefacts, whereby we may establish some correlation between Britain and the expansion westward of Hallstatt culture in Europe.

In an attempt to identify foreign influences – of whatever source or stimulation – in the British Iron Age, we should not assume that these need stem from a single movement at any given time. From its geographical relationship with the Continent, Britain was naturally vulnerable to colonisation from at least two principal directions. From across the Straits of Dover, the most direct access into the country was afforded in prehistoric, as in historic, times to martial invaders from north-eastern France, the Low Countries and ultimately from Central Europe. To the west, the cross-channel route could have been used by traders from Brittany and the Atlantic seaboard, or by refugees displaced from homelands further east.

At the outset of the Iron Age, both these natural routes played their part in bringing southern Britain into contact with the mainstream of events on the Continent. Already by the end of the seventh century, Hallstatt bronzes, including swords of bronze, were being imported into the country, as at Taplow, Bucks (C. F. C. Hawkes, 1938; Cowen, 1967, 443, no. 179), or of iron – with local adaptations – as at Llyn Fawr in Glamorgan (C. Fox and H. A. Hyde, 1939). A clue to the source of these innovating types is provided by the cheek-piece in the Llyn Fawr hoard, which is paralleled at Court St Étienne in Belgium (Marien, 1958). It is the Hallstatt C long swords and equipment which C. F. C. Hawkes attributes to 'adventurers' who reconnoitered the land, in order that settlements like Staple Howe might follow, and the widespread if sparse distribution of finds, extending well up the east coast of England, and even to the borders of Wales, is consistent with his view that the Hallstatt pioneers were concerned with prospecting for iron.

If a subsequent period of colonisation from the Continent is envisaged, it is reasonable to suppose that this would concentrate, initially at least, within a more restricted zone than that which was infiltrated by the adventurers. And since the source of late Hallstatt settlement in Britain continued at least in some considerable part to be Belgium – the nearest

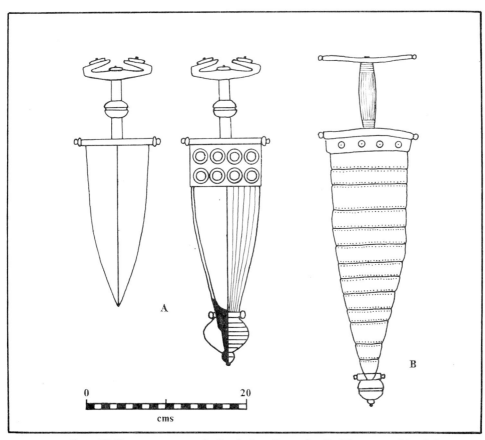

32. *Late Hallstatt weapons. A, St Andrä, Bavaria. B, Thames at Mortlake*

parallel for the Hallstatt D antennae sword from the Thames (R. A. Smith, 1925, Fig. 84) (Fig. 32, B) is again Court St Étienne (Marien, 1958, Fig. 19, 207) – it is scarcely surprising that a fair proportion of Hallstatt D metal finds should come from the lower Thames and south-east of England, including the six fragmentary daggers from the river itself, identified and discussed by Jope (1961, 309–12, Figs 1 and 2). Certainly late Hallstatt bronzes have been found as far afield as Scotland and northern Ireland (C. F. C. Hawkes and M. A. Smith, 1957, 197), but the dating and significance of these need not detain us here.

What is required to reassert the importance of the late Hallstatt phase in Britain is the

135

correlation of this metalwork with a recognisable corpus of contemporary pottery forms. Unfortunately for the purposes of analysis, the fusion of external fashions and insular styles is achieved much more readily in pottery than in metalwork, partly because of the domestic, rather than commercial or industrial, basis of the craft. In consequence, we should not anticipate pottery assemblages which are outstanding as direct imports from the Continent, so much as elements of ornamental style, or small technical details which have been assimilated into the repertory of insular potters. Among the pottery styles of the earliest Iron Age for which a Bronze Age derivation has sometimes been postulated is the use of applied bands around the shoulder or neck, frequently bearing finger-tip or cable decoration. The technique of decoration is common on barrel- and bucket-urns of the middle Bronze Age, and subsequently appears on a number of sites in a transitional late Bronze Age–early Iron Age context from Scarborough (Smith, 1927) to the Isle of Purbeck. More recently, pottery with this kind of applied band has been found in excavations at Ivinghoe Beacon, where fragmentary bronzes of seventh century date, though not in close association with the pottery, are strongly suggestive of a final Bronze Age dating for the re-introduction of the applied cabled cordon (Cotton and Frere, 1968, Fig. 20, 134–5, 137–41). To regard the applied band as a survival from middle Bronze Age decorative modes would have seemed, until recently, to invoke an inordinately long 'folk memory', but at least two examples from Staple Howe (Brewster, 1963, Fig. 38, 2, 3) bear a marked resemblance to barrel urns, particularly the vertical cordons of the latter (Fig. 33, G). In the absence of a well-dated ceramic for the tenth, ninth and eighth centuries B.C., and in view of the increasing uncertainty as to how long any bucket- and barrel-forms lingered on, it is not easy to substantiate an inherent conservatism of pottery styles which might account for the resurgence of the applied cable technique. The general affinities between the finger-tip decorated jars of the Fen-Breckland region and the 'retarded Urnfield' culture pottery of the Low Countries is fairly apparent, but the applied finger-tip band is not a prominent element in this ceramic style. The characteristic form of finger-tip ornament on late Urnfield wares in the Low Countries is the random application of impressions all over the surface of the vessel and along the top of the rim, a style which also appears in Britain at West Harling (Clark and Fell, 1953, Fig. 12, 26) and Ivinghoe Beacon. The superficial evidence for connections across the North Sea with the Low Countries, however, should not be allowed to obscure the duality of cultural influences which could have been introduced into Britain by Hallstatt immigrants, who had themselves already suppressed the late Urnfield population in Belgium. At Staple Howe, such a duality of origin would not only explain the ceramic parallels with the Low Countries, but would also account for the two Hallstatt C razors (Fig. 33, B, C), which are certainly of western German type. And it is in precisely this region that the applied finger-tip cordon is most common, albeit on pots of rather different form, in the Hunsrückeifelkultur of western Germany (Hermann, 1966, Taf. 124, 2; Taf. 147, 8 etc.; Kimmig, 1940, Taf. 9, 1; Taf. 12, 2 etc.; Kossack, 1959, Taf, 76, 10, 25–30; Joachim, 1968, Taf. 6B, 1; Taf. 8, A, 1, 4, etc.). A closed association with an item of dateable metalwork is available in Pit A at Fengate, Peterborough (C. F. C.

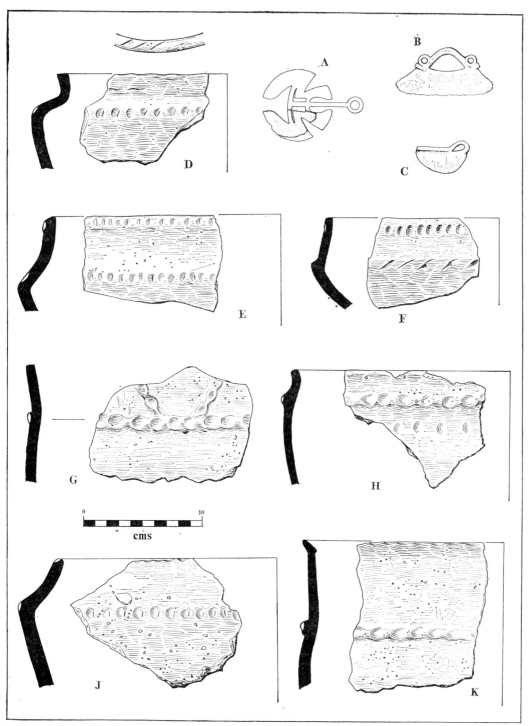

33. *Pottery and metalwork, Staple Howe, Yorkshire*

Hawkes and Fell, 1943, Fig. 1), where a jar with an applied cordon around its neck was accompanied by an iron swan's-neck pin with bronze sunflower-derived disc-head (Fig. 34 A), a type whose distribution is concentrated mainly in eastern Germany. The applied cordon does not appear to survive long into the Iron Age in Britain, and the fact that the Fengate example is quite plain and lacking any kind of finger-tip or cabled ornament may lend weight to Miss Fell's view that the pottery from this site was somewhat later than that from Scarborough and West Harling. Examples are rare in the Upper Thames region, which at this period shows closer contacts with Wessex than with East Anglia. But one fragment from Frilford displays an applied cable around its neck below a short, everted

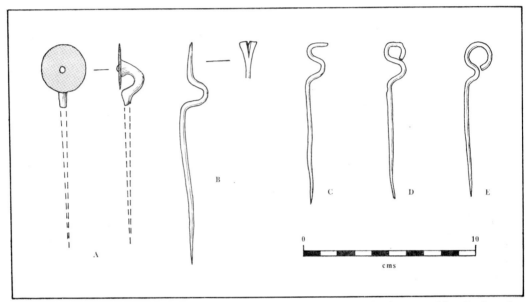

34. *Swan's-neck and ring-headed pins. A, Fengate, Peterborough, Northamptonshire. B, C and E, Woodeaton, Oxfordshire. D, Chinnor, Oxfordshire*

rim, while a very worn sherd from Wytham, which Bradford (1942a, Fig. 12, 25) claimed had an applied cable on its shoulder, is certainly an east coastal form, with a short, concave neck closely paralleled by many of the coarse-ware jars at West Harling.

From these east coastal sites, the coarse-ware pots which bear finger-tip or applied cable ornament are generally not curving, S-shaped vessels of evidently Continental Hallstatt ceramic derivation, but are jars with high and sometimes fairly pronounced shoulders, conventionally grouped within the category of early Iron Age pottery *situlas*. Hitherto pre-historians have been far too ready to assume for early Iron Age pottery forms a derivation from metal prototypes, without sufficient residual features to substantiate the pedigree. This trend was reflected in the frequency with which the term *situla* has been applied to almost any early Iron Age pottery jar, irrespective of its relationship to any of the Continental bronze bucket types. It has also been assumed that a metal prototype necessarily implied an angular profile, and, in consequence, pottery jars which displayed a sharply angular profile were regarded as typologically closer to the metal model, and therefore chronologically earlier, than those with a slack or rounded profile, which were described as 'devolved' or 'degenerate' *situlas*, and attributed to a later phase of the early Iron Age (cf. Savory, 1937, 6; Myres, 1937, 25–6; Bradford, 1940, 19; Williams, 1951, 16; Kenyon, 1952, 38).

The object of this section is to attempt a clarification of the material hitherto confused under the general heading of *situlas*, and to assess the degree to which pottery forms adhere to actual metal prototypes. First, we must distinguish and discount from the present discussion the kind of jar which has a sharp shoulder and tall, flaring rim, which at Long Wittenham Savory described as a situliform vessel with flaring rim (in which he was followed by Dr Kenyon), since its tripartite profile is characteristic, not of the *situla* directly, but of the early La Tène *vases carénés*. Discussion of this group and its Continental affinities will be reserved until a later section. Second, it must be emphasised that sharpness in profile need not, in itself, indicate chronological priority, since many of the metal *situlas*, including some of the earliest, display not an angular but a rounded shoulder. It should, of course, be recognised that features which were characteristic of the metal type may undergo modification when applied to a pottery imitation, since certain functional requirements of the metal model may no longer be practical or necessary in the pottery version. Finally, pottery vessels could have derived from any one of several metal types, and if the derivation is to be regarded as valid, it should be possible to distinguish to which variant the pottery form is related.

In an attempt to identify ceramic derivatives of bronze *situlas*, therefore, we should not be content with the generalised formula that angularity is indicative of a metal prototype. On the contrary, a pottery rendering of Italian or Rhineland *situlas* might be expected to display a high shoulder, not necessarily sharply angular, and might preserve the rolled-over rim or bead-rim, which as a functional feature of the metal prototype served to reinforce the brim of the sheet-bronze vessel. On the Continent, this detail very clearly betrays the derivation of the pottery *situla* identified by Kimmig from Hundersingen (1963, Abb. 6), and a comparable survival of the bead-rim as a non-functional feature of the ceramic form may be seen in the pottery *situla* from Grave 188 in the Marnian cemetery at Les Jogasses (Wheeler, 1943, Fig. 62, 1).

In Britain, the site which most clearly produced pottery to which the term *situla* in this sense may be applied is West Harling (Fig. 35), where there are vessels which display profiles very close to the metal form, including the short, upstanding neck and the rolled-over rim (Clark and Fell, 1953, Fig. 12, nos 20 and 21). Familiarity with the bead-rim as a feature of British Iron Age pottery should not be allowed to conceal the fact that it is more commonly related to later Iron Age contexts, and is not at all usual in the Iron A phase; this renders the derivation from the metalworker's stock-in-trade in the present context more apparent. It might be argued that the use of vertical finger-tipping on one jar from

West Harling (Fig. 35, E), not a common application of the finger-tip style of ornament in Britain, itself derives from the vertical rivets of a sheet-bronze *situla*. (Compare the vertical finger-tipping from West Harling with the example in the cemetery at Pernant in the Aisne, Lobjois, 1969, Fig. 114, 027.01.) Closely allied to the pottery *situlas* of this class are the jars from Staple Howe (Fig. 33, D) which embody a high shoulder and short upstanding rim (e.g. Brewster, 1963, Fig. 43, 2), and the vessel recognised as a pottery *situla* by Hawkes from Linford, Essex (C. F. C. Hawkes, 1962, Fig. 1, i), in which the shoulder is more

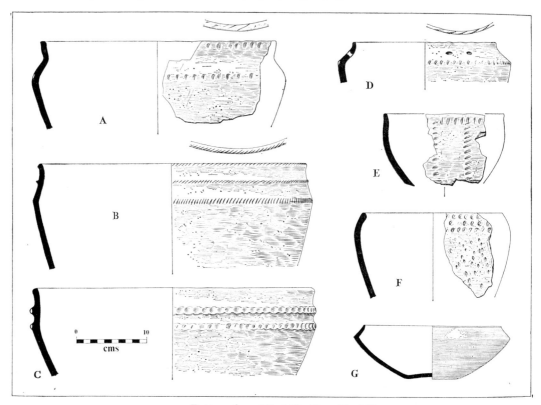

35. *Pottery from West Harling, Norfolk*

obviously angular, but which retains the upright neck and thickened rim. In the upper Thames region, few early Iron Age jars approximate closely to this definition of a pottery *situla*, though a vessel from Standlake might be counted in this category on account of its high shoulder, relatively short neck, and very slightly rolled-over rim (Bradford, 1942c, Fig. 4, 3).

The necked *situla*, which was the prototype for the West Harling, Linford and Standlake jars, is not, of course, the only type of metal *situla*, and correspondingly, the necked version is not the only form in pottery. In his study of Continental bronze *situlas*, Kimmig (1963, e.g. Abb. 3 and Taf. 26) identified a variant which was distinguished by its high shoulder and simple bipartite form, having no true neck at all, which he termed the Meppen-Gladbach type. This bipartite *situla* type he explains as having its rim assimilated to that of the Hallstatt D cauldron, which turns inwards and is characteristically thickened as a result of being hammered inwards. Though there are no examples of this type in metal in

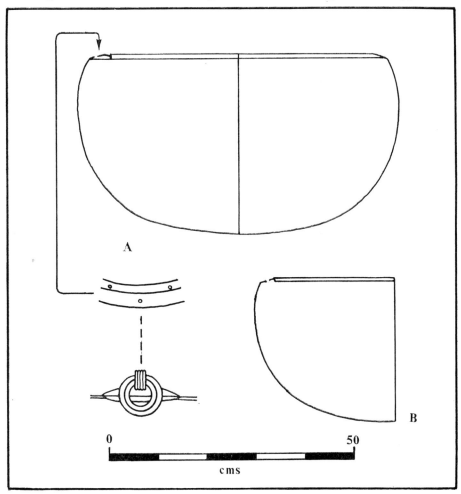

36. *Hallstatt D cauldrons. A, London, with ring-handle inferred from Continental analogies. B, Vilsingen, Hohenzollern*

Britain – they are concentrated mainly in south-east Holland and north-west Germany – one such *situla* did reach as far as Croissic at the mouth of the Loire, so that the stimulus for a pottery copy might very well have extended into Britain. The Hallstatt D cauldron-type itself, at any rate, reached as far as London (Fig. 36, A). Once again, the closest examples in pottery to the bronze bipartite *situla* are to be found at West Harling, where there are jars which quite accurately reproduce both the profile and the proportions of the bronze model (Clark and Fell, 1953, Fig. 14, 52, 60). Further examples may be cited from Fengate (C. F. C. Hawkes and Fell, 1943, Fig. 5, K3 and K4), Staple Howe (Brewster, 1963, Fig. 37, 5), and Stiffkey, Norfolk (R. R. Clarke and Apling, 1935, Fig. 3, 9), all of which have acquired a form of beaded rim, which, though not integral to the Meppen-Gladbach *situla*-type, nonetheless has been assimilated from the metalworker's repertory to be applied to any pottery *situla*, irrespective of its functional origin.

In its primary form, the bipartite *situla* is apparently found mainly in a south-eastern and east coastal distribution. Probably related to this group are a number of bipartite jars, including examples from the Upper Thames, in which the proportions of the vessel vary, the shoulder being lowered, and the profile above it acquiring a slight concavity, as on an example from Mount Farm, Dorchester, Oxon (Myres, 1937, Fig. 8, *ι* 11). Though the derivation from metal models is here undoubtedly no more than secondary, it seems likely that the indirect relationship between such variants and the metal prototype remains essentially valid, since the general form of these vessels is alien to the mainstream of Hallstatt ceramics, in which the tall rim and curving S-shaped body-profile are dominant.

Closely allied to the bipartite *situla* is the bipartite bowl, which at West Harling and Staple Howe was no less common. The very close relationship between the two is indicated not only by their similarity in profile, but also by their comparable distributions, which both concentrate primarily along the east coast and the south-east of England, occasionally extending along the south coast or into Wessex. Once again, the slightly beaded rim is a feature of the West Harling and Staple Howe bowls, which differ from their jar counterparts only in their shallower bodies. It is difficult to avoid the connection of this form of bipartite bowl with the shallow bowls from Minnis Bay (Fig. 37, E, F), which are certainly within the main distribution area of the form. If such a relationship is valid, it serves to emphasise the chronological priority of the bipartite form over the early La Tène tripartite jars and bowls, which nonetheless probably succeeded it generally with no significant chronological break.

In view of the derivation from metal prototypes outlined above, it is significant that the parallelism observed between jars and bowls in Britain in pottery is also a characteristic of the Continental metal series. Already in the eighth century B.C., there existed north of the Alps a type of handled bronze cup, whose shape resembled the larger *situlas*, with the addition of a large handle mounted between shoulder and rim. The function of such cups was almost certainly connected with the *situlas* themselves, serving for ladling and drinking wine from the major container. On the Continent such cups were imitated in pottery, just as were the *situlas* themselves. The association in Britain, therefore, of a large pottery *situla* form with an allied bowl form, is especially consistent with the individual derivations here proposed for a range of vessels whose function was for wine, or other socially superior drink.

Not unrelated to this convivial theme is another class of metal vessel for which pottery copies and derivations may be presumed, namely, the sheet-bronze cauldron. If the development of pottery imitations of bronze *situlas* stemmed from Continental models, the pottery cauldron can be traced to purely insular antecedents. Both, however, arose in comparable circumstances, with the need for domestic vessels in quantities which could not be supplied by the sheet-bronze industry. How long the production of Atlantic cauldrons continued in the highland zone may be open to question; but in south-eastern Britain, where the influx of Hallstatt settlers would have had a greater impact upon insular cultures, we must imagine that sheet-bronze working was on the wane by the end of the seventh century (C. F. C. Hawkes and M. A. Smith, 1957). In consequence, it is reasonable to suppose a

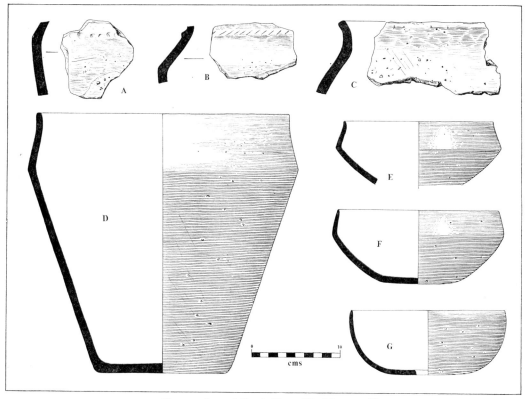

37. *Pottery from Minnis Bay, Birchington, Kent*

growing demand for pottery substitutes at a time when, as we have seen, there must have been a variety of influences affecting the potters' range of products. I have attempted to demonstrate elsewhere (1972, 75ff.) that the principal concentration of pottery vessels for which a derivation from bronze cauldrons may be suggested was within the Upper Thames basin, including examples from Mount Farm, Dorchester, in particular, whose outward and upward projecting rims are strikingly reminiscent of the rims of Class B Atlantic cauldrons of the seventh century (Fig. 38). Other pottery fragments, whose rims display a marked inward flange, may conceivably have been modelled upon the Hallstatt D cauldron type, which in Britain is exemplified by a single example from the Thames at London

143

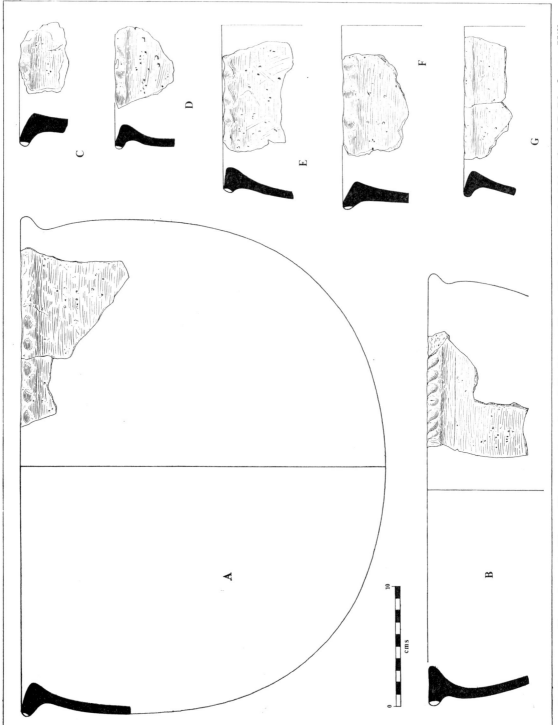

38. *Pottery cauldrons from the Upper Thames region. A and B, Mount Farm, Dorchester, Oxfordshire. C and F, Blewburton Hill,*

(Fig. 36, A). As in the case of pottery *situlas*, the identification of the metal prototype rests largely upon the shape of the rim, which in the original constituted the most vulnerable part of the vessel, and which in consequence was reinforced with special attention. There can be little doubt, however, that the experimental rendering of a cauldron in pottery would not have been very successful, particularly if an attempt was made to retain the hemispherical base of the model. The distribution of pottery vessels, for which this tentative derivation may be advanced, therefore, remains limited, and it was not long before the rim shape itself was assimilated in less exaggerated form to the common stock of Iron Age coarse-ware jars.

If we are to imagine Hallstatt colonists in any numbers in the coastal regions of southern and eastern England in the late seventh and sixth centuries B.C., it would not be unreasonable to expect that, in addition to metal-derived ceramic forms, they would have introduced a fashion for pottery in the Continental Hallstatt tradition. Half a century ago, when direct Continental origins for the British Iron Age had not been seriously called into question, R. A. Smith (1927) had recognised the Hallstatt affinities of the pottery from Scarborough, which included several distinctive curving-bodied profiles as well as vessels with applied cordons of the kind discussed earlier. A comparable group could be cited at Chalbury in Dorset (Whitley, 1943, Figs 3–5), again significantly from a coastal provenance. From the fringes of the Upper Thames region, a number of fragments from Blewburton Hill, in fine grey ware with a light tan burnished surface and curving S-shaped body-profile, are sufficiently unlike local early Iron Age pottery forms and fabrics to suggest that they may be related to such an intrusive late Hallstatt element. But the most outstanding pottery assemblage, the Hallstatt characteristics of which have always been recognised, is that from Eastbourne (Budgen, 1922; Hodson, 1962). Three of these vessels, including one which is decorated with a series of black, concentric lozenges around its shoulder (Fig. 39, B), were found together in a pit, and may reasonably be regarded as a closed association. All have been distorted by firing, and in consequence have been regarded as wasters, a conclusion which, if accepted, necessarily implies local manufacture. The basic curving-bodied shape of the Eastbourne vases, and the particular style of ornament Hodson has traced to Hallstatt C origins in the Rhineland, where the footring or pedestal base, however, is significantly absent at this period. It is in the more westerly extension of Hallstatt culture on the Continent that the pedestal first makes an appearance, as Hodson rightly observed, in the peripheral late Hallstatt cemetery at Les Jogasses. Here we may find parallels, not only for the round-bodied and slightly shouldered profiles from Eastbourne, but also for their combination with the pedestal base (e.g. Favret, 1936, Figs 45, 47). In view of this connection, the use of painted decoration at Eastbourne must surely derive from the Mont Lassois or 'Vix' style of pottery painting, confirming the westerly late Hallstatt origins of the group. The appearance of pedestals at Eastbourne, therefore, need cause us no embarrassment. On the Continent, they continued in fashion into the early La Tène period, when Britain once again was subject to ceramic influence, this time from the Marne region in the fifth century B.C. To this subject we shall return later; for the present it will be sufficient to remark that the Eastbourne vases need in no way be inconsistent with a dating within the second half of the sixth century.

Another Hallstatt pottery form which has received too little attention in the past is the round-bodied bowl. Quite widely distributed in southern England from West Blatchington in Sussex (Norris and Burstow, 1950, Pl. I, 9) to Chalbury in Dorset (Whitley, 1943, Fig. 5, 24, 26), these bowls continued to be current into the early La Tène period. Among the earliest examples were two from the Upper Thames region. One from Old Marston, near Oxford, is decorated around its girth with an incised zig-zag panel and punched dots, filled with white inlay, in a manner clearly derived from the early Wessex style of pottery ornament (Fig. 40, D). The second fragment from Mount Farm, Dorchester,

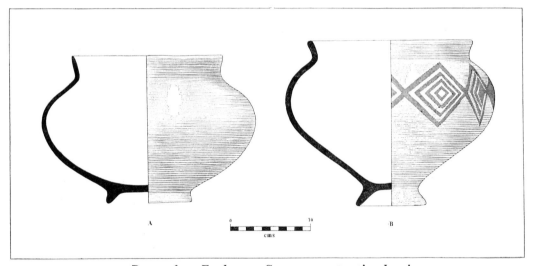

39. *Pottery from Eastbourne, Sussex: reconstruction drawings*

was coated with a deep red haematite slip, and was found in a pit in association with the out-turned rim of a pottery cauldron. Both are instructive, being the products of insular potters who have absorbed into their repertory of shapes an innovating Hallstatt form, and combined this with ornamental fashions adopted from their neighbours in Wessex. The Continental origins of the form itself are not hard to trace. A number of close parallels may be cited from the cemetery at St-Vincent, in Belgian Luxembourg (Marien, 1964), including examples with simple, flat bases and others with the characteristically Hallstatt omphalos base (Fig. 40, A). Ultimately, they are derived from earlier models in the Niederrheinische Hügelgräberkultur (Kersten, 1948), in effect, from the same region which was one of the sources proposed earlier for the applied cable technique in Britain. A variant of the form from Walthamstow (Fig. 40, B) may be quite closely paralleled at Kalbeck, where two vessels display the same tall, flaring rim, though their body-profiles are slightly more biconical than round. At the same time, it is worth recalling that both Les Jogasses (e.g.

146

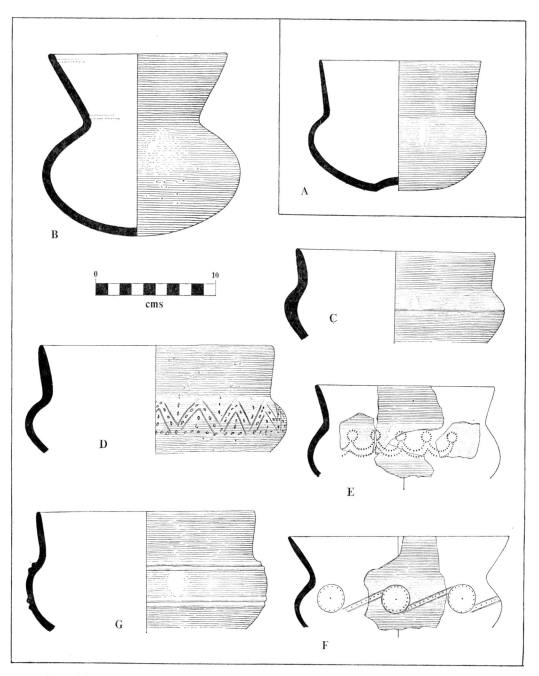

40. *Round-bodied bowls. A, St-Vincent, Luxembourg. B, Walthamstow, London. C, Chinnor, Oxfordshire. D, Old Marston, Oxfordshire. E, F and G, Blewburton Hill, Berkshire*

Favret, 1936, Fig. 45) and Mont Lassois (Joffroy, 1960, Pl. 47, 2) have their own provincial variant of round-bodied bowls, which might well account for the Wessex element within the southern British distribution. In terms of absolute chronology, the Walthamstow pot should probably be regarded as a precursor of the main distribution in Britain, dating perhaps to the end of the seventh century, while the remainder doubtless extended through the sixth and fifth centuries B.C. Some indication of a terminal horizon is afforded by two fragmentary bowls from Blewburton Hill, Berks (Fig. 40, E, F), one of which is decorated with a kind of swag-motif, executed in a series of dotted loops dependent from dotted rosettes, the other being ornamented with an extremely mechanical and prosaic attempt to form a running scroll by joining a sequence of inscribed circles with straight lines extending from the bottom of one to the top of the next. With the accumulation of more evidence for Hallstatt ceramic forms in Britain, the Eastbourne assemblage may eventually appear not as an isolated find or freak but as an outstanding product of a process which embraced a wide area of the Channel coast from the outset of the Iron Age. And though the 'Jogassien' element has not appeared especially prominent in Wessex, this perhaps is only the result of its being overshadowed by more distinctive pottery forms and decorative styles, generally regarded as characteristic of the earliest Iron Age in that region, to which our attention must next be directed.

The principal characteristic which is generally associated with the early Iron Age fine-wares of Wessex is the application of a haematite slip. In practice, powdered haematite (anhydrous sesquioxide of iron) was applied as a slip to the surface of the vessel, which was then burnished to a high red-brown lustre to give an appearance similar to that of polished copper. The widespread distribution of pottery embellished in this fashion has tended to obscure the fact that there is no direct correlation between it and the natural occurrence of mineral deposits suitable for the large-scale production of haematite-coated wares. In view of current controversy concerning the origins of British Iron Age cultures, Oakley's conclusions relating to his analysis of haematite samples from Maiden Castle, Dorset, are instructive: 'The use of haematite burnish is a fashion which would no doubt have arisen in a country where deposits of haematite or red ochre were conspicuous. The fact that the fashion spread into areas like Wessex, where haematite could be found only in small quantities and after exhaustive search, indicates that its ultimate distribution was governed by cultural rather than geological factors' (1943, 380). In Britain, such sources do exist in the carboniferous limestones of Cumberland, Lancashire, North and South Wales and the Forest of Dean, with less significant deposits in the Mendips, Devon and Cornwall; none of these areas has produced pottery which displays a haematite slip. On the Continent, on the other hand, there are suitable mineral deposits from the Loire to the Marne, which were undoubtedly being exploited by this time. *A priori*, therefore, there are grounds for supposing that the technique may have been introduced into southern Britain by immigrants, or refugees from late Hallstatt expansion, via the westerly Channel route. A distribution of haematite-coated pottery in Britain was published by Wheeler (1943, Fig. 55), and a number of easterly outliers were added by Frere (1947, Fig. 20), but no further attempt has been made to subdivide the various kinds of pottery upon which this slip occurs in southern Britain, nor to plot an independent distribution for each.

Haematite is applied regularly to a variety of pottery forms, including both bowls and decorated jars, but it is especially, and invariably, associated with fine-ware bowls which are ornamented with horizontal rilling above their shoulders. These 'furrowed' bowls (Fig. 41) were first defined as a group in Wiltshire as long ago as 1912, by the Cunningtons in their first report on excavations at the classic site of All Cannings Cross, since when they have passed into the literature as one of the pottery forms diagnostic of the earliest Iron Age culture in Wessex. As a result of more recent research, we may now propose a provisional division of furrowed bowls, into those with a short neck above the carination, surmounted by a short, everted rim, and those which display a taller, concave neck terminating in a simple rim. From the limited number of stratified groups at present available, it appears that this typological sequence might well prove to correspond to a chronological progression in which the earlier, short-necked examples are gradually superseded by bowls with taller, concave necks. Approximately corresponding to this change in profile is a change in the kind of rilling, from broad wavy furrows of shallow U-section to narrower channels of V- or ⊔-section, which in some examples becomes nothing more than a linear incision. The derivation of the furrowed technique itself can scarcely be in doubt. Examples are plentiful, particularly with the short neck and everted rim, in late Bronze Age contexts in France (e.g. Sandars, 1957, Fig. 78, 10, from Fort Harrouard), with a widespread distribution in central and north-western Europe. The southerly distribution of the type in England would be consistent with the view that these bowls were the product of a population which was fundamentally late Urnfield in cultural affiliations, but which had acquired certain Hallstatt techniques such as the use of haematite and the omphalos base, brought into Wessex in a movement of withdrawal from the reach of Hallstatt influence and possible incursion towards the Channel. The British furrowed bowls should, therefore, begin in the second half of the seventh century, towards 600, rather than much later, as would have been believed according to the short chronology for the British Iron Age formerly current. If further corroboration for this dating is required, it is provided by the Welby bronze hoard from Leicestershire (Powell, 1948). Although the proportions of the Welby bowl (Fig. 42) are much smaller than those of the majority of pottery examples, it otherwise demonstrates in bronze the selfsame features – broad furrows, short neck with everted rim, and omphalos base – which are characteristic of the early group of furrowed bowls. The dating proposed by Powell for the Welby bowl has since been modified by Hawkes (C. F. C. Hawkes and M. A. Smith, 1957, 155), who attributes it firmly to the second half of the seventh century, which would be quite consistent with the early series of furrowed bowls in southern England. The omphalos base, in pottery, could well derive from a metalworking tradition, while the application of a red-brown haematite coating likewise is evocative of the colour of polished copper or bronze. But in spite of these affinities in technique and dating, it is difficult to conceive of the Welby bowl as a metal prototype for the pottery series, not least because the location of the hoard is well outside the Wessex-centred pottery distribution.

And though Powell considered the possibility that it was itself an import from Central Europe (cf. the bronze bowl handle-holders from the same hoard, 1948, Fig. 3, 14–15), the Welby bowl remains unique; its furrowed technique in particular is quite alien to any Continental metal series, though well represented in the Urnfield pottery tradition. The

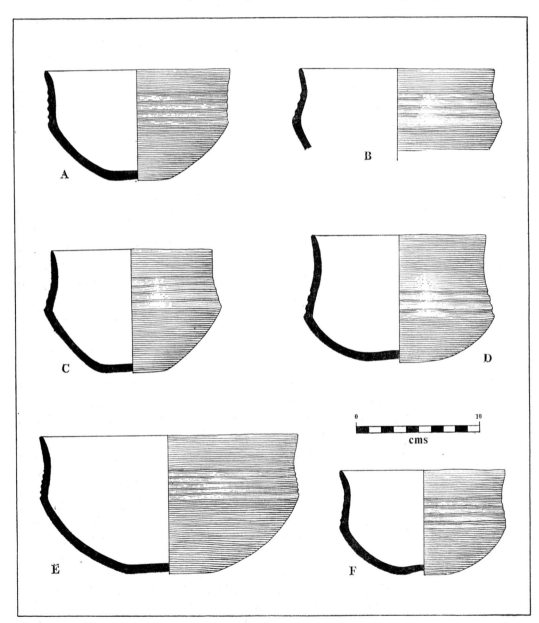

41. *Furrowed bowls from All Cannings Cross, Wiltshire*

XXI *Early La Tène pottery from Swallowcliffe Down, Wiltshire (heights: c. 16 cm)*

XXII *Ornamental chamfrein, Torrs, Kirkcudbrightshire (length of cap: c. 30 cm)*

relationship between the Welby bowl and the Wessex furrowed bowls could, therefore, be a reciprocal one, for in accordance with the chronology outlined above, there is nothing to prevent the bronzesmith incorporating in the Welby bowl a feature which was much more common in the pottery version, which itself owed certain of its other characteristics to the metalworker's craft.

The distribution of haematite-coated furrowed bowls (Fig. 43) is restricted to the Wessex counties of Dorset, Wiltshire and Hampshire principally, with only infrequent outliers further east, or extending into the Upper Thames valley. Significantly, those

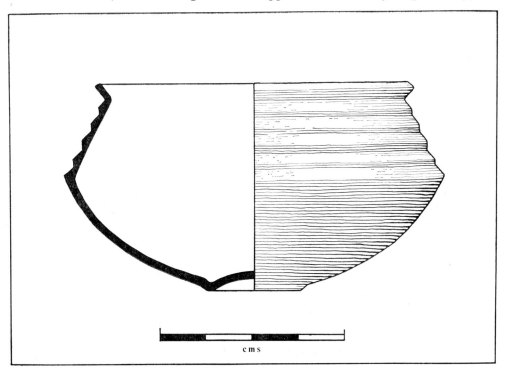

42. Bronze bowl from Welby, Leicestershire

dubious examples which occur peripherally to this distribution are frequently of the later class with narrower, incised furrows, and generally lack the haematite slip which characterises the true furrowed bowls of Wessex. The technique of narrow, horizontal incisions is assimilated on to later pottery forms as far afield as East Anglia, where it appears on bowls from Darmsden, Suffolk (Cunliffe, 1968, Fig. 2, 1–8; Fig. 4, 61; Fig. 5, 63–4). But here the process of diffusion must be regarded as sufficiently secondary to be no longer part of the same ceramic story.

Not all haematite-coated bowls in Wessex, of course, bear the distinctive furrowing. Towards the end of the sequence, the fashion for ornamenting bowls with horizontal rilling declined, and some of the later variants with tall, concave neck are lacking in any

43. *Distribution of furrowed bowls*

further embellishment. By the fifth century B.C., furrowing as an ornamental style was on the wane, and was being progressively superseded in Wessex by a new class of haematite-coated bowl, one which was elaborated by the addition of a footring base and horizontal, applied cordons around its girth. To these new and exotic haematite bowls we shall return in due course.

The application of a haematite slip was not restricted solely to bowls. To larger jars alike the burnished coppery lustre was added, together with distinctive geometric ornamental designs, deeply incised into the surface of the pottery. The incised pattern was then filled with a white chalky paste, so that the design would stand out in sharp – even gaudy – contrast with the burnished haematite backing. Horizontal and vertical zig-zag panels, interlocking triangles filled with linear hatching, and a variety of other rectilinear, and more rarely curvilinear, motifs were traced around the surface of fine-ware jars in this fashion (Fig. 44). It may be argued that such incised hatching was only for the purpose of keying a larger area of ornament in white, rather than delineating the ornamental design itself. Were this really so, however, we might expect the incised lines to be more random, like the random scratching used by a plasterer, and it seems more likely that those instances where the inlay has spread slightly beyond the limits of the incisions are the result of carelessness in the application of the paste. The jars on which this style of ornament appears are almost without exception in fine pottery, the table-ware of early Iron Age communities in Wessex. Few vessels have survived complete, or sufficiently so to restore a complete profile. One example from All Cannings Cross (Cunnington, 1923, Pl. 29, 1) displays a curving body reminiscent of Continental Hallstatt forms. Others, more especially from Longbridge Deverill, present a very different profile, with a fairly high shoulder-angle, which, though obtuse and sometimes quite blunt, is nonetheless readily perceptible. The shoulder and the body below the shoulder are very slightly convex, while the rim is everted and lens-shaped in section, in a manner which recalls the early form of furrowed bowl, and Hallstatt B antecedents on the Continent. This form of early Wessex jar should not be confused with the early La Tène angular jars, whose affinities are with the *vases carénés* of the Marne. The major differences are the obtuse or blunt shoulder-angle of the Wessex jars; their moderate length of rim, neither tall nor extremely short as in the two chief variants of the Marnian models; and the proportionately greater breadth of shoulder which the Wessex jars all display. Furthermore, the convexity in profile of the early Wessex jars contrasts with the marked concavity of some of the Continental *vases carénés*.

On whatever form of jar, the use of this style of deeply incised or deeply punched ornament is by no means exclusively restricted to Wessex, though it is here that the main distribution concentrates. At Hawk's Hill, Fetcham, Surrey (Hastings, 1965, Fig. 12, 12–15), for instance, incised ornament filled with white inlay on jars coated with a deep red haematite slip is as vigorous in its application as on any Wessex site, and may even have been the work of an expatriate Wessex potter. The extraordinary 'concertina' bowls from this site (Fig. 45), however, are without close parallel, in Wessex or elsewhere, and suggest an independent development at Hawk's Hill after the initial contact with Wessex had been

153

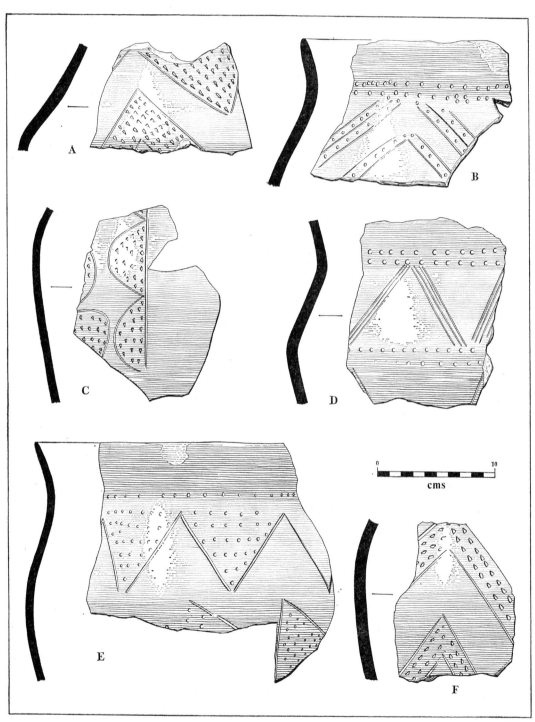

44. *Decorated pottery from All Cannings Cross, Wiltshire*

broken off. As with the technique of 'furrowing', and the use of the haematite slip, the Continental origins of the incised style of ornament can scarcely be doubted. Though the French material itself is not well documented, the incised linear panels filled with deeply punched dots, characteristic of early wares at All Cannings Cross and Longbridge Deverill, are in technique not unlike the style of ornament found at the Fort Harrouard (Philippe, 1927, Pl. XIX), itself derived from the incised (or excised, viz. Kerbschnitt) and punched decoration which Urnfield pottery received, and passed on to Hallstatt, probably from west Continental Bronze Age antecedents.

Coarse pottery, the everyday kitchen ware of the earliest Iron Age in Wessex, as elsewhere, is not especially amenable to classification, its variety reflecting the individuality

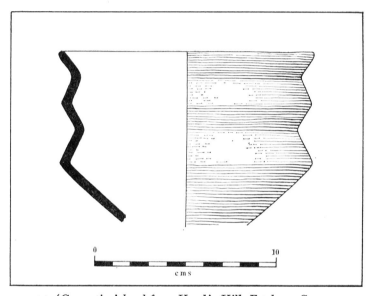

45. 'Concertina' bowl from Hawk's Hill, Fetcham, Surrey

which we might expect from domestic and local production. Even though no specific models, either insular or Continental, can be pin-pointed for the majority of coarse-pottery forms, nonetheless a certain uniformity emerges in the use of simple finger-impressed ornament, generally applied to jars along the rim or shoulder of the vessel. Jars tend to display a shoulder which, though not always very pronounced, is sufficient to distinguish them from many of the slacker profiles of the ensuing Iron B phase. But, in summary, it must be admitted that the range of early Iron Age pottery in Wessex, as in the rest of lowland Britain, is extremely limited, lacking the subtler distinctions between bowls, vases, cups or platters which appear with the Belgic Iron Age.

At the same time, the number of metal utensils and ornaments, which are found on early Wessex settlements like All Cannings Cross, is equally limited. Hallstatt brooches are conspicuously absent from properly associated contexts (e.g. Harden, 1950), the only small personal trinkets which appear in any numbers being pins of the swan's-neck and ring-headed series, generally in bronze, though occasionally in iron. The typological development of such pins was defined by Dunning some years ago (1934). In his primary swan's-neck group he included two variants, one with a bent neck with its head projecting at right angles to the stem, the other having a flattened, spatulate terminal which continues the alignment of the stem beyond the swan's neck (Fig. 33). Both versions are probably to be dated early in the sixth century. The ring-headed pin, in which the terminal is bent round to meet the stem, represents an insular development, probably by the fifth century, and was taken by C. F. C. Hawkes to be characteristic of his Second A culture in southern Britain (1959, 179). Thereafter, the ring-headed pin remained in fashion, with modifications, and examples have even been discovered on the sites of Roman villas like Ditchley in Oxfordshire, though here we cannot be certain that they are not disturbed survivals from earlier settlement.

One further metal type deserves to be mentioned at this point. Among the material remains from All Cannings Cross was a fragment of a bronze socketed axe of the characteristic Breton class (Cunnington, 1923, Pl. 18, 3), which is distinguished by its straight-sided shape and square-ended cross-section. Such axes were being imported widely into southern Britain around the beginning of the sixth century B.C. (Dunning, 1959), not necessarily to be used for their original function as axes, but conceivably as raw material for melting down and recasting for other purposes. The necessity for such imports, C. F. C. Hawkes (1959, 177) has argued, arose from the fact that Hallstatt adventurers were infiltrating the south of England, 'alien to the country and its metalmerchants', and that, in consequence, commercial relations with the metal-producing regions of the highland zone had broken down. Whatever the reason, the appearance of imports from Brittany at this time affords coincidental corroboration for a reference in the Massiliote Periplus of the sixth century B.C., which is quoted in Avienus' *Ora Maritima*, to trade between the people of the Oestrymnides, which are generally taken to have been the regions of the Breton peninsula, and the islands of Ierne and Albion (Powell, 1958, 25–6, Fig. 1). The role which Ireland played in the commercial liaison archaeologically remains obscure, but the reference seems to reinforce the notion that the westerly channel-route into Britain played no small part in the formation of what emerged as our insular Iron Age culture.

10

The early La Tène phase: the 'Marnian' problem

ANY SYSTEM of classification of the Iron Age carries with it the danger of excessive rigidity, just as the use of an absolute chronology is liable to hamper through inflexibility. No subject has been more bedevilled by these problems than the so-called 'Marnian' issue, which in recent years has stimulated considerable controversy concerning the value of certain categories of evidence as an index of cultural change. The ceramic affinities between certain early La Tène groups in the south-east of England, and assemblages from the Marnian hinterland of northern France had long been recognised, and generally accepted as valid. By 1939, an attempt had been made by Hawkes to rationalise the fragmentary evidence then available into a coherent historical interpretation. The appearance of certain outstanding classes of pottery, including pedestal bases, vases with sharply angular shoulders, and tub-shaped 'saucepan' pots, he regarded as the product of a widespread invasion of Continental Celts from the Marne region around 250 B.C. This martial immigration was further witnessed by notable metal types, including La Tène I brooches, and the distinctive Swiss bent silver ring from Park Brow. The native response to this threat by the warrior aristocracy of the Marne was the hasty construction of hillforts in the third century throughout southern England. In retrospect, we may feel that any attempt to explain as the product of a single historical event such a multiplicity of diverse cultural phenomena was bound to result in over-simplification and error. The loopholes which appear in any theory after thirty years of further research are not hard to expose, as Hodson has adequately demonstrated. (For the principal arguments of the 'invasion controversy', see C. F. C. Hawkes, 1959; Hodson, 1960; 1962; 1964a; 1964b; Clark, 1966; C. F. C. Hawkes, 1966; D. W. Harding, 1970.) But we should remember that the relatively short time-scale into which the Iron Age in Britain then had to be compressed inevitably resulted in the conflation of material types which might now be regarded as representative of successive cultural phases. Within the chronological framework now available, hillfort construction, for instance, must be diffused over a much greater span of time, extending conceivably back into the late Bronze Age. And though some hillforts may well have been built and others re-occupied, in the early La Tène period, as a result of renewed contact between southern Britain and the Continent, the intensity of such activity no longer demands interpretation in terms of a single historical invasion. Fundamental to this question, of course, is the extension of the chronological scale for the Iron Age, which enables us now to attribute the important ceramic links with the Marne, defined by Hawkes, to the fifth and fourth centuries B.C., rather than significantly later. The date of 250 B.C., which Hodson was still shadow-boxing in 1962, and which was being quoted as the period of Marnian incursions as recently as 1964 (Simpson), can now be firmly consigned to the archaeological archive, and hopefully

157

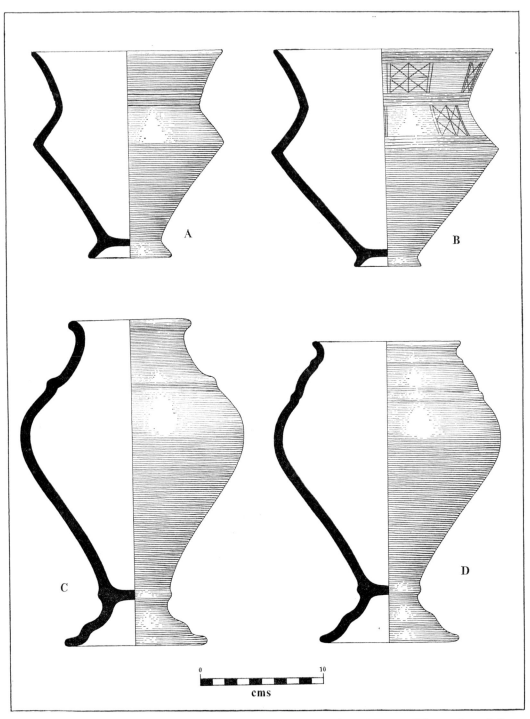

46. *Continental* vases carénés *and* vases piriformes. *A and B, Marson, Marne. C and D, Somme-Bionne, Marne. All from British Museum Morel Collection*

forgotten. As for the case for a Marnian invasion itself, though we may no longer attach such significance to the evidence of hillforts, the ceramic evidence certainly merits serious attention, as do the broadly contemporary groups of early La Tène daggers and brooches.

In the early La Tène burials of the Marne, two principal pottery forms predominate (Fig. 46). The first is the *vase caréné*, distinguished by its sharply angular profile, and often accompanied by a pedestal base. The second, the *vase piriforme*, has a characteristically high, rounded shoulder and pear-shaped body, likewise with a pedestal base. Both occur in the chariot burial at Somme-Bionne (Morel, 1890; R. A. Smith, 1925, 55–8, Pl. III), together with an Attic red-figure vase which provides a *terminus post quem* of around 420 B.C. for the grave. The two forms need not have been contemporary in general, however. The evidence from the Marne region suggests that the *vase caréné* was in circulation earlier in the fifth century, and was gradually supplanted and superseded by the innovating *vase piriforme*, whose origins lay further east in the region of the Hunsrück-Eifel. Angular bowls, with a Hallstatt omphalos base, of course, had been current already in the late Hallstatt phase at Les Jogasses, and these continued in use, with the progressive adoption of the pedestal base, into the early La Tène phase. In Britain, therefore, we should see the introduction of pottery which displays a sharply angular profile as an equally progressive process. At Long Wittenham in Berkshire, for instance, angular bowls still retain in some instances an omphalos base (Fig. 47, A), which is replaced at Chinnor, Oxon, by the pedestal or low footring form (Fig. 47, G, H, J). An angular shoulder in itself was not entirely new in Britain in the early La Tène period. Apart from the bipartite bowls of the kind represented at West Harling, even the late haematite-coated bowls of Wessex, which lack furrows, could be paralleled in general terms among late Hallstatt pottery from Les Jogasses. Nonetheless, the widespread appearance in south-eastern England of jars and bowls of tripartite, angular shape, frequently in fine black, burnished ware – the egg-shell thin fabrics which Savory remarked upon at Long Wittenham (1937) – does seem to represent a sufficient innovation to merit their treatment as a group.

The fine-ware jars of this insular series (Fig. 48) significantly do not display the pedestal bases of Marnian models, nor are they decorated as lavishly as their Continental counterparts. Where decorated examples do occur, as at Allen's Pit, Dorchester-on-Thames (Bradford, 1942a, Fig. 8, 3; D. W. Harding, 1972, Pl. 51b; Kenyon, 1952, Fig. 6, 1), and at Fengate, Peterborough (C. F. C. Hawkes and Fell, 1943, Fig. 2, D1), the ornament consists of simple geometric designs incised around the shoulder of the vessel, or occasionally, as on a second example from Fengate (C. F. C. Hawkes and Fell, 1943, Fig. 1, A2; Fig. 2, D1), and on another from the Caburn (C. F. C. Hawkes, 1939, Fig. A1; Fig. B, 7), the application of a plain cordon around the neck of an otherwise undecorated vessel. Under the influence of the new ceramic fashion, local coarse-ware jars, too, acquire more pronounced shoulders, with tall and sometimes flaring rims, though potters evidently experienced some difficulty technically in achieving the same degree of angularity (D. W. Harding, 1972, 88 ff and Pls 52, 53). The decoration on these local imitations, however, retains exclusively the old, native plastic style of finger-tipping or roughly slashed incisions

159

around the shoulder and rim of the jar, which had characterised coarse-wares of the preceding insular phase. The contrast between these two groups extends to fabric, the fine-ware jars from Long Wittenham and the Caburn lacking beneath their burnished exterior the coarse, untreated temper which in the Upper Thames can amount to shell grits in the order of 15 mm in thickness. Whether this distinction argues an element of professionalism

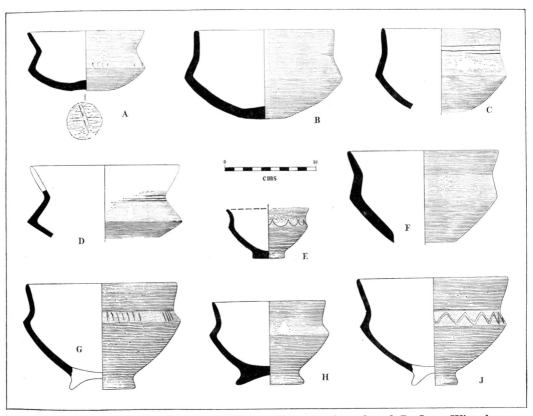

47. *Fine-ware angular bowls from the Upper Thames region. A and B, Long Wittenham,
Berkshire. C and D, Allen's Pit, Dorchester, Oxfordshire. F, Blewburton Hill, Berkshire.
E, G, H and J, Chinnor, Oxfordshire*

in the production of the finer angular wares is debatable; but certainly the marked uniformity of the bowls from Woodeaton in Oxfordshire (Fig. 49), for instance, suggests strongly that they were the work of a single potter whose output was not only numerically prolific, but in quality standardised to a remarkable degree. The bowls, indeed, show even greater affinities with the Continental series. The parallels for the Long Wittenham bowls, with omphalos base, with Continental assemblages which are transitional from late Hallstatt to early La Tène have already been remarked. With the progressive adoption of the pedestal, analogies in the early La Tène cemeteries of the Marne become more pronounced; the comparison between the black, burnished, angular bowl from Chinnor (Richardson and Young, 1951, Fig. 8, 52; Fig. 9) and a pedestal vase from La Sablonnière (Hubert, 1906, Fig. 44, 3 and 4) is convincing. The Chinnor pottery is especially outstanding, not only because of the high lustre of its burnished bowls, but also because of the exotic 'arcaded' decoration which is repeated on several separate examples. Whatever its inspiration – the

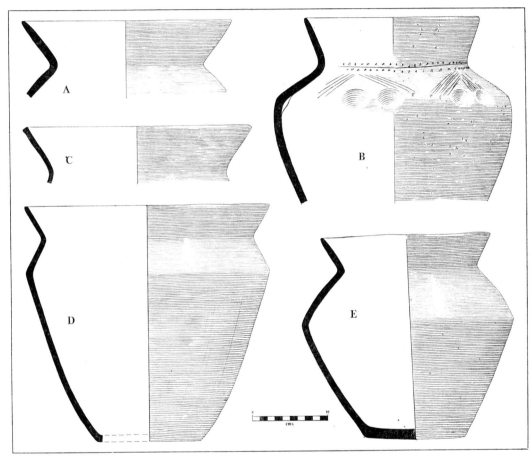

48. *Fine-ware angular jars from the Upper Thames region. A and B, Allen's Pit, Dorchester, Oxfordshire. C, D and E, Long Wittenham, Berkshire*

excavators supposed that the arcaded motif itself was in imitation of the looped handles of a metal prototype – the style is restricted to the northern escarpment of the Chilterns, being represented at the neighbouring settlements at Lodge Hill, Bledlow (*Records of Bucks*, 14, 189–209 and 149) and Ellesborough (Cocks, 1909, Fig. 11), with a single sherd from across the Thames at Hagbourne Hill on the Berkshire Downs executed in the same style. Once again, we may be inclined to think in terms of a specialist group of potters operating in the region on a professional commercial basis, since it is otherwise hard to imagine such a disparity in quality in the output of domestic craftsmen or craftswomen at a settlement like Chinnor. One of the puzzling factors about the Chinnor assemblage is the continued use of white inlay in the incised decoration of the fine-ware bowls (Fig. 50), a technique which is reminiscent of the early style of ceramic ornament in Wessex, but which we would not have expected from a site so peripheral to the Wessex distribution at a time when the style was in any case in the process of decline. In view of the discovery of pottery

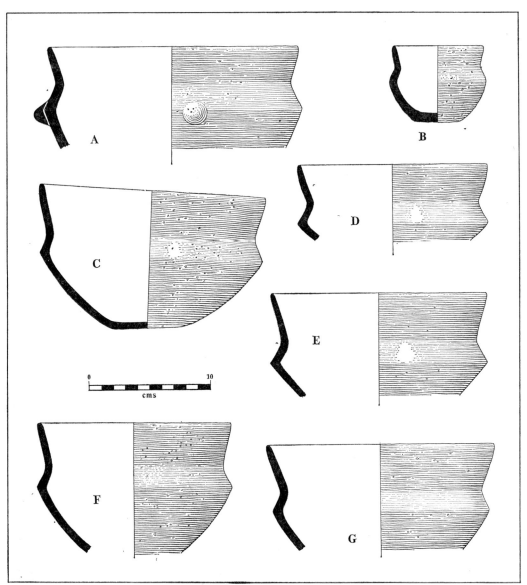

49. *Angular bowls from Woodeaton, Oxfordshire*

decorated in the Chinnor style at Hagbourne Hill, it is not difficult to establish a physical link with Wessex, of course, along the Icknield Way and Berkshire Ridgeway route, and we could perhaps evoke the originality and artistic ingenuity of the Chiltern potters to account for its resurgence at this time. But equally we may wonder how much later pottery with impressed and shallow-tooled (if not actually incised) ornament had originally such inlay, which has not survived because the paste has dissolved out in the ground. Certainly, one of the two saucepan-like pots from Compton Beauchamps in Berkshire retained a

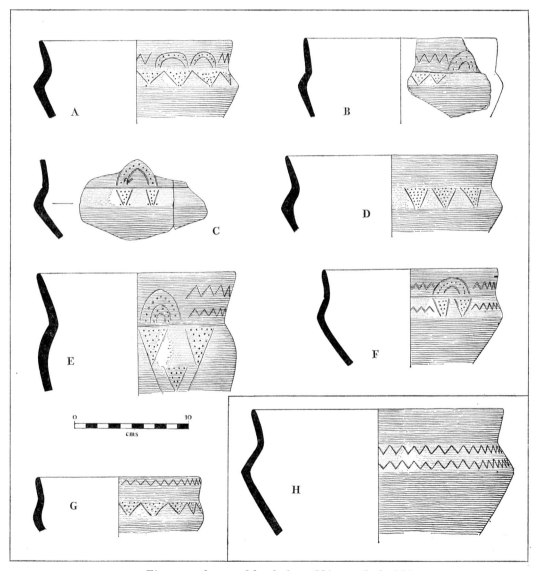

50. *Fine-ware decorated bowls from Chinnor, Oxfordshire*

white pasty filling in its panel of triangles and impressed dots, probably as late as the third century (D. W. Harding, 1972, 101–2, Pl. 65, F). The extent to which the style of ornament of the Chinnor bowls is indebted to the early Wessex fashion for deeply scored and punched decoration is, therefore, questionable. In Wessex, this style was seldom applied to bowls, and in consequence the outline of the design on the large Wessex jars is much cruder and bolder than the delicately incised geometric patterns at Chinnor. In fact, the Chinnor style, and in particular the use of the zig-zag motif, is in many respects closer to the early style of ornament exemplified on metalwork of the period, like the early La Tène dagger sequence from the Thames.

If there was a significant relationship between the ornamental style of the south-eastern angular bowls and Wessex, it should be sought, not in the early series there, but among the latest of the haematite-coated bowls, those which are distinguished by the addition of horizontal cordons and footring bases. The distribution of this group (Fig. 51) is concentrated mainly within a region little more than thirty miles in extent, around the valleys of the Bourne, Avon, Wylye, Nadder and Ebble in Wiltshire, and within this restricted zone the uniformity in style of decoration and fineness of fabric is remarkable. It was recognised long ago that these cordoned, haematite bowls and furrowed bowls did not regularly occur together on the same sites, except where there was evidently a prolonged occupation. Very few of the cordoned variety were found at All Cannings Cross or Longbridge Deverill, where the furrowed bowl was predominant. Conversely, at Meon Hill, Hants (Liddell, 1937, Pls 25 and 26), and in Wiltshire at Fifield Bavant Down (Clay, 1924, Pl. VI), Yarnbury (Cunnington, 1933, Fig. XIV), Figsbury (Cunnington, 1925, 51, footnote 1) and Swallowcliffe Down (Clay, 1925, Pl. VI), the cordoned bowls were in evidence almost to the exclusion of the furrowed bowl altogether. The lack of correspondence in the occurrence of these two major forms cannot be explained on grounds of geographical distribution, since the extremely localised cordoned bowl distribution is virtually at the hub of the furrowed bowl zone. If the difference is not geographical, it must surely be chronological; the two forms were successive and not contemporary. We have already seen that the furrowed bowls have a strong claim to chronological priority on the basis of the relationship to Continental antecedents. In the light of this, and considering the fact that the cordoned bowls are associated in general terms on several Wiltshire sites with pottery displaying Iron B characteristics, it seems likely that they are secondary in the haematite series to the furrowed bowls, and should probably be assigned initially to the fifth century B.C., rather than much earlier. That they were a purely indigenous development, however, is suggested not only by their limited geographical distribution but also by the absence of any obviously comparable group on the Continent. And though the very angular, plane-sided examples appear to be so alien to the ceramic traditions of the early Iron Age in Britain, a fairly simple process of development is indicated by the rounder profiles from Meon Hill, Hants, and Blewburton Hill in Berkshire (Fig. 52, B, C, D). The application of multiple cordons to bowls that are essentially still round-bodied vessels of Hallstatt derivation, as at Meon Hill and Blewburton Hill, eventually has the effect of sub-dividing

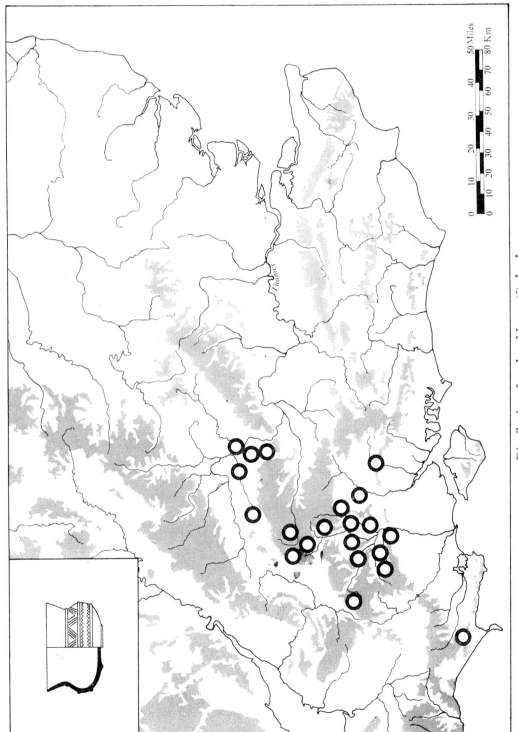

51. *Distribution of cordoned haematite bowls*

the surface of the pottery into panels, and a progressive angularisation of the profile. With the addition of a footring base, the fully developed cordoned haematite bowl is well illustrated by those from Swallowcliffe Down and Little Woodbury.

Whether or not, with the accumulation of stratified groups, the type-sequence proposed

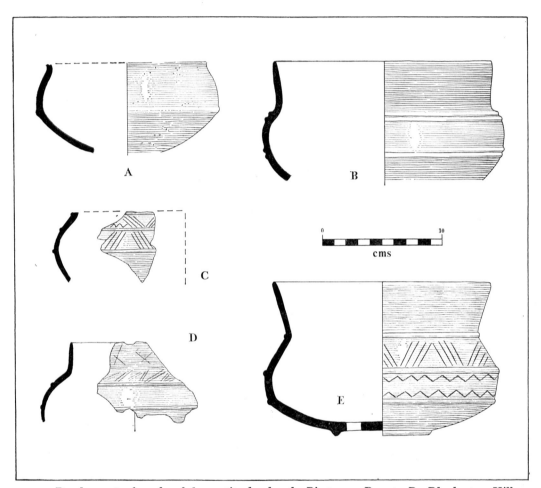

52. Development of cordoned haematite bowls. A, Pimperne, Dorset. B, Blewburton Hill, Berkshire. C and D, Meon Hill, Hampshire. E, All Cannings Cross, Wiltshire

here will be exonerated, the stylistic affinities between the Wessex cordoned bowls and the angular series of the Thames valley and the south-east of England are supported by the occurrence in both regions of fine, applied cordons and footring or pedestal bases. All three of these elements can also be traced to the Marne, the only point of divergence being that, whereas the south-eastern angular jars and bowls owe their shape very largely to Continental influence, in Wessex incised geometric designs, footrings and cordons are applied to a well-established insular variety of bowl. The zig-zag motif is common to all three ceramic groups, the British examples being abundantly paralleled on *vases carénés* at Sogny (Thiérot, 1930, Fig. 3), Marson and Étrechy (Morel, 1898, Pl. 6, 11, Pl. 19, 9) in the Marne or at Pernant (Lobjois, 1969, Fig. 103, 008.02) in the Aisne. In metalwork, the same design is incorporated in the openwork of the dagger-chape from Windsor, and again in the top of the sheath from Richmond. (Jope, 1961, Fig. 4, 20; Fig. 12. Dr Frank Schwappach has pointed out to me that all three motifs on the Richmond scabbard, the zig-zags, the dotted rosette and the H-motif are repeatedly found in the repertory of Central European girdle-plaques of Hallstatt D. The similarity of the Richmond design argues strongly for a dating of the scabbard hardly later than the first half of the fifth century, rather than mid-fourth, as suggested by Jope.) If further evidence for the stylistic relationship between the angular pottery and early La Tène daggers is required, we may compare the dot-filled triangles of the Chinnor bowls with the dotted infilling of the Hammersmith sheath (Richardson and Young, 1951, Fig. 7, 38, 41, 43 etc.; Jope, 1961, Pl. XXI, E).

In the light of such stylistic affinities between the angular pottery of the south-east and the early La Tène daggers of the Lower Thames region, and the independent chronologies advanced for each, there can be little doubt any longer that they both formed part of a contemporary cultural assemblage. The concentration of La Tène 1 daggers in the Lower Thames basin, with only the occasional example above Richmond, at first sight would appear to stand in contrast to the wider south-eastern distribution of angular wares (Fig. 53). But allowing for the fact that the greater number of daggers have been recovered from the river as a result of the dredging activities of the Thames Conservancy Board and the Port of London Authority, whereas settlement sites for the most part are notoriously unproductive of elaborate metalwork, the distribution of pottery and daggers seems reasonably complementary. But even if we accept the angular, black burnished pottery and the daggers as part of the same material culture, and assign both to the early La Tène phase in the south-east, we can hardly doubt that the daggers themselves were of insular manufacture, if we accept Jope's analysis of their construction and typology.

The crucial elements in the classification of these La Tène 1 daggers are technical details of their sheaths – the method of belt suspension and the construction of the chapes (Fig. 54). Jope has shown that the usual means of suspension of Continental sheaths was a broad strap, generally attached to the back plate of the bronze sheath, whereas in the British examples this is replaced by twin, parallel loops which served to suspend the sheath from the belt. This device was by no means a new departure in Britain; it had already been employed by armourers in the late Hallstatt phase, so that the indigenous origin of this technique requires no further demonstration. At the same time, there are several La Tène 1 daggers in Britain which do display the Continental strap-suspension, though sometimes imperfectly, as at Minster Ditch, near Oxford. In classifying the chapes of the British La Tène 1 sequence, however, Jope argued for a further development independent from Continental practice. Both have the common ancestry of the anchor-chape, which is illustrated by two sheaths from a late Hallstatt context at Les Jogasses (Favret, 1936, Fig.

9), and one from the Thames at Chelsea (Jope, 1961, Fig. 3, 11) (Fig. 54, A, B and E). But whereas the British chapes thereafter display a development in which the anchor terminals are bent back towards the stem of the sheath to form an open ring, the Continental series includes an alternative form, lacking in Britain, in which the terminals of the anchor are first tied back to the sheath by a chain or flexible strip of metal. Subsequently

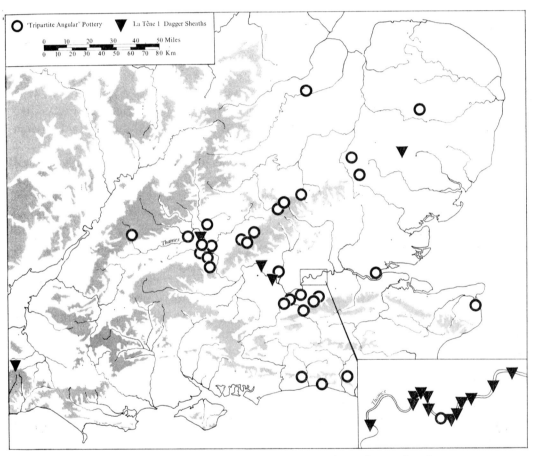

53. *Distribution of angular pottery and La Tène I dagger sheaths*

when the whole unit is cast in one piece many of the Continental chapes retain this notional division into two stages, clearly betraying the typological progression. In the light of this contrast it has been accepted generally that the British sheaths – in their surviving form – were of native manufacture. More puzzling is the continued absence in Britain at this period of the *long* sword, which on the Continent reappears in La Tène I after an intermission in the Hallstatt D phase; further research might still perhaps result in a revision of the chronology of our insular sequence. But we should beware of concluding that Jope's researches necessarily militate against the case for fifth-century incursions. The technical

168

details which he highlighted should not be allowed to obscure the fact that the slender La Tène I dagger in Britain differs markedly from earlier Hallstatt D types, and is essentially of Continental inspiration. In tracing any intrusive movement from abroad, the likelihood of locating archaeologically the original imports of invaders is fairly slight; the pottery and

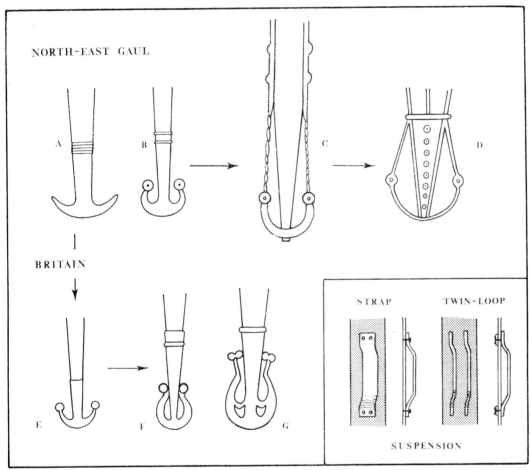

54. *Early La Tène dagger sheaths: chape development and suspension techniques. A and B, Les Jogasses, Marne. C, Marne (British Museum, Morel Collection). D, Varilles de Buoy, Marne. E, Thames at Chelsea. F, Thames at Westminster. G, Minster Ditch, Oxfordshire*

daggers, therefore, both clearly of insular manufacture, might nonetheless be regarded as the products of an intrusive population, manifesting itself archaeologically in modified form only after a period in which settlement has taken root. It is important to note, however, that certain of the Continental sheaths have already developed a complete ring from the knobbed-anchor tube-chape (Favret, 1936, Fig. 11, 3); it is the technique of casting the chape with solid metal between knobs and tube which is characteristically British. As far as the daggers are concerned, the closest the surviving British examples come to the Continental series is in the Chelsea sheath, whose anchor chape might be taken to indicate an early dating for the original cross-channel links. Thereafter, with sheaths requiring repair or replacement, we might anticipate that an element of insular independence would assert itself, if only as a result of an amalgamation of population.

Such an interpretation would be perfectly consistent with Jope's conclusion regarding the Minster Ditch sheath (Fig. 55), that it was 'the product of a continental-trained crafts-man at work (but not in full control) in a British workshop'. The chape, with its terminals cast in a single unit with the tubular stem, is clearly of British La Tène 1 form, as are the raised mouldings of the sheath. The belt attachment, on the other hand, is inspired by the Continental single-strap design, though here constructed less expertly by cutting parallel incisions in the back plate of the sheath, instead of attaching a separate strip of metal to it by means of rivets, as on the Continental models. The three circular mouldings above and below the strap are therefore purely ornamental, simulating the rivets of the original. The decorative design of the back plate itself may well have been a similar attempt to emulate the new Continental 'Waldalgesheim' style, with its more sinuous, curvilinear scrolls. (The term is derived from a chariot-burial, excavated in the later nineteenth century in the Rhineland, which included several gold bracelets ornamented in a vigorous curvilinear style. (Weerth, 1870.) See also Jacobstal, 1944; Jope, 1971a; Megaw, 1970; Driehaus, 1971; Zahlhaas, 1971.) But the British craftsman, lacking the feeling for, or the ability to achieve, the confident freehand mastery of the Waldalgesheim artists, resorted instead to the use of compasses to achieve his writhing, serpent's form design, which is stiffer and more mechani-cal in consequence. But this unsure and experimental move away from purely rectilinear, geometric motifs towards more flowing, curvilinear ornament represents the genesis of the mature La Tène ornamental style in Britain. In spite of its echoes of Continental themes, the Minster Ditch scabbard is probably well advanced in the La Tène 1 dagger series, and can scarcely be dated before the middle of the fourth century at the earliest. Thereafter, insular metalwork was to develop a style which, though parallel to, was not directly deter-mined by, the La Tène art style of Continental Europe.

If a similarity in ornamental style forms any basis for chronological equation, it would be tempting to assign the Blewburton Hill round-bodied bowl with proto-curvilinear decora-tion (Fig. 40, F) to the same period as the Minster Ditch scabbard. Here is the same use of compass-drawn curvilinear designs, and the same mechanical striving after a freehand, flowing style in which the potter never achieved quite the same freedom of expression as the metalsmith, even in the mature La Tène 2 phase. In terms of pottery form, as we have seen, the Blewburton bowl probably represents the latest in the Hallstatt-derived round-bodied bowl series, its only concession to the innovating angular style being its more pronounced and outward-flaring rim.

Not least among the innovations of the early La Tène period is the safety-pin type of brooch (Fig. 56). Hitherto, Hallstatt brooches of Continental type had occurred infre-quently in Britain and Ireland, and rarely in proper archaeological contexts. Now, for the first time, La Tène 1 brooches appear among the material artefacts from Iron Age settlements throughout southern Britain in significant numbers. For our present purposes, the most important of these is the La Tène 1a type, since it must have been in circulation by 400 B.C., during the period of angular pottery in the south-east of England. The characteristics diagnostic of the type are its high-arched bow, its high, often squarish, foot, and the

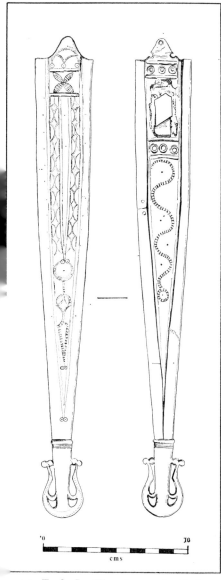

55. *Early La Tène dagger sheath from Minster Ditch, Oxford*

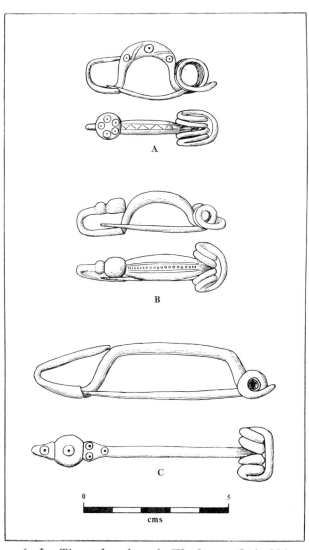

56. *La Tène 1 brooches. A, Woodeaton, Oxfordshire. B, Blandford, Dorset. C, Ham Hill, Somerset*

large coil-springs which provided tension for its pin. The design of this kind of brooch is not so eccentric as it may appear at first sight. The function of the spring and the pin is self-evident; the high bow is intended to take the folds of material of the garment; the foot incorporates the catch-plate which retains the pin in position when the brooch is closed. But in order that the foot should not catch in the clothing, it is bent round towards the bow, the essential characteristic of the La Tène 1 variant being that the foot is not attached directly to the bow. Frequently, the foot terminates in a small knob or disc, which, like the arch of the bow itself, may be the subject of simple, geometric decoration like the ring-and-dot motif on examples from Woodeaton, Oxon, and Maiden Castle, Dorset. The zig-zag, too, is an element of brooch decoration, as it was of both ceramic and scabbard ornament of the period. Some of these brooches, like those from Box, Wilts, Hunsbury, Northants, and Deal in Kent, Jope has suggested (1958, 74, note 31; 77, note 40. For other instances of the assimilation of Continental fashions, see Hodson, 1971) may even have been imports from the Continent, though this aspect is not especially crucial to our interpretation of their significance. Precise dating of these brooches on stylistic and typological grounds remains extremely problematical, though they must have continued well into the fourth century. The dotted and linear design on the side of the bow of the Woodeaton brooch, however, is so strikingly similar to the proto-curvilinear ornament of the fragmentary Blewburton bowl that we must surely consider the possibility that they were contemporary products.

From this brooch-type developed subsequently a variant form in which the bow and the foot are slightly lower, and the springs likewise become proportionally smaller. In due course, by the third century, this type was itself overtaken by the latest in the insular La Tène 1 series, characterised by a flattened and elongated bow, with flattened or sloping foot. From this type, a number of transitional examples lead into the La Tène 2 series, which will be the subject of a later chapter.

In dealing with the pottery and metal types which appear at the outset of the early La Tène phase, it has been necessary in some measure to anticipate subsequent developments of the insular Iron Age. We must now return to consider how long the fashion for angular pottery continued, and those ceramic forms which superseded it. In the absence of more conclusive evidence, we may suppose that angular profiles were on the wane by the second half of the fourth century, and that by 300 they were being replaced by various forms of vessel in the so-called 'smooth dark ware' of sites like Little Woodbury.

In Wessex meanwhile, beyond the primary angular zone, the duration of the broadly contemporary cordoned haematite bowls is equally a matter of speculation, though a clue to their ceramic successors is afforded by the early La Tène assemblage from Swallowcliffe Down in Wiltshire (Clay, 1925, esp. Pl. IV, 4 and 6). Here, several fragments of haematite bowls, some apparently lacking cordons, but of the same plane-sided category, occurred together with various coarse-ware vessels of Iron B character, and two fine-ware jars, the significance of which in the context of early La Tène connections with the Continent has attracted little attention since (Pl. XXI). Both vessels are in smooth, brown ware with traces of external burnishing, and are of similar profile, having a high, rounded shoulder with concave neck and short, everted rim, tapering below the shoulder towards a pedestal base, immediately above which, on one example, is an applied cordon. The two jars were found in separate pits, and unfortunately neither had useful associations. The origin of the pot form is not difficult to trace, however, for we have already seen that the round shouldered and frequently cordoned, pedestal jar (*vase piriforme*) constituted the second major pottery type of the early La Tène period in the Marne, where it was introduced from the Rhineland to become established side by side with the *vases carénés*, which it eventually superseded (Fig. 46). Since the connections between southern Britain and the Marne-culture region have already been amply witnessed by the angular pottery of south-eastern Britain, it is not especially surprising to find that these contacts were periodically renewed into the subsequent phase when the pear-shaped pedestal vase was dominant in the Marne.

It must be conceded, however, that good parallels in Britain for the Swallowcliffe Down jars are not numerous. The example cited by Clay from Fifield Bavant (1924, Pl. VII, 4) is not complete to the rim, but most probably was correctly restored by the excavator, while the reconstruction offered by Miss Richardson for the high-shouldered jars from Boscombe Down West, Wilts (1952, Fig. 10, 59), seems not unreasonable in view of the presence of a number of pedestals in similar fabric from pits elsewhere on the site. More recently, a complete profile was recovered from an Iron B context at Longbridge Deverill, the form of which is quite closely paralleled by the example without cordon from Swallow-cliffe Down. If a handful of examples seems insufficient to sustain substantial contact with the Continent, it may be countered that it is equally difficult to attribute any of the numerous pedestals from southern English sites to any other specific pottery form. Yet to one or other of the limited possibilities available they must have belonged, and it is probable that some at any rate were from vessels of the Swallowcliffe Down kind. It may be significant that the examples listed here are from a fairly restricted region in Wiltshire, as were the cordoned haematite bowls before them. Whether this points to the continuing activities of a local group of potters, anxious to explore and exploit new fashions from the Continent, or whether we should see these pedestal jars, as Hawkes believed, as evidence for renewed incursions from the Marne, remains a matter for debate. To some extent the question hinges on whether we should relate the Wessex jars to another group of pedestal pots, the footring bowls of the south-east of England. If the evidence propounded by Ward-Perkins for Oldbury (1944, 144–6) is valid, it would appear that the footring vessels of his 'Wealden culture' survived as late as the first century B.C., but it is clear from the material he cites that not every example in the south-east need, or should, be dated so late. The two vessels from Findon Park (Wolseley, Smith and Hawley, 1927, Figs 11 and 12), at any rate, must be earlier on account of their association with an iron La Tène 1 brooch, and we may wonder whether such instances point to a similar origin for both the south-eastern and Wessex pedestal vases.

Before attempting to draw this evidence together, we should consider the chronology of the outstanding and unique La Tène groups in eastern Yorkshire (Stead, 1965). Even opponents of the 'invasion hypothesis' have recognised that the combination of the distinctive cart-burials and square-ditched enclosures of the Arras culture, with their accompanying grave-goods of vehicle fittings and horse-gear, must signify an intrusive population whose origins lay somewhere in the vicinity of the Champagne. As yet, however, there is less agreement concerning the date when this invasion into eastern Yorkshire took place. The type-site itself should be assigned to the second century B.C., and for the most part the remaining evidence accords with a late dating for the Arras culture, which Hawkes classified as 'Eastern Second B'. But most important in the present context is the Cowlam grave,

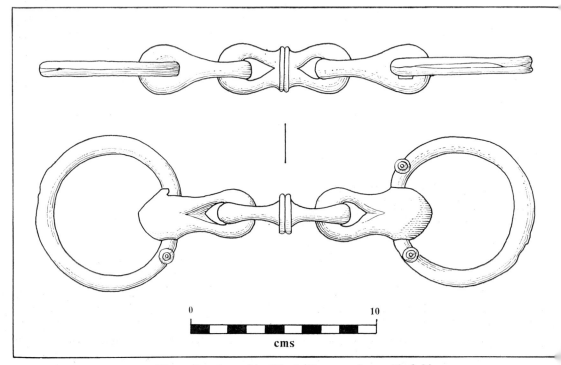

0   10

cms

57. Three-piece horse-bit, King's Barrow, Arras, Yorkshire

which included among its grave-goods a brooch of La Tène 1a type, together with two bracelets, both of which can be paralleled at Arras itself, but which otherwise are not common forms in British or Continental La Tène contexts. Since a bracelet comparable to one of these Cowlam examples was found some years ago with a similar La Tène 1a brooch at Yvonand in Switzerland (Viollier, 1916, Pl. 2, no. 39; 22, no. 122; Stead, 1965, 81–2), Stead is rightly reluctant to dismiss the Cowlam association, which would seem, therefore, to argue an early – perhaps fifth century – inception of the Arras culture. Corroborative evidence for this early initial dating might be inferred from the typology of horse-bits from the Yorkshire graves. Continental analogues for these distinctive three-piece bits (Fig. 57) are concentrated in the Marne and Aisne regions, where associated grave-goods suggest

XXII *Bronze scabbard-mount, Standlake, Oxfordshire (width: c. 5 cm)*

XXIV *and* XXV *Bronze shield, Witham, Lincolnshire: (left) general view; (below) detail (length: 1·13 m)*

XXVI *Grave-group from Aylesford, Kent (diameter of bucket: c. 26·7 cm)*

XXVII *Silver cups from Welwyn, Hertfordshire (rim diameter of handled cup: c. 10·8 cm)*

they belong to a La Tène I horizon (Ward-Perkins, 1939; C. Fox, 1946, 27 ff; Barber and Megaw, 1963; Stead, 1965, 37 ff). In fact, the closest parallel for the Yorkshire series is from the famous chariot burial from Somme-Tourbe – 'La Gorge-Meillet' (Fourdrignier, 1878) which included not only two La Tène Ia brooches, but also an imported Etruscan beaked flagon of the late fifth century. The introduction into Britain of the three-link bit cannot be much delayed beyond this date, before on the Continent its popularity declined in favour of its counterpart, the two-link snaffle-bit. The available evidence therefore, consistently argues a late fifth- or early fourth-century dating for the beginning of the La Tène immigration into eastern Yorkshire, at which time such a movement might be seen as an extension of the fifth-century connection between the south-east of Britain and the Marne. (In 1939, Ward-Perkins had placed this event at the close of the La Tène I phase, 'on the most deflated chronology, . . . hardly later than about 250 B.C.', i.e. the key date then assigned to the Marnian invasion. With the currently extended framework, these events must now be placed nearer the end of the fifth century B.C.)

If we accept this dating for the Cowlam grave group, however, a comparison between Cowlam and the Arras cemetery introduces consequential complications. In addition to the bracelets mentioned above, a string of beads from Cowlam is quite closely paralleled by the necklace in the Queen's barrow at Arras. The comparison between the two sites is further sustained by the fact that both incorporate the same burial rite of single inhumation under a small barrow. If Cowlam is to be dated to the end of the fifth century, there opens up a hiatus of two hundred years or more between it and the main Arras group, with a marked paucity of sites to fill the intervening span of time. Nonetheless, Stead concludes, 'there can be little doubt that Cowlam belongs to this very early La Tène phase, and the similarity between the graves there and at Arras provides an argument in favour of an early date for the Yorkshire invasion' (1965, 82). If we accept Stead's assessment of the Yorkshire evidence, we are faced with the prospect of an invasion at the end of the fifth or perhaps the beginning of the fourth century B.C., which, at that date, has left remnants, both structural and material, which are even more meagre in the archaeological record than that which has been furnished by Hawkes and others for a Marnian immigration into south-eastern England at very nearly the same period.

Though the general affinities between the cart-burials of the Arras culture and the burials of the Champagne are self-evident, the precise origins of the Yorkshire immigration are more difficult to determine. Equally, the Arras culture itself is defective in certain categories of evidence, such as pottery of clearly Continental manufacture or inspiration. Even the grave-goods of the Arras burials are limited in their range by comparison with the variety of ornamented metalwork from the Champagne. To explain this discrepancy, a number of reasons could be contrived: that the invaders were warrior bands who left their womenfolk at home and were dependent for their pottery upon the local population whom they suppressed; that the graves were of the aristocracy only, and therefore not representative of a true cross-section of the culture. Neither of these explanations really rings true. The fact remains that the evidence for an early La Tène invasion of eastern Yorkshire, telling as it is, is very incomplete archaeologically, and the inconsistencies of the burial evidence are only further exacerbated by the absence of innovating settlement patterns or house-types. The real lesson of the Yorkshire material is that, for reasons which we can only guess at, an invasion may only make its true impact felt in the archaeological record some time – even centuries – after the initial immigration has taken place. And had it not been for the survival of its distinctive mode of burial, the Arras culture, as represented by other material or structural types, would probably never have been accepted by prehistorians as the product of an invasion at all.

With this salutary warning in mind, we may review the evidence for a Marnian invasion into southern Britain. Ceramically, the south-eastern distribution of angular jars and bowls affords the most reliable reflection of the area which came under the influence of the early La Tène culture of the Champagne, supplemented in some measure by the La Tène I daggers from the Lower Thames basin. Other metal types – such as the La Tène Ia brooches – might be expected to have a wider distribution, since they would readily have been traded from one neighbourhood to the next; nonetheless they, too, could have been introduced initially, together with horse-bits of the three-link variety, by immigrants and traders in the second half of the fifth century. If the Lower Thames basin formed the focus of innovation, secondary influences certainly permeated westward into Wessex, where first the haematite-coated, cordoned bowls represent an insular reaction to the new ceramic fashions, to be followed before the end of the fourth century by pedestal vases whose affinities with the Marne were more direct. And if the primary settlement of the south-east set off repercussions in Wessex, so, too, did it stimulate a secondary immigration, not necessarily from exactly the same point of departure, into eastern Yorkshire, where subsequently the Arras culture was to emerge as a distinctive entity two centuries or more later. In the south-east, the case for direct colonisation from the Marne would evidently be enhanced by the location and identification of settlement remains, perhaps even rectangular houses, and a class of burials which could be associated with such an intrusive population. Such a complete reflection of a prehistoric culture is seldom likely to survive, however, as the Yorkshire evidence itself indicates. In the meantime, the accumulation of evidence for an early La Tène immigration, centred upon the south-east of England, seems to the present writer to extend beyond the limits that can be accounted for by trade alone.

The middle La Tène phase: consolidation and insular developments

WE HAVE already seen in the previous chapter that, by the middle of the fourth century B.C., attempts were being made by British metalworkers and potters to achieve a freer, curvilinear style of ornament, uninhibited by the rigid geometric symmetry of the early La Tène phase. The elementary spirals of the Box brooch, the writhing snake design of the Minster Ditch scabbard, and even the rudimentary and mechanical scrolls of the Blewburton bowl attest an increasing interest in the sinuous, flowing style which came to characterise mature Celtic art in Britain and on the Continent.

The emergence of this Celtic art-style in Central Europe was first analysed in detail by Jacobstal (1944), whose classification has remained the basis for all subsequent studies. Its earliest manifestation he termed the 'Early Style', which represented a fusion of indigenous Hallstatt geometric and bird motifs with formal plant designs adopted from classical Greece, and even more exotic elements derived ultimately from Scythian or oriental sources. The chronology of the Early Style is fairly well attested from a number of princely burials, especially in the Rhineland and south-west Germany, where lavishly ornamented grave-goods are accompanied by imported Etruscan bronze flagons and Greek black-figure pottery. By the middle of the fourth century, Continental craftsmen had developed a more vigorous, curvilinear style which Jacobstal named after the type-site of Waldalgesheim on the Middle Rhine. (For principal published references, see Megaw, 1970, and Jope, 1971a. For a recent contradiction of the view that the site comprised two successive graves, see Driehaus, 1971, and for a recent study of the bronze *situla*, see Zahlhaas, 1971.) The rich grave-goods from this barrow reflect the transition from the Early Style to the style to which the burial gives its name. The earlier material at Waldalgesheim included a Campanian bronze *situla* with Greek palmette-derived ornament, which was probably manufactured towards the end of the fourth century, and a beaked flagon, decorated in the Early Style with a panel of tightly-interlocking S-shaped curls, which may well have been old when buried. The goldwork from the grave included a pair of hollow bracelets, an armring and a torc, ornamented in the classic Waldalgesheim style. To define the particular quality which characterises the Waldalgesheim art-style is not a simple task, though particular motifs can certainly be isolated. Various writers have referred to its sinuous, fleshy scrolls, its use of the *triskele*, often in a continuous curvilinear sequence, or its writhing and asymmetric plant spirals. In a more flippant vein, we might be tempted to use phrases like 'spaghetti ornament' or 'sweet-pea ornament' in order to describe its twisting, flowing tendril patterns. Perhaps the vigorous, confident and yet subtly experimental quality

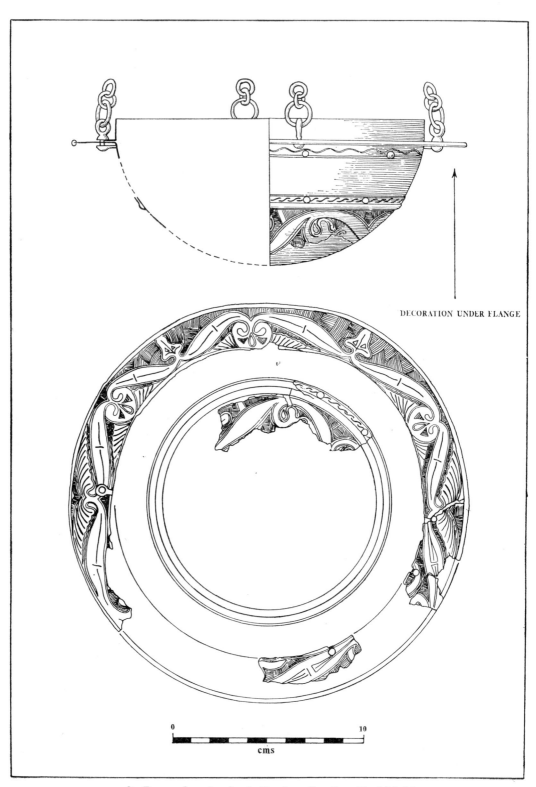

DECORATION UNDER FLANGE

0   10

cms

58. *Bronze hanging-bowl, Cerrig-y-Drudion, Denbighshire*

of the style is best summarised by Megaw's allusion to its 'assured irrationality' on the lower panel of the Amfreville helmet. Subsequent to the Waldalgesheim phase, there developed an exuberant relief-style of ornament known as the Plastic Style, and simultaneously the low relief plant motifs were increasingly adopted by scabbard-engravers to produce what Jacobstal termed the Sword Style. It is to the transition from the Waldalgesheim style to the Sword Style on the Continent that Jope has traced the genesis of the La Tène style in the British Isles (1958).

In the early La Tène period, the kind of ornament which typifies the pottery of the angular series, and many of the La Tène 1 brooches in Britain, generally consists of symmetrical and rather uninspired geometric designs, comparable in some aspects to the repetitive border panels of the Continental Early Style, developing parallel, though not necessarily in response, to it. One outstanding item of metalwork, which Fox related to this Early Style (1958a, 1 and Fig. 1), is the fragmentary hanging-bowl from Cerrig-y-Drudion in Denbighshire (Fig. 58). The underside of the flange of the bowl is decorated with an arrangement of split-palmette motifs, fanning out against a background of alternate linear hatching, a method of background infilling which can be paralleled on the Continent in early La Tène contexts, but which subsequently becomes a characteristic of the western style of La Tène ornament in the British Isles. Both Fox and Jope were inclined to attribute the Cerrig-y-Drudion bowl to a Gaulish workshop of the later fourth or early third centuries B.C., but we may prefer to compromise by suggesting that it was the product of an immigrant metalworker operating under the patronage of a British master. Also derived from the split-palmette motif is the fleshy scroll design on the scabbard plate from Wisbech in Cambridgeshire (Fig. 59), which likewise has been regarded as a Continental import. The ornament itself is executed by means of a rocked tracer, the technique whereby the craftsman holds his implement at an angle to the working-surface, and traces out a line by a series of rocking movements to produce a kind of *tremolo*-effect. The technique is characteristic of engraving in the Sword Style, both on the Continent and in Britain, where it can be seen in an early context on the Minster Ditch scabbard. The relationship between the interlocking S-scrolls of the Wisbech scabbard and the split-palmette design of the Cerrig-y-Drudion style has been taken as evidence that the Wisbech piece was the product of a 'western' school, a view that cannot be contradicted by the uncertain provenance of the find. On the other hand, the border ornament of alternate hatched and plain triangles which frames the central design has been compared by Piggott (1950, 4–5) to the geometric decoration of the early La Tène dagger-sheaths from the Thames. Crude though its execution may be, the Wisbech ornament is evidently aspiring towards the sinuous quality of Continental Waldalgesheim models.

The extent to which the Waldalgesheim style made any real impact upon the insular metalworkers is questionable. Attempts have been made to recognise the inspiration of the Continental fashion in several individual items from Britain, among them the 'horn-cap' from Brentford (C. Fox, 1958, Pls 3 and 4; Megaw, 1970, 97–8, No. 130), which Megaw would prefer to see in the first century B.C., divorced from any Waldalgesheim affiliations.

Other possible illustrations include the ornament on the foot-plates of the Beckley and Woodeaton involuted brooches (Fig. 64), in which the use of fragmented Waldalgesheim motifs may be recognised. In this instance, of course, there can be no doubt that the brooches were the product of British bronze-smiths, since the type itself, as we shall see in due course, is an insular invention of La Tène 2. On the other hand, the bracelet from Newnham Croft, Cambridgeshire (Fig. 29, A) has been claimed as a possible import. Found in 1903, in a 'chariot-burial' with a con-tracted male inhumation, it is decorated with a spindly, twisting, curvilinear design which winds around the armring, in low relief, in a manner not unlike Continental Waldal-gesheim antecedents. At the same time, the combination of this style with the use of background hatching could be taken to indi-cate its insular manufacture. This view is reinforced by the elaborate coral-studded brooch from the same assemblage, which incorporates a positively insular swivel-pin mechanism instead of a spring. Among the remaining grave-goods was a cast bronze harness-fitting, in shape not unlike the Brentford 'horn-cap', and two penannular brooches which could date anywhere from the fourth century B.C. onwards. In spite of Megaw's propensity for late dating, there seems no reason to invoke an unnecessary degree of artistic archaism for the Newnham Croft grave-group; a third century date would not seem out of keeping with its com-bination of Continental and insular styles.

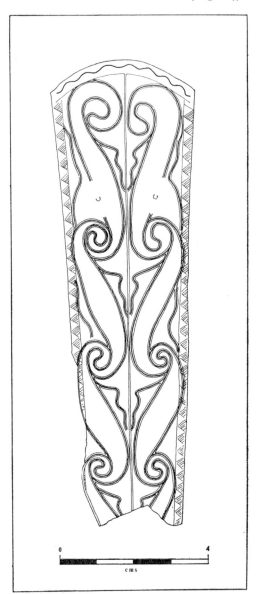

59. *Bronze scabbard-plate, Wisbech, Cambridgeshire*

Metal objects whose ornamental motifs have been attributed to Continental inspira-tion are by no means restricted to southern Britain. Waldalgesheim elements were re-cognised by Piggott in his stylistic analysis (Atkinson and Piggott, 1955; Megaw, 1970, 145–6, Pls 244–5; Stevenson, 1966, 24, Pl. 1) of the Torrs Chamfrein (Pl. XXII), originally discovered in 1829 in a peat bog in Kirkcudbrightshire, and for some years in the possession of the novelist Sir Walter Scott. The chamfrein comprised a pony-cap, with two circular openings for the animal's ears, and two bronze horns, said to have been found on the same site, and subsequently re-stored rather eccentrically in a position surmounting the pony-cap itself. The decoration of the two components is not identical stylistically. That of the cap, hammered up from the inside in the *repoussé* technique, consists of two principal elements, based upon the open-looped *pelta*, each element terminating in a characteristic coiled motif in which the knobbed tendrils apparently simulate a stylised bird's head, in a fashion which is quite closely paralleled in northern Ireland by the bronze horn-mount from Lough-na-Shade in Co. Armagh (Megaw, 1970, 147, No. 246). The feathery ornament of the horns, on the other hand, is much more reminiscent of the scabbard-engravers' style, while its incorpora-tion of a miniature human head, rare in insular Celtic art, certainly recalls a variety of Continental prototypes.

A development which more clearly equates with the Continental Sword Style may be illustrated by a series of swords, dating from the third century B.C. onwards, from the neighbourhood of the River Bann in Co. Antrim, including those from Lisnacrogher, Toome and Coleraine (Jope, 1954; Megaw, 1970, 148, Nos 248–9). Jope has argued that this localised group represents the parade armour of several generations, produced in a tradition first inspired by the work of an immigrant master-craftsman (1958, 79–80). In spite of a current trend towards later dating of these Irish swords, there can be no doubt that Jope was right to emphasise the Continental derivation of the Lisnacrogher swords, the open chape of one in particular being clearly in the Continental, and not British, La Tène I tradition. Further evidence for an intrusive movement into Ireland at the end of the fourth century has been inferred from the famous Turoe stone (Megaw, 1970, 97, No. 129), which shares with certain of the swords the use of the stepped design derived ultimately from the Greek-key motif. Originally located within the fortified enclosure, or rath, at Feewore, the stone is sculptured in low relief with an intricate design of fleshy, swirling tendrils reminiscent of the Waldalgesheim ornament carved on the Pfalzfeld pillar (Jacob-stal, 1944, No. 11).

Whether or not we can really isolate a significant Continental inspiration for these artefacts depends upon a detailed analysis of their component elements: recognition of a generalised aspiration towards more sinuous, curvilinear designs is scarcely sufficient to sustain direct links with the Continental mainstream of metalwork. In any analysis, we should be cautious in assuming that an item of ornamented metalwork will necessarily be the product of a single phase or workshop. Unlike pottery which, once broken, is useless, scabbards, armour and other items of ornamental bronze are likely to have been repaired frequently, and handed down from generation to generation.

Such a process results in composite pieces, like the Standlake scabbard, from Oxford-shire (D. W. Harding, 1972, 103–4, Pls 78–9 and frontispiece; Case, 1949). All that survives of the scabbard is the chape and side-binding, made of iron and enclosing an ornamental bronze strip, and a bronze mount originally attached near the hilt. The remainder of the scabbard was presumably of leather or some similar perishable material, and the surviving fragments are now held together only by the iron blade of the sword, which was in its sheath at the time it was deposited. The chape terminal is formed by an arrangement of four leaf-shaped elements in open ring form, in the tradition of La Tène I weapons described in an earlier section. Unlike the La Tène I daggers from the Thames, however, with their bronze sheaths, the chape of the Standlake sword was attached to its leather scabbard by means of iron side-binding, held taut at its upper end by an iron cross-bridge, which is modelled on the bird-bridges of Swiss middle La Tène sword scabbards. This particular feature argues a dating towards the end of the third century at earliest. On the other hand, the plate which the side-binding encloses and overlaps is ornamented with a freehand, curvilinear design with swirling branches, reminiscent of the Waldalgesheim style, set against a background of irregular hatching which may be compared with that of the Cerrig-y-Drudion bowl. The upper plate (Pl. XXIII) is rather better preserved than the chape-plate. It is dominated by a central *pelta* suspended from a loop, in relief, from which there extend spatulate branches for which Waldalgesheim parallels could be cited, though the curious sycamore-leafed shape of these appendages can also be found on a number of Continental gold ornaments in the Early Style. Once again, the central motif is backed with irregular hatching, executed with a rocked tracer. If the Standlake scabbard was plainly an insular product, the elements which it had absorbed from Continental sources are equally clear.

In general, British swords of the middle La Tène period (Fig. 60) owe little to the development of the parallel Continental series. Like the Continental swords and scabbards, however, their classification has been based very largely upon individual features such as the form of chape, the shape of the hilt and other aspects of scabbard embellishment. Few of the British examples come from good associated contexts, and dating therefore remains fairly subjective, and based entirely upon our interpretation of these typological and decorative traits. The Hunsbury group of scabbards – Piggott's Group II (1950) – are characterised by their heart-shaped chapes, often terminating in a slight lobe: at the point where the chape itself meets the side-binding, several examples display a slight moulding on either side. This type is not obviously related to Continental chapes, which for La Tène itself have been studied and classified in detail by de Navarro (1959; 1972). On the British series, the side-binding is frequently supported by continuous metal strips from one side to the other, and these, as at Hunsbury, may form a surface for ornamentation. Very occasionally, as on the back of the Bugthorpe scabbard, and on the chape from the Thames at Little Wittenham, the space between the side-binding may be used to enclose an openwork design. At the top of the scabbard, the British examples, like their Continental counterparts, had an arched profile, the function of which was presumably to guide the sword into the mouth of the scabbard. Even so, the Continental scabbards tend to differ from the rounded cocked-hat mouths of the insular sheaths, being frequently more elaborate in their pointed crown-shaped extensions. As Piggott has shown, the distribution of this class of scabbard is fairly widespread over southern, central and eastern England, with a noteworthy outlier at Llyn Cerrig Bach in Anglesey, which might well be later than the main distribution series.

A significant variant upon this type had a more limited circulation in the north-east of England and south-eastern Scotland. It is well represented by the scabbard found in the nineteenth century in a burial at Bugthorpe in the East Riding, which Piggott chose as representative of the group (Fig. 61). Unlike the remainder of the series, however, the Bugthorpe scabbard has an iron back-plate, while the bronze front from hilt to chape is more extensively decorated than any other British scabbard. Most characteristic of the type is the heavy cast chape, the upper ends of which bend inwards across the body of the scabbard to meet, forming a closed heart shape. At the tip of the chape, the lobe of the Hunsbury type is developed into distinctive twin lips, which, Megaw has aptly observed, resemble the pouting mouth of a fish, particularly if the chape is viewed sideways, when its trumpet decoration could be taken to form one eye. At the top of the side-binding are two circular 'buttons', which probably retained inlay of coral or enamel; these are matched by a similar pair of studs just below the mouth of the scabbard. The decoration consists of an irregularly repetitive trail of curvilinear designs, filled with matted hatching in a manner which has been frequently compared to the late La Tène mirror style of ornament. In fact, though there clearly is a stylistic affiliation, the Bugthorpe decoration still has not quite achieved the emphasis upon squared hatching which is the especial characteristic of mirror ornament. The openwork on the back of the scabbard between the side-binding of the chape has already been compared to the chape from Little Wittenham, which belongs within Piggott's Hunsbury class of Group II scabbards; both doubtless should be assigned to a first century B.C. context. As for the north-eastern group, which includes the sword from a warrior's grave within the hillfort at Grimthorpe, also in the East Riding, Stead's proposal that they should be interpreted as the weapons of warriors driven north from Lincolnshire or East Anglia as a result of Belgic invasions into the south-east of England around, or shortly after, 100 B.C. seems plausible, and need raise no conflict with the stylistic affiliations of the group.

From this north-eastern series, a group of weapons emerges in the first century A.D., of which the sword discovered in the Stanwick hoard may be regarded as typical (Piggott, 1950, Fig. 9; MacGregor, 1962, Fig. 2). The Stanwick scabbard displays two particular developments. One is a reversal of the previous position of the belt-mount, which is now attached centrally to the front plate of the scabbard; the second is the exaggeration of the twin-lips of the chape into really solid, cast projections, which, on the swords from Morton-hall, Edinburgh and Embleton, Cumberland, begin to resemble a seal's flippers or the whiskers of an aged walrus. Further adaptations in the hilt-typology of this group have been analysed in detail by Piggott, and need not detain us here.

One further class of weapons deserves to be mentioned at this point, the so-called anthropoid swords and daggers which have been studied and classified by Hawkes (R. R. Clarke and C. F. C. Hawkes, 1955). These peculiar weapons derive ultimately in their design from late Hallstatt models, though in their properly developed form they belong entirely to the

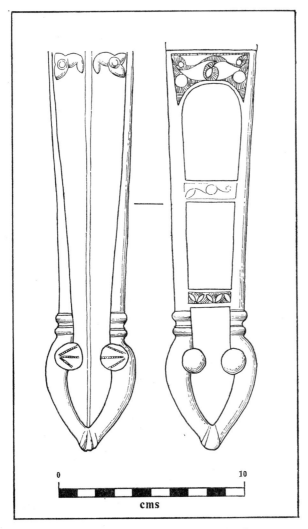

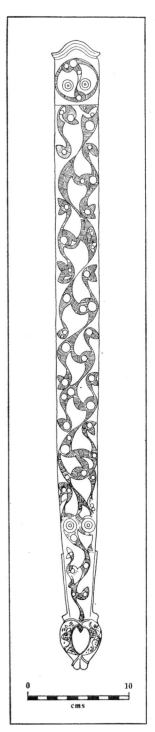

60. *La Tène scabbard-chape from Hunsbury,*
    Northamptonshire

61. *Scabbard from*
    Bugthorpe, Yorkshire

period of La Tène 1–3. The classification of the daggers depends entirely upon the design of their hilts, which are shaped like an outstretched human form (Fig. 62). The arms and legs are essentially functional, providing protection for the hand and a firmer grip for use in thrust-and-parry combat. The head corresponds to the pommel, and it may project outwards, or alternatively may sometimes be retracted between the branches of the arms, or even occasionally, in some of the early examples, omitted altogether. Both arms and legs may vary in shape, including V, Y and U profiles. Whichever pattern is adopted, there is generally a uniformity displayed by the hilt, though sometimes the shape of the legs may be adapted to suit the blade of the sword or the cocked-hat mouth of its scabbard. The critical trait for distinguishing the position of the weapon in the chronological sequence is

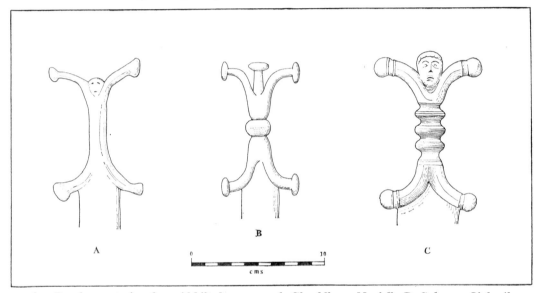

62. *Development of anthropoid hilted weapons. A, Shouldham, Norfolk. B, Sulmona, L'Aquila degli Abruzzi, Italy. C, North Grimston, Yorkshire*

the design of the central hand-grip of the hilt. In the early La Tène examples, this is invariably a simple straight grip, sometimes showing a slight swelling towards the centre. In La Tène 2, the hilt acquires a raised moulding in the grip, which evidently facilitated a more snug fit within the user's hand. Towards the end of the La Tène 2 phase, and continuing into La Tène 3, this develops into a multiple arrangement of three or more raised mouldings. From about 100 B.C., the heads of these La Tène 3 weapons acquire classical features, in those regions of Gaul and Britain which had not yet come under direct Roman subjugation.

The European distribution of this class of weapon includes a limited number of examples from Britain. Among the earliest of these is the sword from Shouldham, in Norfolk, which was the stimulus for Hawkes' enquiry. Also within the La Tène 1 group is the extraordinarily elaborate weapon from 'Hertford Warren' near Bury St Edmunds, Suffolk, which has the appropriate, early form of hand-grip, but with the arms and legs developed to include an openwork arrangement between the individual limbs. This dagger is closely paralleled by an example from Havelte, Drenthe in the Netherlands, to such an extent that we might wonder whether they were the work of the same armourer (Jope, 1961, Fig. 13). The middle category, with single raised moulding, is as yet not represented in Britain at all. The late La Tène group, on the other hand, is represented by several insular examples, including one from Ballyshannon Bay, Co. Donegal, in which the head displays certain limited 'classicising' features. Historically it is not easy to equate any of these weapons with any particular culture or movement of population into Britain. Even though the British distribution is so sketchy as to permit no sound inferences at present, there is certainly a contrast between the occurrence of late types of anthropoid swords in Britain and the areas of primary Belgic settlement. It seems improbable, therefore, that the arrival of these later weapons has any direct correlation with Belgic immigration into the south-east of England, though the La Tène 1 examples might in due course be shown to correspond in their distribution to the area into which early La Tène immigrations from the Continent have been postulated.

Another composite work which was doubtless old when lost, or deposited, was the ceremonial shield found in the river Witham, in Lincolnshire, in 1826 (Pl. XXIV). The later Bronze Age type of circular shield may well have continued in use into the early Iron Age; but by the end of the third century, there is the evidence of Pergamon sculptures to supplement archaeological information concerning the introduction of the long Celtic shield. Powell (1958, 107, Pls 3, 47, 48 and notes) has aptly cited the shield on which the famous 'Dying Gaul' (modelled on a bronze original erected by Attalos I), is kneeling, and the carvings from the temple of Athene Nikephorus at Pergamon, executed in the reign of his son, Eumenes II (197–159) as evidence for the currency of the long shield, with its pronounced midrib and central boss, in Central Europe by middle La Tène times. The Witham shield, with its parallel-sided and round-ended form, was originally constructed of two large sheets of bronze, whose joint is concealed by the central spine of its later embellishment. To its outer face was riveted a boar image, whose spindly, long-legged outline is still visible as a 'ghost' staining the bronze backing. Subsequently, this apotropaic or cult image was replaced by the more elaborate central boss, with its mature, swelling loop-and-*pelta* design and red glass inlay. From this central *umbo*, whose raised form conceals the functional hand-grip behind the shield, extend the arms of the spine towards a pair of terminal discs, supported on stylised horses' or bulls' heads. The background of these discs is filled with an engraved design comprising split-palmettes and hair-spring spirals which, as Megaw has observed (1970, 149–50, No. 252 and Pl. VII), reproduce in circular form the linear ornament of the Irish scabbards, though rather more elegantly. Finally, the whole applied fixture is bordered with a punched line, produced by alternately-angled blows of the metalsmith's tool, in the same technique as is displayed on the Torrs chamfrein.

The Witham shield probably belongs to the second century B.C. Together with the sword found nearby, and the shield bosses from the Thames at Wandsworth, it represents the culmination of the mature Celtic art-style on parade armour of the British Iron Age.

The insular character of the metalworkers' craft, which we have seen witnessed by many of the swords and scabbards of the middle La Tène phase, is equally reflected from the end of the third century by a growing independence, and indeed new inventiveness, in the production of small personal bronzes like brooches. The basic Continental type of La Tène 2 brooch is certainly represented in Britain, though not in great numbers (Fig. 63). Typologically, it is distinguished from all its La Tène 1 predecessors by its foot, which, instead of merely turning back towards the bow, actually clasps the arch of the bow by means of

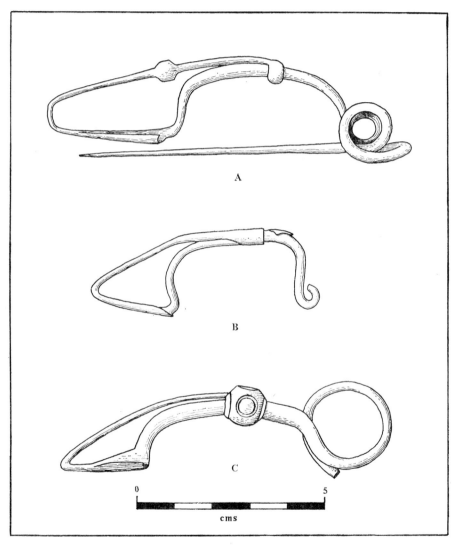

63. *La Tène 2 brooches. A, La Tène, Switzerland. B, Royal Exchange, London. C, Maiden Castle, Dorset (partly restored)*

a collar. We have already noted that the latest in the foregoing sequence of La Tène 1 brooches was one in which the bow became elongated and flattened, as at Swallowcliffe Down. The long, flat-bowed brooch now appears, particularly in eastern Yorkshire, with its foot attached to the bow in the La Tène 2 manner, though generally not to the centre, but to the end, of the arch. The example from Sawdon is of especial interest, since it displays not only this feature, but a second element which is an insular development in La Tène 2, the substitution of a hinge-mechanism for the spring. Quite evidently, British brooch-makers found the traditional spring was prone to break under constant flexing, and in consequence they devised a variety of alternative mechanisms, including a system of hingeing

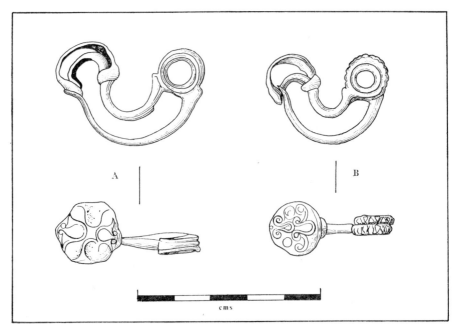

64. *Involuted brooches. A, Beckley, Oxfordshire. B, Woodeaton, Oxfordshire*

which Stead has termed the drum-swivel, incorporated in the Sawdon brooch. In some instances, like Sawdon, this device is concealed within the framework of a skeumorphic spring, perhaps indicating that innovation was less readily accepted among a conservative population than it was among the technicians themselves.

At sites as far afield as Danes Graves in the East Riding (Stead, 1965, Fig. 26, 1–3) and Cold Kitchen Hill in Wiltshire (Goddard, 1894, Pl. facing p. 285, 2, 3), these flat-bowed brooches have been found together – though not in direct association – with another innovating and distinctively insular type, the involuted brooch (Fig. 64), which typologically would appear to be derived from it. In essence, the involuted brooch is a flat-bowed brooch with its back broken, that is, with the ends bent upwards to create the reverse of an arch in the bow. At the same time, the foot is bent back and attached to the sagging bow by means of a collar in the La Tène 2 fashion, and then frequently elaborated by the expansion of the foot-disc into a large sub-circular plate which forms a convenient surface for decoration. Both the Woodeaton and Beckley, Oxfordshire, involuted brooches are ornamented in this manner, with fragmented Waldalgesheim-derived motifs. Like the advanced variety of flat-bowed brooch, the involutes also incorporate a hinge mechanism instead of the earlier form of coil-spring. The distribution of involuted brooches is quite wide (Jope, 1965, Fig. 6), though not especially intense: examples are spread from the Thames valley into Wessex, with a regional group in Yorkshire, and outliers in Cornwall and Wales. Chronologically, they must have been in circulation by the end of the third century, continuing in use probably quite late in the first century B.C.

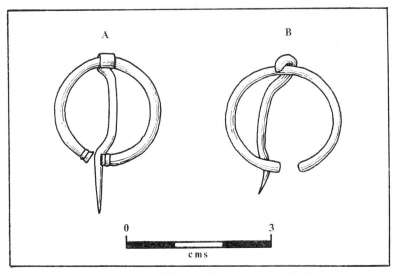

65. *Penannular brooches. A, Maiden Castle, Dorset. B, Meare, Somerset*

One other type has been claimed as an insular invention of this period, the penannular brooch, the early equivalent, as Megaw has described it, of the modern kilt-pin (Fig. 65). Brooches of this kind are known in Spain and Portugal, but otherwise are not widely represented on the Continent. Since the British brooches appeared to be typologically simpler than their peninsular counterparts, Mrs Fowler (1960b) was inclined to regard them as a product of this phase of insular ingenuity and inventiveness, whence they were subsequently exported to Spain and Portugal. Their origin in Britain she traces to a native development from the ring-headed pin, though this view has been challenged by Stead, who prefers to regard them still as ultimately of Continental derivation via an Atlantic trade route (1965, 48–9).

Up to now, nothing has been said regarding the pottery of the period following the early La Tène phase, in which angular vessels and, subsequently, pedestal vases provided a point of reference to Continental fashions. Though there are certain outstanding fine-ware forms which can be attributed to the third and second centuries B.C., the greatest problem is posed by coarse pottery, which at present cannot be related to parallel developments on the Continent, and which, in consequence, is probably better referred to in the conventional terminology as Iron Age B coarse-ware. The difficulty is to isolate recognisable and re-current forms, especially, of course, from useful associations. But this process is hampered by the intractable nature of the material, which includes a large number of pottery vessels whose shape appears at first sight to be utterly nondescript and lacking in diagnostic features. In such circumstances, prehistorians are liable to resort to phrases like 'devolved' or 'degenerate *situlas*' to embrace a variety of pottery shapes that offer no other means of classification.

But if we approach the problem from the opposite end of the spectrum by considering which traits formerly characteristic of Iron A coarse pottery continue or reappear in the ensuing Iron B phase, a certain uniformity might be derived from the absence of these characteristics. By and large, the application of finger-tip ornament to the rim or shoulder of coarse pottery does not appear to survive much after the fourth century or thereabouts, and hardly at all among classic Iron B assemblages like that from Little Woodbury (Brails-ford, 1948). The decline in finger-tipping is quite consistent with the increasing adoption of slack body-profiles, in which the shoulder, formerly the focus of plastic ornament, is much less pronounced, or even indistinguishable. Below the rim, which itself need only be short and slightly everted, the body curves gently towards the base, with no obvious change of plane. Decoration of any kind is conspicuously absent; beneath the rim, impressions of 'thumbing' were sometimes left in shaping the rim, while the external surface of the jar sometimes shows traces of vertical smoothing. All of these features are displayed by the early B jars from City Farm, Hanborough, Oxon (D. W. Harding, 1964), from pits which also produced a flat-bowed iron brooch of the transitional phase from La Tène 1 – 2; like-wise at Maiden Castle, Dorset, the majority of coarse-ware jars – captioned Iron Age A by the excavator – evidently belong to this early B category (e.g. Wheeler, 1943, Figs 57–9). This kind of jar, then, with slack profile and slightly everted rim, forms the 'common denominator' of the Iron B phase (e.g. Fig. 66, R), and indeed, for the highland zone, is the model for a range of derivative forms in the pre-Roman and Roman native periods. We have only to examine the native wares from Stanwick to see the same 'nondescript' charac-teristics re-appearing in the first century A.D. with remarkably little variation (Wheeler, 1954, Fig. 12).

It will be recalled from an earlier chapter that such slack profiles were also characteristic of those few vessels which could be assigned, on the basis of their metal associations, to the late Bronze Age; the lack of examples in greater numbers for the latter period could, per-haps, be partially due to a confusion of the two groups. A comparison of the Worthing pot for instance, with Iron B jars from Little Woodbury and Maiden Castle, shows a marked similarity in terms of pot shape. It is this slack pottery form which constitutes the lowest common denominator in Britain for the best part of a millennium or more, extending from the later Bronze Age at least until the Roman native phase in the north of England. For the

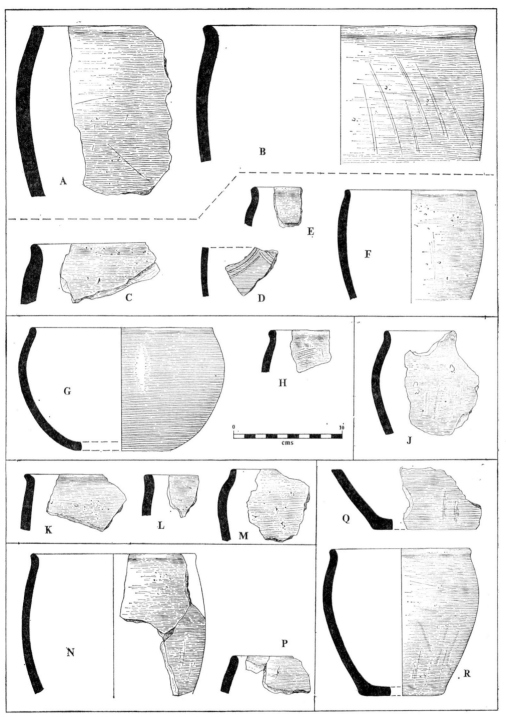

66. *Iron B coarse pottery, Cassington, Oxfordshire*

most part it fails to impress because it is so basic, and systems of classification depend in preference upon more outstanding forms, where these are superimposed upon this non-descript substratum. But when we have to deal with a period in which there are few fine-wares, or superior coarse-ware forms, we are obliged to consider the substratum itself, and, in consequence, classification breaks down, as in the late Bronze Age at present, and perhaps even in the early Iron B period before the emergence of distinctive decorated wares. In this context, it can now be seen that the majority of early Iron Age A shouldered jars are not strictly of this lowest level of pottery. The emphasised shoulder, in fact, even on the coarsest vessels, is probably an indirect result of the effect upon ceramic tradition of the more direct imitations of shouldered *situlas* discussed earlier.

In spite of the apparent predominance of slack-bodied jars of this kind in the third and second centuries, other coarse-ware forms can be recognised, including barrel jars (Fig. 67) and a larger variant, the globular jar (D. W. Harding, 1972, 100 and Pl. 59). The former has a simple, convex outline, with flat base and plain rim, that is, one which terminates with no internal or external flange or evertion. With slight regional variations, like the more hunched, incurving profiles of the Upper Thames basin, this form displays a marked uniformity throughout southern Britain, whence again it might be regarded as the source of similar jars with incurving rim further north and west at Traprain Law, East Lothian (e.g. Cree and Curle, 1922, Fig. 23; also sherds in the Ashmolean Museum, Oxford) and at Dinorben in Denbighshire (Gardner and Savory, 1964, Fig. 32, 3), normally assigned there to a late Iron Age or para-Roman date. Its currency in southern England, however, must begin much earlier: at Swallowcliffe Down (Clay, 1925, Pl. V, 8), for instance, a dating nearer 300 B.C. is suggested by the pedestal vases and flat-bowed brooch of La Tène 1c type. Its fabric is usually coarse, though sometimes the form appears in smooth, dark ware, as in the Iron B occupation at Longbridge Deverill. Decoration, nonetheless, is rare. Handled versions of the barrel-jar, in evidence at the Hunsbury hillfort near Northampton (Fell, 1936, Fig. 7, L. 3), display not the small peg-handles which had characterised Iron A pottery, but much heavier lugs that are moulded into the curvature of the pot wall.

The larger version of this form, here termed the globular jar, displays much the same profile as the barrel-jar, but with a less obvious tendency for the rim to curve inwards, with the result that the diameter of its mouth is generally greater than that of its base. At the same time, the rims of globular jars are sometimes rolled over, as at Cassington and Mad-marston, Oxfordshire, to produce a marginal evertion which amounts very nearly to a proto-bead-rim. Fewer examples of this form can be cited with certainty, not because they do not exist, but because with this, as with other very basic pottery forms, its identification cannot be confirmed without a virtually complete profile, unlike more distinctive groups, such as the earlier furrowed bowls or later Belgic butt-beakers, where a small fragment may be sufficient to betray their class.

Occasionally, of course, even a body-sherd is sufficient to convey useful information about a vessel, as, for example, in the case of Iron B pottery from the south-east Midlands, with its characteristic scored ornament. Originally included by Dr Kenyon in her survey

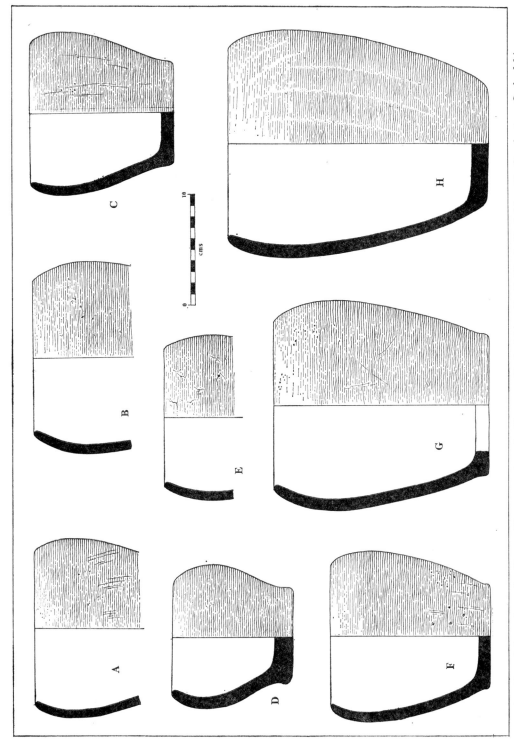

67. *Barrel jars from the Upper Thames region. A, Yarnton, Oxfordshire. B, Frilford, Berkshire. C, Cassington, Oxfordshire. D, Chadlington, Oxfordshire. E, Blewburton Hill, Berkshire. F and G, Stanton Harcourt, Oxfordshire. H, Hatford, Berkshire*

as a feature of the Trent valley AB culture (1952, 71 ff and Figs 22, 23), and typified by the random scoring at Breedon-on-the-Hill (Kenyon, 1950), this fashion can now be seen as a more widely distributed element of Iron B coarse pottery in the Midlands. Recent work in Northamptonshire, in particular, has indicated that it may be possible in due course to distinguish subsidiary groups within the overall category of scored ornament, from the earlier random scoring to a more regular cross-scored style which appears in later B contexts. The form of vessel upon which this style appears certainly includes the slack-bodied jars with short, everted rims, which have been discussed above.

Reference has already been made to pottery in 'smooth, dark ware'. This phrase, first adopted by Brailsford in his report on the pottery from Little Woodbury, is applied to a variety of vessels which have a somewhat superior finish to that of Iron B coarse-wares, often with some attempt at burnishing. Pottery in smooth, dark ware is certainly current by the second half of the fourth century, though the vessels themselves are seldom distinguished in any other respect at this stage. By the third century or thereabouts, however, more outstanding pottery forms emerge, of which the best known is the so-called saucepan pot (Fig. 68). The basic form of the saucepan pot ranges from a straight-sided, tub-shaped profile to one in which the sides of the vessel are more convex and barrel-shaped. Examples do not vary greatly in size, approximating to the capacity of the domestic modern counterpart, though lacking the characteristic handles of the latter. The earlier examples of the form generally display plain, simple rims, though some, as at Blewburton Hill, have a shallow, tooled groove running horizontally around the vessel immediately below its rim, in a manner which seems to foreshadow the sharply-beaded rims of the Wessex saucepans of the first century B.C. A pronounced beading, not necessarily related to the later Wessex fashion, also distinguishes a regional group of saucepan pottery on the South Downs, as at Findon Park and the Caburn, where the heavy, rolled-over rim is matched by a similar projection or moulding around the base of the vessel. Examples of this kind are not apparently restricted to Sussex; a related series has more recently been published from the Iron B occupation of Hawk's Hill, Fetcham in Surrey (Hastings, 1965, Fig. 7, 16; Fig. 8, 26, 31, though here lacking the basal projection). It remains to be seen, however, whether future research will be able to demonstrate any correlation between such localised distritions and the emergence of historically documented tribal divisions.

Decoration on saucepan pottery can be either rectilinear or curvilinear. Rectilinear ornament is usually restricted to a panel around the top third of the external surface of the vessel, and comprises simple, diagonal, hatched or cross-hatched designs, which have been studied and listed by Cunliffe (1964, esp. Fig. 2, A–G). Curvilinear decoration is not quite so regular and mechanical, and tends to utilise the surface of the vessel more fully. Designs include the recumbent figure-of-eight motif illustrated on vessels from Little Woodbury and Blewburton Hill, and the pendent swag, composed of double lines with dotted infilling, as at Findon Park. The range of ornament, however, remains fairly limited; the running scroll of the Caburn saucepan, or the radiating arcs of one from Blewburton Hill, indicate the broad limits of the potters' repertory. The sole exception is, of course, the pottery from

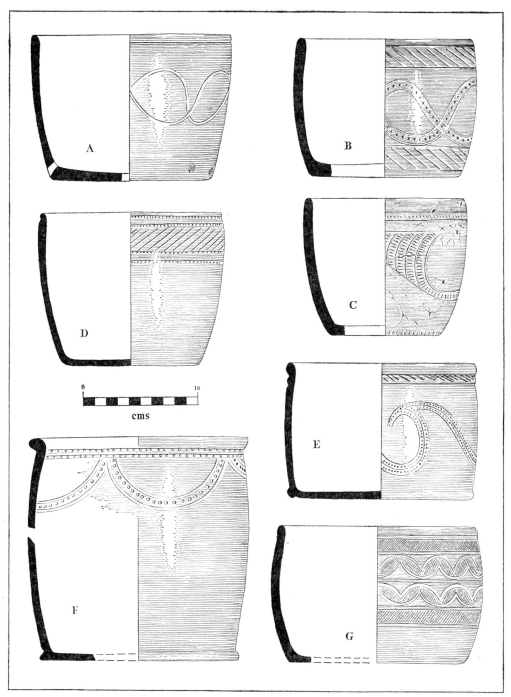

68. *Saucepan pottery. A, Little Woodbury, Wiltshire. B and C, Blewburton Hill, Berkshire. D, Maiden Castle, Dorset. E, the Caburn, Sussex. F, Findon Park, Sussex. G, Meare, Somerset*

195

the Somerset 'lake-villages'. Though the saucepan pot is not among the most common forms represented at Glastonbury and Meare, those which are in evidence display the normal range of leaf-motifs and cross-hatched backing which is characteristic of the south-western style.

Somerset, in fact, is on the extreme western extremity of the saucepan pot distribution, which eastwards extends as far as Surrey and Sussex. A few outliers only extend beyond the Berkshire Downs and into the Upper Thames valley, with a single example only reaching as far as the Chilterns (D. W. Harding, 1972, Pl. 7). The absence of saucepan pottery in the extreme south-east, and north of the Thames in Essex, Middlesex, Hertfordshire and Buckinghamshire, with this one exception, is marked. The distribution, therefore, concentrates in central southern England, and ignores those areas of the south-east and the Thames valley where, in an earlier period, the angular bowls were firmly established, and where in a subsequent phase the impact of the Belgic invasions was first felt. For such a distribution, it should be relatively simple to offer a Continental source. Vessels of saucepan or allied forms are known from the early La Tène period in the Marne (e.g. Favret, 1936, Fig. 58; Brisson, Roualet and Hatt, 1972, Fig. 4, H), whence the form was diffused north-westwards in the ensuing centuries. But without a close analysis of the Continental material, it is difficult to be certain at what point in this process southern Britain might have come into contact with the saucepan-pot fashion. It is possible, however, that the initial appearance of the saucepan coincided with the same phase of contact as introduced the pedestal vases to Swallowcliffe Down and its neighbouring sites in Wiltshire, in the second and westerly extension of Marnian ceramic influence around the end of the fourth century. It must be conceded, however, that relatively few examples of the saucepan group can be shown at present to belong to such an early phase in southern Britain. Wheeler has argued that the ultimate origin of the form was the metal *cista a cordoni* (1943, 228, no. 156 and Fig. 62, vi), a derivation which would certainly account for the use of the beaded or rolled-over rim on a number of examples. An alternative view was that put forward by C. F. C Hawkes (1939, 238), who related the saucepan pots from the Caburn to lathe-turned wooden tubs of the kind exemplified at Glastonbury (Glastonbury I, Fig. 64, Pl. L, X2; Pl. LI, X2). The two interpretations clearly need not be contradictory: the form is a very basic one which could have been produced in bronze, wood or pottery.

Complementary to the saucepan pot, but centred in the Upper Thames basin and the south Midlands, is the distribution of a class of vessel whose shape most closely resembled a small goldfish bowl, which I have referred to elsewhere as the globular bowl form (Fig. 69). Throughout its distribution area it displays a general uniformity of shape, admitting only a variation in rim from a short, upstanding kind to something approaching an incipient beadrim, and a tendency to become progressively less bag-shaped in profile and more truly globular in the later examples. In the Upper Thames region, this slight progression in shape and rim-form appears to correspond to a parallel improvement in the standard of potting, from the brown/black fabrics of the earlier examples to the harder pink/orange wares of the second half of the first century B.C. But it is the decoration of the

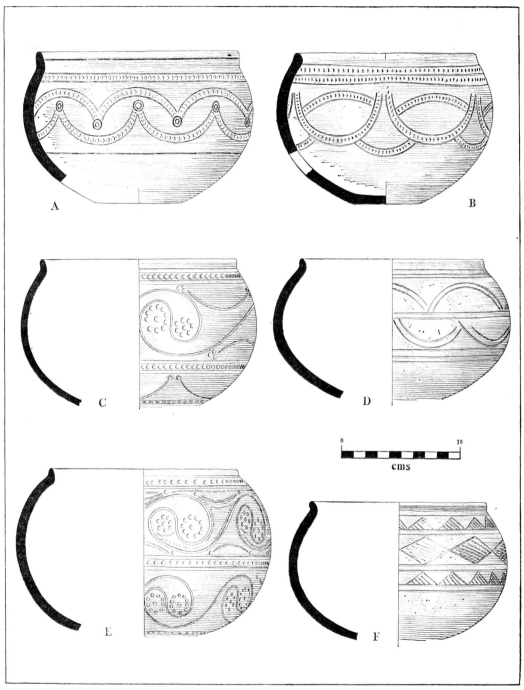

A   B   C   D   E   F

0   10
cms

69. *Globular bowls. A and B, Frilford, Berkshire. C–F, Hunsbury, Northamptonshire* (drawn *by courtesy of Northampton Museum*)

south Midlands globular bowls which particularly distinguishes the form. This may be divided into two subsidiary style-zones, the one characterised by the bowls at Hunsbury (Fell, 1936), the other by those from Frilford (Bradford and Goodchild, 1939, Fig. 7, 78, 84, 85; D. W. Harding, 1972, Pl. 67). The Hunsbury series is decorated in horizontal panels around the body of the bowl, sometimes with rectilinear but more often with flowing curvilinear designs, executed in a rather spindly technique which is reminiscent of the tendrils of the Newnham Croft bracelet. The rosette or rosette-with-dimple is a recurrent element of the Hunsbury style, and one which is also found on bowls of allied form at Desborough and Draughton, Northants (Grimes, 1951, Pl. VI, A; Fig. 41, 3), frequently figuring in the characteristic double looped scroll of the Northamptonshire series.

The Upper Thames bowls, by contrast, are more mechanical and geometric in their style of ornament. Rectilinear designs from the region, like the hatched lozenge design of the Cassington bowl, can be paralleled by the use of hatched triangles at Hunsbury, but it is the pendent swag, or continuous looped design, which is particularly typical of the Frilford globular bowls (Fig. 69). The swags themselves are made up of two or more shallow tooled lines, which form four, eight, or more rarely six loops around the body of the bowl, suspended generally from a series of stamped circlets or rosettes. This basic pattern may be elaborated by the use of stamped infilling of dotted, oblong or crescentic impressions within the tramlines of the swags, or by weaving a system of interlocking swags into a more complex design. Unlike that of the Hunsbury bowls, the Frilford ornament is not subdivided into panels, but freely occupies the full depth of the bowl. Around the top of the vessel, there is frequently a frieze, comprising tramlines with stamped infilling, which is occasionally repeated at the base of the main design. The base of the vessel, too, may be decorated with geometric, compass-drawn designs (D. W. Harding, 1972, Pl. 65, A–D), partly as an ornamental device to be displayed when it was being stored on the shelf upside down, partly as a technical means of facilitating the division of the external surface of the bowl into approximately equal divisions for the swags themselves.

Dating of globular bowls in the south Midlands and Upper Thames basin is as problematical as it is elsewhere. Though the Hunsbury bowls were found in a site-context which included a good deal of metalwork, this itself evidently spanned an extended period of occupation, and direct associations are lacking. At Frilford, however, a fragment of scabbard-chape, found in a pit which appeared to belong to the later occupation of the site, might be taken as provisional evidence that the more advanced form of globular bowl lasted well into the second half of the first century B.C. Concerning the origins of this distinctively insular form, we can only speculate; but it is conceivable that the earliest examples were already in evidence in the early second, if not the later third, century.

Though the globular bowl is especially characteristic of the south Midlands, occasional outliers of this distribution include the example with swag-decoration from Hawk's Hill, Fetcham (Hastings, 1965, Fig. 6, 1), where we have already noted the presence of saucepan pottery in the later phase of occupation. The distribution of the two forms also coincided at Blewburton Hill, where both appeared with the refortification represented by the dump-

XVIII *Ceremonial bucket, Marlborough, Wiltshire (height: 52 cm; diameter: 60 cm)*

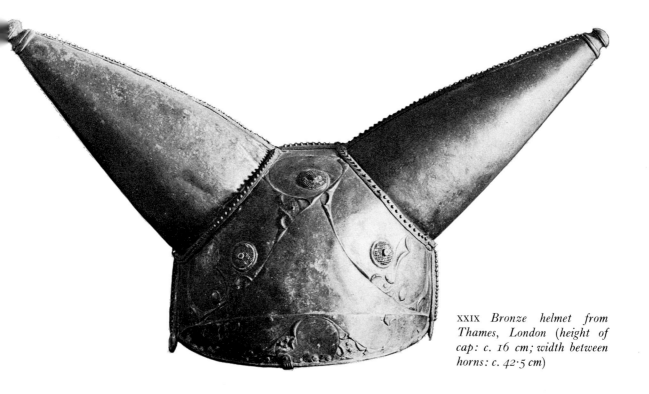

XXIX *Bronze helmet from Thames, London (height of cap: c. 16 cm; width between horns: c. 42·5 cm)*

XXXI *The Battersea shield: detail of terminal design*

XXX *The Battersea shield: general view*
(length: c. 77.5 cm)

XXXII *The Wandsworth shield (diameter: c. 38 cm)*

ramparted phase of the defences. Their broad contemporaneity, otherwise, is attested by the common use of ornamental designs like the swag with dotted infilling, which suggests a wider tradition in artistic usage which to some extent transcended local ceramic boundaries.

The same elements of the swag-motif, more frequently inverted to produce the effect of exaggerated 'eyebrows', characterise the ornamental style of Ward-Perkins's Wealden culture (1944, esp. 146 ff. For omphalos bowls, 1938, Fig. 10, 1–4 etc.). The two principal pottery forms of this south-eastern group are the dumpy pedestal vase and an omphalos-based form with bulbous body-profile and short, everted or sometimes incipient bead-rim. The eyebrow-swag is well illustrated on such an omphalos vessel from Saltdean, near Brighton, which, like the Upper Thames bowls, also incorporates the impressed circlet at the terminals of the eyebrows. Stylistically, there can be little doubt that these vessels share features in common with other regional Iron B groups in southern Britain. Their dating remains problematical, however, and their distribution in the lower Thames and south-east coastal zone, corresponding to the primary areas of Belgic settlement, is certainly provocative.

So far we have seen that there is very little evidence from pottery or metalwork for any significant invasion or immigration from the Continent in the middle La Tène phase. Invasion has been invoked, however, to account for a series of innovations, both ceramic and structural, in one region of southern Britain, the south-west, more especially in Devon and Cornwall (C. F. C. Hawkes, 1959, 182). The appearance of new and distinctive classes of fortification, together with the introduction of curvilinear-ornamented and stamped pottery, in the south-west, has been variously attributed to invaders from Brittany and to immigrants from north-western Spain and Portugal. In his publication of excavations at Chun Castle in Cornwall, Leeds remarked the Spanish and Portuguese parallels for this kind of stone-built cliff-castle, and inferred its introduction into Britain from this source (1926) In fact, there are relatively few such forts in the south-west, and current opinion has tended to favour an origin in south-western Brittany. Similar origins have been postulated for the characteristic type of south-western hillfort with widely spaced bivallate ramparts. Lady Fox has pointed out that these are relatively uncommon in northern France, and has suggested an alternative source in north-western Spain (1958). Once the notion of a bivallate defence system is established in the south-west, it evidently spread eastwards, to be adopted at sites like Maiden Castle, where Wheeler's Phase II clearly demonstrates south-western affiliations.

The adoption of bead-rims – and perhaps countersunk handles as well – at Maiden Castle can probably be traced to the same secondary influence from Devon and Cornwall. Though Wheeler regarded both as an abrupt innovation provoked by Venetic invaders in the mid-first century B.C., it is quite evident from site contexts that the introduction of these new ceramic forms was by no means so abrupt or decisive as he implied. In Brittany, the earliest pottery associated with cliff-castles appears to be the kind of simple bead-rim ware found at Castel Coz, which probably belongs to the early second century B.C. (Wheeler and Richardson, 1957, Fig. 24, 1–15). By the time Breton invaders were infiltrating Cornwall, they may well have been using finer wares with curvilinear ornament, and stamped decoration in the Braubach fashion, from which in due course the native potters of the south-west derived their characteristic insular style. A movement into Cornwall around the middle of the second century, with various influences emanating outwards thereafter, would equally well accord with revised estimates relating to the structural sequence at Maiden Castle, as discussed in an earlier chapter.

The origins of the distinctive 'duck-stamped' style in the south-west must presumably be related to this same immigration, and should not be treated in isolation from the wider ambience of curvilinear ornament in north-western France and Spain. In Britain, on the other hand, the clarification of the problems of this class of pottery must await the publication of current research. North of the Bristol Channel, outside the primary south-western zone, a variant style of duck-stamped pottery occurs at Croft Ambrey in Herefordshire and Bredon Hill in Worcestershire (Hencken, 1938, 88 ff., Figs 13, 14), which may well be the result of the widened influence of south-western potters. The Bredon Hill ornament, however, differs from the true south-western style, in that its stamping is confined more often to a cable-like frieze immediately beneath the rim, rather than around the body of the vessel as on Continental models. Its relationship to the south-west, therefore, still remains open to question: its chronology even more so.

By way of a postcript to this chapter, we may remark the distribution of Allen's two principal classes of currency-bars, the sword-shaped and spit-shaped types (1967, Figs 1 and 2). With the sole exception of the hoard at Ashburton, neither extends into Devon or Cornwall, concentrating rather in central southern England and the Midlands, and substantially overlapping the distribution of the saucepan pot and globular bowl forms, with which they may well have been contemporary. Furthermore, Allen's survey has shown that these groups of currency bars appear overwhelmingly in pre-Belgic contexts, and are significantly lacking in those areas of the south-east which subsequently became the region of primary Belgic settlement. It is to this phase of Belgic invasion that we must now direct our attention.

12

The late La Tène phase:
the Belgic invasions

THE PRINCIPAL FACTOR in the general acknowledgment of the Belgic invasion of Britain is that it is documented historically. Caesar records (*de bello Gallico*, 5, 12; 2, 4) that, prior to his own expeditions of 55 and 54 B.C., the population of the coastal regions of south-eastern Britain had themselves migrated from Belgic Gaul, first in search of plunder, and subsequently in order to settle permanently. In his earlier description of the tribes of Gaul he had further reported that, within his own lifetime, Diviciacus, king of the Suessiones, had been not only the most powerful ruler in all Gaul, but also had exercised sovereignty in Britain. That there was an invasion of south-eastern Britain from Belgic Gaul in the first half of the first century B.C., therefore, can scarcely be disputed; more problematical is the identification of the settlement and material remains of the invaders, and the chronology of the events they witness.

The first archaeological evidence to be equated with these Belgic immigrations was that of the cremation cemetery excavated at Aylesford in Kent by Sir Arthur Evans and published by him in 1890. The complementary urnfield at Swarling, which, with Aylesford, has been taken as the type-site of this intrusive south-eastern culture, was published in 1925 by J. P. Bushe-Fox. Shortly afterwards, the British evidence was related to contemporary late La Tène groups on the Continent by C. F. C. Hawkes and Dunning (1930) in their classic study of the problem, which has remained the basis for all subsequent research. The interpretation then put forward was that two principal movements brought Belgic culture to Britain, the first, around 75 B.C., to the south-east, and the second, dating to the period shortly after Caesar's return to Gaul, being that which Commius led in flight across the Channel, resulting in the Atrebatic colonisation of Wessex. This early conclusion can now be seen to have been an oversimplification, and it was revised by Hawkes in his scheme of 1959 for the British Iron Age, and in a subsequent re-appraisal of the Continental origins of the Belgic immigrants (1959; 1968). Meanwhile, the evidence from the burials of the Aylesford-Swarling series, and in particular the pottery, has been the subject of a detailed survey by Dr Birchall (1965), who endeavoured to reconcile the relatively late dating of these material remains with the evidence for pre-Caesarian invasion.

The major contribution to a revised chronology for the Belgic period has been Allen's exhaustive study of the coin evidence (1958; 1962). The coins which occur in Britain may be divided into two principal categories, those which were minted on the Continent, whence they were imported into Britain as a result of invasion or trade, and those which comprise British imitations of the former. The first category Allen has classified as Gallo-Belgic A–F, dating their inception to the last decades of the second century B.C. (Fig. 74). Celtic coinage was originally struck in imitation of Greek and Roman models: most important are coins whose origins can be traced back to the gold staters of Philip II of Macedon, and indeed it has been argued that the beginnings of Gaulish coinage stem from the influx of Macedonian gold into the Roman world in the 180s and 170s. Most of the Gaulish and Belgian models from which insular coinage stems reflect in debased form the design of the Apollo head on the obverse, with horse and chariot on the reverse. Even so, the antecedents are in most cases comparatively remote, and afford no basis for a firm chronology. Allen's early date for the introduction of Gallo-Belgic A coins in Britain, therefore, is based upon alternative evidence, working from the lower end of the scale. It begins with the famous hoard from Le Catillon in Jersey (Colbert de Beaulieu, 1957; 1958; 1959; Allen, 1958, Appendix IV), thought to have been deposited by refugees fleeing from Caesar at the time of his Venetic campaign about 56 B.C. The hoard contained a worn Gallo-Belgic D quarter-stater and a similarly worn gold stater of Allen's British B class. This latter group was itself derived from Gallo-Belgic C prototypes, and its occurrence in the Le Catillon hoard, in a worn condition, was therefore taken by Allen to indicate a currency for British B around 80–70 B.C., and perhaps about 100 for Gallo-Belgic C. In consequence, Gallo-Belgic A and B coins must have been in circulation in Britain before 100 B.C., the original imports perhaps being as early as 125–120. This dating evidently depends very much upon the length of time which we are prepared to allow for the various coinages in Gaul to develop and then spread to Britain. But even if we choose to reduce the interval assumed by Allen, we must none-the less surely accept that the initial wave of coinage was entering Britain around the turn of the century, and rather earlier than the conventional pre-war date of 75 B.C.

It is the coins of Gallo-Belgic A and B (Fig. 70) which Hawkes believed were indicative of the Belgic invasions to which Caesar alluded. In Britain, A coins are distributed widely in Kent, along the coast around Maidstone, and westward into east Sussex. Thence they spread north-west towards the Chilterns. A secondary grouping concentrates around the Essex coast, doubtless reflecting an alternative point of entry into the country. By contrast, the coins of Gallo-Belgic B are not found in the coastal regions where their immediate pre-decessors are found, but cluster further up the Thames estuary, on both sides of the river. Though they overlap with Gallo-Belgic A in some measure, they may be seen as comple-menting, rather than supplanting that distribution. On the Continent, Gallo-Belgic A coins are found in the Somme and the regions around Amiens, the centre of the tribe of Ambiani. B coins are distributed more widely, as far as it is possible to tell at the present time, when insufficient research has been carried out on Continental coinage. One con-centration, however, is located between the Somme and lower Seine, in the territory of the Caleti. Both these tribes are within the area which Hawkes has defined as Belgic Gaul, and could well be equated with Caesar's invaders who crossed over to Britain, *ex Belgio*, as it would now appear, already before 100 B.C. One further piece of evidence in relation to these coins seems to corroborate this conclusion. The coins of Gallo-Belgic B, without exception, have been struck from dies which have been defaced, some being partially obliterated on both sides, the majority on the obverse alone. This attempt to erase the emblem on the face of these coins seems consistent with the notion of a breaking-away from the homeland of a group of immigrants, who were cutting all ties with the Continent and settling, rather than merely trading, in the south-east of England. As Allen has rightly emphasised, the complementary, rather than overlapping, distributions of Gallo-Belgic A and B coins are more consistent with negotiated settlement in areas not yet fully occupied

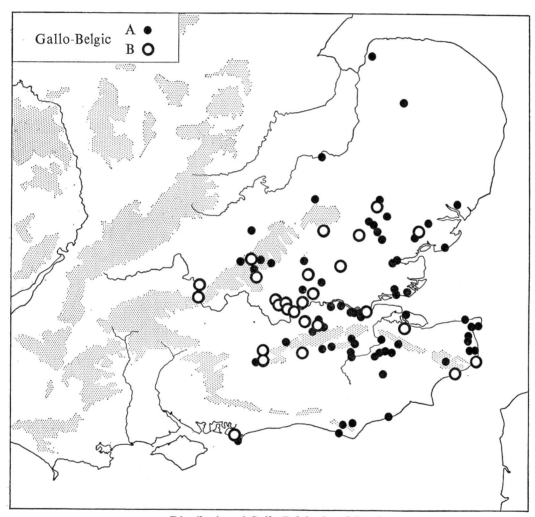

70. *Distribution of Gallo-Belgic A and B coins*

by immigrant Belgae than with commercial relations, which would scarcely be mutually exclusive.

The next series of Continental coins, Gallo-Belgic C, though not intensely distributed in Britain (Fig. 71), is nonetheless of considerable importance, since most of the independent British series derived from it. These coins are found in a limited distribution in Kent,

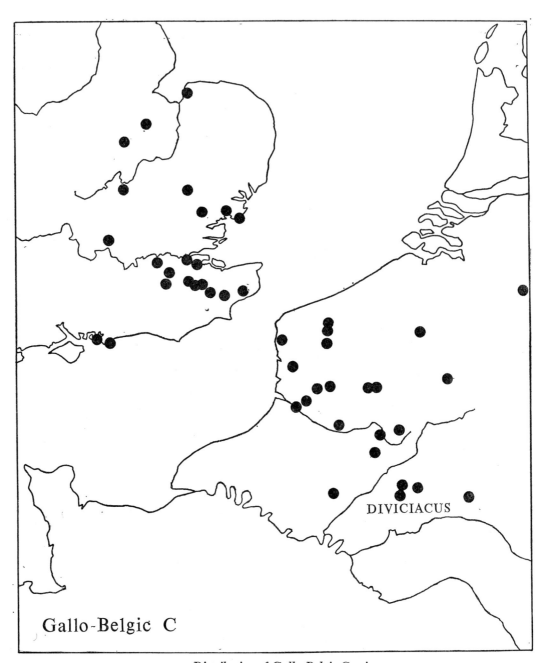

Gallo-Belgic C

DIVICIACUS

71. *Distribution of Gallo-Belgic C coins*

extending marginally towards the Thames, but scarcely into the area of Gallo-Belgic B. It is perhaps difficult to justify a further wave of invasion on the strength of such a distribution, and yet we cannot deny the apparent prestige of the series in view of its impact upon subsequent British coinage. On the Continent, Gallo-Belgic C coins extend from Calais in a broad band right up to the Oise and Marne regions, including the territories of the Gaulish Atrebates (whose name has been conventionally assigned to this coinage), the Ambiani, Viromandui and the Suessiones. And it was the king of this latter tribe, Diviciacus, who was said to have held sway not only in Gaul, but also in Britain, within the lifetime of the envoys who had come to Caesar from their neighbours, the Remi, in the spring of 57 B.C. Hawkes's equation of the Gallo-Belgic C coins, which Allen independently has dated to between 100 and 80 B.C. (when they gave rise to the British B derivative series), and Diviciacus, whose dominion was still vividly recalled by the elder statesmen of the Remi in Caesar's day, is very attractive (though the Suessiones are somewhat peripheral to the Continental distribution). Such an interpretation would certainly account for the authority of his coinage in Britain, albeit limited numerically.

We have noted that Gallo-Belgic C inspired a variety of insular derivatives in Britain, of which only the more important need concern us here. British A, often associated with the hoard from Westerham in Kent, but in fact more widely distributed in Sussex, Surrey and Hampshire, and British B, concentrated mainly in west Hampshire and Dorset, both gave rise in due course to a large body of silver and bronze coins which are generally attributed to the historical tribe of the Durotriges. Allen is inclined to regard the British series A–D as evidence for the westerly expansion of Belgic immigrants, though in the present state of knowledge archaeologically, we cannot be certain that this is not a case of adoption of an innovatory form of coinage by the indigenous Iron B population of Wessex.

Broadly parallel with this development is an extension northwards of British derivatives from the same source, Gallo-Belgic C. In particular, these include British H, in Lincolnshire, and British I, distributed in an arc around H, from the coast north of the Humber to the upper Trent. It is from these insular models that there developed, around the middle of the century, coins of the British L_A group (Fig. 72), more commonly known as the Whaddon Chase type, after the hoard from which a large number was recovered in Buckinghamshire in 1849. First, however, we must return to the primary Gallo-Belgic series.

Gallo-Belgic D is not an outstanding group in Britain. The distribution of the several variants which Allen includes in this category extends from east Kent and along the coast of Sussex. The coins are exclusively quarter-staters, and, though based ultimately upon Gallo-Belgic A models, they are extremely devolved and in some cases unintelligible. Nonetheless, their currency is established once again by the occurrence of a single, worn example in the Le Catillon hoard, from which we may infer that they were broadly contemporary in Britain with the British B group. The principal derivative of Gallo-Belgic D in Sussex is British O, which, like British A, was disseminated westward to become the model for Durotrigian quarter-staters. On the basis of Allen's chronology, this movement westward must have taken place before or by 60 B.C., and he therefore argues that the stimulus for this process of withdrawal was the introduction of the most widespread of all the imported coinages, Gallo-Belgic E.

Gallo-Belgic E coins, with their extensive distribution in northern France and Belgium, are also found throughout south-eastern Britain, along the Sussex and Kent coasts, in the

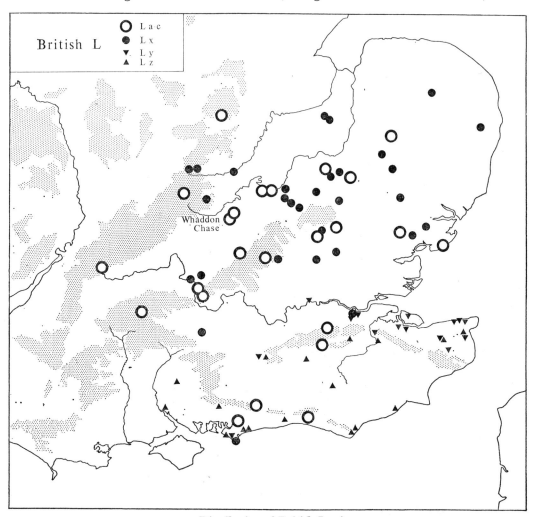

72. Distribution of British L coins

Lower Thames basin, and north of the river in Buckinghamshire, Bedfordshire, Hertfordshire and Cambridgeshire, in particular, with sporadic distribution beyond (Fig. 73). In the hoard from Scartho, Lincolnshire, they were found in association with both British Q and British L coins, the principal constituents of the Whaddon Chase hoard, indicating the overlapping currency of the imported series with insular variants which are normally assigned to a post-Caesar context. Indeed, Gallo-Belgic E coins were undoubtedly being struck for a considerable span of time, and the latest in the series differ little in weight from the coins of the Whaddon Chase hoard.

Even if we accept – as doubtless we should – Allen's case for the introduction of Gallo-Belgic E immediately before Caesar's raids in 55 and 54 B.C., we can hardly regard them as

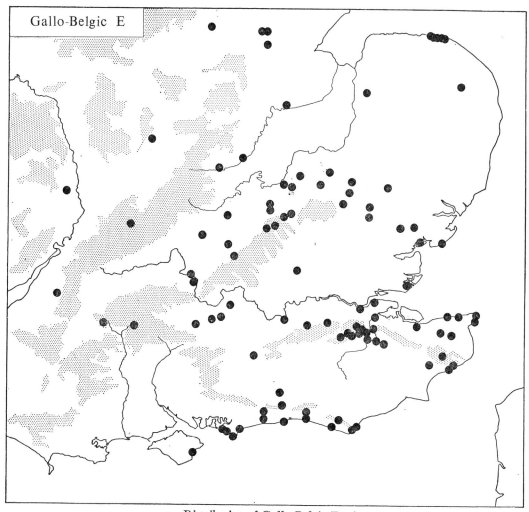

Gallo-Belgic E

73. *Distribution of Gallo-Belgic E coins*

the coins of the invaders from Belgic Gaul to whom Caesar referred. Not only are the majority of these coins on the Continent well outside the area of Belgic Gaul, but also their late arrival in Britain scarcely allows time for the continuous wars which took place between the invaders and the native tribes before the latter's eventual alliance under the supreme command of Cassivellaunus. On the other hand, Allen is reluctant to recognise the Gallo-Belgic E series as the coinage of Cassivellaunus himself, since its distribution extends well beyond the known centres of Catuvellaunian dominion, and even includes the territory of the Trinovantes, with whom the Catuvellauni were at enmity in Caesar's day. Though he has reminded us that the chiefs of the Bellovaci of Belgic Gaul, who had unsuccessfully tried to muster opposition to Caesar, fled to Britain in 57 B.C. (*de bello Gallico*, 2, 14), it is hard to imagine that such refugees could have been responsible for the widespread British distribution of these coins. Caesar, of course, claimed the political liaison between Britain and Gaul as one of the pretexts for his own punitive expeditions, and it may well have been that the union of the British tribes, both north and south of the Thames, in face of the invasion threat, encouraged the circulation of Gallo-Belgic E coins over a wider area than might otherwise have been possible. As for Cassivellaunus, it is still tempting to attach his name to the circulation of British L coins, in spite of their post-Caesar dating, for reasons to which we shall return later.

The final wave of Gallo-Belgic numismatic influence to reach Britain is represented only in the Whaddon Chase hoard, and at Portland in Dorset. But if actual imports are scarce, the effect which Gallo-Belgic F coins had upon the insular series is clearly demonstrated by the adoption on British Q of the triple-tailed-horse motif which characterised the Continental prototypes. It is these coins, dated by Allen to the approximate time-bracket 40–20 B.C., which have been generally associated with the historical Commius, who, Frontinus records, fled while Caesar was still in Gaul (*Stratagems*, 2, xiii, 11). The relative paucity of Gallo-Belgic F coins in Britain, Allen has explained, may be accounted for by the fact that Caesar had suppressed the use of gold coinage in Gaul, and in consequence we should not expect gold coins to be imported in any quantity by a refugee movement in the later 50s. In Britain, the derivative British Q staters divide into two classes: single-faced coins with the triple-tailed horse on the reverse, and those with the same design on the reverse supplemented by a patterned obverse. It is from the latter group that are derived those coins in Britain on which the names of Commius and Tincommius subsequently appear, which would seem to reinforce the view that the introduction of Gallo-Belgic F and British Q is indeed to be connected with Commius' arrival in Britain.

Details of other regional coinage in Britain need scarcely detain us further. The object of the survey (Fig. 74) has been to assess which of the major waves of imported Gallo-Belgic coinage are most likely to have corresponded to periods of actual immigration, as recorded by Caesar. We have seen that the most widespread of these groups, Gallo-Belgic E, must be dated too close to the invasions of 55 and 54 to match the historical record adequately. Both Gallo-Belgic C and D are scarcely sufficient to sustain significant invasions, which leaves only the A and B coins, dating to the end of the second century, rather than later, as contenders for the title. The problem which now arises is to identify any other material remains, either pottery or metalwork, for which such an early dating is acceptable.

To begin with, hardly any of the grave-goods from the classic cemeteries at Aylesford (Evans, 1890) and Swarling (Bushe-Fox, 1925) can be shown to date earlier than the middle of the first century B.C. The pottery from these Belgic cemetery sites introduces a marked contrast with any previous pottery group in Britain, not least because, for the first time, it is

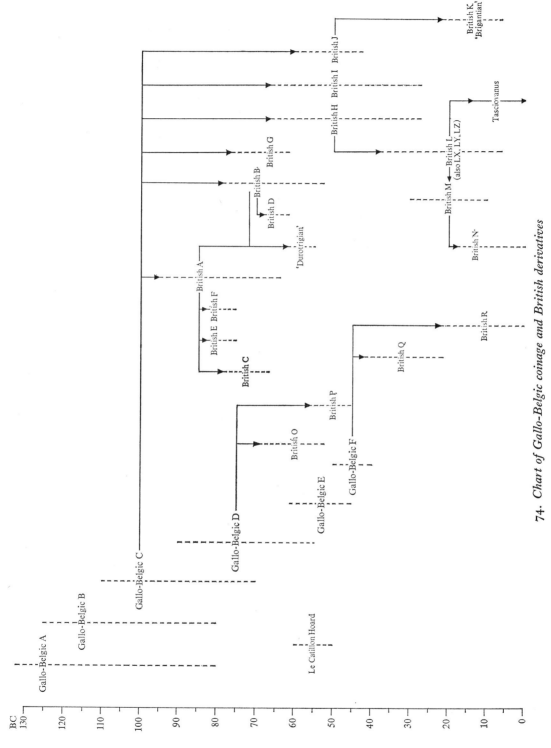

74. *Chart of Gallo-Belgic coinage and British derivatives*

209

wheel-thrown. Because of this technical improvement in the production of pottery, and the more professional commercial structure which it seems to betoken, it is possible now to recognise distinctive pottery-types which occur with sufficient regularity to be treated as such. Among the pottery which Dr Birchall has classified in her 'early' group, the principal type is a pedestal urn which is characterised by a series of horizontal grooves deeply impressed around the body of the vessel (Fig. 75, A). Pedestal jars of this type (Birchall Ia) were found at Swarling in Graves 2, 7 and 14, but unfortunately with no associated grave-goods, either ceramic or of metalwork. A related form of pedestal urn (Fig. 75, B), also with girth-grooving, but with a straighter-sided profile (Birchall IX) was represented in Grave 6. Grave 4, however, included a base-fragment which has been provisionally identified as belonging to a grooved urn of this type, together with an early form of La Tène 3 brooch and a second vessel of cruder manufacture, which was ornamented with vertical and random-scored ornament (Birchall Va), not unlike the style of ornament discussed earlier in connection with Iron B pottery in the south-east Midlands (Birchall, 1965, Fig. 1). The fact that this vessel belongs within an early context suggests that a further group of crude jars, with similar combed ornament, from Aylesford, might equally be earlier than the main body of material from the cemetery (Birchall, 1965, Fig. 10, 73-8). Three other vessels are singled out by Dr Birchall, as being typologically early, from Aylesford. All are in crude, handmade fabrics, but lacking in proper context, and not even positively associated with cremations. The two principal early forms do occur elsewhere, though not commonly; Type Ia, for instance, is represented at Shoebury, Type Va at Heybridge, in Essex. By comparison with the considerable body of wheel-thrown pottery from burial sites of the Aylesford-Swarling series in the south-east, however, these few examples for which a pre-Caesarian dating has been tentatively advanced will hardly fill the ceramic vacuum which we are faced with at present. Indeed, even were they more numerous, it is doubtful whether these pottery-types can be extended chronologically to coincide with the coinage of the earliest immigrants of the period before 100 B.C. And it is equally hard to imagine that cemeteries await discovery which will dramatically produce a new set of types to fill the hiatus.

Two possible contenders for a place alongside the earliest Gallo-Belgic coins have already been considered in the previous chapter, as representative of the south-eastern B culture, the dumpy pedestal vases and omphalos-based bowls whose distribution, plotted by Ward-Perkins (1938a, Fig. 2; 1944, Fig. 6), could be regarded as complementary to that of the coins. Could it be that these forms were adopted by the immigrant Belgic population *in lieu* of better wares during the initial stages of settlement? The apparent absence of Belgic pottery – and indeed of cemeteries too – of the late second and early first centuries B.C. recalls a comparable lack of evidence for the burials and material remains of the intrusive culture of eastern Yorkshire between Cowlam and Arras. For some reason, in each instance, the presence of the invaders does not make its impact upon the archaeological record until some time has elapsed after the initial period of settlement.

The bulk of the material from the Aylesford cemetery, dated largely on the basis of associated metalwork, belongs to the period from around 60 B.C. onwards. The richest of

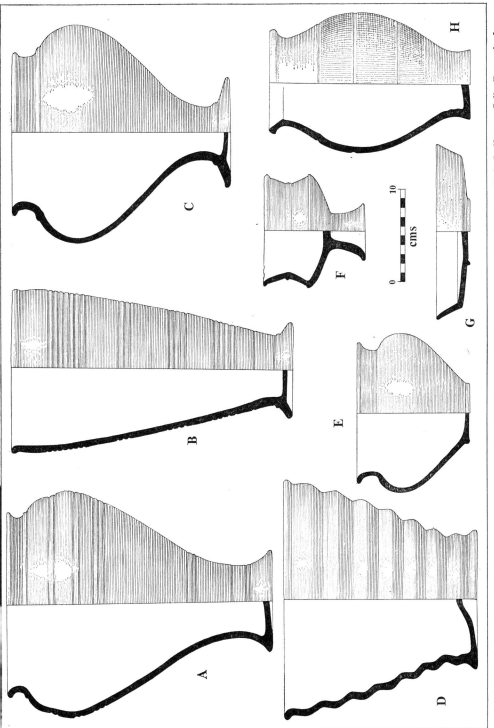

75. *Principal classes of 'Belgic' pottery. A, pedestal urn with horizontal grooving, Swarling, Kent (Birchall type IA). B, conical urn with horizontal grooving, Swarling, Kent (Birchall type IB). C, plain pedestal urn, Swarling, Kent (Birchall type IX). D, corrugated urn, Swarling, Kent (Birchall type II). E, necked bowl with low footring, North Leigh, Oxfordshire. F, carinated cup (tazza) with tall pedestal, Welwyn, Hertfordshire. G, platter with low footring, Watlington, Oxfordshire. H, butt-beaker, Watlington, Oxfordshire (Birchall type VI)*

the burials were graves in which the cremated remains were contained, not in pottery urns, but in wooden buckets, one of which was plated with sheet-bronze and decorated with *repoussé* ornament. Together with this elaborate funerary container were a bronze *patella* and jug of the distinctive Kelheim type (Pl. XXVI), which are also paralleled in Britain at Welwyn, Herts (R. A. Smith, 1912, Figs 17–19).

This class of bronze jug, which occurs widely in La Tène 3 (D) contexts in Europe, has been studied, and its distribution plotted, by Werner (1954), who believed that it was produced during the period 70–15 B.C. He maintained that a widespread circulation prior to that initial date was improbable in the circumstances of political instability and internal upheaval which had prevailed almost continuously within the Roman provinces since the invasion of the Cimbri and the Teutones in 112 B.C. With the suppression of the slaves' revolt in 72–70, and Pompey's success in crushing piratical activities in the Mediterranean in 67, the political climate would have been more favourable for the kind of widespread trading which Caesar claims already prevailed within Gaul. Werner's proposal of a pre-Caesar date for the trading of Kelheim flagons in Central Europe is reinforced by the grave-goods from Chatillon-sur-Indre (R. R. Clarke and C. F. C. Hawkes, 1955, 223, no. 28), which included such a vessel, together with an anthropoid sword which shows some classical influences in the features of its pommel-head, and fragments of a long iron sword, as well as a bronze *patella* and seven pottery *amphorae*. Since the Gauls were said to have been disarmed by Caesar – and we have no grounds for supposing that this was not a fairly thorough operation – the Chatillon grave with its parade of weapons would suggest a date before the Gallic campaign for the associated artefacts, including the *patella* and Kelheim flagon. And at Aylesford, it is worth noting that an initial dating just before Caesar, with continuing use for perhaps half a century thereafter, would coincidentally accord with the two unassociated coins from that site, one of which was of the Gallo-Belgic E series, the other of British Q, derived, it will be remembered, from Gallo-Belgic F.

The pottery characteristic of this middle phase at Aylesford and Swarling includes a variety of cordoned or girth-grooved pedestal jars, together with two other distinctive types of vessel. One is an open-mouthed jar with slightly splayed, corrugated sides, and generally an omphalos base (Birchall II); the other is a small-necked bowl, with slight footring base and broad corrugations between its shoulder and neck (Birchall IVa). This latter form is evidently related to a series of necked bowls, more often found without the broad corrugation, but frequently with narrow cordons, widely distributed on settlement sites like Wheathampstead (Wheeler, 1936, Pl. XLIX, 10; Pl. L, 11, 12), and those of the Upper Thames Valley (D. W. Harding, 1972, Pls 8 and 69).

North of the Thames at this time, the custom of cremation burial is also maintained. Among other burials in Hertfordshire, which share many of the features of the Kentish graves, is the use of bucket-burial at Harpenden and Welwyn. Two of the Welwyn graves, furthermore, contained a set of iron firedogs (Fig. 76), also found elsewhere as part of the late La Tène grave-furniture (Piggott, 1971, including earlier refs.). Pottery from these Hertfordshire graves includes the pedestal urn, but lacks one specific Kentish type (Fig.

75, D), the corrugated urn (Birchall II). Instead, there appears a new form altogether, the *tazza* (Fig. 75 F), a vessel with sharply carinated shoulder and tall, pedestal foot, and grooved or cordoned body (Birchall X). The fact that this elegant cup-form is associated at Welwyn with imported bronzes indicates a date broadly contemporary with the Aylesford bucket-burials: the absence of this pottery type in Kent, therefore, must be accounted for by differences in regional ceramic convention.

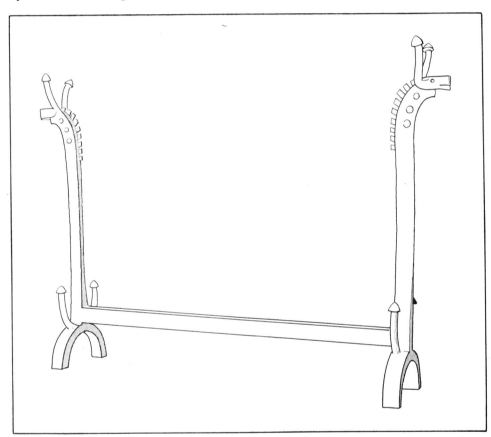

76. Iron firedog from Welwyn, Hertfordshire

The Hertfordshire pattern is repeated, with slight variations, in Essex. Here the bucket-burial custom persists, and is illustrated at Lexden, near Colchester, and at Great Chesterford. The Kentish corrugated urn is also absent, though the remainder of the series, including pedestal urns and the *tazza*, as in Hertfordshire, are present in the Essex burials. An interesting variation on the ceramic series is afforded by the Great Chesterford graves, which included a pedestal urn (Birchall Ib) and a *tazza* (Birchall X), made, not of pottery, but of Kimmeridge shale.

Finally in the ceramic sequence, Dr Birchall identifies a late group at Aylesford and

Swarling, a development which is also reflected north of the Thames. The characteristic innovations of this phase are the butt-beaker (Birchall VI) (Fig. 75, H) and shallow platter (Birchall VII) (Fig. 75, G) types. The former is a particularly distinctive form of vessel, having a barrel-shaped body which is generally divided by horizontal grooves or cordons into a series of panels, frequently ornamented with vertical combing. Its rim is thickened into a wedge-shape, and everted; its base is generally flat or marginally concave. The introduction of the butt-beaker, together with girth-beakers and other Gallo-Belgic forms, is generally attributed to the period following 15 B.C., when, it has been argued, a treaty with Rome, signed by Tincommius, resulted in the promotion of commercial links between Britain and occupied Gaul (Stevens, 1951). From Horace's letters, written around 31 B.C., we may infer that the Romans still regarded Caesar's campaigns in Britain as a triumph which had subdued the native population. At the same time, there had been talk of Augustus mounting a further expedition to press home the conquest initiated by Caesar in 34 B.C., and again in 28–27. But, according to Dio, other problems pressed more urgently, and in due course Augustus abandoned the idea of a military campaign in Britain. The idea of annexing Britain more closely to Rome, however, may not have waned so soon, and by 15 B.C. Horace was able to write that the 'ocean [generally thought to mean Britain, the islands in the Atlantic] listens to the word of Augustus' (Horace, *Odes*, 4, XIV, 45–8. For a discussion, see Stevens, 1951, 338). This in itself may not seem sufficient to justify the inference of a treaty between Britain and Rome, but archaeologically Stevens's interpretation is supported by the fact that it is at about this time that the coins of Tincommius acquire their Romanising elements. And when Tincommius and Dubnovellaunus were supplanted by Verica and Eppillus respectively, these kings continued to strike coins with the word *rex* upon them. Stevens's conclusion, therefore, is that by 15 B.C. the Britons were *clientes*, and that the imports of butt-beakers, platters and Arretine pottery should all be dated from this period.

It has been suggested that this treaty was in essence an alliance between Tincommius and the Romans against Caesar's former principal enemy, the Catuvellauni. Certainly under Cassivellaunus' successor, Tasciovanus (c. 15 B.C.–A.D. 5), the Catuvellauni consolidated their power north of the Thames (Fig. 77), driving the distribution of coins of Tincommius well back within the area which had been formerly occupied by the British Q coins, which presumably had marked the extent of the early kingdom of Commius around 50–20 B.C. Had this treaty been negotiated principally with the Atrebates, we might have expected the initial imports to concentrate in Sussex and Hampshire, and only spread north of the Thames thereafter. The distribution of Arretine ware in Britain follows a quite converse pattern, the principal area of imports being north of the Thames, and even into Gloucestershire and East Anglia. In the Catuvellaunian heartland, the move from Wheathampstead to Verulamium must have taken place about this time. At Wheathampstead, Wheeler's excavation revealed neither butt-beakers nor platters, which presumably means that the *oppidum* was occupied earlier than the introduction of Gaulish wares following the treaty with Rome. At Verulamium, however, butt-beakers, girth-beakers and

Arretine platters are all represented (Wheeler, 1936, Pl. XLIX, 10). Furthermore, it is only shortly after the coins of Tasciovanus acquire a Romanising aspect that they are also found bearing the mint-mark VER, providing further confirmation of the change of tribal capital.

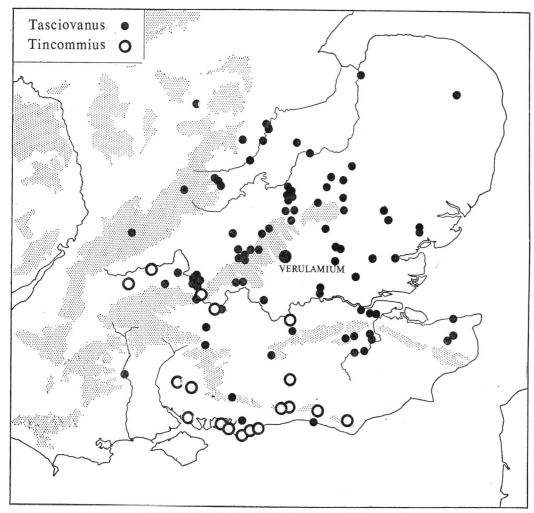

Tasciovanus   ●
Tincommius   ○

VERULAMIUM

77. Distribution of coins of Tasciovanus and Tincommius

Early in the first century A.D. under Cunobelinus, the Catuvellaunian capital was to be moved yet again, this time to the coast at Camulodunum (Colchester) (C. F. C. Hawkes and Hull, 1947). By this time red glazed Arretine ware, the immediate predecessor of Samian, and dateable to the period A.D. 1–40, was being imported in increasing quantities, and Hawkes has postulated that the move to Camulodunum may well have been in response to the need for a major port on the east coast to handle the increased volume of foreign trade. Roman potteries had certainly been established at Trier and elsewhere in northern France and western Germany, for the purpose of supplying the intended Roman province east of the Rhine. When this proposed expansion was abandoned, possibly following the defeat of Varus in A.D. 10, these centres would have needed to seek an outlet for their products elsewhere. The fact that much of the pottery from Camulodunum is well paralleled at Haltern on the Rhine suggests that Cunobelinus may have become one such alternative customer.

The new pottery types do appear in Wessex, however, at Hurstbourne Tarrant in Hampshire (C. F. C. Hawkes and Dunning, 1930, Fig. 32), where a bucket-cremation was accompanied by an early example of a butt-beaker, and at Worthy Down near Winchester (Hooley, 1930, Figs 51–68), where there were platters and butt-beakers in association with bead-rim pottery. These sites, in fact, are west of the main concentrations of coins of Commius and Tincommius; but from the presence of butt-beakers at Rotherley on Cranborne Chase (Pitt-Rivers, 1888, Pl. CXVI, i; C. F. C. Hawkes, 1947, 44 and Fig. 5, f), and at Maiden Castle (Wheeler, 1943, Fig. 75, 231), we may infer that the trade in Gaulish pottery had also made an impact upon the territory of the Durotriges (though not sufficiently as to merit inclusion in Brailsford's list (1957) of diagnostic pottery types). The source of imports into central southern England, on the other hand, would almost certainly have been situated further west than that proposed for the trade with East Anglia; centres at the mouth of the Seine or within reach of Le Havre would seem more probable in this instance. Supplemented in this way by Continental imports, the pottery of the Belgic period provides a more reliable guide to dating for the century following Caesar's raids, than for any previous period in the British Iron Age. At this point, we must return to consider other groups of metalwork, apart from direct imports like those at Aylesford, to see whether these too might afford any aid to chronology.

In the period around 100 B.C. when Belgic migration into Britain was already under way, metalwork on the Continent is in a state of transition from La Tène 2 types to those of La Tène 3. For the brooch series, this entailed a further development in the relationship between bow and foot-return. In the basic La Tène 2 brooch, it will be recalled, the foot had been attached to the bow by means of a collar. In La Tène 3 successors, the bow and foot are now cast as a single unit, the space between the two, in some developed forms, being filled with openwork ornament (Fig. 78). As evidence for the gradual nature of this change, we may cite a number of examples, cast in one piece, which nonetheless retain a ridge or knob on top of the bow, a non-functional feature which evidently is representative of the functional collar of its predecessor. In the genuine La Tène 3 brooch, this residual element is abandoned, and the whole brooch may become more triangular and streamlined, with further variations of the spring-mechanism as on the example from Grave 1 at Swarling. A further modification, the 'trumpet-headed' brooch, is also present in the Swarling cemetery, in Grave 13 (Birchall, 1965, Fig. 3), with a bucket-burial and pottery of Dr Birchall's middle period, suggesting a currency for the type between 50–15 B.C.

In addition to these brooches, occasional examples are known in Britain of a distinctive

216

class of Continental La Tène 3 brooches, the so-called Nauheim brooch (Werner, 1955), named after a type-site in the Rhineland (Fig. 78, b). This type is characterised by its elongated form, and a generally slender, triangular profile of its bow when viewed from above. The foot-plate is frequently the subject of openwork ornament, and the spring is further distinguished by the fact that the loop which crosses over from the coils on one side

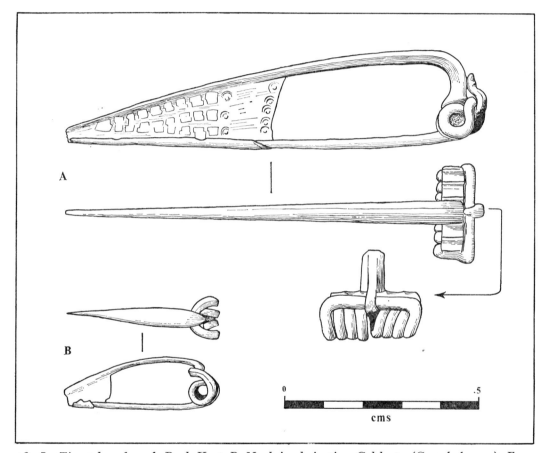

78. *La Tène 3 brooches. A, Deal, Kent. B, Nauheim-derivative, Colchester* (Camulodunum), *Essex*

to those on the other passes between the pin and the bow, instead of forming an external chord as on many standard La Tène 3 forms. The Continental distribution of this type concentrates around Mainz, extending up the left bank of the Rhine and into Switzerland. An example has been found at Manching in a context which should belong to the middle of the first century B.C., but unfortunately the Nauheim brooch still cannot be used confidently to indicate a pre-Caesarian date. The end of its currency on the Continent is indicated by the fact that it is superseded by other types in the later graves at Nauheim itself, and that it is virtually absent from contexts later than mid-Augustan. A date around the middle or third quarter of the first century B.C. would seem appropriate for the example from Wheathampstead, in view of the absence of pottery forms which require a later date.

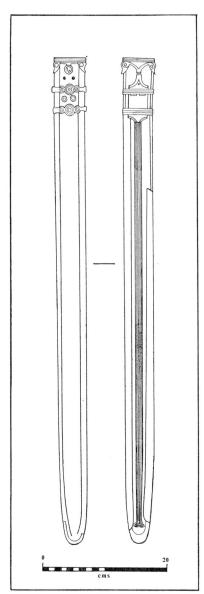

79. *La Tène 3 scabbard from Battersea*

The development of swords and scabbards of the distinctive anthropoid-hilted variety, as we have already seen, shows a similar transition from La Tène 2 to La Tène 3, with increasing classical or 'Romanising' influence depicted in the features of the pommel head (R. R. Clarke and C. F. C. Hawkes, 1955). Otherwise, scabbards of basically La Tène 2 design continued to be used well into the first century, as the chapes from Little Wittenham and Frilford have shown, at least outside the areas of primary Belgic settlement and influence. One innovating type has been noted by Piggott, however, and classified by him in his Group V (1950, 21–2, Fig. 10, 6). Scabbards of this class are distinguished by their parallel-sided shape, with simple rounded chape, and by their abandonment of the cocked-hat form in favour of an open-ended mouth. Examples of this type are known from St Albans, Battersea (Fig. 79) and Boxmoor, Hertfordshire, around the primary Belgic zone, and it would be tempting to regard these as weapons introduced in the first century by Belgic invaders into the south-east. Sporadic outliers in Lincolnshire, Westmorland, Anglesey, and even as far as the coast of Ireland, however, are less readily explained as offshoots from a Belgic distribution which is itself so sparsely represented.

Related to the weapons are two other classes of armour, helmets and shields. Few helmets of the pre-Roman Iron Age have survived in Britain, and the one recovered from the Thames in 1868 is unique in its form (Pl. XXIX). The main cap is constructed from three sheets of bronze, riveted together; to this have been attached twin conical horns which protrude from the temples of the main fitting. The cap itself is decorated in *repoussé* with a trail of stringy plastic designs, incorporating also the use of 'matting', likewise executed in *repoussé*. In addition, the helmet was embellished with a series of circular discs, originally six in number, which are scored with cross-hatching to receive enamel inlays. This technique of enamelling was apparently a feature of the first half of the first century B.C., being superseded thereafter under Roman influence from Gaul by the later *champ levé* method of application. The finest of the Thames shields, that discovered at Battersea in 1857 (Pls XXX, XXXI), is probably rather later in date, since its method of enamelling, or more strictly glass inlay, has been shown by recent analysis to be similar to the technique used in grave-goods from the wealthy La Tène 3 burials of the first century A.D. at Lexden and Hertford Heath. In its shape, the Battersea shield is within the tradition of elongated shields which we have already seen exemplified at Witham, except that it has a much more waisted form than the latter. To its thin sheet-bronze surface have been riveted, as a continuous symmetrical ornament, three circular discs with central bosses. It is within these bosses, and within a series of other roundels incorporated in the curvilinear design, that the red glass inlay is retained. One other point of comparison with the earlier Witham shield is very apparent: the manner in which the lateral discs are supported by grotesque and exaggerated animal heads. Facing outwards from the central device, their bulbous noses overlap the outer discs; their eyes are formed by a pair of rivets in each case, and their heads are crowned with branching horns which incorporated pairs of glass studs. In spite of the recollections of the Witham shield which the Battersea animals provoke, we must surely acknowledge the technical affinities, which Megaw has pointed to (1970, 150–1), with the Catuvellaunian royal graves; even if we permit an earlier introduction of this technique, therefore, we can hardly date the Battersea shield earlier than the end of the first century B.C.

In no single class of artefact is the Belgic artistic and technical achievement better demonstrated than in the lavish gold torcs of the mid-first century B.C. Of these none is finer than the large electrum torc from hoard E at Snettisham (R. R. Clarke and Dolley, 1954, esp. Pls XV and XVI; Megaw, 1970, No. 291) in the county of Norfolk. The main ring of the torc, 20 cm in diameter, is composed of eight twisted strands of wire, each individual wire itself being made up of eight finer strands. The ring has then been soldered to its terminals, which were hollow, cast loops, themselves decorated with relief, plastic ornament and chased background-patterning of squared matting. In one of these ring-terminals was enclosed a quarter-stater of Gallo-Belgic D type, the currency of which was between approximately 80–60 B.C. Nonetheless we should exercise caution in adopting this *terminus post quem* as the date of manufacture of the torc. Not only was the coin itself worn, but furthermore we might anticipate that for an ornamental piece such as the Snettisham torc, an old coin might well have been deliberately chosen, in much the same fashion as caused a previous generation to attach sovereigns to watch chains. In fact, other coins from Snettisham, including *speculum* coins which are more likely to represent the craftsman's earnings, indicate that the workshop which produced these torcs continued in operation probably until the last quarter of the first century B.C.

Few La Tène 3 torcs achieve the degree of elaboration displayed by this outstanding example from Snettisham. By comparison, the torcs discovered recently at Ipswich (Owles and Brailsford, 1969) are constructed with two thicker strands of gold rod, and, with one exception only, have simple looped terminals, rather than separately cast rings which have to be added subsequently to the main body of the torc. The Ipswich series (Pl. XXXIII) is nonetheless instructive, since it appears that some of the constituent examples have not been finished with the degree of elaboration, particularly in respect of the terminals, which might be expected. In fact, the one example with independent cast ring-terminals had apparently only been assembled, and still required completion of its ornament, since the traced outline of the intended design is faintly discernible on the terminals. Though torcs of allied kind are known elsewhere in Britain, there would appear to be increasing justification for Megaw's conclusion that there was in East Anglia a Snettisham–Ipswich 'school' of goldsmiths, who specialised in this ornate and skilful craft.

Finally, we should consider one other class of insular metalwork which has been regarded as characteristic of the later first century B.C. and early first century A.D., the ornamented mirror. The earliest mirrors known in Britain were both found in the Arras culture zone of eastern Yorkshire (Stead, 1965, 55–7). One only survives, from the Lady's Barrow at Arras. The plate of the mirror is circular in shape, plain and made of iron; its handle is also of iron, with bronze mounts at either end. Mirrors are certainly known on the Continent, in the Haute-Marne, in Germany and as far east as Chotin in southern Czechoslovakia, but at the same time are so rare after the early La Tène period that it is difficult at present to see the elaborately decorated mirrors of the British series as anything other than a purely insular development.

The fashion for ornamental mirrors cannot be associated exclusively with the primary areas of Belgic settlement in the south-east, though the variety with kidney-shaped plate seems more typical of this region than elsewhere. Equally elaborate mirrors, however, have been found outside this zone, particularly at Desborough (R. A. Smith, 1909, esp. Pl. XLIII; Powell, 1966, Fig. 243) in Northamptonshire (Pl. XXXV), and in a grave at Birdlip (Pl. XXXVII) near Cheltenham: indeed C. Fox (1958, 84–105) was inclined to favour the territory of the Dobunni as a centre of mirror production. Characteristic of these mirrors is that one face of the plate is subject to incised curvilinear ornament, generally set against a background of regular-squared matting to produce what is known as the mirror style. A comparison of the basic design of the Mayer mirror (Pl. XXXIV) with the ornament of the spearhead from the Thames (Pl. XXXVI), for instance, is sufficient to show that the style was not restricted exclusively to mirrors. Close dating of the mirrors is still not possible, however, on the basis of ornament alone, though the more elaborate cast handles may well be an indication of a first century A.D. dating.

To trace the expansion inland of Belgic culture from the regions of primary settlement in the south-east, and subsequently Wessex, we must once more turn to the evidence of coinage. Whether or not it is feasible to attach the name of Cassivellaunus to the British L series, there can be no doubt from the distribution of dynastic coins that a policy of territorial expansion was pursued by his successor, Tasciovanus, whose coins appear in increased numbers beyond the Ouse, into the margins of the Upper Thames basin and even south of the Thames (Fig. 77). Following the death of Tasciovanus around A.D. 5, Catuvellaunian aggression was apparently directed more particularly under Cunobelinus (Fig. 80) towards the Atrebates, whose pro-Roman policy, adopted by Tincommius, was continued when the latter was succeeded by his younger brother Verica. The territories thus annexed by Cunobelinus, Hawkes has suggested, were subsequently ruled by client kings allied to the Catuvellaunian dominion; their existence is indicated by the coins of Cunobelinus'

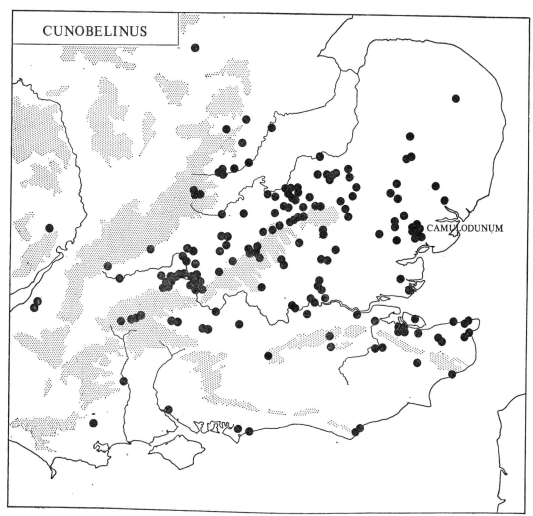

80. *Distribution of coins of Cunobelinus*

brother, Epaticcus, across the Middle Thames, and those of Andoco in the south-east Midlands (C. F. C. Hawkes, 1961, 54).

Meanwhile, the emergence of another Belgic or para-Belgic power in west Oxfordshire, Gloucestershire and Somerset is attested by coins of the Dobunni. The earliest coins of the Dobunni were based upon the distinctive Atrebatic staters which depicted a three-tailed horse on the reverse, and in consequence it has been argued that the Dobunni were themselves an offshoot of the southern Belgic invaders, infiltrating inland into Worcestershire around 30–20 B.C. The massacres witnessed by the cemeteries at Worlebury, near Weston-super-Mare (C. F. C. Hawkes, 1931, 80, 85, 96) and at Bredon Hill, Worcestershire (Hencken, 1938), could thus be attributed to the military resistance which naturally ensued. That the overlords of the Dobunni really were Belgic intruders is perhaps corroborated by the strongly Belgic aspect of their culture as witnessed by Mrs Clifford's excavations at the *oppidum* of Bagendon (1961). Yet when, shortly after 15 B.C. and the conclusion of the treaty with Rome, Tincommius chose to abandon the barbaric emblems on his coins in favour of a Romanising style, the Dobunni nonetheless displayed their evident independence by retaining the traditional designs. For perhaps fifteen or twenty years they continued this practice until the Catuvellauni themselves, with their increasing commercial contacts with the Roman world, eventually adopted a more Roman style of coinage.

Indeed, in terms of material remains, the Bagendon excavation has demonstrated very clearly that the Gloucestershire Dobunni by the early decades of the first century A.D. enjoyed a closer cultural liaison with the Catuvellauni to the east than with the Atrebates to the south. Quite evidently, Arretine pottery, platters and butt-beakers at Bagendon were introduced via the commercial routes from the east, perhaps, as Hawkes has plausibly argued, in return for supplies of metals, iron and copper, possibly lead and tin from sources further west, and conceivably even Irish gold, brought by sea-routes up the Bristol Channel. The form of the earthwork itself at Bagendon, not a hillfort in the earlier Iron Age manner, but a system of extensive dykes, was surely derived from the essentially Catuvellaunian form of *oppidum* like Wheathampstead or Camulodunum. So long as this alliance could be sustained, to the exclusion of the pro-Roman faction in Wessex, Cunobelinus was doubtless content to leave the Dobunni politically independent.

Between these two blocs, on the other hand, the situation is by no means so clear. Though the Upper Thames basin was clearly subject to Belgic influence, the range of Belgic pottery types which were introduced into the region is extremely limited, with only the necked bowl with footring base appearing in significant numbers. Likewise, the coins of Cunobelinus barely extend west of the Cherwell or north of the Thames, where settlement on the gravel terraces continued unabated into the first century A.D. I have therefore argued elsewhere (1972, 117 ff.) that this region was not occupied by an intrusive Belgic population, but by indigenous communities who had been influenced by the east-west trade route from Camulodunum to Bagendon only to the extent of adopting certain superficial aspects of Belgic culture (I am obliged to Mr Leslie Alcock who has pointed out to me that the necked bowl with cordons is less characteristic of Wheathampstead and sites of the Belgic south-east than of Class B pottery at Hengistbury Head – Bushe-Fox, 1915).

Whether we still regard the Dobunni as Belgic invaders from among the Atrebates of Wessex, or whether their apparent rejection of the pro-Roman policies of Tincommius and Verica, and their greater commercial ties with the Catuvellauni are indicative of an antagonism towards Rome which stemmed from insular ancestry, remains in balance for the

222

XXXIII *Gold torcs from Ipswich, Suffolk (maximum diameter: 20 cm)*

V *The Mayer mirror (height: c. 22·5 cm)*

XXXV *Mirror from Desborough, Northamptonshire
(height: c. 35 cm)*

XXXVI *Ornamental spearhead from Thames, London (total length: c. 30 cm; length shown: c. 13 cm)*

XXXVII *Grave-group from Birdlip, Gloucestershire (height of mirror: c. 38·7 cm)*

moment. Indeed, with their tradition of staunch chauvinism, from Cassivellaunus to Caratacus, we must now question the extent to which the Catuvellauni themselves were truly Belgic in an immigrant sense.

For a possible resolution of this dilemma we must return to Caesar's account of the

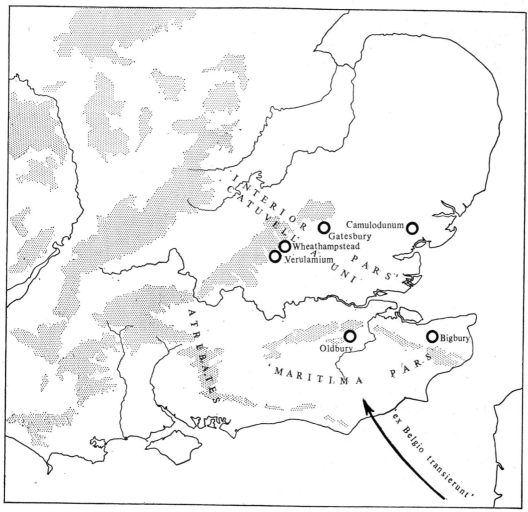

81. *Map: Caesar and the Belgic Invasions*

political structure of south-eastern Britain at the time of his expeditions (Fig. 81) (*de bello Gallico*, 5, 11–14). The passages describing the state of Britain are inserted in a fashion which has sometimes seemed an irrelevant interruption of the historical narrative, at the point where he has introduced for the first time the name of Cassivellaunus, who had been appointed supreme commander of the native resistance. Cassivellaunus' kingdom, he writes, is divided from the maritime states (*a maritimis civitatibus*) by the river Thames. Hitherto, there had been a succession of wars between this chief, Cassivellaunus, and those coastal states; their unity was therefore an expedient provoked by the common adversary, Caesar. At this point, Caesar inserts the apparent digression – no irrelevancy, in fact, for it immediately takes up the division, between the coastal states and the trans-Thames tribes, which has just been noted. The inland region (*pars interior*), he records, is inhabited by people who are proud of their native ancestry, by contrast with the maritime regions (*maritima pars*) which are occupied by tribes who migrated from Belgic Gaul, first in search of plunder, and subsequently to settle and till the land. The sustained contrast is evidently intended to take up the sense of the previous paragraph: in fact, it is Cassivellaunus and his tribes from across the Thames who are proud of their insular origins, and who therefore had naturally been waging continuous wars with the invading Belgae of the maritime states prior to Caesar's arrival. And when the truce between the warring tribes was declared, who better to appoint as allied commander than the native chieftain who clearly knew the terrain so well? The equation between the Belgic invaders and the maritime states is further reinforced when Caesar adds that the inhabitants of Kent (*quae regio est maritima omnis*) are in manners and customs most like the Gauls.

This much is clear, then, that from Caesar's account we may infer that the Catuvellaun were not among the invaders from Belgic Gaul, and were even chauvinistic about their native ancestry. How does this match up with the archaeological evidence? Can we sustain the division, apparently drawn, in Caesar's day, along the line of the Thames? Quite clearly from the coins of Tasciovanus and Cunobelinus, the Catuvellauni, as we have seen, expanded over the Thames to make inroads into the territory of the Atrebates. But at the time of Caesar's invasions, the distribution of Gallo-Belgic E coins spread throughout the south-east, with no regard for such a boundary. Not that we should expect them necessarily to do so, for this was the one period in a century or more when the tribes north and south of the Thames were in some kind of political union. But with Caesar's withdrawal, we may see the aggressive independence of the Catuvellauni reasserting itself in the distribution of British L_A coins, derived precisely *not* from 'foreign' models, but based upon British H and I coins, whose centre of distribution lay still further inland. (It is because of this derivation that the equation of British L coins with the name of Cassivellaunus is especially attractive.) The same indignant patriotism was being registered by Cunobelinus, as Stevens has argued (1951, 342), when he chose the ear of corn ('beer is best') emblem for his coins by contrast with the vine-leaf, symbol of Continental, Mediterranean wine, which was adopted by the pro-Roman ruler Verica, to the south of the Thames.

If, on the other hand, we consider those coins for which Allen has claimed a pre-Caesarian date, the sequence of events which led to the Thames being declared a boundary begins to emerge. First, the Gallo-Belgic A coins, indicating the original Belgic invaders, occupy Kent and Sussex on the one hand, and show a landfall in Essex on the other. In due course, the Gallo-Belgic B distribution suggests further penetration into the lower Thames basin, crossing north of the river. Up to this time, there was presumably no division at the Thames.

The native tribes, of course, will have originally held Kent and Sussex, until being driven progressively inland by the invaders from Belgic Gaul. It is with the next wave of Gallo-Belgic coinage, C, which Hawkes has attributed to Diviciacus, that the division begins to emerge. And though the tribal conflict may have continued long after Allen's date of around 100–80 B.C., the division between the native territories north of the Thames, where in due course the Catuvellauni emerge as the dominant power, and the Belgic 'maritime' states to the south, was evidently established *de facto*, even if it had not been ratified by mutual treaty. Indeed, we might wonder whether the obstacles which faced Caesar when he attempted to cross the Thames were designed solely for his benefit, or whether they already existed as part of the tribal frontier-works.

A distinction which can be traced between the Catuvellauni and the invading Belgic tribes is reflected in the kind of fortification employed by each. The distribution of Fécamp-type or Fécamp-derived earthworks (C. F. C. Hawkes, 1968, Fig. 2b), though limited numerically in Britain to just a few sites, is concentrated south of the Thames, notably at Hammer Wood, High Rocks, Oldbury and the Caburn. The Catuvellaunian method of defence, by contrast, was the network of low-lying dykes, embracing a wide area and probably incorporating natural features as part of its defensive system, as at Camulodunum. Similar defensive earthworks are known in the North Oxfordshire Grim's Ditch and at Bagendon, where the adoption of the Catuvellaunian type of earthwork may now be seen as a measure, not of the Belgic origin of the Dobunni, but of their native, non-Belgic sympathies. The fact that the Dobunni rejected the pro-Roman policies of Tincommius, and instead promoted a commercial alliance with the Catuvellauni, is perfectly consistent with this show of independence. The Catuvellaunian style of *oppidum*, of course, was not a continuous earthwork, but probably incorporated natural defences as well. Gaps were an advantage for manœuvring chariots in an assault or tactical withdrawal. The method of chariot warfare, which Caesar emphasised was so unfamiliar to his troops, we can now see was not a Belgic custom in Britain any more than it had been for some time in Gaul. It was Cassivellaunus who had maintained such a large retinue of charioteers, and the custom was clearly a native one which was used to great effect by the native contingent in the resistance to Caesar.

But the temporary alliance against Caesar was scarcely sufficient to repair the underlying enmity between the Catuvellauni and the intrusive Belgic tribes. Even during the campaigns of 55 and 54, there was still a strong element of dissent among the British tribes, which was liable to erupt into open conflict between the Catuvellauni and the Trinovantes. The latter, together with other tribes whose territories were adjacent to the East Anglian coast, were probably of Belgic origin; among them the tribal name of the Iceni could even be related to that of the Gaulish Cenimagni.

The fundamental antipathy between the Catuvellauni and the Belgic invaders of the south-east, however, did not prevent the native tribe from adopting a higher material standard of living comparable to that of the invaders. Though there are some slight differences in pottery-types between the Hertfordshire groups and those from Kent, which Dr

Birchall has indicated, there can be no doubt that the dominant native royal house was prepared to adopt new wheel-thrown wares, and in due course, with the move from Verulamium to Camulodunum, to exploit more fully the opportunities for foreign trade. More surprising, if truly native, may appear its adoption of the rite of cremation in the Belgic manner; though until we know more of the indigenous burial customs of Iron Age Britain, it is difficult to know just how radical a change this represents.

Who were the Catuvellauni, then, if they were not Belgae in the strictest sense (Guyonvarc'h, 1967)? And why should they have achieved a role so dominant in the political structure of later Iron Age Britain? Some years ago, it was thought that the name might be connected with that of the Gaulish Catalauni, and thereby cited as an instance which Caesar had in mind when he said that the Belgic tribes in the south-east of Britain retained the names of the parent tribes of Belgic Gaul. In his recent reappraisal of the Belgic invasions, C. F. C. Hawkes has been obliged to reject this suggestion, since he has clearly demonstrated that the Continental Catalauni occupied a region outside the area of 'Belgium'. Upon closer inspection, it transpires that the territory of these Catalauni was centred upon the Marne. Surely now the link with Britain must become apparent. Until they were driven inland by invading Belgic tribes at the end of the second century, the native population – who subsequently appear as the historical Catuvellauni – must have occupied a much wider territory which embraced much of the south-east of England, territory which under Tasciovanus and Cunobelinus they attempted in some measure to recover. It is precisely this area which, we have seen in an earlier chapter, was covered by the distribution of angular pottery and its allied types. In effect, then, the Catuvellauni were descended from Continental immigrants, not from Belgic Gaul, but from the early La Tène culture of the Marne several centuries earlier. Their adoption of Belgic pottery, and even the innovating burial rite, therefore, need excite less surprise, since, for all their chauvinism, the Catuvellauni were not ultimately native in the same sense as was the remainder of the early Iron Age population of southern and midland England. Ironically, perhaps, it has transpired from this enquiry that the figure who has long been regarded as the epitome of the intrusive culture of Belgic Gaul, may himself have been in fact a descendant of a Marnian invader.

IV. HISTORICAL SUMMARY

13
Invasion, commercial diffusion or insular evolution?

In the foregoing chapters, we have seen that there is a good deal of evidence in the British Iron Age for direct derivation of certain ceramic forms, metal types, and even some structural innovations from Continental Europe. It only remains now to weigh up the arguments for and against regarding any such innovations as evidence for actual immigration or martial invasions from the Continent, and to consider to what extent we can or should recognise an element of social or economic continuity from indigenous Bronze Age cultures.

The case for invasion from abroad at the outset of the Iron Age is inevitably – and possibly misleadingly – emphasised at the present time by the comparative lack of information concerning the nature and extent of late Bronze Age settlement in southern Britain. Against this background, the introduction of Hallstatt C bronzes, including swords and chapes, razors and *phalerae*, might well be seen as representative of immigrant adventurers infiltrating extensively around the coast of Britain, and paving the way for settlement by late Hallstatt colonists in the ensuing phase. With increasing recognition of the importance of pottery studies, it may be possible to identify many more sites like Scarborough, Eastbourne or Chalbury, which may serve as landmarks for this late Hallstatt settlement of southern and eastern England. In Wessex, meanwhile, the distinctive ceramic traditions of haematite-coated wares, horizontal furrowing and deeply incised ornament, with its ultimately late Urnfield ancestry, must surely argue strongly that here we are dealing with an immigrant – perhaps refugee – population whose origins lay in the more westerly province of Hallstatt culture on the Continent. The absence of a regular and consistent burial type for these earliest Iron Age cultures in Britain remains an enigma, and equally so whether we regard the population as largely intrusive or indigenous. The apparent absence of rectangular house-types, – perhaps not so totally unrepresented in Britain as conventionally assumed – need not preclude a Continental origin for insular cultures, once we recognise that the round-house itself had a wider Atlantic distribution, which included parts of France as well as the Hispanic peninsula and the British Isles. On the other hand, the lack of direct site continuity between later Bronze Age settlements and their Iron Age successors has perhaps been over-estimated in the past. Instead of seeking to assign our earliest hillforts to a late Bronze Age date, we might consider their defensive earthworks as an Iron Age manifestation of the importance of hill-top positions, which in the later Bronze Age had already been the focus of settlement, and perhaps even ritual, without the formality of a defensive enclosure. By convention, prehistorians are expected to produce a parade of evidence for any intrusive or innovating culture, including not only material remains but also new settlement-types and modes of burial. In fact, it is becoming apparent that, by the standards of Childe's original definition, most Iron Age cultural groups in

Britain are defective in one or other major aspect, not excluding those whose Continental origins are generally and legitimately acknowledged.

Judged by these standards, the early La Tène invasions from the Marne have been found defective by several authorities. But are not these standards too exacting for any phase of the Iron Age in Britain? Where are the distinctive Continental ceramic forms and rectangular houses which should be present if we are to acknowledge the intrusive nature of the Arras culture? Does not the absence of such house-types even weigh against the accepted doctrine of a Belgic invasion in southern and south-eastern Britain? Can a distinctive burial-type alone compensate for the absence of the full spectrum of cultural evidence demanded by Childe? If, for the sake of a working hypothesis, we are obliged to accept less rigorous criteria, then surely the Marnian invasion now stands upon firmer ground than it has stood upon hitherto. Not only have we a body of ceramic material concentrating in the south-east of England which displays undisputed affinities with the fifth-century angular wares of the Marne, but also this may now be supplemented by other material types, including the early La Tène dagger series and possibly some of the earliest La Tène I brooches. This south-eastern emphasis is reflected subsequently by the (admittedly still fairly meagre, but perhaps not insignificant) distribution of early swords and daggers of anthropoid type, while the wider impact of this phase of contact with the Continent was surely responsible for the original introduction into Britain of horse-bits of the three-link variety.

If the introduction of these new pottery forms and metal types was occasioned by an invasion of settlers from the Marne, this would seem to the present writer to affect only the south-east of England and Thames valley directly. In Wessex, the impact of such cross-Channel movements was certainly felt, and is reflected in such ceramic innovations as the haematite-coated bowls with horizontal cordons, themselves superseded towards the end of the fourth century by pedestal vases like those from Swallowcliffe Down, which owe their shape to more obvious Marnian inspiration. But at the present time we can scarcely sustain an invasion hypothesis on the strength of such a limited pottery distribution, while the brooches which occasionally accompany these pedestal vases are of the distinctly insular flattened-bow La Tène I variety. These secondary developments in Wessex, therefore, can be adequately explained as the product of commercial connections with the primary south-eastern zone, or indeed with the Continent itself, but imply no significant influx of invaders from abroad.

To the north, on the other hand, this period of immigration from the Champagne did result in settlement of newcomers, whose impact in eastern Yorkshire is curiously retarded, being represented in its initial phase by one distinctive burial only, at Cowlam. However distasteful this lack of evidence may be, we must surely accept Stead's contention that the inception of the Arras culture should be traced to the late fifth century or thereabouts, and perhaps reflect upon the implications of this conclusion for our assessment of the evidence for immigrant cultures elsewhere in southern Britain in the Iron Age.

Indeed, a comparison of the evidence from eastern Yorkshire with that from the south-east of England in the early La Tène phase shows that those elements which are present in the one are very largely lacking in the other. The distinctive angular wares of the south-east are not matched by any outstanding ceramic forms in Yorkshire; the cart-burials of the north-eastern group contrast with the marked absence of a regular form of burial in the south-east. Only at Newnham Croft might we claim a burial in the Continental tradition, and this is undoubtedly later than the primary south-eastern incursions. Finally, in respect of house-types, both regions lack the rectangular buildings of Central European derivation which some authorities have insisted should be introduced by an invading population. But with several tentative examples from the Upper Thames region, and the truly classic series now available further west at Crickley Hill, we must be encouraged to hope that excavation can yet throw light upon this vexed question. If a Marnian invasion of the south-east is still lacking in convincing demonstration, therefore, it is no more so than the intrusive La Tène cultures of eastern Yorkshire. *Per contra*, both, I believe, may reasonably be regarded as the most plausible explanation of evidence which by its very nature, we must expect to be less conclusive than we might wish.

The third and second centuries were evidently not marked by any major population movements into Britain. The rise of the insular style of Celtic art, though parallel with Continental developments, shows no direct dependence upon the latter which needs to be explained by further invasions. Moreover, the appearance of particular types, like the insular involuted and penannular brooches, attests the independence of British metal-workers at this period. Only towards the end of the second century, with the appearance, already before 100, of early Gallo-Belgic coins, is there evidence for renewed connections with the mainstream of events on the Continent.

The case for a Belgic invasion of south-eastern and central southern Britain has always seemed so decisive that it has perhaps received less critical attention than it should. The major innovations of coinage and wheel-thrown pottery, together with the existence of a distinctive method of burial in cremation-cemeteries like Aylesford and Swarling, has tended to obscure certain inconsistencies which emerge in a closer examination of the evidence for Belgic invasion. Most important is the disparity in dating between the initial introduction of Gallo-Belgic A and B coins, and the earliest dateable burials, with pottery associations, at least half a century later. As we have seen in the last chapter, the distribution of neither Gallo-Belgic C nor D coins is sufficiently widespread or intense to reflect more than secondary movements of consolidation from Belgic Gaul, while Gallo-Belgic E is dated much too close to the period of Caesar's own expedition to be equated with the invasions to which he referred. Here again, therefore, we have seen in operation the 're-tarded impact' effect whereby the presence of invaders, as in eastern Yorkshire, is barely noticeable archaeologically until several, or even many, generations later. Even then, the evidence of settlement-sites gives no indication of an innovating house-type of the Continental rectangular kind; in fact, Belgic huts rarely seem to achieve the symmetry of groundplan or architectural grandeur of earlier Iron Age houses.

Judged by the rigorous criteria which prehistorians have demanded that we apply to earlier periods of the Iron Age, indeed, the Belgic invasions which have for so long provided the linch-pin of proto-historic archaeology in Britain appear equally unsustained. That they should be so is a measure less of the inherent deficiency of the archaeological record, than of a slovenly and uncritical reading of the historical evidence, which may now form the basis for a new interpretation of the Belgic period in Britain. Building upon Caesar's division of the tribes of south-eastern England, we may now see Cassivellaunus not simply as the architect of resistance to Roman invasion, but as the chauvinistic opponent of Belgic aggression in the pre-Caesarian period as well. And if the result of this enquiry has been to bolster the case for the somewhat discredited Marnian-invasion hypothesis on the one hand, and to qualify the long accepted view of widespread Belgic invasions on the other, the irony of this situation may appear less acute if we regard the two phases as no longer distinct and separate, but as a cumulative process in the colonisation of south-eastern Britain.

Abbreviations

AHR   Agricultural History Review
Ant. J.   Antiquaries Journal
Arch. Aeliana   Archaeologia Aeliana
Arch. Camb.   Archaeologia Cambrensis
Arch. Cant.   Archaeologia Cantiana
Arch J.   Archaeological Journal
BBOJ   Berks, Bucks and Oxon Archaeological Journal
Berks. Arch. J.   Berkshire Archaeological Journal
B.M.   British Museum
BRGK   Bericht der Römisch-Germanische Kommission
C.B.A.   Council for British Archaeology
ERA   East Riding Archaeologist
HFC   Proceedings of the Hampshire Field Club and Archaeological Society
JBAA   Journal of the British Archaeological Association
JRGZM   Jahrbuch des Römisch-Germanischen Zentralmuseums im Mainz
JRIC   Journal of the Royal Institution of Cornwall
JRS   Journal of Roman Studies
Oxon.   Oxoniensia
PCAS   Proceedings of the Cambridge Antiquarian Society
PDNHAS   Proceedings of the Dorset Natural History and Archaeological Society
POAHS   Proceedings of the Oxford Architectural and Historical Society
PPS   Proceedings of the Prehistoric Society
Proc. Soc. Ant. Lond.   Proceedings of the Society of Antiquaries of London
PSANHS   Proceedings of the Somerset Archaeological and Natural History Society
PSAS   Proceedings of the Society of Antiquaries of Scotland
Rep. Oxon. Arch. Soc.   Report of the Oxfordshire Archaeological Society
SAC   Surrey Archaeological Collections
SxAC   Sussex Archaeological Collections
TBGAS   Transactions of the Bristol and Gloucester Archaeological Society
TEHAS   Transactions of the East Hertfordshire Archaeological Society
TLCHS   Transactions of the Lancashire and Cheshire Historical Society
TLAS   Transactions of the Leicestershire Archaeological Society
TWFC   Transactions of the Woolhope Field Club, Herefordshire
WAM   Wiltshire Archaeological Magazine
UJA   Ulster Journal of Archaeology

Bibliography

ABERG, F. A. (1957). 'The early plough in Europe', *Gwerin*, 1, 171–81.

ADAMS, W. Y. (1968). 'Invasion, diffusion, evolution?', *Antiquity*, 42, 194–215.

ALCOCK, L. (1962). 'Settlement patterns in Celtic Britain', *Antiquity*, 36, 51–4.

(1965). 'Hillforts in Wales and the Marches', *Antiquity*, 39, 184–95.

(1969). 'Excavations at South Cadbury Castle, 1968', *Ant. J*, 49, 30–40.

ALEXANDER, J. (1964). 'The origin of penannular brooches', *PPS*, 30, 429–30.

ALLEN, D. (1958). 'The origin of coinage in Britain: a reappraisal', in FRERE (ed.) (1958), 97–308.

(1962). 'Celtic coins', in ORDNANCE SURVEY (1962), 19–32.

(1967). 'Iron currency bars in Britain', *PPS*, 33, 307–35.

ALLEN, G. W. G. (1938). 'Marks seen from the air in the crops near Dorchester, Oxon', *Oxon.*, 3, 169–71.

(1940). 'Crop marks seen from the air, Northfield Farm, Long Wittenham, Berks', *Oxon.*, 5. 164–5.

ALLIBONE, T. E. *et al.* (1970). *The Impact of the Natural Sciences on Archaeology.*

ANDREW, W. J. (1933). 'Report on the first excavations at Oliver's Battery in 1930', *HFC*, 12, 5–10.

APPLEBAUM, S. (1954). 'The agriculture of the British Iron Age . . .', *PPS*, n.s. 20, 1954, 103–14.

(1966), 'Peasant economy and types of agriculture', in *Rural Settlement in Roman Britain* C.B.A. Research Report 7, 99–107.

ARKELL, W. J. (1939). 'The site of Cherbury Camp', *Oxon.* 4, 196–7.

ARTHUR, B. V. and JOPE, E. M. (1962). 'Early Saxon pottery kilns at Purwell Farm, Cassington, Oxfordshire', *Medieval Archaeology*, 6–7, 1–14.

ARTIS, E. T. (1828). *The Durobrivae of Antonius.*

ATKINSON, D. (1916). *The Romano-British Site on Lowbury Hill in Berkshire.*

ATKINSON, R. J. C. (1942). 'Archaeological sites in Port Meadow, Oxford', *Oxon.*, 7, 24–35.

ATKINSON, R. J. C. and PIGGOTT, S. (1955). 'The Torrs Chamfrein', *Archaeologia*, 96, 197–235.

ATKINSON, R. J. C., PIGGOTT, C. M. and SANDARS, N. K. (1951). *Excavations at Dorchester, Oxon.*

AVERY, D. M. E. (1968). 'Excavations at Meare East, 1966', *PSANHS*, 112, 21–39.

AVERY, D. M. E. and CLOSE-BROOKS, J. (1969). 'Shearplace Hill, Sydling St Nicholas, Dorset, House A: a suggested re-interpretation', *PPS*, 35, 345–51.

AVERY, D. M. E. *et al.* (1967). 'Rainsborough, Northants, Excavations 1961–5', *PPS*, 33, 207–306.

BARBER, J. and MEGAW, J. V. S. (1963). 'A decorated Iron Age bridle-bit in the London Museum: its place in art and archaeology', *PPS*, 29, 206–13.

BARKER, H. and MACKEY, C. J. (1960). 'British Museum Radiocarbon Measurements II', *American Journ. Science Radiocarbon Supplement 2.*

BARTON, K. J. (1962). 'Settlements of the Iron Age and Pagan Saxon periods at Linford, Essex', *Trans. Essex Arch. Soc.* Vol. 1, Pt 2, 3rd series, 57–104.

BAYNE, N. (1957) 'Excavations at Lyneham Camp, Lyneham, Oxon', *Oxon.*, 22, 1–10.

BEEX, G. and HULST, R. S. (1968). 'A Hilversum culture settlement near Nijnsel . . ., North Brabant', *Bericht. Rijksdienst Oudheidkundig Bodemonderzoek*, 18, 117–30.

BELLORIUS J. P. (1704). *Columna Cochlis M. Aurelio Antonino Augusto dicata . . . a P.S. Bartolo aere incisa.*

BERSU, G. (1940). 'Excavations at Little Woodbury, Wiltshire . . .', *PPS*, 6, 30–111.

(1945a). 'Celtic homesteads in the Isle of Man', *Journ. Manx Museum*, 5, 177–82.

(1945b). *Das Wittnauer Horn.*

(1948). 'Fort at Scotstarvit, Fife', *PSAS*, 82, 1947–8, 241–63.

BERSU, G. and GOESSLER, P. (1924). 'Der Lochenstein bei Balingen', *Fundberichte aus Schwaben*, NF. 11, 1922–4, 73–103.

BIANCHETTI, E. (1895). *I Sepolcreti di Ornavasso.*

BIDDLE, M. (1965). 'Excavations at Winchester, 1964', *Ant. J.* 45, 230–64.

BIRCHALL, A. (1965). 'The Aylesford-Swarling culture: the problem of the Belgae reconsidered', *PPS*, 31, 241–367.

BOWEN, H. C. (1961). *Ancient Fields*, British Association for the Advancement of Science.

(1967). 'Corn storage in antiquity', *Antiquity*, 41, 214–15.

(1969). 'The Celtic background' in *The Roman Villa in Britain*, ed. A. L. F. Rivet, 1–48.

BOWEN, H. C. and FOWLER, P. J. (1966). 'Romano-British rural settlements in Dorset and Wiltshire', in THOMAS, A. C. (1966), 43–67.

BOYD-DAWKINS, W. (1862). 'Traces of the Early Britons in the neighbourhood of Oxford', *POAHS* n.s. 1, 1860–4, 108–16.

(1902). 'On Bigberry Camp . . .', *Arch. J*, 59, 211–18.

BRADFORD, J. S. P. (1940). 'The excavations of Cherbury Camp', *Oxon.*, 5, 13–20.

(1942a). 'An Early Iron Age site at Allen's Pit, Dorchester', *Oxon.*, 7, 36–60.

(1942b). 'An Early Iron Age site on Blewburton Hill, Berks', *Berks. Arch. J*, 46, 97–104.

(1942c). 'An Early Iron Age settlement at Standlake, Oxon', *Ant. J*, 22, 202–14.

BRADFORD, J. S. P. and GOODCHILD, R. G. (1939). 'Excavations at Frilford, Berks', 1937–8, *Oxon.*, 4, 1–80.

BRADFORD, J. S. P. and LOWTHER, A. W. G. (1946). 'Iron Age pottery from Yarnton, Oxon: further notes', *Oxon.*, 11–12, 175–81.

BRADLEY, R. (1971a). 'Stock raising and the origins of the hill-fort on the South Downs', *Ant. J*, 51, 8–29.

(1971b). 'Economic change in the growth of early hill forts', in JESSON and HILL (1971), 71–83.

BRAILSFORD, J. (1948). 'Excavations at Little Woodbury, Wiltshire (1938–9), Part II: The pottery', *PPS*, 14, 1–18.

(1957). 'The Durotrigian culture', *PDNHAS*, 79, 118–21.

BREWSTER, T. C. M. (1963). *The Excavation of Staple Howe*, 1963.

BRISSON, A., ROUALET, P., and HATT, J.-J. (1972). 'Le cimitière gaulois La Tène Ia du Mont-Gravet, à Villeneuve-Renneville (Marne)', *Mémoires de la Société d'Agriculture, Commerce, Sciences et Arts du département de la Marne*, 87, 7–48.

BRISSON, A. and HATT, J-J. (1955). 'Cimetières gaulois et gallo-romains à enclos en Champagne', *Revue Archéologique de L'Est et du Centre-Est*, 6, 313–33.

BRITTON, D. (1968). 'Late Bronze Age finds in the Heathery Burn Cave, Co. Durham', *Inventaria Archaeologica*, G.B., 9th set.

(1971). 'The Heathery Burn Cave revisited', in *Prehistoric and Roman Studies*, ed. G. de G. Sieveking, B.M.

BROOKS, R. J. (1964). 'The Rumps, St Minver: interim report on the 1963 excavations', *Cornish Archaeology*, 3, 26–34.

(1966). 'The Rumps: second interim report on the 1965 season', *Cornish Archaeology*, 5, 4–11.

BROOKS, R. J. (1968). 'The Rumps, St Minver: third interim report, 1967 season', *Cornish Archaeology*, 7, 38–40.

BUDGEN, W. (1922). 'Hallstatt pottery from Eastbourne', *Ant. J*, 2, 354–60.

BULLEID, A. (1926). *The Lake-Villages of Somerset*.

BULLEID, A. and GRAY, H. ST-G. see GLASTONBURY and MEARE.

BURGESS, C. B. (1970). 'The Bronze Age', *Current Archaeology*, 19, 208–15.

BURROW, E. J. *et al.* (1925). 'Leckhampton Hill', *TBGAS*, 47, 82–112.

BURSTOW, G. P. and HOLLEYMAN, G. A. (1957). 'Late Bronze Age settlement on Itford Hill, Sussex', *PPS*, 23, 167–212.

(1964). 'Excavations at Ranscombe Camp, 1959–60', *SxAC*, 102, 55–67.

BUSHE-FOX, J. P. (1915). *Excavations at Hengistbury Head, Hampshire, 1911–12*, Report of the Research Committee of the Society of Antiquaries of London, 3.

(1925). *Excavations of the Late-Celtic Urnfield at Swarling, Kent*, Report of the Research Committee of the Society of Antiquaries of London, 5, 1–55.

BUTTLER, W. (1936). 'Pits and pit-dwellings in Southeast Europe', *Antiquity*, 10, 25–36.

CALKIN, J. B. (1948). 'The Isle of Purbeck in the Iron Age', *PDNHAS*, 70, 29–59.

(1964). 'Some Early Iron Age sites in the Bournemouth area', *PDNHAS*, 86, 120–30.

CAPRINO, C. *et al.* (1955). *La Colonna di Marco Aurelio*.

CASE, H. J. (1949). 'The Standlake Iron Age sword', *Rep. Oxon. Arch. Soc.*, 87, 7–8.

(1954). 'The Prehistoric period', in *The Oxford Region*, ed. A. F. Martin and R. W. Steel.

(1958). 'A Late Belgic burial at Watlington, Oxon', *Oxon.*, 23, 139–41.

CASE, H. J. *et al.* (1964). 'Excavations at City Farm, Hanborough, Oxon', *Oxon.*, 29/30, 1–98.

CHAMPION, S. (1974). 'Leckhampton', in HARDING, D. W. (1974).

CHEVALLIER, R. and ERTLÉ, R. (1965). 'Un fond de cabane gauloise à Berry-au-Bac, (Aisne)', *Revue Archéologique de l'Est et du Centre-Est*, 16, 206–14.

CHILDE, V. G. (1935). *The Prehistory of Scotland*.

(1940). *Prehistoric Communities of the British Isles*.

(1946). *Scotland before the Scots*.

(1951). 'The balanced sickle', in *Aspects of Archaeology in Britain and Beyond*, ed. W. F. Grimes, 39–48.

(1954). 'Rotary motion', in *A History of Technology*, Vol. 1, ed. C. Singer, E. J. Holmyard and A. R. Hall, 187–215.

(1956). *Piecing Together the Past*.

CLARK, J. G. D. (1936). 'Report on a Late Bronze Age site in Mildenhall Fen', *Ant. J*, 16, 29–50.

(1952). *Prehistoric Europe, the Economic Basis*.

(1966). 'The invasion hypothesis in British Archaeology', *Antiquity*, 40, 172–89.

CLARK, J. G. D. and FELL, C. I. (1953). 'An Early Iron Age site at Micklemoor Hill, West Harling, Norfolk . . .', *PPS*, 19, 1–40.

CLARKE, R. R. (1960). *East Anglia*.

CLARKE, R. R. and APLING, H. (1935). 'An Iron Age tumulus on Warborough Hill, Stiffkey, Norfolk', *Norfolk and Norwich Archaeological Society*, 25, 408–28.

CLARKE, R. R. and DOLLEY, R. H. M. (1954). 'The Early Iron Age treasure from Snettisham, Norfolk', *PPS*, 20, 27–86.

CLARKE, R. R. and HAWKES, C. F. C. (1955). 'An Iron anthropoid sword from Shouldham, Norfolk', *PPS*, 21, 198–227.

CLAY, R. C. C. (1924). 'An Early Iron Age site on Fyfield Bavant Down', *WAM*, 42, 457–96.

(1925). 'An inhabited site of La Tène I date, on Swallowcliffe Down', *WAM*, 43, 59–93.

CLEERE, H. F. (1972). 'The classification of early iron-smelting furnaces', *Ant. J*, 52, 8–23.

CLIFFORD, E. M. (1961). *Bagendon: A Belgic Oppidum*.

CLOSE-BROOKS, J. (1965). 'Proposta per una suddivisione in fasi' [Veii, Quattro Fontanili Villanovan cemetery], *Notizie degli Scavi*[8], 19, 53–64.

COCKS, A. H. (1909). 'Pre-historic pit-dwellings at Ellesborough', *Records of Bucks*, 9, 349–61.

COGHLAN, H. H. (1956). *Notes on Prehistoric and Early Iron in the Old World*.

COLBERT DE BEAULIEU, J. B. (1957). 'Le trésor de Jersey II et la numismatique Celtique des deux Bretagnes', *Revue Belge de Numismatique*, 103, 47–88.

(1958). 'Armorican coin hoards in the Channel Islands', *PPS*, 24, 201–10.

(1959). 'Un troisième lot de la récolte de Jersey-II', *Revue Belge de Numismatique*, 105, 49–57.

COLLINS, A. E. P. (1947). 'Excavations on Blewburton Hill, 1947', *Berks. Arch. J*, 50, 4–29.

(1952). 'Excavations on Blewburton Hill, 1948–49', *Berks. Arch. J*, 53, 21–64.

COLLINS, A. E. P. and COLLINS, F. J. (1959). 'Excavations at Blewburton Hill, Berks, 1953', *Berks. Arch. J*, 57, 52–73.

COMBIER, J. (1961). 'Information archéologiques . . . Grenoble: Sérézin-du-Rhône (Isère)', *Gallia Préhistoire*, 4, 316–18.

COOMBS, D. (1974). 'Mam Tor' in HARDING, D. W. (1974).

COTTON, M. A. (1954). 'British camps with timber-laced ramparts', *Arch. J*, 111, 26–105.

(1957). '*Muri Gallici*', in WHEELER and RICHARDSON (1957), 159–216.

(1961). 'Robin Hood's Arbour and rectilinear enclosures in Berkshire', *Berks. Arch. J*, 59, 1–35.

(1962). 'Berkshire hill-forts', *Berks. Arch. J*, 60, 30–52.

COTTON, M. A. and FRERE, S. S. (1968). 'Ivinghoe Beacon excavations, 1963–5', *Records of Bucks*, 18, 187–260.

COWEN, J. D. (1967). 'The Hallstatt sword of bronze: on the continent and in Britain', *PPS*, 33, 377–454.

CRAWFORD, O. G. S. (1930). 'Grim's Ditch in Wychwood, Oxon', *Antiquity*, 4, 303–15.

CRAWFORD, O. G. S. and WHEELER, R. E. M. (1921). 'The Llynfawr and other hoards of the Bronze Age', *Archaeologia*, 71, 133–40.

CREE, J. E. and CURLE, A. O. (1922). 'Account of the excavations on Traprain Law during the summer of 1921', *PSAS*, 56, 189–259.

CROSSLEY-HOLLAND, P. (1942). 'Iron Age pottery from Chinnor, Oxon', *Oxon.*, 7, 108–9.

CUNLIFFE, B. (1968). 'Early pre-Roman Iron Age communities in eastern England', *Ant. J*, 68, 175–91.

CUNLIFFE, B. and PHILLIPSON, D. W. (1968). 'Excavation at Eldon's Seat, Encombe, Dorset, England', *PPS*, 34, 191–237.

CUNLIFFE, B. *et al.* (1964). *Winchester Excavations, 1949–1960*, Vol. 3.

CUNNINGTON, M. E. (1912). 'A Late Celtic inhabited site at All Cannings Cross Farm', *WAM*, 37, 526–39.

CUNNINGTON, M. E. (1923). *All Cannings Cross*.

(1924). 'Pits in Battlesbury Camp', *WAM*, 42, 368–73.

(1925). 'Figsbury Rings. An account of excavations in 1924', *WAM*, 43, 48–58.

(1933). 'Excavations in Yarnbury Castle Camp, 1932', *WAM*, 46, 198–213.

(1934). *An Introduction to the Archaeology of Wiltshire*, (2nd edition).

(1917). (with CUNNINGTON, B. H.) 'Lidbury Camp', *WAM*, 40, 12–36.

CURWEN, E. C. (1929). 'Excavations in the Trundle, Goodwood, 1928', *SxAC*, 70, 33–85.

(1930). 'Wolstonbury', *SxAC*, 71, 237–45.

(1931a). 'Excavations in the Trundle', *SxAC*, 72, 100–50.

(1931b). 'The date of Cissbury Camp', *Ant. J*, 11, 14–36.

(1932). 'Excavations at Hollingbury Camp, Sussex', *Ant. J*, 12, 1–16.

(1934). 'A Late Bronze Age farm and a Neolithic pit-dwelling on New Barn Down, Clapham, nr. Worthing', *SxAC*, 75, 137–70.

CURWEN, ELIOT and CURWEN, E. CECIL. (1927). 'Excavations in the Caburn, near Lewis', *SxAC*, 68, 1–56.

DAVIS, J. B. and THURNAM, J. (1865). *Crania Britannica*. 2, 18.

DAWSON, G. J. (1961). 'Excavations at Purwell Farm, Cassington', *Oxon.*, 26/27, 1–6.

DEHN, W. (1953). 'A prehistoric wall of sun-dried brick', *Antiquity*, 27, 164.

(1960). 'Einige Bemerkungen zum "Murus Gallicus"', *Germania*, 38, 43–55.

(1961). 'Zangentore an Spätkeltischen Oppida', *Pamatky Arch.*, 52, 390–6.

(1963). 'Frühe Drehscheibenkeramik nördlich der Alpen', *Alt-Thuringen*, 6, 372–82.

DEHN, W. and FREY, O.-H. (1962). 'Die absolute Chronologie der Hallstatt-und Frühlatenezeit Mitteleuropes auf Grund des Südimports', *Atti VI Cong. Internat. Scienze Preist. e Protost.* 1, 197–208.

DETSICAS, A. P. (1966). 'An Early Iron Age and Romano-British site at Stone Castle Quarry, Greenhithe', *Arch. Cant.* 81, 136–90.

DEWAR, H. S. L. and GODWIN, H. (1963). 'Archaeological discoveries in the raised bogs of the Somerset Levels, England', *PPS*, 29, 17–49.

DIXON, P. W. (1972). 'Crickley Hill, 1969–71', *Antiquity*, 46, 49–52.

(1974). 'Crickley Hill', in HARDING, D. W. (1974).

DRIEHAUS, J. (1971). 'Zum Grabfund von Waldalgesheim', *Hamburger Beiträge zur Archäologie*, Bd 1, Ht 2, 101–14.

DUDLEY, D. and JOPE, E. M. (1965). 'An Iron Age cist-burial with two brooches from Trevone, North Cornwall', *Cornish Archaeology*, 4, 18–23.

DUNNING, G. C. (1931). 'Salmonsbury Camp, Gloucestershire', *Antiquity*, 5, 489–91.

(1934). 'The swan's neck and ring-headed pins of the Early Iron Age in Britain', *Arch. J*, 91, 269–95.

(1959). 'The distribution of socketed axes of Breton type', *UJA*, 22, 53–5.

DYER, J. F. (1961). 'Dray's Ditches, Bedfordshire, and Early Iron Age Territorial boundaries in the Eastern Chilterns', *Ant. J*, 41, 32–43.

DYMOND, C. W. (1902). *Worlebury, An Ancient Stronghold in the County of Somerset*.

ELLISON, A. and DREWETT, P. (1971). 'Pits and post-holes in the British Early Iron Age', *PPS*, 37, 183–94.

ERITH, F. H. and HOLBERT, P. R. (1970). 'The Iron Age "A" Farmstead at Vinces Farm, Ardleigh',

Colchester Archaeological Group Quarterly Bulletin, Vol. 13, No. 1, 1–26.

EVANS, A. J. (1890). 'On a Late-Celtic urn-field at Aylesford, Kent', *Archaeologia*, 52, 315–88.

(1915). 'Late-Celtic dagger, fibula and jet cameo', *Archaeologia*, 46, 569–72.

FAVRET, P. M. (1936). 'Les Nécropoles des Jogasses à Chouilly (Marne)', *Préhistoire*, 5, 24–119.

FELL, C. I. (1936). 'The Hunsbury hill-fort, Northants . . .', *Arch. J*, 93, 57–100.

(1952). 'An Early Iron Age settlement at Linton, Cambridgeshire', *PCAS*, 46, 31–42.

FILIP, J. (1960). *Celtic Civilization and Its Heritage*.

FOURDRIGNIER, E. (1878). *Double sepulture gauloise de la Gorge-Meillet, territoire de Somme-Tourbe (Marne)*.

FOWLER, E. (1960). 'The origins and development of the penannular brooch in Europe', *PPS*, 26, 149–77.

FOWLER, P. J. (1960). 'Excavations at Madmarston Camp, Swalcliffe, 1957–58', *Oxon.*, 25, 3–48.

FOWLER, P. J. and EVANS, J. G. (1967). 'Ploughmarks, lynchets and early fields', *Antiquity*, 41, 289–301.

FOX, A. (1954). 'Celtic fields and farms on Dartmoor, in the light of recent excavations at Kestor', *PPS*, 20, 87–102.

(1958). 'South-Western hill-forts', in FRERE (ed.) (1958), 35–60.

FOX, C. (1923). *The Archaeology of the Cambridge Region*.

(1927). 'A La Tène I brooch from Wales', *Arch. Camb.*, 82, 67–112.

(1946). *A Find of the Early Iron Age from Llyn Cerrig Bach, Anglesey*.

(1958). *Pattern and Purpose, a Survey of Early Celtic Art in Britain*.

FOX, C. and HYDE, H. A. (1939). 'A Second cauldron and an iron sword from the Llyn Fawr hoard, Rhigos, Glamorganshire', *Ant. J*, 19, 369–91.

FOX, C. and WOLSELEY, G. R. (1928). 'The Early Iron Age site at Findon Park, Findon, Sussex', *Ant. J*, 8, 449–60.

FRERE, S. S. (1940). 'A survey of archaeology near Lancing', *SxAC*, 81, 140–72.

(1944). 'An Iron Age site at West Clandon, Surrey . . .', *Arch. J*, 101, 50–67.

(1947). 'The Iron Age finds from the Warren, Esher', *Ant. J*, 27, 36–46.

(1958). (ed.) *Problems of the Iron Age in Southern Britain*.

GARDNER, W. and SAVORY, H. N. (1964). *Dinorben*.

GLASTONBURY I: Bulleid, A. and Gray, H. StG., *The Glastonbury Lake Village*, Vol. 1, 1911.

II: *The Glastonbury Lake Village*, Vol. 2, 1917.

GODDARD, E. H. (1894). 'Notes on the opening of a tumulus on Cold Kitchen Hill, 1893', *WAM*, 27, 271–91.

GODWIN, H. (1941). 'Studies of the post-glacial history of British vegetation, VI. Correlations in the Somerset levels', *New Phytologist*, 40, 108–32.

GOODCHILD, R. G. and KIRK, J. R. (1954). 'The Romano-Celtic temple at Woodeaton', *Oxon.*, 19, 15–37.

GREEN, C. (1949). 'The Birdlip Early Iron Age burials: a review', *PPS*, 15, 188–90.

GREENWELL, W. (1894). 'Antiquities of the Bronze Age found in the Heathery Burn Cave, County Durham', *Archaeologia*, 54, 87–114.

GRESHAM, C. A. (1939). 'Spettisbury Rings, Dorset', *Arch. J*, 96, 114–31.

GRIMES, W. F. (1943). 'Excavations at Stanton Harcourt, Oxon, 1940', *Oxon.*, 8–9, 19–63.

(1948). 'A prehistoric temple at London Airport', *Archaeology*, 1, 74–9.

GRIMES W. F. (1951). 'The Jurassic way across England', in *Aspects of Archaeology in Britain and Beyond*, ed. W. F. Grimes, 144–71.

(1952). 'Art on British Iron Age pottery', *PPS*, 18, 160–75.

(1958). 'Settlement at Braughton, Northants., Colsterworth, Lincs. and Heathrow, Middx' in FRERE (ed.) (1958), 21–8.

GURNEY, F. G. and HAWKES, C. F. C. (1940). 'An Early Iron Age inhumation burial at Egginton, Bedfordshire', *Ant. J*, 20, 230–44.

GUYONVARC'H, C. J. (1967). 'Les noms des peuples Belges II', *Celticum*, 18, 299–314.

HALL, D. W., HASWELL, G. A. and OXLEY, T. A. (1956). 'Underground storage of grain', *Colonial Research Studies*, No. 21, H.M. Stationery Office for the Colonial Office.

HAMILTON, J. R. C. (1968). *Excavations at Clickhimin, Shetland.*

HAMLIN, A. (1963). 'Excavations of ring-ditches and other sites at Stanton Harcourt', *Oxon.*, 28, 1–19.

(1966). 'Early Iron Age sites at Stanton Harcourt', *Oxon.*, 31, 1–27.

HARBISON, P. (1969). 'The Chariot of Celtic funerary tradition', in *Marburger Beiträge zur Archäologie der Kelten, Festschrift W. Dehn, Fundberichte aus Hessen*, 1, 34–58.

(1971). 'The Old Irish "Chariot"', *Antiquity*, 45, 171–7.

HARDEN, D. B. (1937). 'Excavations on Grim's Dyke, North Oxfordshire', *Oxon.*, 2, 74–92.

(1942). 'Excavations in Smith's Pit II, Cassington, Oxon', *Oxon.*, 7, 104–7.

(1950). 'Italic and Etruscan finds in Britain', *Atti del I° Congresso Internazionale di Preistoria e Protostoria Mediterranea*, Florence.

HARDING, D. W. (1959). 'Excavation of multiple banks, Thickthorn Down, Dorset', *PDNHAS*, 81, 110–13.

(1964). 'The west settlement', in CASE (1964), 79–88.

(1966). 'The pottery from Kirtlington, and its implications for the chronology of the earliest, Iron Age in the Upper Thames region', *Oxon.*, 31, 158–61.

(1967). 'Blewburton', *Current Archaeology*, 4, 83–5.

(1970). 'The "new" Iron Age', *Current Archaeology*, 20, 235–40.

(1972). *The Iron Age of the Upper Thames Basin.*

(1973). 'Round and rectangular: Iron Age houses, British and foreign', *Archaeology into History*, 1, *Greeks, Celts and Romans*, (eds) C. F. C. and S. C. Hawkes, 43–62.

(1974). (ed.) *Hillforts; a survey of research in Britain and Ireland.*

HARDING, D. W. and BLAKE, I. M. (1963). 'An Early Iron Age settlement in Dorset', *Antiquity*, 37, 63–4.

HARDING, J. M. (1964). 'Interim report on the excavation of a Late Bronze Age homestead in Weston Wood, Albury, Surrey', *SAC*, 61, 10–17.

HARDY, H. R. (1937). 'An Iron Age pottery site near Horsted Keynes', *SxAC*, 78, 253–65.

HARTLEY, B. R. (1956). 'The Wandlebury Iron Age hill-fort, excavations of 1955–6', *PCAS*, 50, 1–28.

HASTINGS, F. A. (1965). 'Excavation of an Iron Age farmstead at Hawk's Hill, Leatherhead', *SAC* 62, 1–43.

HATT, J. J. and HEINTZ, G. (1951). 'Découverte d'une cabane gallo-romaine précoce à Achenheim', *Cahiers d'archéol. et d'hist. d'Alsace*, 9, 47–52.

HAWKES, C. F. C. (1931). 'Hill forts', *Antiquity*, 5, 60–97.

(1935). 'The pottery from the sites on Plumpton Plain', *PPS*, 1, 39–59.

(1936). 'The excavations at Buckland Rings, Lymington, 1935', *HFC*, 13, 124–64.

(1938). 'A Hallstatt bronze sword from the Thames at Taplow', *Ant. J*, 18, 185–7.

(1939). 'The Caburn pottery and its implications', *SxAC*, 80, 217–62.

(1940a). 'The excavations at Quarley Hill, 1938', *HFC*, 14, 136–94.

(1940b). 'The Marnian pottery and La Tène I brooch from Worth, Kent', *Ant. J*, 20, 115–21.

(1940c). 'The excavations at Bury Hill, 1939', *HFC*, 14, 291–337.

(1940d). 'An Iron Age torc from Spettisbury Rings, Dorset', *Arch. J*, 97, 112–14.

(1946). 'Prehistoric Lincolnshire', *Arch. J*, 103, 4–15.

(1947). 'Britons, Romans and Saxons round Salisbury and on Cranborne Chase: reviewing the excavations of General Pitt-Rivers, 1881–1889', *Arch. J*, 104, 27–81.

(1959). 'The ABC of the British Iron Age', *Antiquity*, 33, 170–82.

(1961). 'The Western Third C Culture and the Belgic Dobunni', in CLIFFORD (1961), 43–67.

(1962). 'The Iron Age pottery from Linford, Essex', in BARTON (1962), 83–7.

(1966). 'British prehistory: the invasion hypothesis', *Antiquity*, 40, 297–9.

(1968). 'New thoughts on the Belgae', *Antiquity*, 42, 6–16.

(1971). 'Fence, wall, dump, from Troy to Hod', in JESSON and HILL (1971), 5–18.

(1972). 'Europe and England: fact and fog', *Helinium*, 12, 105–16.

HAWKES, C. F. C. and DUNNING, G. C. (1930). 'The Belgae of Gaul and Britain', *Arch. J*, 87, 150–335.

HAWKES, C. F. C. and FELL, C. I. (1943). 'The Early Iron Age settlement at Fengate, Peterborough', *Arch. J*, 100, 188–223.

HAWKES, C. F. C. and HULL, M. R. (1947). *Camulodunum*, Report of the Research Committee of the Society of Antiquaries of London, No. 14.

HAWKES, C. F. C. and JACOBSTAL, P. (1944). 'A Celtic bird-brooch from Red Hill, near Long Eaton: Notts.', *Ant. J*, 24, 117–24.

HAWKES, C. F. C., MYRES, J. N. L. and STEVENS, C. G. (1930). 'St Catharine's Hill, Winchester', *HFC*, 11.

HAWKES, C. F. C. and PIGGOTT, S. (eds) (1948). *A Survey and Policy of Field Research in the Archaeology of Great Britain.*

HAWKES, C. F. C. and SMITH, M. A. (1957). 'On some buckets and cauldrons of the Bronze and Early Iron Ages', *Ant J.*, 37, 131–98.

HAWKES, J. (1946). 'The beginning of history: a film', *Antiquity*, 20, 78–82.

(1968). 'The proper study of mankind', *Antiquity*, 42, 255–62.

HAWKES, S. C. (1958). 'Early Iron Age enclosures on Longbridge Deverill Cow Down, Wiltshire', in FRERE (ed.) (1958), 18–20.

HEARNE, T. (1717). *Diaries*, 74.

HELBAEK, H. (1952). 'Early crops in Southern England', *PPS*, 18, 194–233.

(1957). 'Carbonised cereals', in BURSTOW and HOLLEYMAN (1957), 206–9.

HENCKEN, T. C. (1938). 'The excavation of the Iron Age camp on Bredon Hill, Worcestershire, 1935–37', *Arch. J*, 95, 1–111.

HERMANN, F.-R. (1966). *Die Funde der Urnenfelderkultur in Mittel-und Südhessen.*

HIGGS, E. S. and WHITE, J. P. (1963). 'Autumn Killing', *Antiquity*, 37, 282–9.

HODGES, H. W. M. (1962). 'Thin sections of prehistoric pottery: an empirical study', *Bulletin of the Institute of Archaeology*, University of London, 3, 58–68.

HODSON, F. R. (1960). 'Reflections on "The ABC of the British Iron Age"', *Antiquity*, 34, 138–40.

HODSON F. R. (1962). 'Some pottery from Eastbourne, the "Marnians" and the pre-Roman Iron Age in Southern England', *PPS*, 28, 140–55.

(1963). 'Les periodes de La Tène en Suisse et dans les Îles britanniques', *Celticum*, 6, 75–80.

(1964a). 'La Tène chronology, Continental and British', *Bulletin of the Institute of Archaeology, University of London*, 4, 123–41.

(1964b). 'Cultural grouping within the British pre-Roman Iron Age', *PPS*, 30, 99–110.

(1968). 'The La Tène Cemetery at Munsingen-Rain', *Acta Bernensia* 5.

(1971). 'Three Iron Age brooches from Hammersmith', in *Prehistoric and Roman Studies*, ed. G. de G. Sieveking, B.M., 50–6.

HOGG, A. H. A. (1960). 'Garn Boduan and Tre'r Ceiri', *Arch. J*, 94, 1–39.

HOLLEYMAN, G. A. (1958). 'Muntham Court, Findon, Sussex', in FRERE (ed.) (1958), 20.

HOLLEYMAN, G. A. and CURWEN, E. C. (1935). 'Late Bronze Age Lynchet settlements on Plumpton Plain, Sussex', *PPS*, 1, 16–38.

HOLMES, J. and FREND, W. H. C. (1959). 'A Belgic chieftain's grave on Hertford Heath', *TEHAS*, 14, 1–19.

HOOLEY, R. W. (1930). 'Excavation of an Early Iron Age village on Worthy Down, Winchester', *HFC*, 10, 178–92.

HOSKINS, W. G. and JOPE, E. M. (1954). 'The Medieval period', in *The Oxford Region*, ed. A. F. Martin and R. W. Steel, 103–20.

HUBERT, H. (1906). 'La Collection Moreau', *Revue Archéologique*, 4-ème série, tome 8, 337–71.

HULL, M. R. (1958). *Roman Colchester*.

HULST, R. S. (1965). 'Zijderveld, gem. Everdingen', *Nieuwsbull. Koninklijke Nederlandse Oudheid-kundige Bond*, 107, 138.

(1966). *ibid.*, 93.

HUNTINGFORD, G. W. B. (1920). 'On the date of the White Horse', *BBOJ*, 26, 19–20.

(1936). 'The ancient earthworks of North Berkshire', *Berks. Arch. J*, 40, 157–75.

ISAAC, G. (1971). 'Whither archaeology?', *Antiquity*, 45, 123–9.

JACKSON, D. A. (1970). 'Fieldwork and excavation in north eastern Northamptonshire', *Bulletin of the Northamptonshire Federation of Archaeological Societies*, 4, 35–48.

JACKSON, K. H. (1964). *The Oldest Irish Tradition: A Window on the Iron Age*.

JACOBSTAL, P. (1944). *Early Celtic Art*.

JANKUHN, H. (1966). 'Zur Deutung der Tierknochenfunde aus La Tène', *Helvetia Antiqua: Festschrift Emil Vogt*, 155–8.

JESSEN, K. and HELBAEK, H. (1944). *Cereals in Great Britain and Ireland in Prehistoric and Early Historic Times*.

JESSON, M. and HILL, D. (eds.) (1971). *The Iron Age and its Hillforts*.

JESSUP, R. F. (1933). 'Bigberry Camp, Harbledown, Kent', *Ant. J*, 89, 87–115.

JOACHIM, H. E. (1968). *Die Hunsrück-Eifel-Kultur*.

JOBEY, G. (1962). 'An Iron Age homestead at West Brandon, Durham', *Arch. Aeliana*, 40, 1–34.

JOFFROY, R. (1954). *Le Trésor de Vix*.

(1960). *L'Oppidum de Vix . . .*

JONES, E. W. (1954). 'Forestry', in *The Oxford Region*, ed. A. F. Martin and R. W. Steel, 63–6.

JONES, G R. J. (1961). 'Settlement patterns in Anglo-Saxon England', *Antiquity*, 25, 221–32.

JOPE, E. M. (1954). 'An Iron Age decorated sword-scabbard from the river Bann at Toome', *UJA*, 17, 81–91.

(1956). 'Ceramics: medieval', in *A History of Technology*, Vol. 2, ed. C. Singer, E. J. Holmyard, A. R. Hall and O. O. Williams, 284–310.

(1958). 'The beginnings of the La Tène ornamental style', in FRERE (ed.) (1958), 69–83.

(1961). 'Daggers of the Early Iron Age in Britain', *PPS*, 27, 307–43.

(1965). (with D. Dudley) 'An Iron Age cist-burial with two brooches from Trevone, North Cornwall', *Cornish Archaeology*, no. 4, 18–23.

(1971a). 'The Waldalgesheim master', *The European Community in Later Prehistory: Studies in Honour of C. F. C. Hawkes*, ed. J. Boardman, M. A. Brown and T. G. E. Powell, 165–80.

(1971b). 'The Witham shield', in *Prehistoric and Roman Studies*, ed. G. de G. Sieveking, B.M., 61–8.

(forthcoming), *Early Celtic Art in the British Isles*.

KELLER, J. (1965). *Das Keltische Fürstengrab von Reinheim*.

KENDRICK, T. D. (1927). *The Druids*.

KENYON, K. M. (1950). 'Excavations at Breedon-on-the-Hill, 1946', *TLAS*, 26, 17–82.

(1952). 'A survey of the evidence concerning the chronology and origins of Iron Age A in Southern and Midland Britain', *University of London Institute of Archaeology, Eighth Annual Report*, 29–78.

(1953). 'Excavations at Sutton Walls, Herefordshire, 1948–51', *Arch. J*, 110, 1–87.

KERSTEN, W. (1948). 'Die niederrheinische Grabhügelkultur', *Bonner Jahrbücher*, 148, 5–80.

KIMMIG, W. (1940). *Die Urnenfelderkultur in Baden*.

(1963). 'Bronzesitulen aus dem Rheinischen Gebirge, Hunsrück-Eifel-Westerwald', *Bericht der Römisch Germanischen Kommission*, 43–4, 31–106.

KING, E. (1812). 'A description of antiquities discovered on Hagbourne-Hill', *Archaeologia*, 16, 348–9.

KIRK, J. R. (1949). 'Bronzes from Woodeaton, Oxon', *Oxon.*, 14, 1–45.

KLEIN, W. G. (1928). 'Roman temple at Worth, Kent', *Ant. J*, 8, 76–86.

KLINDT-JENSEN, O. (1959). 'The Gundestrup bowl: a reassessment', *Antiquity*, 33, 161–9.

(1961). *Gundestrup Kedelen*.

KNIGHT, W. F. J. (1938). 'A Romano-British site at Bloxham, Oxon', *Oxon.*, 3, 41–56.

KOSSACK, G. (1959). *Südbayern während der Hallstattzeit*.

KRÄMER, W. (1960). 'The Oppidum of Manching', *Antiquity*, 34, 191–200.

(1962). 'Manching II: Zu den Ausgrabungen in den Jahren 1957 bis 1961', *Germania*, 40 293–317.

KRÄMER, W. and SCHUBERT, F. (1970). *Der Ausgrabungen in Manching*, I.

KRÄMER, W. *et al*. (1961). 'Neue Funde aus dem Oppidum von Manching', *Germania*, 39, 299–383,

KROMER, K. (1959). *Das Gräberfeld von Hallstatt*.

DE LAET, S. J. (1961). 'Opgravingen en vondsten in de Limburgse Kempen', *Archaeologia Belgica*, 55, 137–67.

LANE-FOX, Col. A. (1870). *Journal of the Ethnological Society of London*, new series 2, 1870, 412–15,

(1881). 'Excavations at Mount Caburn Camp . . .', *Archaeologia*, 46, 423–95.

LAURIOL, J. (1958). 'Un gisement . . . Bronze Final – Ier Age du Fer: les fonds de cabanes du

Baous de la Salle', *Cahiers Ligures de Préhist. et d'Archéol.*, 7, 16–51; summary *Gallia*, 1959, 457–9.

(1963). 'Trois nouveaux gisements du bronze final à Bize (Aude), les habitats de "Boussecos"', *Cahiers Ligures de Préhist. et d'Archéol.*, 12, 131–41.

LAVER, P. G. (1927). 'The excavation of a tumulus at Lexden, Colchester', *Archaeologia*, 76, 241–54.

LEEDS, E. T. (1926). 'Excavations at Chun Castle in Penwith, Cornwall', *Archaeologia*, 76, 205–40.

(1930). 'A bronze cauldron from the river Cherwell, Oxfordshire, with notes on cauldrons and other bronze vessels of allied types', *Archaeologia*, 80, 1–36.

(1931a). 'An Iron Age site near Radley, Berks', *Ant. J*, 11, 399–404.

(1931b). 'Chastleton Camp, Oxfordshire, a hillfort of the Early Iron Age', *Ant. J*, 11, 382–98.

(1935). 'Recent Iron Age discoveries in Oxfordshire and North Berkshire', *Ant. J*, 15, 30–41.

LETHBRIDGE, T. C. (1953). 'Burial of an Iron Age warrior at Snailwell', *PCAS*, 47, 25–37.

LEWIS, M. J. T. (1966). *Temples in Roman Britain.*

LIDDELL, D. M. (1937). 'Report of the Hampshire Field Club's excavations at Meon Hill, 1933', *HFC*, 13, 7–54.

LOBJOIS, G. (1969). 'La Nécropole gauloise de Pernant (Aisne)', *Celticum*, 18, 1–284.

LONGWORTH, I. H. (1960). 'A Bronze Age urnfield on Vinces Farm, Ardleigh, Essex', *PPS*, 26, 178–92.

LOPEZ CUEVILLAS, F. and LORENZO FERNANDEZ, J. (1946–7). 'Las habitaciones de los castros . . .', in *Cuadernos de Estudios Gallegos*, 2.

LOWTHER, A. W. G. (1939). 'Early Bronze Age–Pagan Saxon period', in *A Survey of the Prehistory of the Farnham District*, 153–260.

(1945). 'Iron Age pottery from Wisley, Surrey', *PPS*, 11, 32–8.

(1946). 'Excavations at Purberry Shot, Ewell, Surrey', *SAC*, 50, 9–46.

MacGREGOR, M. (1962). 'The Early Iron Age metalwork hoard from Stanwick, N.R. Yorks', *PPS*, 28, 17–57.

MACKIE, E. W. (1969). 'Radiocarbon dates and the Scottish Iron Age', *Antiquity*, 43, 15–25.

MANNING, W. H. (1964). 'The plough in Roman Britain', *JRS*, 54, 54–65.

MARIEN, M. E. (1958). *Trouvailles du Champ d'Urnes et des Tombelles hallstattiennes de Court-Saint-Etienne.*

(1964). *La Nécropole à tombelles de Saint-Vincent.*

(1971). 'Tribes and archaeological groupings of the La Tène period in Belgium: some observations', *The European Community in Later Prehistory: Studies in Honour of C. F. C. Hawkes*, ed. J. Boardman, M. A. Brown and T. G. E. Powell, 211–42.

MEARE 1 (1948). Bulleid, A. and Gray, H. StG., *The Meare Lake Village*, Vol. 1.

MEARE 2 (1953). Bulleid, A. and Gray, H. StG., *The Meare Lake Village*, Vol. 2.

MEARE 3 (1967). Cotton, M. A., *The Meare Lake Village*, Vol. 3.

MEGAW, J. V. S. (1970). *Art of the European Iron Age.*

VON MERHART, G. (1952). 'Studien über einige Gattungen von Bronzegefässen', *Festschrift des Römisch-Germanischen Zentralmuseums im Mainz*, Band 2, 1–71.

MOREL, L. (1890). *La Champagne Souterraine.*

MURRAY-THRIEPLAND, L. (1956). 'An excavation at St Mawgan-in-Pyder, North Cornwall', *Arch. J*, 113, 33–83.

MUSSON, R. C. (1954). 'An illustrated catalogue of Sussex Beaker and Bronze Age pottery', *SxAC*, 92, 106–24.

MYRES, J. N. L. (1930). 'A prehistoric settlement on Hinksey Hill, near Oxford', *JBAA*, 36, 360–90.

(1937). 'A prehistoric and Roman site on Mount Farm, Dorchester', *Oxon.*, 2, 12–40.

DE NAVARRO, J. M. (1955). 'A doctor's grave of the Middle La Tène period from Bavaria', *PPS* 21, 231–48.

(1959). 'Zu einigen Schwertscheiden aus La Tène', *BRGK*, 40, 79–119.

(1972). *The Finds from the Site of La Tène, Vol. I, Scabbards and the Swords found in them.*

NORRIS, N. E. S. and BURSTOW, G. P. (1950). 'A prehistoric and Romano-British site at West Blatchington, Hove', *SxAC*, 89, 1–56.

OAKLEY, K. P. (1943). 'A note on haematite ware', in WHEELER (1943), 379–80.

ORDNANCE SURVEY (1962). *Map of Southern Britain in the Iron Age.*

OWLES, E. and BRAILSFORD, J. (1969). 'The Ipswich gold torcs', *Antiquity*, 43, 208–12.

PARKES, M. B. (1973). 'The literacy of the laity in the middle ages', in *The Literature of the Western World*, 2, ed. D. Daiches and A. K. Thorlby.

PARSONS, W. J. and CURWEN, E. C. (1933). 'An agricultural settlement on Charleston Brow', *SxAC*, 74, 164–80.

PASSMORE, A. D. (1914). 'Liddington Castle Camp', *WAM*, 38, 576–84.

PATCHETT, F. M. (1944). 'Cornish Bronze Age pottery', *Arch. J.*, 101, 17–49.

PAYNE, F. G. (1947). 'The plough in Early Britain', *Arch. J.*, 104, 82–111.

(1957). 'The British plough: some stages in its development', *AHR*, 5, 74–84.

PEACOCK, D. P. S. (1968). 'A petrological study of certain Iron Age pottery from Western England', *PPS*, 34, 414–27.

(1970). 'A contribution to the study of Glastonbury ware from south-western Britain', *Ant. J.*, 50, 41–61.

(1971). 'Roman amphorae in pre-Roman Britain', in JESSON and HILL (1971), 161–88.

PEAKE, H. (1931). *Archaeology of Berkshire.*

PEAKE, H. J. and PADEL, J. (1934). 'Exploration of three round barrows on Woolley Down, Berks.', *Trans. Newbury and District Field Club*, 7, 30–48.

PENN, W. S. (1960). 'Springhead: Temples III and IV', *Arch. Cant*, 74, 113–40.

PENNIMAN, T. K., ALLEN, I. M. and WOOTTON, A. (1958). 'Ancient metallurgical furnaces in Great Britain to the end of the Roman occupation', *Sibrium*, 4, 97–126.

PERRY, B. T. (1966). 'Some recent discoveries in Hampshire', in THOMAS, A. C. (1966), 39–41.

PÉTREQUIN, P., URLACHER, J.-P. and VUAILLAT, D. (1969). 'Habitat et sépultures de l'Age du Bronze Final à Dampierre-sur-le-Doubs (Doubs)', *Gallia Préhistoire*, 12, 1–35.

PHILIPPE, J. (1927). *Cinq Années de Fouilles au Fort-Harrouard, 1921–1925.*

PIGGOTT, C. M. (1942). 'Five Late Bronze Age Enclosures in North Wiltshire', *PPS*, 8, 48–61.

(1949). 'The Iron Age settlement at Hayhope Knowe, Roxburghshire: excavations, 1949', *PSAS*, 83, 45–67.

(1953). 'An Iron Age barrow in the New Forest', *Ant. J.*, 33, 14–21.

PIGGOTT, C. M. and SEABY, W. A. (1937). 'Early Iron Age site at Southcote, Reading', *PPS*, 3, 43–57.

PIGGOTT, S. (1927). 'A British Village site at Knighton Hill, Compton Beauchamps', *BBOJ*, 31, Part I, 25–7.

(1928). 'Excavation of an Early Iron Age site at Knighton Hill, near the White Horse Hill, Berks', *Man*, 28, 97–101.

(1950). 'Swords and Scabbards of the British Early Iron Age', *PPS*, 16, 1–28.

PIGGOTT, S. (1961). 'Native economies . . .', in *Roman and Native in North Britain*, ed. I. A. Richmond, 1–27.

(1962). 'Heads and hoofs', *Antiquity*, 36, 110–18.

(1965). *Ancient Europe.*

(1968). *The Druids.*

(1971). 'Firedogs in Iron Age Britain and beyond', in *The European Community in Later Prehistory: Studies in Honour of C. F. C. Hawkes*, ed. J. Boardman, M. A. Brown and T. G. E, Powell, 243–70.

PIGGOTT, S. and C. M. (1940). 'Excavations at Rams Hill, Uffington, Berks', *Ant. J*, 20, 415–80.

PITTIONI, R. (1954). *Urgeschichte des Österreichischen Raumes.*

PITT-RIVERS, Lt.-Gen. A. H. L. F. (1888). *Excavations in Cranborne Chase.*

POWELL, T. G. E. (1948). 'The Late Bronze Age hoard from Welby, Leicestershire', *Arch. J*, 105. 27–40.

(1958). *The Celts.*

(1966). *Prehistoric Art.*

POWELL-COTTON, P. H. G. and CRAWFORD, O. G. S. (1924). 'The Birchington hoard', *Ant. J*, 4, 220–6.

RADDATZ, K. (1951). 'Zur Deutung der Funde aus La Tène', *Offa*, 11, 24–8.

RADFORD, C. A. R. (1951). 'Report on the excavations at Castle Dore', *JRIC*, n.s. 1, Appendix.

(1954). The tribes of Southern Britain', *PPS*, 20, 1–26.

RAHTZ, P. and APSIMON, A. (1962). 'Excavations at Shearplace Hill, Sydling St Nicholas, Dorset', *PPS*, 27, 289–328.

RANDALL-MacIVER, D. (1927). *The Iron Age in Italy.*

RHODES, P. P. (1948). 'A Prehistoric and Roman site at Wittenham Clumps, Berks', *Oxon.*, 13, 18–31.

(1949). 'New Archaeological sites at Binsey and Port Meadow, Oxford', *Oxon.*, 14, 81–4.

(1950). 'The Celtic field-systems on the Berkshire Downs', *Oxon.*, 15, 1–28.

RICHARDSON, K. M. (1952). 'The excavation of Iron Age villages on Boscombe Down West', *WAM*, 54, 123–68.

RICHARDSON, K. M. and YOUNG, A. (1951). 'An Iron Age A site on the Chilterns', *Ant. J*, 31, 132–48.

RICHMOND, Sir I. *et al.* (1968). *Hod Hill*, Vol. 2.

RIEK, G. and HUNDT, H. J. (1962). *Der Hohmichele ein Fürstengrabhügel der späten Hallstattzeit bei der Heuneberg.*

RILEY, D. N. (1942). 'Crop-marks in the Upper Thames Valley seen from the air during 1941', *Oxon.*, 7, 111–14.

(1943). 'Archaeology from the air in the Upper Thames valley', *Oxon.*, 8–9, 64–101.

(1946). 'A Late Bronze Age and Iron Age site on Standlake Downs', *Oxon.*, 11–13, 27–43.

RIVET, A. L. F. (1958). 'Some of the problems of hill-forts', in FRERE (ed.) (1958), 29–34.

(1971). 'Hill-forts in action', in JESSON and HILL (1971), 189–202.

RÖDER, J. (1948). 'Der Goloring', *Bonner Jahrbücher*, 148, 81–132.

ROLLESTON, G. (1884). *Scientific Papers and Addresses*, Vol. 2, 939–44.

ROSS, A. (1967). *Pagan Celtic Britain: Studies in Iconography and Tradition.*

(1968). 'Shafts, pits, wells – sanctuaries of the Belgic Britons?', *Studies in Ancient Europe*, ed. J. M. Coles and D. D. A. Simpson, 255–85.

(1970). *Everyday Life of the Pagan Celts.*

ROWLETT, R. M. (1969). 'The Iron Age north of the Alps', *Science*, 161, 123–34.

ROWLETT, R. M. and S. J. and BOUREUX, M. (1969). 'A rectangular Early La Tène Marnian house at Chassemy (Aisne)', *World Archaeology*, 1, no. 1, 106–35.

RYBOVÁ, A. and SOUDSKÝ, B. (1962). *Libenice: Keltská Svatyně ve Střednich Čechách.*

RYDER, M. L. (1966). 'Can one cook in a skin?', *Antiquity*, 40, 225–7.

SANDARS, N. K. (1957). *Bronze Age Cultures in France.*

SAVORY, H. N. (1937). 'An Early Iron Age site at Long Wittenham, Berks', *Oxon.*, 2, 1–11.

(1971). 'A Welsh Bronze Age hillfort', *Antiquity*, 45, 251–61.

SCHWARZ, K. (1958). 'Spätlatènezeitliche Viereckschanzen. Keltische Kultplätze', *Neue Ausgrabungen in Deutschland*, 205–14.

(1962). 'Zum Stand der Ausgrabungen in der spätkeltischen Viereckschanze von Holzhausen', *Jahresber. Bayer. Bodendenkmalpflege*, 22–77.

SEABY, W. A. (1938). 'Early British coins found in Berkshire and the Silchester district', *Berks. Arch. J*, 42, 75–91.

SHEPARD, A. O. (1961). *Ceramics for the Archaeologist*, Washington.

SIMPSON, G. (1964). 'The hill-forts of Wales and their relation to Roman Britain: a recension', in GARDNER and SAVORY (1964), 209–20.

SMALL, A. (1969). 'Burghead', *Scottish Arch. Forum*, Edinburgh, 61–8.

SMITH, I. F. (1961). 'An essay towards the reformation of the British Bronze Age', *Helinium*, 1, 97–118.

SMITH, M. A. (1959). 'Some Somerset hoards and their place in the Bronze Age of Southern Britain', *PPS*, 25, 144–87.

SMITH, M. A. and BLIN-STOYLE, A. E. (1959). 'A sample analysis of British Middle and Late Bronze Age materials using optical spectrometry', *PPS*, 25, 188–208.

SMITH, R. A. (1909). 'On a Late-Celtic mirror found at Desborough . . .', *Archaeologia*, 61, 329–46.

(1912). 'On Late-Celtic antiquities discovered at Welwyn, Herts', *Archaeologia*, 63, 1–30.

(1925). *A Guide to the Antiquities of the Early Iron Age of Central and Western Europe*, B.M.

(1927). 'Pre-Roman remains at Scarborough', *Archaeologia*, 77, 179–200.

STAMPFUSS, R. (1927). 'Beiträge zur Nordgruppe der Urnenfelderkultur', *Mannus, Zeitschrift für Vorgeschichte*, 5, 50–100.

STANFORD, S. C. (1967). 'Croft Ambrey hill-fort – some interim conclusions', *TWFC*, 39, 1, 31–9.

(1970). 'Credenhill Camp, Herefordshire: an Iron Age hill-fort capital', *Arch. J*, 127, 82–129.

(1971). 'Invention, adoption and imposition – the evidence of the hill-forts', in JESSON and HILL (1971), 41–52.

STEAD, I. M. (1965). *The La Tène Cultures of Eastern Yorkshire.*

(1967). 'A La Tène III burial at Welwyn Garden City', *Archaeologia*, 101, 1–62.

(1968). 'An Iron Age hill-fort at Grimthorpe, Yorkshire, England', *PPS*, 34, 148–90.

(1971). 'The reconstruction of Iron Age buckets from Aylesford and Baldock', *Prehistoric and Roman Studies*, ed. G. de G. Sieveking, B.M., 250–82.

STEER, K. (1955). 'The Early Iron Age homestead at West Plean', *PSAS*, 89, 227–51.

STEVENS, C. E. (1940). 'The Frilford site – a postscript', *Oxon.*, 5, 166–7.

(1951). 'Britain between the invasions (54 B.C.–A.D. 43): a study of ancient diplomacy', in *Aspects of Archaeology in Britain and Beyond*, ed. W. F. Grimes, 332–44.

STEVENS, F. (1934). 'The Highfield pit dwellings, Fisherton, Salisbury . . .', *WAM*, 46, 579–624.

STEVENS, L. R. (1953). *Byfleet, A Village of England*.

STEVENSON, R. B. K. (1966). 'Metal-work and some other objects in Scotland and their cultural, affinities', in *The Iron Age in Northern Britain*, ed. A. L. F. Rivet, 17–44.

STONE, S. (1857). 'Account of certain (supposed) British and Saxon remains . . .', *Proc. Soc. Ant· Lond.* 1st series 4, 1856–9, 92–100.

(1858). *Proc. Soc. Ant. Lond.*, 1st series 4, 1856–9, 213–19.

STRACHAN, J. and O'KEEFE, J. G. (1912). *The Táin Bó Cúailnge*.

SUTTON, J. E. G. (1966). 'Iron Age hillforts and some other earthworks in Oxfordshire', *Oxon.*, 31, 28–42.

TAYLOR, H. (1922). 'Third report on Rowberrow Cavern', *Proceedings of the Bristol University Speleological Society*, 2, 1922–3, 40–50.

THIÉROT, M. A. (1930). 'Tombes Marniennes à Sogny-aux-Moulins (Marne)', *Revue anthropologique*, 4-ème année, nos 10–12, 1–7.

THOMAS, A. C. (1966). (ed.) *Rural Settlement in Roman Britain*, C.B.A. Research Report 7.

(1971). *The early Christian archaeology of North Britain*.

THOMAS, N. (1957). 'Excavations at Callow Hill . . .', *Oxon.*, 22, 11–53.

TIERNEY, J. J. (1960). 'The Celtic ethnography of Posidonius', *PRIA*, 60, C, no. 5, 189–275.

TRATMAN, E. K. (1925). 'Second report on Kings Weston Hill, Bristol', *Proceedings of the Bristol University Speleological Society*, 2, 238–40.

TSCHUMI, O. (1940). *Die Ur-und Frühgeschichtliche Fundstelle von Port im Amt Nidau*.

TYLECOTE, R. F. (1962). *Metallurgy in Archaeology*.

UNDERHILL, F. M. (1937). 'Notes on recent antiquarian discoveries in Berkshire', *Berks. Arch. J*, 41, 33–41.

(1938). 'Notes on recent antiquarian discoveries in Berkshire (2)', *Berks. Arch. J*, 42, 20–8.

VÁŇA, ZD. (1967). 'Výzkum Středního Valu Slovanského Hradiště v Bílině', *Archeologiché rozhledy*, 19, 4, 451–71.

VARLEY, W. J. (1948). 'The hillforts of the Welsh Marches', *Arch. J*, 105, 41–66.

(1950) 'Excavations of the Castle Ditch, Eddisbury, 1935–38', *TLCHS*, 102, 1–68.

(1964). *Cheshire before the Romans*.

(1968). 'Barmston and the Holderness Crannogs', *ERA*, 1, Pt 1, 11–26.

VIOLLIER, D. (1916). *Les sepultures du second âge du fer sur le plateau suisse*.

VOUGA, P. (1923). *La Tène*.

WAINWRIGHT, G. J. (1970). 'An Iron Age promontory fort at Budbury, Bradford upon Avon, Wiltshire', *WAM*, 65, 108–66.

WARD-PERKINS, J. B. (1938a). 'An Early Iron Age site at Crayford, Kent', *PPS*, 4, 151–68.

(1938b). 'The Roman villa at Lockleys, Welwyn, Hertfordshire', *Ant. J*, 18, 339–76.

(1939). 'Iron Age metal horses' bits of the British Isles', *PPS*, 5, 173–92.

(1944). 'Excavations on the Iron Age hill-fort of Oldbury, near Ightham, Kent', *Archaeologia*, 90, 127–76.

WATSON, W. (1947). 'Two brooches of the Early Iron Age from Sawdon, North Riding, Yorkshire', *Ant. J*, 27, 178–82.

WEERTH, E. AUS'M. (1870). 'Der Grabfund von Wald-Algesheim', *Festprogramm für Winckelmanns Geburtstag*, Bonn.

WERNER, J. (1954). 'Die Bronzekanne von Kelheim', *Bayerische Vorgeschichtsblätter*, 20, 43–73.
(1955). 'Die Nauheimer Fibel', *JRGZM*, 2, 170–95.

WESTERN, A. C. (1963). 'Wood and charcoal in archaeology', in *Science and Archaeology*, ed. D. Brothwell and E. Higgs, 150–8.

WHEELER, R. E. M. (1943). *Maiden Castle, Dorset*.
(1953). 'An Early Iron Age "Beach-head" at Lulworth, Dorset', *Ant. J*, 33, 1–13.
(1954a). *Archaeology from the Earth*.
(1954b). *The Stanwick Fortifications*, Reports of the Research Committee of the Society of Antiquaries of London, no. 17.

WHEELER, R. E. M. and RICHARDSON, K. M. (1957). *Hillforts of Northern France*.

WHEELER, R. E. M. and T. V. (1936). *Verulamium: A Belgic and Two Roman Cities*.

WHITE, D. A. (1970). 'The excavation of an Iron Age round barrow near Handley, Dorset, 1969', *Ant. J*, 50, 26–36.

WHITLEY, M. (1943). 'Excavations at Chalbury Camp, Dorset, 1939', *Ant. J*, 23, 98–121.

WILLIAMS, A. (1944). 'A promontory fort at Henllan, Cardiganshire', *Arch. Camb.*, 98, 226–40.
(1946). 'Excavations at Langford Downs, Oxon . . .', *Oxon.*, 11–12, 44–64.
(1950). 'Excavations at Allard's Quarry, Marnhull', *PDNHAS*, 72, 20–75.
(1951). 'Excavations at Beard Mill, Stanton Harcourt, Oxon, 1944', *Oxon.*, 16, 5–23.

WILLIAMS-FREEMAN, J. P. (1915). *Field Archaeology as Illustrated by Hampshire*.

WILSON, A. E. (1938). 'Excavations in the ramparts and gateway of The Caburn, August–October 1937', *SxAC*, 79, 169–94.

WILSON, A. E. and BURSTOW, G. P. (1948). 'The evolution of Sussex Iron Age pottery', *SxAC*, 87, 77–111.

WOLSELEY, G. A. and SMITH, R. A. (1924). 'Discoveries near Cissbury', *Ant. J*, 4, 347–59.

WOLSELEY, G. A., SMITH, R. A. and HAWLEY, W. (1927). 'Prehistoric and Roman settlements on Park Brow', *Archaeologia*, 76, 1–40.

WOODS, P. J. (1969). *Excavations at Hardingstone, Northants, 1967–8*, Northamptonshire County Council.

WORSFOLD, F. H. (1943). 'A report on the Late Bronze Age site excavated at Minnis Bay, Birchington, Kent, 1938–40', *PPS*, 9, 28–47.

WRIGHT, E. V. and C. W. (1947). 'Prehistoric boats from North Ferriby, East Yorkshire', *PPS*, 13, 114–38.

WRIGHT, E. V. and CHURCHILL, D. M. (1965). 'The boats from North Ferriby, Yorkshire, England', *PPS*, 31, 1–24.

WYSS, R. (1954). 'Das Schwert der Korisios', *Ur-Schweiz*, 18, 4, 53–8.

ZAHLHAAS, G. (1971). 'Der Bronzeeimer von Waldalgesheim', *Hamburger Beiträge zur Archäologie*, Bd 1, Ht 2, 115–30.

ZÜRN, H. (1971). 'Die keltische Viereckschanze bei Tomerdingen, Kr. Ulm (Württemberg)', *PPS*, 37, 218–27.

Index